D0886906

Parallax Re-visions of Culture and Society

Stephen G. Nichols, Gerald Prince, and Wendy Steiner
Series Editors

Subversive Pleasures

Bakhtin, Cultural Criticism, and Film

Robert Stam

The Johns Hopkins University Press

BALTIMORE AND LONDON

The Johns Hopkins University Press
701 West 40th Street
Baltimore, Maryland 21211
The Johns Hopkins Press Ltd., London

The paper used in this publication meets the minimum
requirements of American National Standard for Information
Sciences—Permanence of Paper for Printed Library Materials,
ANSI Z39.48-1984.

LIBRARY OF CONGRESS CATALOGING-IN-PUBLICATION DATA

Stam, Robert, 1941–
    Subversive pleasures : Bakhtin, cultural criticism, and film /
Robert Stam.
        p.   cm. — (Parallax)
    Bibliography: p.
    Includes index.
    ISBN 0-8018-3814-2 (alk. paper)
    1. Motion pictures and literature.   2. Bakhtin, M. M.
(Mikhail Mikhailovich), 1895–1975—Criticism and
interpretation.   3. Criticism.   4. Popular culture.
I. Title.   II. Series: Parallax (Baltimore, Md.)
PN1995.3.S73   1989
791.43'01—dc20   89-2594
                                                        CIP

62365

Para Ella

Contents

Acknowledgments   xi

Introduction   1

1. Translinguistics and Semiotics   26

2. Language, Difference, and Power   57

3. Film, Literature, and the Carnivalesque   85

4. Of Cannibals and Carnivals   122

5. The Grotesque Body and Cinematic Eroticism   157

6. From Dialogism to *Zelig*   187

Envoi: Bakhtin and Mass-Media Critique   219

Notes   241

Index   259

◼︎ Acknowledgments

Some passages in this text were published, in preliminary and very different form, in various journals. Some of the material in Chapter 1, "Translinguistics and Semiotics," first appeared under the title "Film and Language: From Metz to Bakhtin," in *Studies in the Literary Imagination* 19, no. 1 (Spring 1986). Some parts of Chapter 2, "Language, Difference, and Power," first appeared in an essay coauthored with Ella Shohat entitled "The Cinema after Babel: Language, Difference, and Power," published in *Screen* 26, nos. 3–4 (May–August 1985). (I would like to thank Ella for generously allowing me to include part of the "shared territory" of that essay within this text.) Some passages in Chapter 3, "Film, Literature, and the Carnivalesque," appeared, in modified form, in "On the Carnivalesque," published in *Wedge,* no. 1 (Summer 1982). The material in this chapter concerning Umberto Eco and Roberto da Matta first appeared as "Carnival, Politics, and Brazilian Literature," *Studies in Latin American Popular Culture*, vol. 7 (1988). A version of some of the material in Chapter 4, "Of Cannibals and Carnivals," was published in an essay coauthored with João Luiz Vieira entitled "Parody and Marginality: The Case of Brazilian Cinema," in *Framework,* no. 28 (1985). (I thank João Luiz Vieira for allowing me to include some of that material within this text.) Some of Chapter 5, "The Grotesque Body and Cinematic Eroticism," was first delivered as a paper at the "Semiotics of Eroticism" Conference at the University of Toronto (1987) and subsequently published under the title "Bakhtin, Eroticism, and the Cinema: Strategies for the Critique and Trans-valuation of Pornography," in *CineAction,* no. 10 (Fall 1987). Some of the material in Chapter 6, "From Dialogism to *Zelig,*" appeared in a preliminary version in an article coauthored with Ella Shohat entitled *"Zelig* and Contemporary Theory: Meditation on the Chameleon Text," published in *Enclitic* 9, nos. 1–2, issues 17/18 (1987).

I would like to thank the following persons and institutions for various forms of help and support. The John Simon Guggenheim Foundation provided me with a grant which indirectly helped support this project. A Fulbright Lectureship also gave me breathing time to work on this project. I would also like to thank the members of the various "Bakhtin Circles" of which I have been a part. The first, consisting of Joel Kanoff, Richard Porton, and myself, devoted its energies to reading the fundamental Bakhtin texts, but often veered off delightfully into such topics as the carnivalesque credentials of contemporary stand-up comics. The second circle, linked to the journal *Social Text,* consists of George Yudice, Betsy Wheeler, Jay Lemke, George Otte, Michael Brown, Lee Quinby, Peter Hitchcock, Tom Hays, Bill McClellan, Bruce Dorval, John Dohr, Sonia Sayres, and Lloyd Davis. The dialogic stimulation of both of these groups has been a tremendous source of illumination and pleasure. I would also like to thank the editors of various journals with whom I have worked in connection with Bakhtin-related projects: Bart Palmer of *Studies in the Literary Imagination*; Jennifer Batchelor, Mandy Merck, and Annette Kuhn of *Screen*; Brian Wallis and Phil Mariani of *Wedge*; Kass Banning and Janine Marchessault of *CineAction*; and John O'Kane of *Enclitic*. I would also like to express my thanks to my longstanding colleagues at NYU—Bob Sklar, Annette Michelson, Bill Simon, and Bill Everson—and to Jay Leyda, whose phenomenal and self-effacing generosity will long be remembered, as well as to my more recent colleagues Antonia Lant and Richard Allen. I am also indebted to the many fine graduate students I have had the privilege to teach in various Bakhtin seminars at NYU. Finally, I would like to thank the following for their support over the years: my brothers James and David Stam, Robert Allen, Robert Alter, Bertrand Augst, Catherine Benamou, Warren Dean, Lucia Guimaraes, Randall Johnson, E. Ann Kaplan, Ernest Larson, Ana Lopez, Richard Macksey, Ivone Margulies, Christian Metz, Sherry Millner, Margaret Morse, Roswitha Mueller, Laura Mulvey, Michael O'Toole, Richard Pena, Ella Shohat, João Luiz Vieira, Kathleen Woodward, and Ismail Xavier. Finally, I would like to thank Penny Moudrianakis, my editor, for her impeccably professional and sympathetic help with the manuscript.

■■■■■■■ Introduction

In the last few years, the Russian author Mikhail Bakhtin has become one of the most influential and controversial thinkers on the contemporary scene. Called by his biographers one of the "leading thinkers of the twentieth century," Bakhtin published, under his own name or in collaboration, books and essays on subjects ranging from linguistics (*Marxism and the Philosophy of Language,* 1929) to psychoanalysis (*Freudianism: A Marxist Critique,* 1927) to literary criticism (*The Formal Method in Literary Scholarship,* 1928; *Problems of Dostoevsky's Poetics,* 1929; *Rabelais and His World,* 1965). The two series of essays gathered under the titles *The Dialogical Imagination* and *Speech Genres and Other Late Essays* have been translated into English, while other works by the "Bakhtin Circle" have been reappraised in the light of Bakhtin's burgeoning reputation. Recently, Bakhtin's influence has spread to many parts of the world, crucial Bakhtinian terms have gained wide dissemination, and the exegetical application of his ideas is proceeding apace.

Bakhtin began writing in the twenties, but it is only now that the magnitude of his accomplishment has begun to be appreciated. In France, when his books on Dostoevsky and Rabelais appeared in translation in the late sixties, Bakhtin was initially seen as a kind of protostructuralist working out of the formalist tradition. In two landmark articles, "Bakhtin, le mot, le dialogue et le roman" (1967) and "Une Poetique Ruinée" (1970), Julia Kristeva presented Bakhtin as a precursor of the most sophisticated literary theoreticians of structuralism and poststructuralism. And in 1981, Tzvetan Todorov performed a major reevaluation of Bakhtin's *oeuvre* in his *Mikhail Bakhtine: Le Principe Dialogique*. In the anglophonic world, Bakhtin was at first viewed largely as the theorist of carnival and ritual inversions of hierarchy; only recently, with the translation of numerous books by or about him, has Bakhtin come to be seen as a major theoretician of language and literature. A profoundly anticipatory thinker, Bakhtin managed to foreshadow aspects of Lacan's "linguistic" reading of Freud in *Freudianism: A Marxist Critique* (1927), aspects of contemporary sociolinguistics (Pêcheux, Halliday, Lakoff) in *Marxism and the Philosophy of Language* (1929), and aspects of cultural anthropology (Victor Turner and Mary Douglas) and historical ethnography (Emmanuel le Roy Ladurie) in *Rabelais and His World* (written in 1940).

Bakhtin's concern with the dialogical relationship between self and other "mirrors" the similar concerns of such thinkers as Heidegger, Sartre, and Lacan, but Bakhtin was addressing such questions in the teens and twenties of this century, long before the others. Only Bakhtin's nonproprietary attitude toward authorship and the vicissitudes of Stalinist repression kept the world unaware of Bakhtin's accomplishment. Some of Bakhtin's writings were published under pseudonyms, many of his collaborators were persecuted or killed, and he himself was condemned to internal exile during long periods. Indeed, it is astonishing that a man who was systematically kept distant from the great cultural centers of the Soviet Union and who presumably had great difficulty gaining access to key texts, managed to anticipate so many of the ideas that came to dominate the latter half of the twentieth century. Bakhtin intuited, with extraordinary clairvoyance, the future aporias of Saussure-derived structuralism, and thus anticipated crucial features of poststructuralism. As Julia Kristeva noted in her late-sixties essays, Bakhtin uncannily foreshadowed major poststructuralist topoi: the denial of univocal meaning, the infinite spiral of interpretation, the negation of originary presence in speech, the unstable identity of the sign, the positioning of the subject by discourse, the untenable nature of inside/outside oppositions, and the pervasive presence of intertextuality.[1] In a very real sense, Bakhtin's "time," as Allon White points out, is now, not only after structuralism but also after Stalin (one imagines Bakhtin applauding the lively debates on *glasnost* and *perestroika* now sounding from the Soviet Union) and after Bakhtin's own death, for his work addresses central issues of language, culture, and politics, and only now have the discourses emerged which, in dialogue with Bakhtin's, can fully raise the "question of his questions."[2]

Between 1924 and 1929, Bakhtin personally completed or coauthored four major books. The authorship of three of the collaborative texts—*Marxism and the Philosophy of Language* (with Voloshinov), *Freudianism: A Marxist Critique* (with Voloshinov), and *The Formal Method in Literary Scholarship* (with Mededev)—is disputed, but there is considerable evidence that Bakhtin wrote substantial portions of these books or at least worked in extremely close collaboration with his two coauthors. Many commentators have pointed out the irony that Bakhtin, who spent much of his intellectual energy theorizing the question of authorship, should himself be the subject of disputes concerning authorship. But of all the debates swirling posthumously around the head of Bakhtin, the attempt to separate out categorically, under distinct proper names, the utterances of the disputed texts, is the one that interests us the least. Such a preoccupation shows insensitivity to what Allon White calls the "hybrid and collaborative composition" chosen by Bakhtin and is diametrically opposed to Bakhtin's view of writing as always dialogical, impure, citational.[3] For the purposes of this text, therefore, the name "Bakhtin" will be used stenographically, to refer to Bakhtin himself together with his close collaborators, under the assumption that the works in question represent a mingling of voices, a view that strikes us as perfectly in keeping with the Bakhtinian conception of authorship.

In preparation for my larger argument, it will perhaps be useful at the outset to trace Bakhtin's overall intellectual trajectory and briefly sketch out the basic arguments of some of the key texts. *Freudianism: A Marxist Critique* (1927) mingles a sociologistic critique of what Bakhtin sees as the ahistorical character of Freudian "biologism," with a celebration of the specifically linguistic dimension of the psychoanalytic project, seen as a "special kind of interpretation of utterances." (Although Julia Kristeva, in "Une Poetique Ruinée," suggests that Bakhtin had a "presentiment of the Freudian intervention," in fact Bakhtin knew that intervention directly). Bakhtin situates Freudian thought, somewhat simplistically, as part of a broader bourgeois, subjectivist, ideological current characterized by a "sui generis fear of history, an ambition to locate a world beyond the social and the historical, a search for this world precisely in the depths of the organic," a feature that pervades "all systems of contemporary philosophy and [constitutes] the symptom of the disintegration and decline of the bourgeois world" (p. 14). Insisting on the verbal nature not only of the psychoanalytic method but also of the psyche itself, Bakhtin salutes Freud's emphasis on language but critiques the model of language adopted. The Freudian model, according to Bakhtin, fails to recognize the politicohistorical dimension of language. It fails to see that every exchange of words, including that between analyst and patient, is "ideological," characterized by specific social intonations through which it gains historical specificity and momentum.

In line with this "socialization" of the Freudian problematic, Bakhtin audaciously recasts the Unconscious/Conscious distinction as one not between two orders of psychic reality but rather between two modalities of verbal consciousness. Official consciousness refers to that which social and ideological structures allow one to express openly, while unofficial consciousness expresses that which deviates from socially accepted norms, that which is taboo, beyond the pale, a kind of mental carnival whose favored linguistic mode is "inner speech." At certain points, Bakhtin anticipates the Delleuze-Guattari critique, in *Anti-Oedipus,* that Freudianism, in a quasi-totalitarian manner, reduces all human narratives to the Ur story of "Daddy, Mommy, and Me." In contrast to Freud, who explains processes that are "essentially social from the perspective of a purely individual psychology," Bakhtin sees self-awareness as indissociable from social norms and evaluations. "In becoming aware of myself, I attempt to look at myself, as it were, through the eyes of another person, another representative of my social group, my class." Thus Bakhtin attempts, admittedly with partial success and with only an incomplete knowledge of Freud's work, to historicize, politicize, and socialize the Freudian idea of the Unconscious.

Since Bakhtin at times seems to anticipate the language and thought of Jacques Lacan, it is important to stress the areas where the two men converge as well as the points on which they clearly differ. They clearly converge in emphasizing the linguistic dimension of Freud's thought, although the linguistics to which Bakhtin would have appealed would not have been the structuralist, Saussurean variety. Bakhtin shares with Lacan a preoccupation with the image of the mirror and the role of the other in our psychic life. To be, for Bakhtin, signifies to be for and through the other. The human being is not the sovereign master of an interior domain, but exists in the shadowy region between self and other. Consciousness of self is constantly perceived against the background of others' consciousness: "I for myself" against the background of "I for another." In the early sixties, contemplating a new edition of his book on Dostoevsky, Bakhtin wrote in his notebook, under the heading "Underground Man before the Mirror," that Dostoevsky reveals the "impossibility of a direct relation with oneself, even in confession."[4] Even when looking within oneself, one looks in and through the eyes of the other; one needs the other's gaze to constitute oneself as self. Even the apparently simple act of looking in the mirror, for Bakhtin, is complexly dialogical, implying an intricate intersection of perspectives and consciousnesses. To look at ourselves in the mirror is to oversee the reflection of our life in the plane of consciousness of others; it is to see and apprehend ourselves through the imagined eyes of our parents, our brothers and sisters, through the supportive look of our friends or the hostile regard of our enemies, as well as through the more abstract panoptical "eyes" of mass-mediated culture, with its implicit norms of fashion and acceptable appearance.

Repeatedly, then, we find ideas and language that seem to anticipate Lacanian thought but that are conceived in a quite different spirit. Bakhtin too might have affirmed that "l'inconscient, c'est le discours de l'autre," but rather than the abstract otherness of Lacan's impersonal symbolic order, Bakhtin would presumably have meant the ongoing and reciprocally modifying interpersonal exchange of historical subjects. When Bakhtin reminds us that even our name is given us by another, he is calling attention not to a repressive "nom du père" but rather to evidence of the theoretical impossibility of solitude, since every word, even the solitary word, presupposes an interlocutor. (Only Adam in Eden, hypothetically, was in a position to name objects without hearing the answering echo and resonances of other voices). For Bakhtin we do not "fall" into language/the symbolic, but are enriched and fulfilled by it. Although both Lacan and Bakhtin concern themselves with the mirror and its symbolic role in psychic life, Bakhtin does not limit his interest to a "stage" of psychic development; rather, he continually returns to the evolving role of dialogism and to the problem of confession. The realities of dialogism render impossible any direct relation to the self, for all human relations, including that to oneself, are mediated by language and by the other; we see ourselves in what Bakhtin calls the "mirror of others' words." The Lacanian intervention makes subjectivity dependent upon the recognition of an irreducible distance separating self from other, and in so doing, turns psychic life into a series of irremediable losses and misrecognitions. But while Lacan seems to see human beings as eternally susceptible to the lure, as ontologically defined by lack and imperfection, as subject to a desire that can only lead to an impasse of dissatisfaction, Bakhtin foregrounds the human capacity to mutually "author" one another, the ability to dialogically intersect on the frontiers between selves. One becomes "oneself" not by shedding others to disinter an originary essence, but rather by revealing oneself to another, through another, with another's help.

A Bakhtinian approach is in this sense quite compatible with the feminist critique of Freudianism developed by Jessica Benjamin in *The Bonds of Love* (1988).[5] In her analysis of the early phases of development in childhood and infancy, Benjamin focuses on the importance of the mother-child dyad in psychic development, ultimately painting a portrait of intersubjective communication that is markedly different from the Lacanian model. In a very Bakhtinian vein (although Bakhtin is not her explicit point of reference), Benjamin sees the child as evolving against the backdrop of the responsive understanding of the mother. Rather than stress physiological dependency à la Freud, Benjamin highlights the "emotional attunement, mutual influence, affective mutuality" inhering in a "life-giving exchange with others." Benjamin's notion of "intersubjectivity" reorients the conception of the psychic world from a subject's relation to its object toward a subject meeting another subject. The mother is not only provider, caretaker, and mirror, but interlocutor as well. Citing recent infancy research, Benjamin points out that already at three or four months, the infant has the capacity to participate in sophisticated facial play, the main motive of which is social interaction, responding to the mother's voice and face with wriggles and smiles. Benjamin rejects the Freudian notion of psychosexual phases within the individual in favor of tension between interacting individuals. Rather than a dual relationship, an exercise in misrecognition and the lure, the mother-child relationship is a "dance of interaction," an apprenticeship in communication.

Bakhtin's interest in "the formal method" (as Russian formalism referred to itself) culminated in *The Formal Method in Literary Scholarship,* which appeared under Medvedev's name in 1928, but which bears the unmistakable imprint of Bakhtin's thought and style. Although Bakhtin has himself occasionally been labeled a "Russian formalist," in fact his attitude toward that movement mingles appreciation and critique. *The Formal Method* credits the formalists with "posing the essential problems of literary scholarship," but criticizes them for isolating the study of literature from the other arts and from social context. The literary phenomenon, Bakhtin argues, is simultaneously determined from without (extrinsically) and from within (intrinsically). From within it is conditioned by language and literature itself, and from without it is influenced by the other spheres of social life. In contrast to the antecedent "flabby eclecticism," the formalists brought great sharpness to problems of literary specification, seeing the artistic signifier not as a mere technical auxiliary for conveying "reality" or "grand thoughts" but rather as a self-valuable part of reality. The formalists' attempts to "free the word," unfortunately, were marred by a mechanical rejection of tradition—Bakhtin's notion of intertextual dialogism allows for no such simple undialectical hostility to the past—and by an impoverished view of the text as a modish arsenal of "devices" whose tautological purpose was to "make themselves perceptible." And while formalism saw the artistic text as closed within some "permanent contemporaneity," Bakhtin sees every utterance, including artistic utterances, as social and historical "events" resonating not only with their actual time and context but also with the echoes and reverberations of their past usages.

   Marxism and the Philosophy of Language (1929) constitutes Bakhtin's first direct intervention in the contemporary reflection on language. Here Bakhtin offers a comprehensive account of what he calls "translinguistics," a theory of the role of signs in human life and thought and the nature of utterance in language. Bakhtin rejects what he sees as the "psychologism" of the Saussurean linguistic tradition, arguing that individual consciousness cannot be used to explain anything but rather is itself in need of explanation from a sociological and translinguistic perspective. Bakhtin's twin targets in *Marxism and the Philosophy of Language* are a reductive Marxism that would relegate the world of signs and ideology to a "superstructure" determined by an economic "base," on the one hand, and a rationalist "abstract objectivist" view that would reduce language to a stable system of normative forms, on the other. For Bakhtin, the reality of language-speech is not the abstract system of linguistic forms but rather the social event of verbal interaction implemented in language exchange, for signs can arise only on "interindividual territory." What Bakhtin calls "the word"—that is, language in the broadest sense—is the "ideological phenomenon par excellence" and the "purest and most sensitive medium of social intercourse."

Bakhtin shares with Marxism the assumption that cultural processes are intimately linked to social relations and that culture is the site of social struggle. His specific contribution, however, is to highlight what might be called the *linguistic* dimension of class struggle. Human beings are not simply born into language as a master code; they grow into it, and help shape it, as woman or man, worker or boss, peasant or landowner. Every apparently unified linguistic or social community is characterized by heteroglossia, whereby language becomes the space of confrontation of differently oriented social accents, as diverse "sociolinguistic consciousnesses" fight it out on the terrain of language. Utterances and their types, Bakhtin writes in "The Problem of Speech Genres," are the "drive belts" that intervene between the history of society and the history of language. While the dominant class strives to make the sign "uniaccentual" and to endow it with an eternal, supraclass character, the oppressed, especially when they are conscious of their oppression, strive to deploy language for their own liberation. To speak of dialogue without speaking of power, in a Bakhtinian perspective, is to speak meaninglessly, in a void. For Bakhtin, language is thus everywhere imbricated with asymmetries of power. Patriarchal domination and economic dependency make sincere interlocution impossible. There is no "neutral" utterance; language is everywhere shot through with intentions and accents; it is material, multiaccentual, and historical, and is densely overlaid with the traces of its historical usages.

These Bakhtinian formulations have the advantage of not restricting liberatory struggle to purely economic or political battles; instead, they extend it to the common patrimony of the utterance. Bakhtin locates ideological combat at the pulsating heart of discourse, whether in the form of political rhetoric, artistic practice, or everyday language exchange. Discursive relationships, in this perspective, can be deciphered as microhistorical encounters. Bakhtin's language-oriented view of social practice brings discursive precision to the countercultural axiom "everything is political." Indeed, a good deal of quotidian politics operates in the microcosmic form of everyday language exchange. Oppression often "passes" not only in the form of state repression and the "dull compulsion" of economic dependency (the billy club and the pink slip) but also in the more subtle forms of face-to-face discursive interaction: the male doctor's condescending tone and choice of words toward his "hysterical" woman patient, the policeman's subtly or not-so-subtly discriminatory language, the welfare bureaucrat's censorious intonation toward the welfare recipient, the boss's patronizing tone when he compliments "the girls" in the office. Language intersects with power even in the forms of the one-upmanships of cocktail parties and the verbal muggings and discursive violences of everyday life. Power is exercised in the right to speak, the right to interrupt, the right to remain silent. Politics and language intersect in the form of attitudes, of talking down to or looking up to, of patronizing, respecting, ignoring, supporting, misinterpreting.

In *Problems of Dostoevsky's Poetics* (1929), Bakhtin extends to literature some of the ideas on verbal interaction developed in *Freudianism: A Marxist Critique* and *Marxism and the Philosophy of Language*. Less than a simple work of literary criticism, the book offers in embryo a number of suggestive theses concerning the polyphonic novel, dialogism, carnivalization, along with an innovative conception of literary genres and their transformation in Dostoevsky's work. Bakhtin's point of departure is what had always been the pivotal question within Dostoevsky criticism—the relation between Dostoevsky as author and his vociferous gallery of flamboyant characters. Dostoevsky is to be identified not with one or another voice within his novels, Bakhtin argues, but rather with the agency that orchestrates a multiplicity of distinct and even antithetical voices. Dostoevsky's art is "polyphonic"—that is, it engenders a textual plurality of unmerged voices and consciousnesses. It deploys juxtaposition, counterpoint, and simultaneity in its treatment of its favored subject—the dialogue of consciousnesses within the sphere of ideas. The lack of an originary personality or homogeneous style is not a flaw in Dostoevsky's work; it is, rather, "of the essence," the means by which Dostoevsky juxtaposes discourses in a process of mutual illumination and relativization. This does not mean that the author is the passive compiler of others' points of view; rather, he is profoundly active, alert to the dialogical tissue of human life, to the array of voices the author reproduces, answers, interrogates, amplifies.

Bakhtin sees Dostoevsky's work as existing in the satiric tradition of the "Menippea," a perennial artistic genre intimately linked to a carnivalesque vision of the world and marked by oxymoronic characters, multiple styles, violation of the norms of decency, and the comic confrontation of conflicting points of view. Bakhtin's broad conception of the Menippea, although obviously not originally conceived as an instrument of cinematic analysis, has the capacity, I will be arguing, to deprovincialize a film-critical discourse too often tied to nineteenth-century European conventions of verisimilitude. The mainstream cinema, as countless commentators have pointed out, has shown itself to be the aesthetic and narrative heir of the nineteenth-century mimetic novel and the "well-made play." Dominant journalistic and televisual criticism—what Metz calls the "linguistic appendage of the industry"—has also molded itself within the confines of an aesthetic appropriate to such forms. Even the rebels against the hegemony of dominant cinema have often been indirectly parasitical on the mainstream illusionistic tradition, proposing little more than a festival of negations of the dominant conventions, a cinema of sterile transgressions which shatters the image, fractures the narrative, explodes character, and generally refuses the decorum of the "well-made film." But if we are to see such filmmakers as Bunuel, Godard, Ruiz, and others not as the mere negation of the dominant tradition but rather as perpetuators of *another* tradition, our perspective must be quite different. We would see them as the renovators of a perennial mode whose protean vitality derives not only from individual invention but also from renewed contact with an often repressed but ultimately irrepressible generic tradition.

In *Problems of Dostoevsky's Poetics,* Bakhtin had already sketched out his ideas concerning "carnivalization" as the transposition of the spirit of carnival festivities into art, but it was in *Rabelais and His World* (first submitted as a thesis in 1940 but not published until the sixties) that Bakhtin gave this notion its fullest and richest formulation. Rabelais has been misunderstood, Bakhtin argues, because scholars have failed to discern Rabelais' profound links with popular culture (especially in the form of festivities such as carnival), and have failed to appreciate the literary modes associated with carnival—parody and grotesque realism. Carnival, for Bakhtin, is at once a historical reality in early modern Europe, the hermeneutic key to Rabelaisian writing, and an "anticipatory" mode of socialist gregariousness. In *Rabelais and His World,* Bakhtin develops his ideas concerning key topoi of the carnivalesque—the grotesque body, gay relativity, free and familiar contact, banquet imagery, marketplace speech, and the bodily lower stratum—in reference to Rabelais but with implications that go far beyond him.

The essays gathered in *The Dialogical Imagination,* generally written after the Dostoevsky book and before the Rabelais book, develop such ideas as the anti-epic distinctiveness of the novel form, its penchant for "heteroglossia" (literally, "many-languagedness") and "dialogization," defined as the necessary relation of any utterance to other utterances. In *The Dialogical Imagination,* Bakhtin also develops his concept of the literary "chronotope" (literally, "time-space") as a means for understanding the ways in which spatiotemporal structures in the novel evoke the existence of a life-world independent of the text and its representations. The notion of the chronotope refers to the constellation of distinctive temporal and spatial features within a genre defined as a "relatively stable type of utterance." In "Forms of Time and Chronotope in the Novel," Bakhtin suggests that time and space in the novel are intrinsically connected since the chronotope "materializes time in space." The chronotope mediates between two orders of experience and discourse: the historical and the artistic, providing fictional environments where historically specific constellations of power are made visible. The chronotope offers specific settings where stories can "take place" (the atemporal otherworldly forest of romance, the "nowhere" of fictional utopias, the roads and inns of the picaresque novel, the merchant and whaling ships of Conrad's or Melville's tales). These concrete spatiotemporal structures in the novel are correlatable with the real historical world but not equatable with it because they are always mediated by art. (We must never confuse the represented world of the text, Bakhtin warns us, with the world outside the text, for "the represented world, however realistic and truthful, can never be chronotopically identical with the real world it represents.")

Through the idea of the chronotope, Bakhtin shows how concrete spatiotemporal structures in literature limit narrative possibility, shape characterization, and mold a discursive simulacrum of life and the world. And although Bakhtin once again does not refer to the cinema, his category seems ideally suited to it as a medium where "spatial and temporal indicators are fused into one carefully thought-out concrete whole." Bakhtin's description of the novel as the place where time "thickens, takes on flesh, becomes artistically visible," and where "space becomes charged and responsive to the movements of time, plot, and history," seems in some ways even more appropriate to film than to literature, for whereas literature plays itself out within a virtual, lexical space, the cinematic chronotope is quite literal, splayed out concretely across a screen with specific dimensions and unfolding in literal time (usually 24 frames a second), quite apart from the fictive time/space specific films might construct.

The notion of the chronotope has the potential of historicizing the discussion of filmic genre. In her "Lounge Time: Post-war Crises and the Chronotope of Film Noir," Vivian Sobchack extends chronotopic analysis to the spatiotemporal features of film noir as a cinematic space/time in which the postwar crises in cultural values and in economic and sexual identity found vernacular expression.[6] Chronotopes, Sobchack argues, are not merely the spatiotemporal backdrop for narrative events but are also the literal and concrete ground from which narrative and character emerge as the temporalization of human action. The diacritical contrast that structures film noir, for Sobchack, is between the impersonal, discontinuous rented space of cocktail lounge, nightclub, hotel, and roadside café, on the one hand, and the familiar, unfragmented secure space of domesticity, on the other. The noir chronotope has no room for children or for rituals of family continuity: "no weddings, no births, no natural death, no familial intimacy and connection can be eventful here." Even leisure is more suffered than enjoyed in the "lounge-time" of the shadowed spaces of film noir. The characters generated by this chronotope are transient, without roots or occupation, in a world where murder is more natural than death. The chronotope of noir, Sobchack argues, perversely celebrates the repressed hysteria of a postwar cultural moment when domestic and economic coherence were fractured, spatializing and concretizing a "freedom" at once attractive, frightening, and ultimately illusory.

The pieces gathered in *Speech Genres and Other Late Essays,* like those gathered in *The Dialogical Imagination,* are drawn from different periods in the author's life. In these essays, Bakhtin makes general observations about the state of literary studies, expatiates on the *bildungsroman* and on the "problem of the text." Most important, for our purposes, Bakhtin elaborates his conception of a continuum of "speech genres," which move from the "primary" speech genres derived from everyday language exchange to the more complex literary and scientific speech genres, a conception rich in potential, as we shall see, for the analysis of film.

Although there is no vertical hierarchy among Bakhtin's interrelated conceptual categories, it is useful to regard "dialogism" as a category that "horizontally" embraces and comprehends the others. The privileging of just one of Bakhtin's many interrelated concepts is reflected not only in the popularity, within literary and film-critical discourse, of the qualifier "dialogic," but also in the titles of some of the books about Bakhtin: *The Dialogical Principle*

(Todorov) and *Bakhtin: Essays and Dialogues on His Work* (Morson). Bakhtin himself seems to authorize the impression that "dialogism" is central to all his work. "I hear voices everywhere," Bakhtin was fond of saying, "and the dialogical relations between them." The word *dialogism,* however, is almost too rich in philosophical and literary reverberations, too embarrassingly polysemic, whence its appropriation by the most diverse and politically heterogeneous currents. How is it, Paul de Man asks, that "dialogism can be so enthusiastically received by theoreticians of very diverse persuasion and made to appear as a valid way out of many of the quandaries that have plagued us for so long?"[7]

Without presuming to answer de Man's question—in a way this entire book is an attempt at an answer—I hope to illuminate some aspects of dialogism and its relevance to film specifically and cultural studies generally. In a preliminary way, we can define dialogism as the necessary relation of any utterance to other utterances, using *utterance,* as always, in Bakhtin's inclusive sense of that word. In all his writings, Bakhtin tirelessly reiterates this idea of the dialogical or relational nature of the utterance. Any verbal performance, he writes in *Marxism and the Philosophy of Language,* "inevitably orients itself with respect to previous performances in the same sphere, both those by the same author and those by other authors, originating and functioning as part of a social dialogue."[8] Bakhtin sees dialogism as a defining characteristic of the novel, cognate with its openness to the social diversity of speech types. The word *dialogism* in Bakhtin's writings progressively accretes meanings and connotations without ever losing this central idea of "the relation between the utterance and other utterances." Although Bakhtin often refers to dialogue in the literal sense to provide examples of the dialogic, the dialogic cannot in any way be equated with dialogue itself. Nor can dialogue and monologue be seen as absolute opposites, since a monologue can also be dialogic, given the fact that every utterance, including the solitary utterance, has its "others" and exists against the backdrop of other utterances.

It is not my purpose to exhaust or "finalize" the discussion of dialogism—"the possibilities and perspectives embedded in the [dialogic] word," Bakhtin writes in "The Problem of the Text," "are essentially infinite"—but rather to highlight several points relevant to my present purposes. First, there is a constant back and forth, within Bakhtin's discussion of dialogism, from the literal to the metaphorical plane, from the specific to the general, and from

the close to the more distant. Dialogism refers to the relation between the text and its others not only in the relatively crude and
obvious forms of argument—polemics and parody—but also in
much more diffuse and subtle forms that have to do with overtones,
pauses, implied attitude, what is left unsaid or is to be inferred. In
"The Problem of the Text," Bakhtin suggests some of the more subtle forms of this more implicit, often unacknowledged dialogism:
"confidence in another's word" (the tacit faith in the believability of
the word of the other); "reverential reception" (one thinks, in life, of
worshipful attitudes toward persons, and in criticism, of fawning
attitudes toward admired sources); "apprenticeship" (a dialogism
in which there is a fledgling attempt at mastering a jargon or a
style); the "layering of meaning upon meaning, voice upon voice"
and "the combination of voices."9 Even agreement comes in "infinite gradations and shadings" ranging from grudging acknowledg-
ment of the factual validity of another's statement to total affirmation and solidarity with the other's thrust and purposes. For
Bakhtin, even an agreed-upon sentence can embrace difference; as
pronounced by two different people, "What a beautiful day!" involves two distinct but verbally identical utterances, each with its
own voice and intonation, but linked by a "dialogical relation of
agreement." Furthermore, while dialogism at its root is interpersonal, it applies by extension to the relation between languages, lit-
eratures, genres, styles, and even entire cultures, a fact whose
ramifications we will be exploring throughout this text.

Dialogism entails a view of the individual and, by extension,
of the literary or film author, as existing in, and even in some measure created by, dialogue. "Dialogic theory," Bakhtin writes, leads
to a "new statement of the problem of authorship." Although he
never invokes the somewhat apocalyptic tones of the "death of the
author" school, Bakhtin too deflates the romantic myth of the artist as visionary, sage, or "unacknowledged legislator." He questions the notion of author as primary and sacrosanct source of the
text, while at the same time restoring a kind of dignity and importance to the author as the stager and *metteur-en-scène* of languages
and discourses. In *Problems of Dostoevsky's Poetics*, Bakhtin portrays the author ideally, as a kind of democratic parliamentarian
who "gives the floor" to his characters, who allows them to exist au-
tonomously alongside and even "in rebellion against" him, but who
retains control of the overall conception of the whole. But apart from
this quasi-political question of the power relations between author
and character, the author is further relativized in Bakhtin's work

by the idea of his or her necessary (one is tempted to say "ecological") dependence on the linguistic and literary environment. The author lives, in short, within, and thanks to, "intertextuality."

Bakhtin traces literary dialogism as far back as the Socratic dialogues, with their agonic staging of the contest of two competing discourses. He opposes the dialogic and polyphonic texts of Rabelais, Cervantes, Diderot, and Dostoevsky to "monologic" and "theological" texts that unproblematically assert a single truth. The concept of dialogism suggests that every text forms an intersection of textual surfaces where other texts may be read. "The literary word," according to Bakhtin, "is aware of the presence of another literary word alongside it." All texts are tissues of anonymous formulae embedded in the language, variations on those formulae, conscious and unconscious quotations, conflations, and inversions of other texts. (Gore Vidal refers to this textual process in his novel *Duluth* by having a character tap out romantic novels on a word-processor with a memory bank of 10,000 other novels.) In the broadest sense, intertextual dialogism refers to the infinite and open-ended possibilities generated by all the discursive practices of a culture, the entire matrix of communicative utterances within which the artistic text is situated and which reach the text not only through recognizable influences but also through a subtle process of dissemination.

Although Bakhtin has had a world-wide impact on cultural studies, affecting not only the Soviet Union but also Western Europe, Japan, North America, and South America, it is not always clear which "Bakhtin" is having the impact. Each country and school seems to nurture its own Bakhtin, and often multiple Bakhtins can be found to coexist within the same country. The last few years have witnessed, in fact, a kind of posthumous wrestle over the soul and legacy of Bakhtin. As an extraordinarily complex, contradictory, and at times even enigmatic figure, Bakhtin has been appropriated by the most diverse ideological currents.[10] In political terms, we find Bakhtin the populist, Bakhtin the Marxist, Bakhtin the anti-Marxist, Bakhtin the social-democrat, and Bakhtin the anti-Stalinist. There is a left reading of Bakhtin (Fredric Jameson, Terry Eagleton, Tony Bennett, Ken Hirschkop, Allon White/Peter Stallybrass, Graham Pechey) and a liberal reading (Wayne Booth, David Lodge, Tzvetan Todorov).[11] Here, however, I will be reading him as a kind of "para-Marxist" or radical populist working "alongside" Marxism (certainly not *against* it, as some of his commentators would have it), and as a "trans-" or "post-Marxist" in the sense that he remedies some of the blind spots of Marxist theory. Although I am indebted to all of Bakhtin's commentators (notably to Katerina Clark, Michael Holquist, Gary Saul Morson, and Caryl Emerson), my ideological affinities incline toward those who try to push Bakhtinian ideas in radical directions rather than toward those who recruit him as a kind of liberal pluralist. My argument is not essentialist—the "real" Bakhtin was radical—but pragmatic and personal—this is the use to which I would like to see Bakhtin put.

I will not attempt here to iron out the manifest "wrinkles" in Bakhtin's work—his penchant for simplistic dichotomies, his frequent oscillation between idealist and materialist categories, his failure to deeply theorize power relations, his blindness to the potential co-optability of popular discourses—or to fill out its obvious lacunae. Nor will I seek to explain away the numerous points where Bakhtin was clearly and demonstrably wrong—for example, his occasional essentialist denigration of epic, drama, and poetry as necessarily "monological" and his corollary idealization of the novel as intrinsically "dialogical." At times we will have to pursue Bakhtin's ideas where they lead, ignoring the somewhat arbitrary limits he himself placed on them, while remaining within the spirit of his enterprise. Rather than emphasize the shortcomings of Bakhtin's *oeuvre*, I will focus on the richness of its potential applicability. I plan to engage in a kind of "threshold encounter" with Bakhtin's ideas, here "reaccentuated" as if they had been addressed directly to our concerns, in hopes of "fleshing out" what Kristeva called Bakhtin's "intuitions," extrapolating Bakhtinian concepts "beyond" their original field of reference, deploying them as a kind of trampoline for broader cultural exegesis.

What follows is an affectionate dialogue with Bakhtin's work, here extended in its implications to cultural areas about which he himself rarely if ever spoke. Bakhtin, as far as we know, never addressed himself to the film medium. He says nothing, for example, of the theory of film that so fascinated his contemporaries the Russian formalists and the avant-garde in the twenties. Nevertheless, just as Bakhtin suggested that we should not "squeeze" Shakespeare into the Elizabethan period, but rather should view his work as unfolding within "great time," so too we should not restrict Bakhtin's relevance to those media and subjects he himself happened to address. The "rightness" of a Bakhtinian approach to film derives, I would suggest, not only from the nature of the field and the nature of the medium but also from the "migratory" cross-disciplinary drift of the Bakhtinian method. As a self-defined "liminal" thinker, Bakhtin moves on the borders, at the junctures and points of intersection of academic disciplines as traditionally defined and institutionally regulated. The most productive interdisciplinary relations, Bakhtin argues, occur at the borders between the diverse sectors, and not when those sectors close themselves within their specificity. Given the film medium's own variegated roots in popular as well as erudite culture, and given the historical permeability of the medium by developments in literary theory and criticism as well as its traditional openness to new and often radical methodologies, the encounter of Bakhtin with film might be viewed as virtually inevitable.

This encounter is facilitated, furthermore, by the open and "nonfinalizing" style of Bakhtinian thought and by what Bakhtin himself calls "the internal open-endedness" of his ideas, their inherent potential for giving rise to surprising extrapolations. For Bakhtin no writing is complete without the readers/interlocutors who fill in meaning from their particular position in space and time. My interest, then, will not be in disinterring a "real," originary Bakhtin, or in situating his work within the context of the intellectual history of the Soviet Union—tasks for which I lack the requisite training in Slavic Studies and the Russian language—but rather in exploring the analytic relevance of Bakhtinian categories for the cinema and for cultural criticism. To advance the circulation of Bakhtin's ideas into the bloodstream of other disciplines is appropriate to their being, in Graham Pechey's words, "constitutively migratory."

Up to this point in the history of reflection on cinema, Bakhtin has been viewed largely as the theoretician of carnival and ritual inversions of power as reflected in the diegeses of films, and, as filtered through the work of Julia Kristeva and Gerard Genette, as one of the seminal source-thinkers of "intertextuality"—that is, the interanimation and the interfecundation of texts. The ready, anarchic appeal of the "carnivalesque," however, and the facile, almost "technocratic" applicability of the notion of "intertextuality" have at times led to the slighting of other, more radical dimensions of Bakhtin's thought. My project here will be to speak not only of the critical use-value of "carnival" but also of other Bakhtinian concepts, particularly of his politicized vision of language as pervaded by "dialogism" (i.e., the transindividual generation of meaning), "heteroglossia" (the interanimation of the diverse languages generated by sexual, racial, economic, and generational difference), and "tact" (the ensemble of codes governing discursive interaction). Bakhtin, I will argue, can serve as a corrective to structuralism, particularly in the area of the social context of languages and actual linguistic, literary, and cinematic praxis. Bakhtin promotes the subversive use of language by those who otherwise lack social power in ways that extend well beyond the sterile neutrality of structuralism.

What Bakhtin offers cultural analysis, as Todorov points out in *The Dialogical Principle,* is nothing less than a unitary transdisciplinary view of the human sciences and of cultural life based on the common *textual* nature of their materials. Bakhtin believed in the fundamental unity of all those spheres of knowledge that are dependent on the text as their object of study: "Where there is no text," he writes, "there is no object of study, and no object of thought either."[12] Not only are texts, oral and written, the primary given of all those disciplines (linguistic, philological, literary, or any kind of analysis) and of all thought in the human sciences and philosophy in general, but also even nonverbal actions are "potential texts," understandable "in the dialogical context of their time."

It is this methodological *parti pris* for seeing the objects of study of the human sciences as texts to be deciphered and interpreted (rather than as objects or substances to be cognitively "known") that "authorizes" us to extrapolate Bakhtin's ideas to media that he himself never discussed. Bakhtin's definition of *text* as "any coherent complex of signs" encompasses everything from literature to visual and aural works of art—Bakhtin specifically cites the study of music and the fine arts as "textual"—as well as everyday action and communication. We do not "need" Bakhtin, of course, to learn that films are texts—the notion of the film/text is a commonplace of contemporary discourse, even if Bakhtin was among the first to formulate the pantextual idea. But Bakhtin's view of all cultural utterances as texts does facilitate the passage from literary to film theory. Bakhtin develops, in effect, a wide-ranging semiotic embracing both everyday discourse and the entire spectrum of artistic practices. As "coherent complexes of signs," films not only *include* texts; they *are* texts, necessarily susceptible to a Bakhtinian "translinguistic" analysis. Bakhtin's view of all language, including artistic language, as exhibiting conflicting utterances and as inflected both by other similar "utterances" and by social context suggests valuable reading strategies that are as valid for film and media texts as they are for the novel. Bakhtin's metaphors for textual processes, moreover, are both aural ("the orchestration of voices") and visual ("the multiplicity of focuses"), which further facilitates the passage from a verbal medium like literature to an audiovisual medium such as film.

Bakhtin's insistence on the presence of "voices" as well as "images," I would suggest, corresponds to a privileging of hearing over sight in recent feminist texts, as well as to the developing anthropological critique of Western "visualism." Many cultural commentators (e.g., Walter Ong, James Clifford, Johannes Fabian, Frances Yates, and Mary Louise Pratt) have argued, in different ways, that the Western masculinist imagination is strongly "visualist," positing cultural facts as things observed or seen rather than heard, transcribed, or invented in dialogue.[13] The Bakhtinian predilection for aural and musical metaphors—voices, intonation, accent, polyphony—argues an overall shift in priority from the visually predominant logical space of modernity (perspective, evidence in empirical science, domination of the gaze) to a "postmodern" space of the vocal (oral ethnography, peoples' history, slave narratives), all as ways of restoring voice to the silenced. The visual organization of space, George Yudice suggests, with its limits and boundaries and border police, is a metaphor of exclusions and hierarchical arrangements, while voice suggests a metaphor of seepage across boundaries which redefines spatiality itself.[14] The task of the Bakhtinian critic, then, is to call attention to the voices at play in a text, not only those heard in aural "close-up," but also those voices dominated, distorted, or drowned out by the text.

Another favorite term for Bakhtin, and here also he anticipated contemporary thought, is *discourse,* a term to which Bakhtin gave, again, the broadest possible definition. *Discourse* refers to language in its concrete, living totality. In his methodological critique of the discipline of "stylistics," Bakhtin contrasts a small-minded preoccupation with the "petty vicissitudes of stylistic modifications" with a broader concern for the "great historical destinies of genres" and the "anonymous destinies of artistic discourse itself."[15] Stylistics, he complains, too often limits itself to the nuances of "private craftsmanship," rather than open itself to the "social life of discourse outside the artist's study, discourse in the open spaces of public squares, streets, cities and villages, of social groups, generations and epochs."[16]

Bakhtin's broad view of *text* and *discourse* as referring to all cultural production rooted in language—and for Bakhtin no cultural production exists *outside* language—has the advantage of breaking down not only the walls between popular and elite culture but also those between text and context. The barrier between text and context, between "inside" and "outside," for Bakhtin, is an artificial one, for in fact there is an easy permeability between the two. The context is already textualized, informed by the "already said" and by "prior speakings," while the text is "redolent with contexts," at every point inflected by historical process and shaped by social events. In this regard, it is significant that virtually all of the key Bakhtinian categories—dialogism, heteroglossia, polyphony, carnival, tact, intonation—simultaneously embrace the textual, the intertextual, and the contextual. Like the formalists, Bakhtin is sensitive to the specificity of textual mechanisms—literature as literature, film as film—but unlike them, he refuses to dissociate these mechanisms from other signifying practices (including those of everyday life) or from larger social and historical processes as a whole.

Bakhtin, I will argue, points the way to transcending some of the felt insufficiencies of other theoretical grids. His concept of dialogism, of language and discourse as "shared territory," inoculates us against the individualist assumptions undergirding romantic theories of art, while still allowing us to be attuned to the specific ways in which artists orchestrate diverse social voices. His emphasis on a boundless context that constantly interacts with and modifies the text helps us avoid the formalist fetishization of the autonomous art object. And his emphasis on the "situated utterance" and the "interpersonal generation of meaning" helps us avoid both the static ahistoricism of an apolitical "value free" semiotics and the implicit hermeneutic nihilism of some poststructuralist thought.

Bakhtin's careful attention to the interlocutor of the text, meanwhile—his conviction that all discourse exists in dialogue not only with prior discourses but also with the recipients of the discourse—aligns him with the concerns of the contemporary reception theory of Jauss and Iser as well as with the "reader response" criticism of Stanley Fish and Norman Holland. Like the reception theorists, Bakhtin rejects referential models of artistic discourse. Rather than reflect a protextual situation, discourse *is* a situation, an event shared by author and reader. Artistic speech is interlocution, the in-between of text and a reader whose responsive understanding is sought and anticipated and on whom the text depends for its concretization. In his essays on "speech genres," Bakhtin speaks of the "addressivity" of the utterance, its quality of always being addressed to someone. This addressee can be an immediate participant/interlocutor in an everyday dialogue, or a differentiated collective of specialists, an ethnic group, or "like-minded people, opponents and enemies, a subordinate, a superior, someone who is lower, higher, familiar, foreign . . . or even an indefinite, unconcretized other," or a "loophole addressee" existing at a metaphysical distance or in far-off historical time.[17]

Bakhtin also speaks of the "active influence of the reader," whose "apperceptive background of responsive understanding" must be taken into account. Both Bakhtin and reception theorists resist the formalists' closing off of the text, positing real, active readers, with the crucial difference that Bakhtin gives a more specific social density to the "virtual," "implied," and "ideal" readers and "interpretative communities" of reception and reader-response theory, furnishing them with a local habitation and name, a gender, a class, a nation. Rather than appeal to a phenomenology of consciousness ("horizons of expectation"), Bakhtin appeals to a socialized world of discourse, ideology, language. In this sense, Bakhtin's work is compatible with, and at times concretely influenced, the television and film-reception studies performed by analysts such as Robert Allen, Ian Eng, Charlotte Brunsdon, Tania Modleski, John Fiske, David Morley, and Stuart Hall, who document and theorize the process whereby specific audiences "negotiate" mass-media messages from particular angles and perspectives.[18]

Bakhtinian categories, I will be arguing, display an intrinsic identification with difference and alterity, a built-in affinity for the oppressed and the marginal, a feature making them especially appropriate for the analysis of opposition and marginal practices, be they Third World, feminist, or avant-garde. Although Bakhtin did not specifically address himself to all oppressions, a conceptual space is staked out for them, as it were, in advance. Indeed, Bakhtinian thought provides a "loophole" for the discussion of all oppressions, as in the following passage from *Problems of Dostoevsky's Poetics* (pp. 122–23):

What is suspended [in carnival] first of all is hierarchical structure and all the forms of terror, reverence, piety, and etiquette connected with it—that is, everything resulting from sociohierarchical inequality or any other form of inequality among people (including age).

The formulation could not be broader—"everything resulting from sociohierarchical inequality or any other form of inequality among people." Although Bakhtin does not speak directly to Third World or minoritarian concerns, for example, his categories are eminently well-suited to them, offering a corrective to certain Euro-centric prejudices. In *The Formal Method in Literary Scholarship,* Bakhtin speaks of non-European cultures as the catalysts for European modernism's surpassing of a retrograde culture-bound verism. And Bakhtin's oxymoronic carnival aesthetic, in which everything is pregnant with its opposite, implies an alternative logic of nonexclusive opposites and permanent contradiction that transgresses the monologic true-or-false thinking typical of Western rationalism.

Although Bakhtin seldom speaks specifically of the oppression of women, similarly, his work can thus be seen as intrinsically open to feminist inflection. It is interesting, in this connection, that Bakhtin consistently heaps scorn, throughout his writings, on the "canon" and on the "canonical," expressions that enjoy their own "homecoming festival" in a context of feminist and minoritarian contestation of the canon as a fixed body (implicitly masculine and Eurocentric) of "great works." In *Feminist Dialogics,* Dale Bauer argues that Bakhtin's social theory of the utterance is "congenial to a feminist approach to the normative discursive practices of patriarchal culture, which feminism would subvert."[19] She distinguishes between Bakhtinian "multivocality" and a conservative "pluralism" that invites women to join a community and then promptly drowns out their voice. While criticizing the dominant mode of Bakhtin scholarship for its lack of interest in gender theory or sexual difference, she attempts to "refashion Bakhtin's sociological stylistics into a feminist dialogics." Noting the lack, in Bakhtin, of an adequate theory of power, she ultimately finds Bakhtinian dialogism "an empowering model" in the combat against patriarchy.

Apart from the points of coincidence mentioned by Bauer, there are important congruences of approach and sensibility between Bakhtinian dialogism and feminism. It is certainly no accident that Bakhtin's positively connoted words—*polyglossia, dialogism, polyphony*—so frequently feature prefixes that designate plurality or alterity. Rather than find difference and multiplicity threatening, Bakhtin finds them exhilarating, and in this sense his thought opens to what Luce Iragaray calls feminine "plurality" and "multiplicity." Bakhtin shares with feminism a preference for process over product, a distrust of "mastery" and the "last word." Bakhtin's sensitivity to "tact" and "intonation" also is congenial to feminists, since it is women who have been taught by experience under patriarchy to distinguish between what is said and what is meant, between what is said and how it is said.

Bakhtin, I would suggest, offers us a powerful analytic, one that has the capacity, if used well, to make its object of study come alive, scintillate, and resonate with previously unheard overtones and voices. Over the course of the book, I will be attempting to elaborate a Bakhtinian critical method and to apply it successively to diverse areas of film and mass-media inquiry: first to theory (translinguistics and semiotics), then to a specific language-related problematic (language difference in the cinema), then to issues involving auteur and genre (carnivalesque strategies in literature and film), then to the cultural productions of a specific nation (Brazil), then to a thematic (eroticism) and a genre (pornography), then to a specific text (*Zelig*), and finally to a social pragmatic (the uses of Bakhtin for mass-media critique). At the same time, each chapter will foreground one or more Bakhtinian concepts to be defined, elaborated, and exemplified. The concepts will then reappear throughout the text, rather like musical leitmotifs (in keeping with Bakhtin's notorious fondness for musical metaphors), accreting meanings and reverberations with each new context. Bakhtin's concepts taken as a whole, furthermore, will be viewed as a kind of ideational polyphony in which ideas regarding the body, power, language, and carnival resonate complexly and reciprocally.

The book deals, overall, with four major conceptual areas— language, carnival, the body, and dialogism. The first two chapters delineate Bakhtin's invaluable contribution to a sociomaterialist theory of language, focusing especially on *Marxism and the Philosophy of Language* (written in collaboration with V. N. Voloshinov) as the first systematic attempt to ground a Marxist theory of language within a thorough and critical knowledge of contemporary linguistics. Chapter 1, "Translinguistics and Semiotics," foregrounds Bakhtin's potential contribution to the semiotics of the cinema. The ideas adumbrated in *Marxism and the Philosophy of Language,* I will argue, provide a corrective to the blind spots of film linguistics based on the Saussurean model, just as the Bakhtin/Medvedev critique of the formalists in *The Formal Method in Literary Scholarship* provides the theoretical basis for going beyond an asocial, ahistorical, purely formalistic analysis of cinematic texts. This chapter, in some ways the most aridly theoretical of the book, nevertheless "enables" the larger argument by exploring the extendibility of Bakhtin's language-based tropes to media that are not at first glance "linguistic."

While Chapter 1 stresses film *as* language, Chapter 2, "Language, Difference, and Power," addresses language *in* film, and specifically the ways in which Bakhtin's nonunitary approach to language can help illuminate the impact of language difference (polyglossia and heteroglossia) on the cinema in terms of such issues as translation, postsynchronization, subtitles, and the like. How do language and language difference "enter" the cinema? How do differences between and within languages impinge on film as a discursive practice thoroughly penetrated by relations of power?

Chapters 3 and 4 deal with diverse aspects of the Bakhtinian notion of carnival. Chapter 3, "Film, Literature, and the Carnivalesque," explores Bakhtin's notions of carnival (developed especially in *Rabelais and His World*) and Menippean satire (elaborated in *Problems of Dostoevsky's Poetics*) as exegetical keys for literature (Rabelais, Shakespeare, Jarry) and for the cinema, drawing examples from the films of the Marx Brothers, Luis Bunuel, Jean Vigo, Jean-Luc Godard, Lina Wertmuller, Mel Brooks, Monty Python, and Shohei Imamura.

Chapter 4, "Of Cannibals and Carnivals," explores the import of Bakhtin's notions of the carnivalesque and parodic carnivalization for the cultural productions of a country where carnival, in its literal denotation, retains its protean vitality. Bakhtinian categories, I will argue, are ideally suited to the analysis of the carnivalesque images and strategies that permeate Brazilian artistic productions, from music and literature to the cinema. Conversely, Brazilian textual examples serve to "flesh out" and actualize a theory of carnival rooted in the European Middle Ages and the Renaissance.

The next area of concern is Bakhtin's semiotic of the body. Bakhtin contrasts the open, protruding, grotesque body—associated with process and becoming—with the static, closed, monumental body of the classical aesthetic. In Chapter 5, "The Grotesque Body and Cinematic Eroticism," I will attempt to draw out the implications of Bakhtin's corporeal semiotic for an analysis of cinematic eroticism, emphasizing its potential for enabling both a critique and a transvaluation of pornography. How might Bakhtin contribute to the partial reframing of a debate that too often lapses into the formulaic repetition of Manichean binarisms: bad porn versus good erotica, bad censorship versus good freedom, and so on? How might Bakhtin's categories be enlisted in a nonmoralistic critique of pornography, one that does not invoke retrograde notions of "good taste" and "seemly behavior"?

Chapter 6, "From Dialogism to *Zelig*," invokes a number of Bakhtinian categories under the general rubric "dialogism." The chapter particularly focalizes the concept of cultural and intertextual dialogism. Drawing examples from popular culture (hip hop) and Woody Allen, it focuses especially on *Zelig* as the ideal point of convergence for a Bakhtinian textual analysis deploying an array of Bakhtinian concepts. This "meditation" on the Woody Allen text attempts to disengage the film's generic intertext and to delineate, through such Bakhtinian concepts as "dialogism," "heteroglossia," and "the in-between," the variegated strata of that film's allegorical palimpsest.

The envoi—"Bakhtin and Mass-Media Critique"—recapitulates crucial Bakhtinian concepts, this time in the context of the relevance of Bakhtin to cultural and mass-media critiques. How might Bakhtin help us transcend some of the sterile analytical dichotomies of the traditional left? How can Bakhtin aid in the elaboration of a radical hermeneutic that goes beyond dogmatism, beyond puritanism, beyond economism, and beyond cultural defeatism? How might Bakhtinian conceptualizations help us analyze, teach, and finally generate mass-mediated culture? Why, in short, do we "need" Bakhtin?

1

■■■■■■■ Translinguistics and
Semiotics

It has become a commonplace to proclaim that our century has
been relentlessly language haunted. If ours is the century of the
atom and the cosmos, Julia Kristeva has suggested, it is also the
century of *langage*. Although language has been an object of philosophical reflection for millennia, only recently has it come to constitute a fundamental paradigm, a virtual "key" to the mind, to artistic and social praxis, and indeed to human existence in its
entirety. Central to the project of thinkers as diverse as Wittgenstein, Cassirer, Heidegger, Lèvi-Strauss, Derrida, and Merleau-
Ponty is a concern with the crucial importance of language in human life and thought. The metadiscipline of semiotics, in this
sense, can be seen as a local manifestation of a more widespread
"linguistic turn," an attempt, in Jameson's words, to "rethink everything through again in terms of linguistics."

As the methodological success story of the twentieth century,
linguistics has generated a plurality of structuralisms, most of them
premised on seminal Saussurean dichotomies such as diachrony/
synchrony and langue/parole. Thus the scientific advance represented by Saussure's *Course in General Linguistics* (1916), decisive
in its area, was applied to other disciplines, such as literary study,
by Jakobson and the School of Prague, after which the Saussurean
method "passed" to Lèvi-Strauss, who used it with great intellectual
audacity in anthropology and thus founded structuralism as a
movement. By seeing kinship relations as a "language" susceptible
to the kinds of analysis applied by Troubetskoy and Jakobson to

questions of phonology, Lèvi-Strauss took the fundamental step
that made it possible for us to extend the same structural-linguistic
logic to all social, mental, and artistic structures. A wide range of
domains—fashion, cuisine, comic strips—came under the jurisdic-
tion of structural linguistics. Economics, in its semiotic dimension,
came to be seen as a symbolic system comparable to the symbolic
exchange of words in a language, and psychoanalysis, with Lacan,
came to view the Unconscious itself as "structured like a language."

The cinema, for its part, has not been immune to this spreading linguistic "contamination." Indeed, the notion of "film language" appears in the writings of some of the earliest theorists of
the cinema. One finds the metaphor in the writings of Riccioto
Canudo in Italy and Louis Delluc in France, both of whom saw the
languagelike nature of the cinema as linked to its nonverbal nature, its status as a "visual esperanto" transcending the barriers of
national language.[1] One finds it as well as in the work of Bela Balazs, who repeatedly stressed the languagelike nature of film in his
work from the twenties through the late forties.[2] Also beginning in
the twenties, the Russian formalists developed the analogy between language and film in a somewhat more systematic way. In
their anthology *Poetica Kino* (1927), with contributions by Eichenbaum, Shklovsky, Tynyanov, and others, the formalists stressed a
"poetic" use of film that was analogous to the "literary" use of language they posited for verbal texts.[3] Tynyanov spoke of the cinema
as offering the visible world in the form of semantic signs engendered by cinematic procedures such as lighting and montage, while
Eichenbaum viewed the cinema in relation to "inner speech" and
"image translations of linguistic tropes." The cinema, for Eichenbaum, was a "particular system of figurative language," the stylistics of which would treat film "syntax," the linkage of shots into
"phrases" and "sentences."

Subsequent to the work of the Russian formalists, the notion
of film language came to form the implicit topos grounding the
many "grammars" of cinema—for example, Raymond Spottiswoode's *Grammar of Film* (1935) and Robert Bataille's *Grammaire
Cinégraphique* (1947). In other presemiotic discussions, the film-
language metaphor became intimately linked to the cognate trope
of "film writing." In post-World War II France, especially, this
"graphological" figure became a key structuring concept subtending film theory and criticism. Only with the advent of structuralism and semiotics in the sixties, however, was the film-language
concept explored in depth by such theorists as Umberto Eco, Pier

Pãolo Pasolini, and Christian Metz. The key figure, of course, was Metz, whose purpose, as he himself defined it, was to "venir à bout de la metaphore linguistique"—that is, to get to the bottom of the linguistic metaphor, by testing it against the most advanced concepts of contemporary linguistics.

But before we return to Metz and cinesemiology, it is important to sketch out Bakhtin's relation to the "linguistic" turn generally, and to Saussurean semiology particularly, for the astonishing fact is that Bakhtin, writing in the twenties, both anticipated and superseded the structuralist project. His thoroughgoing and interlinked critiques of both Saussurean linguistics and formalist poetics point with uncanny prescience to the dialectical transcendence of the aporias generated by those movements. As a kind of proleptic poststructuralist—the one, in A. C. Goodson's words, who "was there all along"—Bakhtin managed to "go beyond" structuralism even before the movement had fully constituted itself as a paradigm. Just as Saussureanism and formalism were about to enter into that paradigmatic shift called structuralism, Bakhtin "mutated" them, as it were, into his own brand of Marxist-inflected transstructuralism. The prolegomenal text, in this regard, is *Marxism and the Philosophy of Language,* which first appeared under Voloshinov's name in 1929, and which constitutes Bakhtin's first direct intervention in the contemporary tradition of reflection on language. The task of this chapter will be to explore the ramifications of that book, and of Bakhtin's other writings on language, for a "social semiotic" of the cinema.

Marxism and the Philosophy of Language must be seen not only against the backdrop of a generally expanding semiotic consciousness growing out of the native Russian tradition of such linguists as Fortunatov, Chakmatov, Kruszewski, and Jan Baudouin de Courtenay, but also in the context of the dissemination, in the Soviet Union of the twenties, of the ideas of Ferdinand de Saussure. Russian intellectuals were acquainted with the work of the Swiss linguist both through his posthumously published *Course* and through the interpretation of his ideas by Sergei Karcaveskij, who returned to Russia in 1917 after studying in Geneva. As is well known, Saussure argued against the historical (diachronic) orientation of the neogrammarians in favor of a "synchronic" approach in which language is studied as a functional totality at a given point of time. Within the domain of the synchronic, linguistics was to focus on *langue*—that is, the language system, with its basic units and rules of combination—rather than on *parole,* the concrete utterances made possible by that system. In *Marxism and the Philosophy of Language,* Bakhtin threw down a radical challenge to both these dichotomies, reversing Saussure's priorities by emphasizing the diachronic, downplaying the language system as abstract model, and stressing instead parole, speech as lived and shared by human beings in social interaction.

The desire to see language as a static synchronic system, according to Bakhtin, is symptomatic of a kind of linguistic necrophilia, a nostalgia for deceased languages, whose systems could be fixed precisely because they were dead. The fundamental categories of Saussurean linguistics, which are phonetic (units of sound) and morphological (units of sense), ultimately derive from the categories of Indo-European comparative linguistics, precisely those categories that are most appropriate to a dead or alien language. As an heir of what Bakhtin calls the "abstract objectivist" tradition, the roots of which can be traced back to the rationalist tradition of Descartes, Leibniz, and Condillac, Saussure emphasizes those phonetic, lexical, and grammatical features which remain identical and therefore normative for all utterances, thus forming the ready-made "code" of a language. Within this system, individual and social variations of speech do not play much of a role; they are seen as random, "messy," too heterogeneous and slippery for the linguist's theoretical grasp, and irrelevant to the fundamental unity of language as system.

Given this static view of language, Bakhtin argues, Saussurean linguistics is completely discomfited by the problem of historical change. It is able to posit only a succession of synchronic states—"a series of infallible popes who happen to contradict each other," in Eagleton's witty formulation—rather than a dynamic process. For Bakhtin, in contrast, languages are alive, constantly changing under the discursive pressure of daily utterance, relentlessly generating new norms and counternorms through the processes of dialogism and heteroglossia. The idea of a language system is an imposed abstraction; what is important is not only the stable self-equivalent sign but also the inherent tendency toward change and dynamism. Premised on a series of untenable binarisms and compartmentalizations, the Saussurean mode, for Bakhtin, cordons off history from structure, the social from the individual, and abstract langue from workaday parole. By refusing to scrutinize language at its point of production—as actually spoken, listened to, written, read, and disseminated—Saussure stripped language of its sociality and historicity.

A systematic approach to language such as Saussure's runs the risk of expressing implicit conservatism, of regarding a living language as arrested and fixed, a kind of "exquisite corpse." Systematic, grammatical thought, Bakhtin writes in *Marxism and the Philosophy of Language*,"

must inevitably adopt a conservative position, i.e. it must interpret living language as if it were already perfected and ready-made and thus look upon any sort of innovation in language with hostility. Formal, systematic thought about language is incompatible with living, historical understanding of language. From the system's point of view, history always seems merely a series of accidental transgressions.[4]

Saussure in this sense is the heir of the conservatism of the official Francophonic attitude, with its traditional endorsement of institutions, such as the Académie Française, authorized to regulate language use. Educated in Switzerland and holding an academic chair in Paris, Saussure was the intellectual product of a Third Republic France that was very much preoccupied with maintaining linguistic hegemony. It is no accident, as Bart Palmer points out, that Saussure formulated his crucial langue/parole distinction at a time when the French educational system was striving to wipe out regional dialects and class usage by imposing the standard literary language on the pupils in its charge.[5] Indeed, it is precisely such contextualizing features that Saussurean linguistics "edits out"— that is, those features having to do with the sociohistorical process by which a language (and by extension a language theory) is constituted as normative, and thus is imposed on others and reproduced as the dominant form.

Bakhtin's "translinguistics," formulated against Saussurean linguistics, emerges from an intellectual context that is radically different from that which shaped Saussure. Bakhtin's work responds to the myriad social, political, economic, and cultural forces shaping the 1917 revolution, and specifically to the polemic concerning language to which much of his work is explicitly or implicitly addressed. Bakhtin's thought finds its inspiration not only in literature but also in the multitudinous voices clamoring from every corner of Russian society in the early decades of this century. Debates on language were nurtured, for example, not only by such formalist groups as the Moscow Linguistic Circle, founded in 1915 by Jakobson, and the Society for the Study of Poetic Language (OPOYAZ, founded in 1916 in Petrograd), but also by Khlebnikov's researches into ultrasignifying "pure sounds," by Eisenstein's pre-occupation with ideography and the origins of sign systems, by Vygotsky's studies of "inner speech" and "thought and language," and by Mayakovsky's abolition of the barriers between poetic sense and nonsense. Bakhtin's intervention took place against the animated backdrop of the contemporaneous debates that pitted the formalist advocates of an exclusively poetic language against the political vanguard's support for a nonelitist language drawn from everyday social praxis. Bakhtin was inevitably conscious, then, of the revolutionary years' boisterous intermingling of speech genres and socially inscribed discourses, conscious of what he called, in reference to Dostoevsky's novels, the "cacophony of voices" typical of the period.

Although Bakhtin's thoughts on language permeate his work, it is in *Marxism and the Philosophy of Language* that he offers the most comprehensive account of "translinguistics," a theory of the role of signs in human life and thought. "Translinguistics" might be compared to Saussure's "semiology" (the science of signs and sign systems) were it not for the fact that it is precisely Saussure's notion of both sign and system that is being attacked. For Saussure, the sign possesses a stability that is based on the orderly matching of signifier and signified which allows it to be placed within a code. Individual texts can disturb this stability through processes of polysemy and displacement, but the displacement is always premised on an initial stability. For Bakhtin, in contrast, the stability of the sign is just one of the mystifications advanced by "abstract objectivism," for "multiplicity of meaning is the constitutive feature of the word." A primordial dynamism, then, animates the sign itself. The stability of the sign is a fiction, since "the constituent factor for the linguistic form, as for the sign, is not at all its self-identity as a signal but its specific variability."[6]

While Bakhtin agrees with Saussure that a discipline should be created that would study the "life of signs within society," he differs in his view of both the nature of signs and their role within social life. Rejecting what he sees as Saussure's mentalistic individualism, which locates language and ideology within the individual consciousness, Bakhtin regards both consciousness and ideology as semiotic, as existing only insofar as they are realized within some kind of semiotic material, whether in the form of "inner speech" or in the process of verbal interaction with others, or in mediated forms like writing and art. Linguistics, for Bakhtin, forms part of the broader study of ideologies, for the "domain of ideology coincides with the domain of signs." The individual consciousness is decentered, for signs can arise only on "interindividual territory." Debunking the cherished myth of the monadic ego, Bakhtin posits the consciousness as a socioideological fact rather than a self-generating cogito. Saussure's langue/parole dichotomy, which places the social (langue) on one side and the individual (parole) on the other, tacitly validates a Vosslerian definition of the speech act as manifesting an individual, creative power, a schema that implicitly reproduces the venerable bourgeois individual-versus-society trope that Bakhtin is at such pains to reject. For Bakhtin, the individual, even in his or her dreams, is permeated by the social; indeed, one develops individuality not against but *through* the social.

Although Bakhtin offers a quasi-Marxist critique of psychologism, he is no less critical of a vulgar, mechanistic Marxism that would relegate the world of signs and ideology to a superstructural "roof" resting on an economic foundation. "It is just as naïve," Bakhtin writes in *The Formal Method in Literary Scholarship*, "to think that separate works, which have been snatched out of the unity of the ideological world, are in their isolation directly determined by economic factors as it is to think that a poem's rhymes and stanzas are fitted together according to economic causality."[7] Bakhtin's "historical poetics" avoids the twin traps of an empty apolitical formalism, on the one hand, and a vulgar Marxism, on the other. Instead of a hierarchical model in which economic base simply "determines" artistic superstructure, Bakhtin proposes a kind of mobile "juxtastructure" (Metz) of mutual and in some ways reciprocal determinations. Bakhtin shares with Marxism the premise that cultural process is intimately connected to social relations, and that culture is the site of social difference and contradiction. For Bakhtin, however, every ideological sign is more than a "reflection, a shadow, of reality; it is also itself a material participant in that reality." Even consciousness is linguistic, and therefore social, and thus an objective fact and a social force. The semiotic form of consciousness is "inner speech," which when translated into outer, public speech, has the capacity to act on the world. Entering into the discursive systems of science, art, law, and ethics, it becomes a powerful force, capable even of exerting an influence on the economic strata.

The Bakhtinian conception of language, then, constitutes a vehicle for avoiding the trap of mechanistic economism: "The category of mechanical causality can most easily be surmounted on the grounds of the philosophy of language."[8] As complex networks of ideological signs, literature and cinema must be conceptualized as much more than mere reflection. Literary study, Bakhtin suggests in *The Formal Method in Literary Scholarship* (and we can easily extend his analysis to film study) is "concerned with the concrete life of the literary work in the unity of the generating literary environment, the literary environment in the generating ideological environment, and the latter, finally, in the generating socioeconomic environment which permeates it."[9] Rather than a hierarchical base/superstructure model, then, Bakhtin sees the mediation between the two as that of superimposed concentric circles, constantly rippling in and out, rather like a vertiginous combination of forward track and backward zoom, each with its own dynamism and specificity.

Whereas the Saussurean tradition regards speech as individual and language as social, and thus the two as antinomies, Bakhtin sees them as constantly imbricated, for speech produces utterances, which are social by definition because they are interindividual, requiring a speaker and an addressee. Imprisoned within the ossified categories of Indo-European comparative linguistics, the broader field of linguistics has tended to neglect the dynamics of the utterance and of syntactic forms.

All syntactic analyses of speech entail analyzing the living body of an utterance, and therefore powerfully resist relegation to the abstract system of language. Syntactic forms are more concrete than morphological or phonetic forms and therefore closer to the real conditions of discourse.[10]

In this regard, Bakhtin is careful to distinguish between the sentence and the utterance. The sentence, Bakhtin argues in "The Problem of Speech Genres," is a purely grammatical unit, while the utterance is a discursive unit. (Bakhtin uses the word *slovo,* which can be translated as "word" but which is used by the Bakhtin School with a strongly social accent, making it closer to "utterance" or "discourse".) The utterance has a context and an intertext, and is demarcated on each side by a change of speaking subject, whereas the sentence, like the individual word, is merely a signifying unit rather than a communicative one. Depending on our perspective, the same unit of speech can be a sentence or an utterance. "The sun has risen," taken abstractly, is a sentence; but a wife telling her husband that "the sun has risen" and therefore "we had better get up and go to work" is an utterance. The utterance, unlike the sentence, has an "author," an "expressive intonation," as well as a context and an addressee.[11]

Equally pertinent to an evaluation of cinesemiology is Bakhtin's critique of formalism. In *The Formal Method in Literary Scholarship* (coauthored with Medvedev), Bakhtin develops a thoroughgoing critique of the underlying premises of first-phase Russian formalism. This is not the place to sum up Russian formalism or to reiterate the details of Bakhtin's critique, but it is the place to stress the points that will be relevant to our discussion of cinesemiology. It is important to note at the outset that Bakhtin's "sociological poetics" and its dialogical adversary, formalist poetics, share a number of common features. Both schools, for example, refuse a romantic view of art as the expression of the artist's vision. Both insist on the autotelic specificity of art, resisting a vulgar Marxist reduction of art to questions of class and economics. ("Literary works," writes Bakhtin, "have their own independent ideological role and their own type of refraction of socioeconomic existence.") Both see "literariness" not as inhering in texts per se, but as a differential relation between texts, which the formalists refer to as "defamiliarization" and which Bakhtin refers to under the more comprehensive rubric "dialogism." Both reject naïvely realistic or referential views of art. (A literary structure does not reflect reality, writes Bakhtin; instead, it "reflects and refracts the reflections and refractions of other ideological spheres.") *The Formal Method,* furthermore, gives considerable credit to formalism, praising it for its "productive role" in formulating "the most important problems of literary scholarship" and for doing so "with such sharpness that they can no longer be avoided or ignored."

Bakhtin, it is important to note, engages formalism on its own chosen ground: the question of "specification" and the notion that the object of literary scholarship is not literature but "literariness." Recognizing this issue as a legitimate one, Bakhtin proposes a translinguistic and materialist solution, as opposed to what he sees as the inadequate solution proposed by the formalists. Within this double operation, Bakhtin in *The Formal Method* essentially "deconstructs" a number of crucial formalist dichotomies—for instance, practical/poetic language, material/device, and story/plot—each time proposing his own, more comprehensive formulation. In most cases, Bakhtin argues, the formalists, in their polemical extremism, simply reverse preexisting dyads, turning them inside out in an undialectical manner, enthroning intrinsic form, for example, where extrinsic content once was supreme. For Bakhtin, however, the implicit spatial metaphor underlying the separating-out of the extrinsic and the intrinsic is simplistic and misleading. Every artistic phenomenon is simultaneously determined from within and without. The barrier between "inside" and "outside" is an artificial one; indeed, there is an easy permeability between the two. In the process of history, Bakhtin points out, things extrinsic and intrinsic dialectically change places; what was once "within" can easily become "without," and vice versa. The analyst need not choose between the "inner" and the "outer," for the two are inextricably linked.

Bakhtin similarly deconstructs the formalist binarism that separates practical from poetic language, arguing that in fact the two types of language thoroughly interpenetrate each other, that poetic speech can acquire a practical dimension, just as practical speech is capable of the disruptions, breaks, and defamiliarizations that the formalists posit as unique to poetic speech. The formalist view of poetic language as the mere converse of practical language, with the only "plus" of art consisting in disruption, is for Bakhtin an impoverished view that turns poetic language into the "parasite of a parasite." "This contrast [of poetic and practical language], which determined all the formulations of the formalists, was a fatal one. Anything fruitful could only appear in spite of it."

In their hypostatization of the aesthetic, the formalists gave little theoretical place to the diverse apparatuses—the academy, the literary establishment, the publishing industry, the censors— which govern the production, dissemination, and legitimation of the artistic product. Bakhtin's communicative model, in contrast, highlights what he calls "the varied forms of artistic intercourse." Participation in the perception of an ideological object such as art, Bakhtin argues, presupposes special social relationships; the very process is intrinsically social. The forms of artistic intercourse, Bakhtin writes, "are extremely varied and differentiated," from the "intimate" audience of the drawing room lyric to the immense "multitude" of the tragedian or novelist. Although Bakhtin does not mention the cinematic audience, his words are evocative of it: "The poet's audience, the readers of a novel, those in the concert hall—these are collective organizations of a special type," and "without these distinctive forms of social intercourse there are no poems, no odes, no symphonies." The formalists, in contrast, according to Bakhtin, ultimately adopt a culinary, consumerist attitude toward art, seeing it as an object of individual consumption:

"The conception of a work of art as an object of individual pleasure and experience is essentially an expression of a tendency to equate an ideological phenomenon to a product of individual consumption." But this doctrine, for Bakhtin, no matter what "subtle and ideal forms it assumes (artistic pleasure, intellectual enjoyment of truth, bliss, aesthetic ecstasy) . . . is inadequate to the specific social nature of the ideological phenomenon."

Formalism, for Bakhtin, failed to discern the social nature of literature in its *specificity;* it failed to note the historicity of forms themselves. By dissolving history into an "eternal contemporaneity," the formalists created a model that was inadequate to support even the immanent evolution of literature, not to mention its relation with the other series. In Bakhtin's view, the formalists' fetishization of the work of art as the "sum of its devices" left formalist readers with nothing more than their own empty sensation, the hedonistic pleasure of "defamiliarization" experienced by the individual consumer of the artistic text. Art, the formalists argued tautologically, is "about" being aesthetic, about renewing perception, about making the reader/spectator feel the "artfulness of the object" and the "stoniness of the stone." The technique of art," Shklovsky wrote, is to "make forms difficult, to increase the difficulty and length of perception because the process of perception is an aesthetic end in itself and must be prolonged."[12] While not denying that the renewal of perception is a legitimate function of art, Bakhtin also emphasizes the intense social meaningfulness of art, since the very language in which art is spoken is already social and dialogical. The artistic utterance is irremediably social because it is addressed to historically situated subjects. Without ever falling into vulgar sociologism or what Barthes called the "veristic idiocy," Bakhtin called for a poetics sensitive to the "whole generating series" of literature—what Kristeva later called the "genotext"—not only to the literary series, but to all the "prior speakings" to which art responds, including those of everyday life and dialogue.

It might be objected at this point that Bakhtin was somewhat unfair to formalism, treating it as a unified system or *langue.* Formalism, at the same time or even before Bakhtin's critique, was transforming itself into "socioformalism" and beginning to address precisely the questions that preoccupied Bakhtin. In their famous 1928 theses, Jakobson and Tynyanov emphasized the need for dynamizing and "diachronizing" the formalist model and stressed the relation between the literary series and the other series, while still insisting that immanent analysis should come first. And the

Prague School structuralists, building on the insights of Jakobson and Tynyanov, did go much of the way—but not the entire way—toward vindicating formalism against the charge of ahistoricism. By shifting their focus from the immanent formal analysis of the technical facets of poetic construction to the broader study of literary history, Prague School theorists foregrounded the intrinsic link between literature and the "historical series." The Prague School model still lacks the social dynamism of Bakhtinian dialogism, however, and too often the Prague School theorists limited their attention to the historicity of the literary series, without pointing to a dynamic multileveled connection with all the other series.

But what, one might reasonably ask, does this long excursus have to do with film theory? A Bakhtinian "translinguistics," I hope to show, offers a more adequate basis for cinesemiotics, since it is capable of clarifying some of the theoretical and ideological ambiguities generated by both the Saussurean and the formalist framework. Bakhtin's location of meaning not in petrified linguistic forms but rather in the use of language in action and communication (the utterance), his insistence that these meanings are generated and heard as social voices anticipating and answering one another (dialogism), and his recognition that these voices represent distinct socioideological positionings whose conflictual relation exists at the very heart of language change (heteroglossia) are immensely important for the theory, analysis, and even the praxis of cinema.

But before suggesting the theoretical and analytical potential of the Bakhtinian model, we must first address the tradition that calls for supersession. Beginning in the sixties, a number of cinesemiologists—Pasolini, Bettetini, and Eco, among others—explored the question of "film language." It was the French semiologist Christian Metz, however, who examined the question with the greatest rigor and sensitivity. Metz attempted to "get to the bottom" of the perennial trope of film language by testing the comparison against what he saw as the most advanced concepts in contemporary linguistics. Metz took the metaphor seriously, but also skeptically, in order to discern its quantum of truthfulness. In the background of Metz's discussion was Saussure's founding methodological question regarding the "object" of linguistic study. Thus Metz looked for the counterpart, in film theory, of the conceptual role played by langue in the Saussurean schema—that is, the "object" of the filmolinguistic endeavor. And much as Saussure concluded that the rightful object of linguistic investigation was to disengage the abstract signifying system of a language—that is, its key units and their rules of combination at a given point in time—so Metz concluded that the object of cinesemiology was to disengage the cinema's signifying procedures, its combinatory rules, in order to see to what extent these rules resembled the doubly articulated diacritical systems of "natural languages." The question that oriented Metz's early work, then, was whether the cinema was *langue* (language system) or *langage* (language), and his well-known conclusion to his own question was that the cinema is a language, not a language system. Because the cinema lacks an arbitrary sign, minimal units, and double articulation, film texts cannot be conceived of as being generated by an underlying language system, but they do manifest a languagelike systematicity. Cinema, for Metz, is a language in a double sense: first, as a "technico-sensorial unity" grounded in a given matter of expression; and second, as a discourse or signifying practice with specific codifications and recognizable ordering procedures.

Film became a discourse, Metz argued, by organizing itself as narrative and thus producing a body of signifying procedures. The true analogy between film and language consists, then, in their common syntagmatic nature. Both language and film produce discourse through paradigmatic and syntagmatic operations. Language selects and combines phonemes and morphemes to form sentences; film selects and combines images and sounds to form "syntagmas"—that is, units of narrative autonomy in which elements interact semantically. It was in this context that Metz explored the comparison (familiar from the earliest days of film theory) of the shot to the word and the sequence to the sentence. Metz points out a number of problems with this analogy: shots are infinite in number, unlike words but like statements; shots are the creation of the filmmaker, unlike words but like statements; and the shot is an actualized unit, unlike words, which are virtual lexical units, but again like statements. In all these respects, individual shots reveal themselves to be more like statements or utterances than like words. Metz's view of the shot as *énoncé* is compatible with Bakhtin's emphasis on the "utterance" as opposed to the individual word, but a translinguistic approach would go farther, "dialogizing" such filmic utterances even more, to see their existence in relation to a theme, to other similar utterances, and to an addressee.

Metz's most thorough exercise in filmolinguistics was *Langage et Cinema,* first published in French in 1971 and translated (badly) into English in 1974.[13] Here Metz develops the concept of cinema as a necessarily "pluricodic" medium. Although lacking in a grammar or phonemic system, film still constitutes a quasi-linguistic practice because of the generating force of its "codes." For Metz, filmic texts interweave codes that are specific to the cinema and codes that are shared with languages other than the cinema. These codes range from the very specific—codes that are linked to the cinema's definition as deploying moving, multiple images (e.g., codes of camera movement and continuity editing)—to codes that are demonstrably nonspecific because they are widely disseminated in the culture and are in no way dependent on the specific modalities of the medium (e.g., the codes of narrative or of gender roles).

Metz's discussion of cinematic specificity was obviously indebted to the Russian formalist emphasis on literary specificity, or *literaturnost*. And it was precisely in this area that Bakhtin gave the formalists the most credit. In *The Formal Method in Literary Scholarship,* Bakhtin lauds the formalists for posing "the essential problems of literary scholarship" and bringing "great sharpness and principle to the problem of artistic specification." Against vulgar Marxists and with the formalists, Bakhtin refuses an instrumentalist view of artistic technique; the artistic signifier is not merely a technical auxiliary for conveying "grand thoughts," but rather is a self-valuable part of reality. The analyst of any text, then, must pay attention to what Bakhtin calls the "representing body of the text"—what semiologists call the signifier—and not pass immediately to what is represented.

Similarly, one of Metz's most important contributions was to call attention to the cinematic signifier, in a critical atmosphere formerly dominated by naïve referentialism and vulgar sociologism. But if Metz can be credited with bringing great "sharpness and principle to the problem of [cinematic] specification," he was somewhat less adept at linking the specific and the nonspecific, the social and the cinematic, the textual and the contextual. Bakhtin's work, written long before Metz's work but disseminated concurrently or subsequent to it, provides, I would suggest, a means to recuperate and "dialogize" the immense portion that is valuable in Metz's work. Precisely to the extent that Metz "inherits" the interrelated blind spots of structural linguistics and Russian formalism, a Bakhtinian perspective can serve as a corrective. My purpose here will not be to develop a full-blown "Bakhtinian Translinguistics of the Cinema," but rather to sketch out some of the directions such a project might take.

Metzian filmolinguistics is largely premised on just one linguistics and its derivatives—to wit, what J. G. Merquior calls the "Saussurean disaspora," the linguistics of Saussure and his latter-day descendants Martinet and Hjelmslev, among others. A familiarity with Bakhtin's work might have spared the pioneer cine-semiologists considerable effort by warning them against undertaking what turned out to be a futile search for the cinematic equivalents of Saussure-derived entities such as langue, the arbitrary sign, minimal units, and double articulation. (Metz deserves credit for being among the first to discern the absence of such entities and the futility of trying to make forced, procrustean comparisons.) Bakhtin's critique of the abstract objectivist premises undergirding langue, and his urging of a displacement of interest from phonetic and morphological categories to the "dynamics of the utterance and of syntactic forms," are clearly relevant to the inaugural phase of cinesemiology. Bakhtin shares with the Saussurean tradition a kind of "relational thinking," but the relations in question no longer form part of a closed, homeostatic system. Bakhtin retains the linguistic paradigm, but opens it to the diachronic, to history and struggle. Like the semiologists, Bakhtin discerns language everywhere, but unlike the semiologists, he also sees language as everywhere imbricated with power. A Bakhtinian "social semiotic" would thus avoid the prudish scientism of a certain "value free" structuralism, enabling us to reintroduce both politics and culture into the abstract model so skillfully constructed by Metz.

While Metz, somewhat "blocked" by the Saussurean langue/parole schema, tends to bracket questions of history and ideology, Bakhtin locates both history and ideology at the pulsating heart of all discourse. Purely linguistic definitions of a language and its elements, Bakhtin suggests in "The Problem of the Text," can serve only as "initial terms for description," for what is most important "is not described by them and does not reside within them."[14] What matters "is not elements (units) of the language system that have become elements of the text, but aspects of the utterance." It is not phonemes and morphemes that enter into dialogism, but utterances, and it is as utterance that "the word" acquires relation to an addressee and to life. The signifying units of language lack the quality of being addressed to someone: "Speech is always cast in the form of an utterance belonging to a particular speaking subject, and outside this form it cannot exist."[15]

The sensitivity to context that characterizes a translinguistic approach to language as complexly situated utterance allows the film analyst to draw distinctions between similar shots where a more rigid "stylistics" would not. Take, for example, the often-repeated assertion that the point-of-view shot—a shot purporting to represent the literal perspective of a character in the film—necessarily entails identification and sympathy with the character in question. But Griffith's archracist film *Birth of a Nation* offers a number of shots from the point-of-view of Gus, the sexually aggressive black man, a figure with whom the film has no sympathy whatsoever. A translinguistic analysis, however, would clarify the apparent paradox, since these isolated shots must be seen in the context not only of the film as a whole as an ode to white supremacy and the Ku Klux Klan but also within the historical context of the ambient racism of the period. Griffith uses these subjective shots only to convey the white projection of the black man as the incarnation of all that is base and animalic. The choice of subjectivizing a black character cannot be separated from the other choices informing the film—the choice of players (the use of a white in blackface rather than a black actor who might have injected some form of resistance or subversion into the role) and the character construction, here inflected by the projection of white sexual paranoia and guilt onto the black male, in the case of Gus, and the projection of patriarchal chivalry, in the case of his girl-victim, Flora. The black character's point of view, then, is filtered through a racist imaginary, in a case where the presumed interlocutor is the spectator at least potentially sympathetic to the white supremacist ideology of the Ku Klux Klan.

The Bakhtinian notion of the "chronotope," meanwhile, allows us to historicize the question of space and time in the cinema. The "chronotope," we recall, is a means for understanding the ways in which spatiotemporal structures in the novel evoke the existence of a life/world independent of the text and its representations. Since the chronotope provides fictional environments implying historically specific constellations of power (Gary Saul Morson proposes that *chronotope* be translated as "a particular complex of socio-historical relations"), it is ideally suited to a medium where "spatial and temporal indicators are fused into one carefully thought-out concrete whole."[16] Paraphrasing Bakhtin, we could say that film forms the textual site where "time thickens, takes on flesh, becomes artistically visible," and where "space becomes charged with and responsive to the movements of time, plot, and history." In this sense, Bakhtin's chronotopic project recalls the "grande syntagmatique," Metz's attempt to isolate the principal

syntagmatic figures of narrative cinema, those units that organized spatial and temporal relations as part of the "denotation" of a
plot. Bakhtin's (admittedly incomplete) attempt to provide an all-
embracing theory of time-space in the novel might be synthesized
with the efforts of Metz, Burch, Heath, Bordwell/Thompson, and
others to define the spatiotemporal categories of filmic discourse.
With its suggestive linkage of typical decor (in film the bars,
lounges, and city streets of film noir), temporal articulations (in
film the *faux raccords* of Resnais, the nervous montage of a
Richard Lester, the slow pacing of a Satyajit Ray film), and characteristic deployment of space (the flattened perspectives of a Godard, the oblique angularity of a Welles), a chronotopic model might
be of help in constructing a more comprehensive model for the
analysis of time-space in the cinema, one that would simultaneously take into account questions of history, genre, and the specifically cinematic articulation of space and time.

A Bakhtinian concern with the interlocutor of the text, moreover, allows for all the ways that the filmic experience is inevitably
inflected by the cultural or political awareness of the audience itself, constituted outside the text and traversed by the conflicting
social determinations implicit in heteroglossia. Individual shots
and entire films might be seen on one level as utterances with their
own rhetoric, their own persuasive or provocative relation to their
own assumed interlocutor: the popular audience of *Rambo,* the
artsy upscale audience of Rohmer films, the politically committed
audience of many Third World films. At the same time, a translinguistic approach would allow for what Bakhtin calls the "rights
of the reader" and the "rights of the listener—that is, for the possibility of "aberrant" readings that go against the grain of the textual
discourse. Although fiction films are constructed as persuasive machines designed to produce specific impressions and emotions, they
are not all-powerful; they may be read differently, and even sub-
versively, by different audiences. Thus the audience's knowledge
or experience can generate a counterpressure to oppressive representations. Hollywood's ill-informed portrayals of Latin American
life in such films as *Tropical Serenade* and *Down Argentine Way,*
for example, were often laughed off the screen when shown in Latin America itself. Larry Peerce's *One Potato, Two Potato* (1964), a
film about interracial marriage, provides an especially poignant
narrative example of this process of "aberrant readings," in which
the experience of oppression inflects a character's reading of a film-
within-the-film. The black husband, enraged by an escalating se-

ries of racially motivated slights, attends a western in a drive-in movie theater. Projecting his anger, he screams his support for the Indians, seen as his analogues in suffering, and his hatred for the white "heroes," in a reading that goes against the drift and grain of the discourse.

Every community comes to film from what Bakhtin would call a distinct "dialogical angle"; each brings its own cultural orientation and political aspirations to bear on the film. The textually constructed reader/spectator does not necessarily coincide with the sociohistorical reader/spectator. Subcultural groups can read popular forms to their own advantage, even without the "authorization" of the text or its producers. Every culture understands the films produced by another culture through an interpretative grid that predisposes it to certain readings as opposed to others. (In Chapter 2 we will see how this process operates with regard to titles and dialogue translation.) The Bakhtinian notion of heteroglossia, as the diverse perspectival languages generated by sexual, racial, economic, and generational difference, is eminently compatible with spectator-oriented approaches. Both Bakhtin and the latter-day reception theorists would combat what might be called "the myth of the single spectator"—usually assumed to be white, male, Western—in favor of a multiplicity of spectatorial positions, sometimes coexisting within a given spectator. Rather than a universal monolithic spectator, we find a diversity of positions having to do with gender (the ways in which women "negotiate" patriarchal texts, for example), with race (the black experience of *Birth of a Nation* is distinct from that of even the most sympathetic whites), with class (a welfare mother is more likely to empathize with the protagonist of Haile Gerima's *Bush Mama* than a middle-class suburbanite), with culture (an Indian audience brings a different "cultural preparation" to the films of Mrinal Sen than that brought by a Western audience), with sexual orientation (gays have developed special angles not only on the films of Carmen Miranda and Pee Wee Herman but also on such mainstream classics as *Strangers on a Train*), and even region (the Manhattan films of Woody Allen or Paul Mazursky are read differently in Peoria than in New York). The spectator is also historically situated, and this in both a biographical and a larger historical sense. The same spectator, at different points in his or her life, sees a film diversely as different discourses become "available." Nor can spectators escape from history. It would be difficult for us as contemporary spectators to "lose ourselves" in the escapism of a Nazi musical comedy;

the knowledge of the holocaust inevitably haunts our experience of such a film.

It must be acknowledged that Metz has repeatedly insisted on the necessity of studying the economic-political-ideological dimension of film along with its semiotic-psychoanalytic dimension; indeed, at times, as in his discussion of the "three industries"—the technical film industry proper, the mental machinery that accustoms us to consuming films, and the critical industry, the "linguistic appendage" of the industry—he brilliantly effects a synthesis of such concerns.[17] He manages this, however, not because of but *despite* the model of language he has adopted. Since history and ideology are largely elided by the Saussurean model, Metz is reduced to a compartmentalized recommendation that film scholars should *also* study (within a kind of amicable division of labor) history, economics, sociology, and so forth. Here Metz recapitulates the approach taken by the formalists themselves, who recommended first the immanent study of the literary text and of "literariness" and only then the study of the relation between the literary series and the other historical series. (Jakobson and Tynyanov, for example, defended such an approach in their famous 1928 "theses.") For Bakhtin's "sociological poetics," in contrast, all artistic languages, given their inherently dialogical quality and the fact that they are addressed to interlocutors, are "already" social. A "translinguistic" view of film as "utterance," therefore, would regard the cinematic text as socially informed communication, and therefore as social and historical "from the outset." The utterance, Bakhtin writes in "Discourse in the Novel," is "a social phenomenon—social throughout its entire range and in each and every of its factors."[18] Film, within a translinguistic perspective, does not only include utterances, it *is* utterance. And every utterance, for Bakhtin, is tied to an object (e.g., the theme or the profilmic phenomenon being registered), to others' speech about the theme (other films and other discourses treating the same theme—i.e., the filmic and extrafilmic intertext), to a reader, listener, or spectator (its addressee), and to its context. The filmic text, then, is incontrovertibly social, first as an utterance, which is social by definition, and second as an utterance that is situated, contexted, historical.

In the social life of the utterance, whether it is a verbally proffered phrase, a literary text, a comic strip, or a film, each "word" is subject to rival pronunciations and "social accents." Bakhtin and his collaborators invented an entire cluster of terms to evoke the

complex social and linguistic codes governing these rival pronunciations and accents (and most of the terms have simultaneous verbal and musical connotations): "social accent," "social evaluation,"
"tact," and "intonation." The appropriateness of these terms to the
cinema becomes obvious when we remember that the fiction film,
and especially the sound film, can be seen as the *mise en scène* of
actual speech situations, as the visual and aural contextualization
of speech. Sound cinema is perfectly qualified to render what
Bakhtin calls "intonation," that phenomenon which lies on the
border of the verbal and the nonverbal, the spoken and the non-
spoken, and which "pumps the energy of the real life situation
into the discourse," imparting "active historical movement and
uniqueness."[19]

In a brief but extremely suggestive passage in *Formal Method in Literary Scholarship,* Bakhtin offers a conceptual tool for
dealing with this intersection of language with history and power.
He speaks of *taktichnost,* or "speech tact," as a "formative and organizing force" within everyday language exchange.[20] The term *tact*
may strike us as somewhat improbable because we associate it
with questions of etiquette and diplomacy, but Bakhtin uses it in
its musical sense as "that which sets down the basic meter." *Tact,*
then, refers to the "ensemble of codes governing discursive interaction," and is "determined by the aggregate of all the social relationships of the speakers, their ideological horizons, and, finally,
the concrete situation of the conversation." "Tact," according to
Bakhtin, should be "understood in a broad sense, with politeness
as only one of its aspects." Tact "gives form to everyday utterances,
determining the genre and style of speech performances." The notion of "tact" is extremely suggestive for film theory and analysis,
applying literally to the verbal exchanges within the diegesis, and
figuratively to the tact involved in the metaphorical dialogue of
genres and discourses within the text, as well as to the "dialogue"
between film and spectator. With regard to this last point—the
dialogue of film and spectator—it is noteworthy that many filmmakers, taking their cue from such "self-conscious" novelists as
Cervantes and Fielding, "literalize" the dialogue with the spectator through direct-address commentary. The "host" of Maax
Ophuls' *La Ronde* introduces himself directly to the audience—
"You are probably wondering what my part in the story is. Author?
Compère?"—ultimately defining himself as "the answer to your
wish to know." With regard to verbal exchanges between characters in the diegesis, meanwhile, it is worth noting that the cinema

is superbly equipped to present the extraverbal aspects of linguistic discourse, precisely those subtle contextualizing factors evoked by "tact." In the sound-film, we not only hear the words, with their accent and intonation, but we also witness the facial or corporeal expression that accompanies the words—the posture of arrogance or resignation, the raised eyebrow, the look of distrust, the ironic glance that modifies the ostensible meaning of an utterance—in short, all those elements that discourse analysts have taught us to see as so essential to social communication.

While a writer such as Proust can evoke such discursive phenomena in sinuous prose, the cinema presents them, as it were, "in tact." As a powerful condenser of unspoken social evaluations, film has the power to represent the complexities of verbal behavior. Words, for Bakhtin, are always "saturated" with "accents" and "intonations"; they carry with them the "aura" of a profession, a party, a generation. Film acting largely consists in getting these accents and intonations right, much as film directing has to do with contextualizing them. With its capacity for contexting words not only through *mise en scène* but also through its other tracks (music, noise, written materials), film is ideally suited for conveying what Bakhtin calls "contextual overtones." Film dramaturgy has its special tact, its ways of suggesting, through camera placement, framing, and acting, such phenomena as intimacy or distance, camaraderie or domination—in short, all the social and personal dynamics operating between interlocutors.

The discursive rules of "tact" operate not only in the fiction film—think, for example, of the evolving tact between master and servant in Losey's *The Servant*—but also in the documentary. In countless documentaries (including "progressive" ones) about oppressed or colonized peoples, the off-screen voice of a narrator takes on intonations of domination and omniscience. Studio-protected, this voice speaks in regular and homogeneous rhythms, while the human subjects of the film speak hesitantly, in direct sound. The off-screen voice speaks of its subjects confidently, in the third person, while they speak of themselves hesitantly, in the first. The narrator becomes the voice of knowledge and mastery, while the narratees are the voice of undiscriminating experience. The voice translates their "alien words" into the impersonal discourse of objective truth. Similarly, the ideologically informed "tact" of television news tends to pit discursively competent adults—the newscasters, the politicians, the managers—against a stammering, infantilized populace. The suave articulateness of the newscasters, underwritten by scripted texts, studio apparatus, and editing, contrasts with the equally constructed inarticulateness of those at the bottom of the speech hierarchy.[21] Or, to take another example, think of the "tact" of Ted Koppel's "Nightline." Since Koppel, thanks to television, repeatedly meets, in an electronic tête-à-tête, with heads of state, and since he is framed in an identical manner, we subliminally begin to see him as a head of state. Furthermore, the technological tact of "Nightline" creates a situation in which Koppel sees his interlocutors while they are placed in an alien perceptual world dominated by the earpiece that conveys Koppel's words. (Indeed, Koppel's invisibility to his interlocutors is itself "invisible" to the spectators.) Koppel has the power to cut off his interlocutors or cage them within a rectangle, relativize them by juxtaposing them with their adversaries, or even reduce them to the size of a postage stamp. We are not surprised, therefore, when Koppel interrupts or rhetorically badgers renowned Third World leaders—"Will you renounce violence, Mr. Tambo?"—it somehow seems within his rights.

Tact also metaphorically evokes the power relations between film and audience. Does the film assume distance or a kind of intimacy? Does the film lord it over the audience like many Hollywood "blockbusters" and "superspectacles" (the terms themselves imply arrogance or aggression), or is it obsequious and insecure? Is it confident of the sympathies of the audience, or is it constantly preoccupied, as in the case of many left-liberal films such as *Missing* and *Latino,* with reassuring a politically mainstream audience? Does a film assume an interlocutor of a specific gender or class or nation? Does a film ignore the possible reactions of women or take them into account? Does it assume a lily-white audience or make room for blacks? Many mainstream films of the fifties gave the impression that there were no black people in America. Hitchcock's documentary-like *The Wrong Man* (1957), for example, shows the subways and even the prisons of New York City as totally devoid of blacks. A film like *Adventures in Babysitting* (1987), to take a more recent instance, seems to assume an audience of well-off white suburbanites for whom blacks, Hispanics, and the working class represent a menacing underworld of difference and otherness. Hollywood films such as *Black Sunday* and *Ishtar,* finally, take it as a given that the cinematic scapegoating of Arabs or Muslims will offend no one. These films, like all films, make specific assumptions about audience ideology and cultural preparation; they take a clearly defined attitude toward what Bakhtin would call their "projected interlocutor."

Tact evokes, finally, the power relations between the diverse elements of the filmic text, between its tracks, its discourses, and its generic strands. This translinguistic view of intratextual conflict suggests affinities with the politicized aesthetic of Bertolt Brecht, and especially with epic theatre's "radical separation of the elements." Brecht favored an aesthetic that would set scene against scene and track—music, dialogue, lyric—against track. Music and lyrics, for example, were designed mutually to discredit rather than complement each other. Epic theatre implies not only a "horizontal" autonomy of autonomous scenes, then, but also a "vertical" tension between the diverse strata or tracks of the text. Godard's *Numero Deux,* for example, exacerbates this tension by having multiple images play with and against one another within the rectangle of the screen, and by having the distinct temporalities of the different tracks enter into fecund interaction and "dialogue." The diverse tracks by turns fall back, catch up, overtake, and dialogically relativize one another. The constantly shifting aural and visual coordinates highlight the film text as the scene of what Metz would call the "perpetual displacement of codes."

In this context, it is worth comparing the Metzian and Bakhtinian accounts of textual contradiction. In *Language and Cinema,* Metz elaborates the notion of "textual systems," formed by the interweaving of cinematic and extracinematic codes. In the book, however, there is a clear tension between a static, taxonomic, structuralist-formalist view of textual systems, and a more dynamic view of text as "productivity," "displacement," and *écriture,* as if within Metz-the-structuralist there breathed a poststructuralist straining to break free. Influenced by the Kristevan critique of the Saussurean paradigm (a critique indebted not only to the Derridean critique of the sign but also to Bakhtin's critique of Saussure), Metz describes the moment of filmic parole as the dissolution of the very systematicity he has elsewhere emphasized.

The system of the text is the process which displaces codes, deforming each of them by the presence of the others, contaminating some by means of others, meanwhile replacing one by another, and finally—as a temporarily "arrested" result of this general displacement—placing each code in a particular position in regard to the overall structure, a displacement which thus finishes by a positioning which is itself destined to be displaced by another text.[22]

The latter, more dynamic view of the text as a "nonfinalized" perpetual displacement constitutes the more dynamic pole in *Lan-*

guage and Cinema, and it is the view that is most easily reconciled with a translinguistic approach. A film's text, within this more dynamic conception, is not the "list" of its operative codes but rather the labor of constant restructuring and displacement by which the film "writes" its text, modifies and combines it codes (playing some codes off against others), and thus constitutes its system. The system of the text, then, is the instance that displaces the codes so that they become inflections and substitutions for one another. What matters is the passage from one code to another, the way in which signification is relayed from lighting, for example, to camera movement, from dialogue to music, or the way in which music plays against dialogue, or lighting against music, or music against camera movement.

Bakhtin's formulations about the novelistic text are at times strikingly anticipatory of Metz's formulations concerning the textual systems of films. The language of the novel, Bakhtin asserts in "Discourse in the Novel," is "the system of its languages."[23] But even here there are differences. First, Metz's abstract objectivist presuppositions oblige him to speak of "codes," while for Bakhtin all utterances, including artistic utterances, are determined not by the systematicity of codes but by the historically unique conjunctural circumstances of the communication. Bakhtin contrasts semiotics, which deals "primarily with the transmission of ready-made communication using a ready-made code," with live speech, where "communication is first created in the process of transmission, and there is, in essence, no code."[24] More important, Metz does not sufficiently emphasize the crucial link between textual and social contradiction. In this sense, Bakhtin's critique of the formalists can be extrapolated so as to apply to the Metzian view of textual systems. As Graham Pechey points out, the formalists described textual contradiction in terms redolent of social struggle. Shklovsky, for example, compared each new school of literature to a revolution, "something like the emergence of a new class," while Tynyanov likened literary succession to a "struggle" involving the destruction of the old unity and a construction of the new.[25] The formalists, speaking more generally, were fond of metaphors of combat, struggle, and conflict. But Shklovsky went on to downplay his own metaphor of revolution as "only an analogy," and literary contradiction remained in a hermetically sealed world of pure textuality. In *The Formal Method in Literary Scholarship,* Pechey goes on to argue, Bakhtin and Medvedev take the formalist metaphors seriously—especially those terms that easily resonate with class struggle and insurrection, terms such as *revolt, conflict, struggle, destruction,* and even *the dominant*—and make them apply equally to the text and to the social itself.[26]

What both Metz and the formalists "need," then, is the Bakhtinian concept of "heteroglossia"—that is, a notion of competing languages and discourses which would apply equally to *text* and *hors-texte.* A social semiotic of the cinema would retain the formalist and the Metzian notion of textual contradiction, but would rethink it through heteroglossia. *Heteroglossia* refers to the shifting stratifications of language into class dialects, professional jargons (lawyers, doctors, academics), generic discourses (melodrama, comedy), bureaucratic lingoes, popular slangs, along with the specific languages of cultural praxis. The languages composing heteroglossia represent "bounded verbal-ideological belief systems," points of view on the world, forms for conceptualizing social experience, each marked by its own tonalities, meanings, and values. A given linguistic community shares a common language, but different segments "live" that common language diversely. The role of the artistic text, be it a novel, a play, or a film, is not to represent real life "existents" but rather to stage the conflicts inherent in heteroglossia, the coincidences and competitions of languages and discourses.

Rather than directly "reflect" the real, or even "refract" the real, artistic discourse, for Bakhtin, constitutes a refraction of a refraction—that is, a mediated version of an already textualized socioideological world. Art does not represent Reality in its changing forms; rather, it exhibits the changing forms of representation. The Bakhtinian formulation thus steers clear of any substantialist belief that art refers back to a preexisting referent against which art's truth might be "tested," without ever lapsing into a "hermeneutic nihilism" that would regard all texts as nothing more than a meaningless play of signification open to an infinity of interpretative projections. Bakhtin rejects naïve formulations of realism, in other words, without ever abandoning the idea that artistic representations are at the same time irretrievably social, precisely because the discourses art represents are *themselves* social and historical. This formulation has the advantage of avoiding the kind of referentialism that sometimes creeps into Metz's account of cinematic representation even against Metz's best intentions. (The "grande syntagmatique," for example, is premised on an impossible comparison of the putative time-space of the diegesis and the actual spatiotemporal articulation of the filmic discourse itself, and thus at times seems to imply that some preexisting anecdotal nucleus precedes the text, when in fact the diegesis is pure construct.) By completely bracketing the question of the real (what Metz would call the "totality of profilmic elements"), and instead emphasizing the representation of languages and discourses, Bakhtin relocates the question altogether so as to avoid what Rifaterre calls "the referential illusion."[27] For Bakhtin, human consciousness and artistic practice do not come into contact with existence directly, but meet it through the medium of the surrounding ideological world. Literature, and by extension cinema, does not no much refer to or call up the world as it represents the world's languages and discourses. Language, in a Bakhtinian view, is not only the material but also the object of representation: "Language in the novel not only represents," Bakhtin writes, "but itself serves as the object of representation."[28]

The languages of heteroglossia, Bakhtin argues in "Discourse in the Novel," may be "juxtaposed to one another, mutually supplement one another, contradict one another, and be interrelated dialogically.[29] This formulation is especially appropriate to any number of postmodernist films which, rather than represent "real" humanly purposeful events within an illusionistic aesthetic, simply stage the clash of languages and discourses. Here one could cite a wide spectrum of films and filmmakers, from Bruce Conner's avant-garde collages of preexisting found footage to the work of such filmmakers as Jean-Luc Godard and Yvonne Rainer. Godard and Gorin's *Tout Va Bien,* for example, is structured around a tripartite play of ideological languages: that of capital, that of the Communist Party, and that of the Maoists. Deploying dialogue consisting primarily of quotations from disparate political sources, the film places languages in collision, thus generating a semantic richness beyond the reach of monologic texts. Rainer's *The Man Who Envied Women* goes even farther by horizontally juxtaposing or vertically superimposing a variety of voices and discourses: the on-screen voice of Jack, the professor-theorist whose discourse consists of a quasi-nonsensical amalgam of Foucault, Lacan, and other poststructuralists (the "droning voice of theory as unrelenting patriarchy," in Patricia Mellenkamp's apt phrase); the off-screen voice of Trisha, the female protagonist, along with the array of voices from answering-machine messages to a videotaped debate concerning New York City housing, the whole regularly "punctuated" by the interpolated snippets of dialogue pilfered from anonymous speakers on New York streets and meeting places. These literal voices are then overlaid with any number of graphic and visual discourses: news photos, advertisements, citations, and film clips. One sequence enacts the tact of gendered power relations and the dialogical encounter of discourses by having the theorist-professor, armed with Foucault, attempt to intellectually seduce a woman (Jackie Raynal), armed with a feminist text by Meeghan Morris, as their bodies play out the evolving positionalities of manipulation, defense, teasing, and double-voiced subversion. Such films practice what Bakhtin called the "mutual illumination of languages," languages that intersect, collide, rub off on and mutually relativize one another. And, as Bakhtin argued in relation to Dostoevsky, the fact that these languages are "borrowed" from the social and discursive atmosphere in no way detracts from the "deep-seated intentionality" and "overarching ideological conceptualization of the work as a whole." Dostoevsky astounds us with a wide diversity of types and varieties of discourse, but we still sense in his work the voice of a unified creative will. Filmmakers like Godard or Ruiz or Rainer similarly offer a dizzying array of filmic and extrafilmic discourses, yet we never lose consciousness of the compositional *écriture* "behind" the discourses.

Bakhtin's emphasis on the pluralism of languages also responds to another problematic feature of Metz's early work—to wit, his privileging of the mainstream narrative film. Film became discourse, Metz argued in this early stage, by organizing itself as narrative: "It was precisely to the extent that the cinema confronted the problem of narration that . . . it came to produce a body of specific signifying procedures."[30] Metz's definition of cinematic language as "first of all the literalness of a plot" excluded both documentaries and the avant-garde film. The "grande syntagmatique" was Metz's attempt to isolate the principal syntagmatic figures of narrative cinema, those units that organized spatial and temporal relations as part of the "denotation" of a plot. After widespread criticism, Metz offered his autocritique in *Language and Cinema,* where he redefined the "grande syntagmatique" as merely a subcode of editing within a historically delimited body of films—that is, the mainstream narrative tradition from the consolidation of the sound-film in the thirties through the death of the studio aesthetic and the emergence of the diverse "new waves." Again, a Bakhtinian formulation would have saved cinesemiologists in the Saussurean tradition a good deal of trouble by rejecting from the outset the very notion of a unitary language. Anticipating contemporary sociolinguistics, Bakhtin argued that all languages are characterized by the dialectical interplay between normativiz-ation (monoglossia) and dialectical diversification (heteroglossia). This approach provides a valuable framework for seeing the classical dominant cinema as a kind of imposed standard language backed and "underwritten" by institutional power and thus exercising hegemony over a number of divergent "dialects" such as the documentary, the militant film, and the avant-garde cinema. A translinguistic approach would be more relativistic and pluralistic about these diverse film languages, privileging, as is characteristic of Bakhtin, the peripheral and the marginal as opposed to the central and the dominant.

Since Bakhtin directly responded to two of the source-movements for cinesemiology—Saussurean linguistics and for-malist aesthetics—it makes obvious sense to deploy Bakhtinian conceptual categories in order to dialogically extend Metzian semiology. It is somewhat more difficult and speculative, on the other hand, to make Bakhtinian concepts productive in relation to second phase "psychoanalytic" and "poststructuralist" semiotics. Insofar as the eclipse of filmolinguistics, in the seventies and eighties, derived from its failure to historicize the study of filmic signification, we can retroactively see Bakhtinian translinguistics as intuiting the necessary complementarity, and mutual imbrication, of historical study (which had generally lacked a theory of signification) with structuralist-semiotic study (which had difficulty incorporating the diachronic). It is more difficult, however, to "place" Bakhtin in relation to Lacanian poststructuralist semiotics, although here too we can speculate on compatibilities as well as differences. In this second psychoanalytic phase, film theory, basing itself on a somewhat unstable amalgam of Althusserian Marxism, Lacanian psychoanalysis, and Barthesian "textualism," shifts discussion away from film as a "languaged" phenomenon to the question of the "apparatus" and the place of the "desiring spectator" within it. The orienting questions become, "What is our investment in film?" and "What are the psychic satisfactions conferred by the cinematic apparatus?" Theorists such as Jean-Louis Baudry, Jean-Louis Comolli, Laura Mulvey, and Metz develop a discourse of positionality, postulating an unconscious substratum in spectatorial identification in the sense that cinema, as a simulation apparatus, not only represents the real but also stimulates intense "subject effects."

Insofar as contemporary film theory in the Althusserian-Lacanian mode is indebted to Saussure, it is of course in some ways incompatible with Bakhtinian translinguistics. A significant difference, moreover, marks their respective theoretical styles. While recent psychoanalytic film theory is fond of overarching abstractions (Desire, Law, the Imaginary, the Symbolic, the Unified Subject), Bakhtin deploys what are essentially metaphors (*dialogism, tact, polyphony*), which are rooted in the everyday and only then spiral outward toward the abstract and the rarefied. There are both similarities and differences, as I suggested earlier, between Bakhtin and Lacan. Both thinkers are concerned with the constitution of the subject through the other and through language. Both undercut the myth of the unified subject. But whereas Lacan seems preoccupied with a subject who is psychically—some would say ontologically—fractured, Bakhtin is more concerned with subjects who are multiple and discursively discontinuous, who simultaneously constitute and are constituted by conflictual social and cultural institutions and contexts. Distinct social experiences, for Bakhtin, engender distinct subjectivities, yet individuals and groups are not passive or helpless in this process. For Lacan, the law is inscribed within language; entry into the symbolic order entails submission to a pre-given place and role. For Bakhtin, as we have seen, the subject does not "fall" into language/the symbolic; rather, the subject is simultaneously constrained and empowered by language. Discourse does not simply "speak" the subject; rather, subject and discourse mutually constitute one another within a constantly changing social field.

Bakhtin also differs from Althusser and his film-theoretical followers, for whom ideology is fundamentally a matter of subject construction. For Bakhtin, ideology is a matter of sociohierarchical power exerting pressure on the interlinked realms of language and subjectivity. A Bakhtinian approach would reject, I think, the defeatism implicit in a monolithic conception of "dominant ideology" and "dominant cinema" which leads us to view cultural products undialectically, as if they were exempt from contradiction. Bakhtin does not say that language *is* ideology, but rather argues that language is the *domain* of ideology, one that must be seen as a contradictory force-field. Insofar as Althusserian-Lacanian film theory projected a totalizing, all-powerful apparatus, virtually foreclosing all possibilities for resistance and subversion, Bakhtin would have had to demur, insisting once again on the "right of the reader" to accept, challenge, or modify the artistic utterance. Bakhtin would doubtless have supported, we may speculate, the movement away from textual and extratextual determinism—

dominant ideology, manipulative text, all-powerful apparatus—
toward multiple textual systems, multiple subject-positions of di-
versified spectators, and multiple, indeed boundless, contexts of
reception.

At the same time, there are important congruences between
Bakhtin and second-phase cinesemiotics. The Metz of *The Imaginary Signifier,* for example, speaks illuminatingly of all the ways
that spectatorial desire impinges on and even partially constitutes
the film experience. His approach can be seen as "dialogical," although he never uses that term, in the sense that it focuses on what
happens "in between" the film and its spectator. In an eloquent
passage, Metz compares the intensity of filmic pleasure to the
shared fantasies of lovers, to the "feeling of a little miracle, as in
the state of shared amorous passion . . . as the temporary rupture
of a quite ordinary solitude."[31] Bakhtin too, I think, could subscribe
to this interest in spectatorial participation—dialogism too presupposes issues of identification and projection—although not in
the strict psychoanalytical sense that Baudry and Metz give it. On
many occasions, furthermore, Metz demonstrates an acute sensitivity to the social and political dimension of the industrial exploitation of cinematic pleasure, of dominant cinema as a "good object"
industry that produces not only films but also its own spectators.
But here too Metz offers such insights not because of but despite
his model—in this case a Lacanian-psychoanalytic model that is
an heir not only of Freud but also of Saussure—and here again
cinesemiotics "needs" a translinguistic approach concentrated on
the "utterance" rather than on the "signifier."

Although Metz often had trouble breaking out of the prisonhouse of the Saussurean and Lacanian schemas within which he
began his research, I in no way wish to disparage his immense
achievement in virtually founding filmolinguistics. Metz tested
the perennial metaphor of film/language against the concepts of
contemporary linguistics and then expanded his research into the
"semiopsychoanalysis" of the cinema. He chose his two grids, linguistics and psychoanalysis, not for arbitrary voguish reasons but
because they are the two sciences that deal with signification per
se. Just as Bakhtin "needed" Saussure and the formalists in order
to "go beyond" them, so a cinematic translinguistics needs Metz in
order to transcend his work. (Even formalist "mistakes," Bakhtin
argues, were productive, helping to focus attention on the problems formulated.) Metz must be credited, to paraphrase Bakhtin's
tribute to the formalist contribution to literary study, with "isolat-

ing the [cinematic] text as such, revealing its structure, determining the forms and variations of this structure, defining its elements and its functions."[32] But if it is not to fall into ahistoricism and scientism, the Metzian model also "needs" Bakhtin. A translinguistic approach to a theory of film language would allow us, after having "discovered" cinematic specificity, to reappreciate the links of film to other "series" or semiotic systems, to reaffirm the affinities of film studies to other disciplines, and to reenvision the relation between film history and the larger historical trajectory of narrative and discursive forms. Bakhtin's emphasis on a boundless and ever-changing context as interacting with the text helps us avoid the formalist fetishization of the autonomous art object. Bakhtin's emphasis on collective speech—the missing term in structural linguistics—and the interpersonal generation of meaning, finally, enables us to critique the static ahistorical aspects of first-phase semiology through a "translinguistics" that is compatible with the linguistic paradigm, but without the positivistic illusion of mastery and hypostatization of system that typifies a certain structuralism.

■■■■■■ Language, Difference, and Power

In its discussion of film as language, I have suggested, cinesemiology was both too linguistic—that is, too constrained by the abstract objectivist presuppositions of the Saussurean model—and not linguistic enough. If one scrutinizes the cinema, within a Bakhtinian translinguistic perspective, as "utterance," as a discursive rather than merely a signifying practice, then one can see language and cinema as having even more in common than cinesemilogy suggested. Here our focus will shift slightly, from the cinema *as* language to language *in* the cinema, and especially to language difference in the cinema. For while contemporary theoretical work has been concerned with the analogies and disanalogies between film and "natural language," it has virtually ignored the role of language difference *within* film. Cinesemiology has rarely delineated the impact on cinema, for example, of the prodigality of tongues in which films are produced, spoken, and received. My purpose here, then, will be to deploy the conceptual apparatus outlined in Chapter 1 in order to explore a number of language-related questions: how does language, first of all, "enter" film, and second, how does the sheer fact of difference, both within and between languages, impinge on film as a discursive practice and on the cinema as an "encratic" institution embedded in multiform relations of power?[1]

Throughout his writings, Bakhtin recurrently returns to the theme of the omnipresence of language within all social life and cultural production. Since experience can be apprehended only through its material embodiment in signs, Bakhtin writes in "The Problem of the Text," "language and the word are almost everything in human life."[2] "All the diverse areas of human activity," he writes in "The Problem of Speech Genres,"involve the use of language."[3] The "word," for Bakhtin, is the "exclusive" medium of consciousness and "functions as an essential ingredient accompanying all ideological creativity."[4] Yet it would be a mistake, Bakhtin continues, to think that this multifaceted, language-saturated reality can be "the subject of only one science, linguistics, or that it can be understood through linguistic methods alone"—hence the need for a *trans*linguistics.[5]

Central to our approach here will be not only Bakhtin's insights concerning the ubiquity of language within cultural production but also his thoroughgoing critique of the notion of any unitary language. Bakhtin traces the idea of a unitary language, of the "one language of truth," to Aristotelian poetics, to Augustine and the poetics of the medieval church, to the Cartesian poetics of neoclassicism, to Leibniz's idea of a "universal grammar," and to all the centripetal forces that served the project of centralizing and unifying the European languages:

The victory of one reigning language (dialect) over the others, the supplanting of languages, their enslavement, the process of illuminating them with the True Word, the incorporation of barbarians and lower social strata into a unitary language of culture and truth, the canonization of ideological systems, philology with its methods of studying and teaching dead languages, languages that were by that very fact "unities," Indo-European linguistics with its focus of attention, directed away from language plurality to a single protolanguage—all this determined the content and power of the category of "unitary language" in linguistic and stylistic thought.[6]

Speech diversity, as Bakhtin puts it,

achieves its fully creative consciousness only under conditions of active polyglossia. Two myths perish simultaneously: the myth of a language that presumes to be the only language, and the myth of a language that presumes to be completely unified.[7]

Every utterance, for Bakhtin, participates in the centripetal "unitary language" and partakes of social and historical heteroglossia—the centrifugal, stratifying forces. Language difference, then, involves both "polyglossia"—the simultaneous world-wide existence of mutually incomprehensible tongues—and "hetero-glossia"—the proliferation of competing and intersecting social "languages" cohabiting within a "single" language. We are refer-ring, then, not only to the clearly distinct idioms (English, French, Russian, Arabic) recognized as linguistic unities by grammars and lexicons, but also to the diverse class, generational, and profession-al languages that coexist within a single culture or speech com-munity. For Bakhtin, the "crude" boundaries separating natural languages represent only one extreme on a continuum. Every ap-parently unified linguistic community is characterized by "many-languagedness," in which the idioms of different generations, classes, genders, races, and locales compete for ascendancy. Every language, then, constitutes a set of languages, and every speaking subject opens onto a multiplicity of languages. All communication entails an apprenticeship in the language of the other, a kind of translation or coming to terms with meaning on the boundaries of another's set of languages as well as one's own. Thus, interlinguis-tic translation has as its counterpart the intralinguistic "trans-lation" required for dialogue between diverse individuals and diverse communities.

Bakhtin's approach, it is important to say at the outset, has a built-in "place" for film. Unlike Saussure, who privileged the lin-guistic sign system, Bakhtin sees verbal language as forming part of a continuum of semioses, a plurality of sign-related discourses that share a common underlying logic and can be "translated" into one another:

Any sign system (i.e. any language), regardless how small the collective that produces its conventions may be, can always be deciphered, that is, translated into other sign systems (languages). Consequently, sign sys-tems have a common logic, a potential single language of languages (which, of course, can never become a single concrete language, one of the languages).[8]

I would like to begin, then, by exploring the implications of Bakh-tin's translinguistic and pansemiotic attitude for the analysis of language and language difference in the cinema. In *Language and Cinema,* Metz stresses the linguistic character of two of film's five "tracks"—namely, recorded phonetic sound and written materials within the image. (These two can also change places, with written materials standing in for phonetic dialogue, as in the celebrated "dialogue of the book covers" in Godard's *Une Femme est une Femme.*) We need not linger here over spoken dialogue, the most obvious form in which language enters film, except to emphasize two points. First, there is a crucial difference between the written transcription and the cinematic presentation of speech. While the written transcription of speech, whether in the form of trial notations, a novel, or a journalistic report, inevitably involves a certain loss of "accent," the sound-film is virtually incapable of representing speech *without* an accent. The sound-film comes inevitably equipped with "accent" and "intonation," even in cases when that accent is false in terms of the diegetic social representation. The actors in the sound-film exhibit a specific "grain" of voice, and they construct, in their creation of characters, particular social tones and accents. Indeed, it was the very literalness of the "accentedness" of film speech that engendered difficulties in the period of the transition from silent films to sound-cinema. With sound, spectators were obliged to confront particular voices with particular accents. Greta Garbo, silent-film fans discovered, had an attractive Swedish accent, while John Gilbert's voice turned out to be irritatingly "reedy" and "unpleasant." (The effect of loss was analogous, in some respects, to that experienced by lovers of a novel when verbally cued fantasized characters are incarnated by disappointingly specific actors with particular voices and physiognomies.)

Second, cinema as a multitrack medium is especially well adapted to the presentation of the multitrack phenomenon called speech-communication. Dialogue, Bakhtin points out, involves more than the exchange of purely verbal utterances: "We usually respond to any utterance made by our interlocutor, if not with words, then at least with a gesture, a movement of the hand, a smile or by shaking the head."[9] As an audiovisual medium, cinema can thus correlate word with gesture, dialogue with facial expression, verbal exchange with bodily dynamics.

The often-neglected role of written materials also merits emphasis. The history of cinema has often been marked by a kind of "logophobia," a recurrent impulse to banish language from a "purely visual" medium. Not only was sound initially resisted as unduly tributary to verbal language, but there was a campaign, within silent cinema, against the written intertitle, both in the commercial feature and in the avant-garde film. A number of contemporary films, as if in response to this hostility, have deliberately foregrounded the words of a film, both oral and written, in a defiant demonstration of "logophilia." In Louis Malles's *My Dinner with André,* for example, Gregory's words are powerfully evocative, virtually obliging us to visualize his verbal narratives, and this in a film whose visuals, in a strict sense, are deliberately underplayed, repetitive, and shorn of interest. Many avant-garde "text films," such as Landow's *Remedial Reading Comprehension* and Michael Snow's *So Is This,* meanwhile, go somewhat farther, literalizing the notion of "reading the film text," while what Noel Carroll calls the " Althusserian-Lacanian new talkies," such as *Dora* (1980) and *Riddles of the Sphynx* (1977), place texts drawn from Anglo-French psychoanalytic semiotics in shifting relations with a diversity of images. *Remedial Reading Comprehension* explicitly refers to the issue of "learning to read" by including a voice-over citing the *Bay State Primer,* an eighteenth-century schoolbook in reading. *So Is This,* for its part, strictly limits its profilmic material to written words, presented silently, one at a time, for durations varying from a single frame—used, for example, for the "subliminal" intrusion of the words *tits* and *ass* and *cock* as a provocation to the Ontario censors—to nearly a minute. Snow's editing thus imposes a particular cinematic temporality on the verbal text, subordinating an audience of reader-spectators to the rhythm imposed by the film. The film also "dialogues" with its spectators, advising us directly to "just think of this as entertainment . . . it's not going to be such heavy going," thus making us conscious of ourselves as the text's interlocutors. And by presenting us with one word at a time, when we are more accustomed to reading and thinking in phrases, the film forces an unnatural delay in understanding, as if to illustrate Bakhtin's point that in communication it is not the individual sign or even the sentence that matters but rather the meaningful utterance. Snow creates a kind of suspense of the utterance, as we wait for the crucial word that will take us from language as a mere succession of linguistic tokens to language as communicative utterance and semantic meaning.

It is interesting to note that the translated subtitles for films in a foreign language often downplay, for practical as well as ideological reasons, the importance of written materials. Subtitles tend to be vococentric, concentrating on spoken dialogue while ignoring other phonetic linguistic messages such as background conversation, radio announcements, and television programs, as well as mixed visual and graphological materials such as posters, marquees, billboards, and newspapers. The non-French speaker, for example, misses the play between text and image generated by the written materials pervading most Godard films, which might be seen as glosses on Barthes' dictum that "we are still, more than ever, a civilization of writing."[10]

From a translinguistic perspective, we can see language as pervading all the cinematic tracks, since "all manifestations of ideological creativity," as Bakhtin and Voloshinov put it in *Marxism and the Philosophy of Language,* "are bathed by, suspended in, and cannot be entirely segregated or divorced from the element of speech."[11] Pursuing this insight, we might see the music and noise tracks in film as also embracing linguistic elements. Recorded music is often accompanied by lyrics, and even when not so accompanied, can evoke lyrics. Purely instrumental versions of popular songs often elicit in the spectator the mental presence of the words of the song. (Kubrick, in *Doctor Strangelove,* exploits this evocation of remembered lyrics when he superimposes the well-known melody "Try a Little Tenderness" on images of nuclear bombers). Even apart from lyrics, music itself is permeated with semantic and discursive values. Musicologist J. J. Nattiez, for example, sees music as deeply embedded in social discourses, including verbal discourses.[12] Moreover, recorded noises are not necessarily "innocent" of language. Setting aside the question of the cultural relativity of the boundaries separating noise from music from language—one culture's "noise" may be another culture's "language" or "music," as in the case of acoustic speech surrogates such as African talking drums, which use pitch to relay tonal languages—countless films reveal the close imbrication of noise and language. The stylized murmur of conversing voices in the restaurant sequences of classical Hollywood films renders human speech as background noise, while Jacques Tati's films give voice to an Esperanto of aural effects—vacuum cleaners that wheeze and vinyl suits that go "poof"—characteristic of the postmodern environment.

But the linguistic presence cannot be confined to the soundtrack or to written materials within the image: the image track itself is infiltrated by the ubiquitous agency of language. I am not arguing, I hasten to add, that film is "essentially" verbal, or to deny that it is *also* visual, or even to deny that there is something in images that "escapes" language. I am insisting only on cinema's "languagedness," on a verbal dimension rather than a verbal "essence."[13] This dimension, this verbal-visual nexus—or the infiltration of the iconic by the symbolic, to borrow Piercean terminology—can take many forms. Boris Eikhenbaum, viewing film metaphor as parasitic on verbal metaphor, speaks of "image translations of linguistic tropes"[14]—the way camera angle, for example, can literalize specific locutions such as "look up to" or "oversee" or "look down on." In the case of such "literalisms," the visual impact is inseparable from fidelity to a linguistic metaphor. At times, whole sequences and even entire films are structured by linguistic formations. Hitchcock's *The Wrong Man* (1957) is informed in its entirety by the quibbling sentence: "Manny plays the bass." The protagonist plays the bass, quite literally, in the Stork Club, but he also plays the role of the "base" when he is falsely accused and forced to mimic the actions of the real thief. Similarly, the interplay of verbal-visual puns and equivalences becomes both subliminal and pervasive in Hitchcock's *Psycho,* where the opening shots prefigure the film's obsession with avian imagery by literalizing the notion of a "bird's-eye view" of a city, appropriately named Phoenix, while airborne "crane shots," which lead us to a character named Marion Crane, visually mimic the soaring movements of a bird through the air.[15]

At times, however, language enters the cinematic experience in ways that are only obliquely related to the five tracks of the film text itself. Within the apparatus itself, in certain locales and at certain historical moments, intermediate speaking figures have been employed to negotiate, as it were, between film and audience. In the silent period, lecturers at times commented on the screen action and thus oriented audience response, while in Japan, "benshis" read and interpreted the images, avatars of an institution that lasted through the late thirties. Some films, furthermore, such as the Argentinian *La Hora de los Hornos* (Hour of the Furnaces, 1968), incorporate into the text itself programmed interruptions of the screenings to allow for political debate, thus opening up the cinema to direct person-to-person dialogue in what amounts to a provocative amalgam of cinema, theatre, and political rally.

Language also enters the cinematic experience in other, more extemporaneous ways. Dialogue, usually present as part of the diegesis, is metaphorically evoked, within a Bakhtinian perspective, by the "dialogue" between film and spectator, a dialogue that is at times literalized, on the part of the audience, through impromptu verbal participation. In some speech-communities, the conventions of spectatorship encourage the "naïve" audience to address verbal warnings or approval to the actors/characters on screen; the collectivity, in such instances, celebrates its own existence. In New York's Forty-second Street movie theaters, for example, boisterous commentary forms part of the ritual of film-going. At times, a full-scale dialogue can break out among the spectators themselves in the form of repartee or argument; the film loses its diegetic hold over the audience as the spectacle is displaced from screen to audience. This linguistic assertiveness reaches its paroxysm in the cult-film phenomenon, for example with the *Rocky Horror Picture Show,* where an audience of repeat viewers elaborates a dynamically evolving parallel parody text, combining the synched repetition of songs and lines from the film with interpolated phrases that "play off" and mock the "official" on-screen dialogue.

Even when verbal language is absent from both film and theater, semantic processes take place in the mind of the spectator through what Bakhtin, following Vygotsky, calls "inner speech": "The processes of understanding any ideological phenomenon at all (be it a picture, a piece of music, a ritual, or an act of human conduct) cannot operate without the participation of inner speech."[16] Inner speech, for Vygotsky as for Bakhtin, refers to intrapsychic discourse, the pulse of thought implicated in language, a mode that is qualitatively different from "other speech" in its personal, idiosyncratic, and fragmentary form. "Inner speech" is not merely speech minus sound. It is a separate speech function deploying not only words (in both phonetic and graphic form) but also images, schemata, symbols, and phonetic fragments. Bakhtin describes inner speech as a "variegated verbal dance" consisting in a "stream of words, sometimes joined up into definite sentences, but more often flowing in a sort of unbroken succession of fragmentary thoughts, habitual expressions, some general merged impressions from some objects or phenomena from life."[17]

A number of filmmakers have shown an interest in rendering inner speech cinematically. Bakhtin's contemporary Eisenstein repeatedly expressed a desire to render the stream-of-consciousness monologues of Joyce's *Ulysses;* and Godard, in both *Une Femme Mariee* and *Two or Three Things I Know about Her,* approximates inner speech through discontinuous and fragmentary voice-over commentaries. Film spectatorship, meanwhile, is, according to Boris Eikhenbaum, "accompanied by a constant process of internal speech" whereby images and sounds are projected onto a kind of verbal screen functioning as a "ground" for meaning.[18] Filmic perception itself, then, is partially oriented by the linguistic, in at least a double sense. First, the codes of iconic recognition and designation, as Metz points out in "The Perceived and the Named," structure the vision of the spectator, who thus "brings language," as it were, "to" the image.[19] But beyond this perceptual-lexical filtration of the image, the spectator has a general predisposition to internally verbalize narrative, to set up a kind of intrapsychic "exchange system" between verbal and visual information. Theoreticians of cinema have not really begun to explore the subtle ways in which this inaudible but nonetheless real accumulative pressure of inner speech constitutes an integral part of the film experience.[20]

Language in art does not appear as undifferentiated "stuff"; it is mediated by specific artistic and discursive forms. In "The Problem of Speech Genres," Bakhtin provides extremely suggestive concepts that are susceptible to extrapolation for the analysis of cinema. Bakhtin here calls attention to a wide gamut of "speech genres" that represent normatively structured clusters of formal, contextual, and thematic features having to do with ways of speaking in particular situations. (Bakhtin's concept is in some ways close to Halliday's notion of "register" as the semantic potential associated with a given type of situation, the systems of rules governing the production, transmission, and reception of "appropriate" meanings by "appropriate" users in "appropriate" forms in particular social contexts.) Both oral and written, simple and complex, these genres, for Bakhtin, range all the way from "the short rejoinders of ordinary dialogue" in everyday narration, to the military command, to all the literary genres (from the proverb to the multivolume novel) and other "secondary (complex) speech genres" such as the major genres of sociocultural commentary and scientific research. The secondary, complex genres draw from the primary genres of unmediated speech communion and influence them as well in a process of constant back-and-forth flow. (It is typical of Bakhtin's method to slide easily from the oral to the written and back without privileging either term.)

A translinguistic approach to speech genres in the cinema would correlate the primary speech genres—familial conversation, dialogue among friends, chance encounters, boss-worker exchanges, classroom discussions, cocktail party banter, military commands—with their secondary cinematic mediation. It would analyze the etiquette by which the classical Hollywood film, for example, deals with typical speech situations such as two-person dialogue (usually by the conventional ping-pong of shot and countershot) and dramatic confrontations (the verbal standoffs of western and gangster films), as well as with the more avant-gardist subversions of that etiquette. Godard's entire career, for example, might be seen as a protracted attack on the conventional Hollywood decorum for handling discursive situations in the cinema (hence his refusal of the canonical back-and-forth of over-the-shoulder shots for dialogue in favor of alternative approaches:

pendulum-like lateral tracks (*Le Mépris*), lengthy single-shot sequences (*Masculin, Féminin*), and unorthodox positioning of the bodies of the interlocutors (e.g., having one speaker's head block the view of the other, as in *Vivre sa Vie*).

Our everyday speech, Bakhtin suggests, is cast in generic forms, which we master fluently even before we study grammar. He cites various everyday genres in which the individual speech-will is manifested and given expressive intonation. A number of films, in this sense, can be seen as dealing quite consciously and reflexively with the question of primary speech genres and their cinematic mediation. The Brazilian avant-garde film *Bangue, Bangue* (Bang, Bang, 1971), by Andrea Tonacci, performs a meta-linguistic examination of the everyday speech genre called "greetings and exchange of trivialities." A man and a woman initiate, five times in succession, the same conversation, concluding, after considerable prolixity, that "Hi" should be systematically substituted for the usual sequence of "Good morning," "How are you?" "I'm fine," and so forth. One of a number of reflexive minisequences in the film, the episode implicitly compares film itself to discourse, to conversation. It consists, more accurately, of metadiscourse, discourse on discourse, just as the film itself constitutes metacinema. The apparent point of the discourse—the desirability of using as few words as possible—is contradicted by the discourse itself, which is wordy and redundant. What matters, the sequence suggests, is not the message but the articulation, or better the inseparable link between the two, a point further illustrated when the same conversation is played against different contextual sound elements, first with harsh, ambient noise and then again with harp music, each time having a completely different effect.

The repertoire of speech genres varies from person to person. Many people who have an excellent general command of a language, Bakhtin points out, feel painfully inadequate in particular spheres of communication because they lack a practical mastery of the requisite generic forms. Japanese director Juzo Itami deals with one such specialized primary speech genre in *The Funeral*. The film chronicles three traumatic days in the lives of an upscale Japanese couple—a middle-aged actor and his actress wife—in the wake of her father's death, from the day they receive the news till the day the corpse is cremated, the ashes buried, and everyone returns home. The trauma consists not in the loss of the father, who was universally regarded as a cruel and gluttonous lecher, but rather in the discursive challenge of coping with the unfamiliar speech situation engendered by the funeral and burial. Out of touch with the venerable Shinto traditions and with contemporary funeral decorum, the couple has to learn both for this special occasion. (Their acting profession presumably equips them especially well for the challenge.) They do so with the help of a videocassette entitled "The ABC's of the Funeral," thanks to which they can learn what formulaic phrases to expect—"our condolences on your tragic loss," "what a blessing he didn't suffer long," "he looks so peaceful in the coffin, as if he were asleep," and so forth—as well as how to master their own equally formulaic responses—"thank you for your condolences," "he would have been so happy to know you were here"—and thus to become proficient in the tragic-loss-of-a-loved-one "speech genre." The husband is expected to give a talk about the deceased at a final dinner, but the "actor" here suffers from stage fright, and it is his wife who ultimately rises to the discursive challenge with a touchingly modest performance.

Bunuel's *Exterminating Angel* (1962), similarly, can be seen as a comic deconstruction of the primary speech genre called "polite dinner conversation." The film's plot, revolving on the inexplicable entrapment of a pride of socialites at an elegant dinner, provides the point of departure for the critical dissection of the elaborate discursive rituals of the *haute bourgeoisie*. On one level, the film is a joke on an everyday social experience, the excruciatingly formal dinner where all the guests are quite miserable but pretend to be having a marvelous time, where everyone would prefer to leave but no one has the courage. The film also offers satirical variants of "speech subgenres," the civil discourse of individuals who detest one another but are constrained to be polite, the encounters of wives and lovers (quite aware of a triangular situation) who conveniently pretend not to know, and so forth. In a kind of *gramatica jocosa* of the language of social etiquette, Bunuel engenders absurd discursive encounters. A couple about to marry, for example, performs a kind of bureaucratized parody of the man-meets-woman-at-social-gathering speech genre, as she asks while they dance, "Name? Age? Profession? Marital Status?" As bourgeois etiquette disintegrates, Bunuel seems to be offering the linguistic-discursive evidence of grave ruptures in the fabric of a pathologically polite society. He mingles the polite and the impolite, the noble and the vulgar: "You smell like a hyena," one socialite tells another. A doctor confides to a friend that one of his patients will soon become "completely bald" (a Spanish expression roughly equivalent to "croak" or "kick the bucket").

Bakhtin compares inner speech to a form of "translation," arguing that "even the most intimate self-consciousness" is an attempt to translate the self into a common language."[21] And if all film experience involves a kind of translation—from the images and sounds of the text into the internalized discourse of the spectator—interlingual cinematic experience entails specific and more complicated mechanisms. In the case of the subtitled film, we hear the more or less alien sounds of another tongue. If the language neighbors our own, we may recognize a substantial portion of the words and phrases. If it is more distant, we may find ourselves adrift on an alien sea of undecipherable phonic substance. Specific sound combinations might remind us of locutions in our own language, but we cannot be certain they are not phonetic *faux amis*. The intertitles and subtitles of foreign films, meanwhile, trigger a process of what linguists call "endophony"—that is, the soundless mental enunciation of words, the calling to mind of the phonetic signifier. But the interlingual film experience is perceptually bifurcated; we hear the other's language while we read our own. The processes of reading and hearing, furthermore, are not identical; each sets in motion a distinct form of inner speech. Reading remains relatively cerebral, while hearing prompts associative processes that are more deeply rooted in our psychic past. It was only as a result of the bifurcation involved with subtitled sound-films, interestingly, that Latin American film critics and spectators, for example, began to complain about the "foreignness" of American films. Thanks to the "visual Esperanto" of the silent film, non-American spectators not only read intertitles in their own language but also presumably fantasized the dialogue as being in their own language. Cinema was only retroactively perceived as foreign precisely because other-languaged dialogue, in combination with subtitles, destroyed the masking effect of silence. The "foreign" spectator became acutely conscious, in Bakhtinian terms, of being forced to see one language "through" another.

There is still another sense, however, in which films are "bathed by" and "suspended in" language. Films are saturated by language from the beginning to the end of their existence; they come from language and ultimately return to it. A film's incarnation as an audiovisual phenomenon, in this sense, is quite ephemeral. Films often take the form, initially, of verbal text or performance—source-play or novel, verbal synopsis, script, story conference. Language also pervades the process of production—written script, verbal memoranda, production meetings, verbal cues to actors, along with the proverbial "Lights! Camera! Action!" Upon completion, the film returns to language, again becoming the subject of verbal representation in the form of verbal synopsis, the negative or positive evaluations of "word-of-mouth commentary," journalistic reviews, scholarly text, classroom exegesis, *TV Guide* capsule summary, Siskel-Ebert banter. Thus filmic representations, which never cease to be partially linguistic (since all the arts, in Bakhtinian terms, represent the languages and discourses thrown up by social praxis), get translated back, by a rough exchange, into words. David Black speaks of "the synoptic tendency"—that is, the notion of verbal/visual exchange as a founding principle for narrative film. Narrative film is understandable, Black argues, only in relation to the principle of verbal recountability as a kind of gold standard for narrative exchange. Like the formalists, Black sees verbal activity as providing the connective tissue for narrative film. Film narrative is "logomorphic"; it tells stories by virtue of its ability to cluster around verbal or verbal-potential discourse.[22] The fiction film, and indeed all films, exist, then, within the powerful gravitational field of what Bakhtin calls "the word."

One filmmaker who constantly foregrounds the ways in which life and the cinema are "bathed in language" is Jean-Luc Godard. In *Two or Three Things I Know about Her,* Godard explores the parameters not only of the "languagedness" of our understanding but also of filmmaking as a "linguistic" practice. Released in 1967, the film came in the wake of the first tentative gropings toward a semiotics of film and was more or less simultaneous with Kristeva's landmark introduction of Bakhtin ("Bakhtin, le mot, le dialogue et le roman"). Godard, always a sensitive barometer to changes in the intellectual atmosphere, registered these language-oriented concerns in what he himself called a "film-essay." Within this language obsession, *Two or Three Things* explicitly cites two of the central figures in the contemporary tradition of reflection on language. Asked "What is language?" by her young son, the protagonist, Juliette, responds with a paraphrase of the famous Heideggerian definition of language as "the house of being," here simplified for a child's understanding: "Language is the house man lives in." And later an extreme close-up of an espresso coffee cup is superimposed on a whispered citation from Wittgenstein's *Tractatus Logico-Philosophicus:* "The limits of my language are the limits of my world." Godard's twenty-eight "commentaries" in the film, furthermore, have constant recourse to the metalanguage of linguistics—"vocabulary," "syntax," "semantic riches," "a new language—and it is the idea of language that links sequences that would otherwise appear to have little connection. Juliette's definition of *language* is immediately followed, for example, by a comic-strip panel suggesting that the languages that "house" us are visual as well as verbal.

We live, Bakhtin writes, "in a world of others' words." Our life can be seen as a "reaction to others' words . . . beginning with [our] assimilation of them (in the initial mastery of speech) and ending with [our] assimilation of the wealth of human culture (expressed in the word or in other semiotic materials)."[23] *Two or Three Things* foregrounds the semiotic "wealth of human culture." More precisely, it calls attention to the signs and sign systems typical of the postmodern semiosphere: cigarette cartons, travel posters, billboards, pinball machines, gas station marquees, paperback books, underwear ads. "Why are there so many signs everywhere," Godard's off-screen voice whispers, "that I end up wondering what language is about, signs with so many different meanings, that reality becomes obscure. . . ?" The multiplicity of consumerist and pop-culture images accompanied by verbal texts gives expression to what Fredric Jameson called, in his critique of Saussurean linguistics and formalist poetics, the "deeper justification of the linguistic model," to wit:

the concrete character of the social life of the so-called advanced countries today, which offer the spectacle of a world from which nature as such has been eliminated, a world saturated with messages and information, whose intricate commodity network may be seen as the very prototype of a system of signs.[24]

Godard's former collaborator Jean-Pierre Gorin also foregrounds language and language difference in his documentary *Poto and Cabengo* (1979). The film explores the linguistic anomaly presented by the apparently invented "twin speech" or "idioglossia" of two six-year-old sisters, Gracie and Ginny Kennedy, who attracted ephemeral national attention in 1977. The San Diego twins, who have nicknamed each other "Poto" and "Cabengo," form the point of departure for a meditation on the nonunitary nature of language. The film, according to Gorin himself, concerns "unstructured discourse (the language of the twins) surrounded by structured discourses (the discourse of the family, the discourse of the media, the discourse of therapy, the discourse of documentary film-making)."[25] *Poto and Cabengo* almost exactly corresponds to Bakhtin's remarks concerning the incorporation of heteroglossia in the comic novel, which is characterized by two distinctive features: first, the inclusion of a "multiplicity of 'languages' and verbal-ideological belief-systems," alternating with "direct authorial discourse" (here Gorin's personal voice-over); and second, the "unmasking" of these languages and belief systems as "false, hypocritical, greedy, limited, narrowly rationalistic, and inadequate to reality."

"To understand the creolized language of the twins," Gorin reflects, "I would have to listen to the voices which had dominated their lives." The emphasis on "voices" recalls Bakhtin, with his capacity to hear "voices in everything and dialogical relations among them."[26] In the attempt to understand the twins, then, Gorin gives us the crucial voices and discourses that have informed and deformed them: that of their culturally limited immigrant mother, their naïvely optimistic Horatio Algerish father, their German grandmother, their teachers and speech therapists, along with the mass-mediated voices of television programs, comic strips, and advertising.

As Vivian Sobchack points out in her excellent essay on *Poto and Cabengo,* the Gorin film virtually pleads for a "translinguistic" analysis. The film foregrounds, first of all, the tension between what Bakhtin calls the "centrifugal" and "centripetal" forces within a language, between "those contingent and contextual forces which push a language far from its central core toward invention and those normative and historically-hardened forces which authorize and unify a language as coherent, systematic, and conventional."[27] Within the film's "active polyglossia," the "unstructured discourse" of the twins is made to challenge the authoritarian discourses of family, therapy, and the media. Their idioglossia erupts as what Sobchack calls a "subversive act of authorship" unendorsed by any social or ideological establishment. The film deconstructs what Bakhtin calls the "double myth": the myth of the language that presumes to be the only language, and the myth of the language that presumes to be completely unified. First, as Sobshack points out, spoken English is "decentered and opened up by a multitude of accented voices": Gorin's French cadences, the caricatural German-American pidgin of a narrator reading from *The Katzen jammer Kids* ("Vat vould happen iff elephinks could fly?"), the professional diction and elocution of a female narrator; the idiosyncratic voices of the twins' speech therapists; the southern accent of the twins' father; the Chicano English of the family's neighbors; and the teachers' mouthing of the patronizing "child speak" adults so often adopt with children. Then, through a kind of inversion, the twin's invented speech, an idioglossic parody of standard English, slowly becomes familiar and "normal" to us while the "respectable" discourses come to seem strange. Much as in Todd Browning's *Freaks,* where by the end of the film the normal people seem like freaks and the freaks normal, in *Poto and Cabengo* the avatars of discursive authority, such as the psychologist and the speech therapist, seem linguistically deficient and ironically incomprehensible and inarticulate.

Apart from language difference as foregrounded by specific films, however, much remains to be said, on a theoretical level, about the implications of polyglossia—the world-wide babble of mutually incomprehensible tongues—for the cinema. Polyglossia, after all, was one of Bakhtin's principal concerns. Not only was he a philologically trained literary critic working in numerous ancient and contemporary languages; he was also the intellectual product of a specific historical situation—that of the Soviet Union in the twenties—which favored a heightened awareness of the importance of the rights of multilingualism and multiculturalism for the diverse peoples making up the Soviet Union and its republics. In "Epic and Novel," Bakhtin stresses the role of polyglossia as a factor in artistic creation. In a polyglot world, the "period of national languages, coexisting but closed and deaf to each other . . . comes to an end." Instead, languages come to throw light on each other: "one language can, after all, see itself only in the light of another."[28] Only polyglossia, Bakhtin writes, "fully frees consciousness from the tyranny of its own language and its own myth of language."[29] I would like here to approach the question of polyglossia in the cinema, within a translinguistic perspective, both in terms of the Bakhtinian notion of the "mutual illumination of languages" and in terms of the interaction of language and power. In practical, analytical, and theoretical terms, what are the consequences of the intersection of film and polyglossia, and in what ways is this intersection imbricated with the asymmetries of power?

The import of such questions, and of a translinguistic approach to them, becomes evident even as we consider the translation involved with titles, subtitles, and postsynchronization. Title translations, for example, often betray the "tyranny of one language" and its "myth of language." Translated titles and subtitles often involve serious miscalculations due to haste, laziness, or insufficient mastery of the source or target language and culture. (While publishers presumably would never engage a hack translator for *A la Recherche du Temps Perdu,* film distributors, perhaps out of a vestigial scorn for a low-status medium, regularly hire incompetents.) A Rumanian bureaucrat, for example, misled by the phonetic resemblance between the Italian word *moderato* and the Rumanian word *moderat* (quiet, cautious), and between *cantabile* and *comtabil* (bookkeeper, accountant), construed *Moderato Cantabile,* the Peter Brook adaptation of the Duras novel, as *The Quiet Accountant.* But the question of film translation is more complex than such an egregious example of the "nonillumination of languages" would suggest. When one language, in Bakhtinian terms, "looks at" another, perfect translations are even in the best circumstances a virtual impossibility. Languages are not ossified nomenclatures, parallel lexical lists from which one need merely choose matching items on the basis of a one-to-one correspondence. Even an untranslated title subtly changes by virtue of entering a new linguistic and cultural environment, while translated titles get caught up in a veritable maelstrom of *différence.* Take, for example, the paradigmatic challenge posed by titular puns and wordplay. The "pieces" in the film *Five Easy Pieces,* for example, are at once musical, filmic, and sexual, yet it is highly unlikely that any other language would feature the same relation between the phonemic and the semantic (what linguists call "paranomasia") and thus be able to orchestrate the same constellation of meanings. Similarly, the "wave" in Michael Snow's *Wavelength* condenses multiple reverberations—sea waves, "see" waves, sine waves, sound waves, new wave—in a simultaneity that would be virtually impossible to convey in another language. Given the challenge of an unattainable adequation, the translator, in "principled despair," must settle for a semantic and affective approximation of the "alien words" of the source text.

Within a Bakhtinian perspective, languages are composed not of self-equivalent signs and sentences but of situated utterances. Translation, in this sense, constitutes a form of what Bakhtin calls "reported speech," the word of the other transmitted by an alien tongue. Since all discourse is intensely conventionalized and embedded in cultural particularity, no absolute transparency is possible. Technically "correct" translations can involve subtle modifications. The English *Day for Night* correctly renders the cinematographic procedure known in French as "La Nuit Américaine," but a nuance is lost with the disappearance of "Américaine," pointing, as it does in the Truffaut film, to the nostalgic memory of the Hollywood film.

Any utterance, within a Bakhtinian perspective, is partially shaped by the addressee whose potential reaction must be taken into account. A translated film title, in this sense, can be seen as one turn taken in a kind of ongoing dialogue between film and spectator. Torn from its usual linguistic environment, the title in translation enters an alien field of what Bakhtin calls "prior speakings." The English phrase "horse's mouth," for example, enters a paradigm of proverbial expressions such as "straight from the horse's mouth" and "don't look a gift horse in the mouth," a point that was lost on the Polish translator, who construed the Ronald Neame film *The Horse's Mouth* (1958) literally, as *Konsky Pysk* ("Mouth of the Horse"). Since the figurative expression "straight from the horse's mouth" does not exist in Polish, the title became inadvertently surrealistic, leading baffled viewers to expect a horse that never materialized. Commercial considerations, meanwhile, sometimes lead to "parasitical" translations that strive to evoke another successful film or genre—the intertextuality of the box office. Israeli distributors, hoping to capitalize on the success of Mel Brooks's *Blazing Saddles* (1974), rereleased his earlier *Twelve Chairs* as *Kis'ot Lohatim* (Blazing Chairs). Or the commercial intertext sometimes leads to the gratuitous eroticization of titles. Bergman's title *Persona,* with its rich resonances, at once psychoanalytic, theatrical, and philosophical, became in Brazil *Quando as Mulheres Pecam* (When Women Sin), a title whose puritanical lasciviousness led local viewers to expect a film in the tradition of the Brazilian soft-core *pornochanchada.*

With the advent of the sound-film, once it became obvious that the production of multiple-foreign-language versions of films was not a viable option, producers, distributors, and exhibitors were left with the fundamental choice of either subtitles (dominant in France and the United States) or postsynchronization (the standard practice in Italy and Germany). Godard's distaste for postsynchronization led him in *Le Mépris* to make a film so multilingual that it would require subtitles *wherever* it was screened. The film, whose diegesis revolves around a cinematic adaptation of *The Odyssey,* touches on the role of translation and interpretation, first in the literal sense of the constant translation required between the diverse nationalities caught up in the polyglot atmosphere of international coproductions, and second in the broader sense of other literal and metaphorical "translations": the translation of classical Greek epic into modern European languages, the translation of the Moravia source-novel into film, the translation of ancient storytelling into modern-day narrative. The interpreter Francesca, in the film, constantly ferries messages back and forth between the American producer, the German director, and the French scriptwriter, but her translations invariably modify the messages transmitted, thus showing the problematic and hazardous nature of all translation. (The Italian distributor's obligatory postsynchronization eliminated the role of the interpreter, leading Godard to dissociate himself from the Italian version of the film.)

In the case of subtitles, the processes that characterize title translation—the filtration of meaning through ideological and cultural grids, the mediation of a social or political superego—operate with equal force. For those who are familiar with both the source and the target language, subtitles provide a kind of "mutual illumination of languages," as well as the pretext for a linguistic game of "spot the error." Subtitles can simply be mistaken—the English version of the subtitle of Godard's *Masculin, Féminin* translates *bruler à napalm* (burning with napalm) as "burning Nepal"—or bowdlerized (common in English translations of French New Wave films), or politically censorious. Subtitles can also inject revolutionary messages into nonrevolutionary films. In the late sixties, for example, French leftists reportedly "kidnapped" Kung Fu films, giving them revolutionary titles such as *La Dialectique Peut-Elle Casser les Briques?* and incendiary subtitles, thus providing leftist political "anchorage" for what were essentially exploitation films.

The choice of postsynchronization (defined for our purposes as the technical procedure by which a voice, whether of the original performer or another, is "glued" to a visible speaking figure in the image) also has significant consequences. With subtitles, the difference in material of expression—phonetic original and graphological translation—allows for the juxtaposition of two parallel texts, one aural and the other written, and thus for the possibility of comparison and "mutual illumination." Errors become potentially "visible" not only to privileged spectators who are familiar with the languages in question but also to the general viewer who is conscious of small inconsistencies: a disproportion in duration between spoken utterance and written translation, for example, or the failure of subtitles to register obvious linguistic disturbances such as a lisp or a stutter. But the single-track nature of dubbing, in contrast, makes comparison impossible. Without the original script or version, there is simply nothing with which to compare the dubbed version. Given our desire to believe that the heard voices actually emanate from the actors/characters on the screen, we repress all awareness of the possibility of an incorrect translation; in fact, we forget that there has been any translation at all.

The marriage of convenience that weds a voice from one language and culture to an imaged speaker coming from another often triggers a kind of battle of linguistic and cultural codes. Linguistic communication, as Bakhtin implies, is multitrack; every language carries with it a constellation of corollary features having to do with oral articulation, facial expression, and bodily movement. The norms of physical expressiveness, moreover, vary sharply from culture to culture; extroverted peoples accompany their words with a livelier play of gesticulations than more introverted peoples. In *Trouble in Paradise* (1932), Ernst Lubitsch practices the "mutual interillumination of cultures" by humorously counterpointing the speech mannerisms of southern and northern Europeans. Recounting a robbery to the Italian police, the Edward Everett Horton character speaks in English (posited as putative French) while the Italian interpreter ferries his words over to the police. Horton's speech is unemotional, efficient, and gestureless, while the interpreter's is flamboyant and animated with lively facial expressions and emphatic Italianate gestures.

To graft one language, with its own system of linking sound and gesture, onto the visible behavior associated with another, is often to foster a kind of cultural violence and dislocation. Relatively slight when the cultures closely neighbor, this dislocation becomes major when they are more distant, resulting in a clash of cultural repertoires. Brazilian television, like television in many countries of the Third World, constantly programs American films and television programs in which American media stars speak fluent dubbed Portuguese. The match of the moving mouths of Kojak, Colombo, and Starsky and Hutch with the sounds of Brazilian Portuguese, however, results in a kind of monstrosity, a collision between the cultural codes associated with Brazilian Portuguese (strong affectivity, a tendency to hyperbole, lively gestural accompaniment of spoken discourse) and those associated with television-cop English (minimal affectivity, understatement, controlled gestures, a cool, hard, tough demeanor).

A number of recent films from countries where postsynchronization is common have thematized the issue of dubbing as part of the plot. The male object of desire in Pedro Almodovar's *Women on the Verge of a Nervous Breakdown* (1988) is rendered as pure voice;

not only does he dub movies, he constantly leaves duplicitous messages on his lover's answering machine. Brazilian Walter Rogerio's
Voz do Brasil (Voice of Brazil, 1981) features one sequence showing
an American television program being dubbed into Brazilian Portuguese. As the film loop of an action-packed scene passes on the
screen, the dubbing technicians do their work and exchange trivialities. We are struck by the disjunction between the glamorous
American stars on the screen and the ordinary Brazilians lending
their voices. The film thus uncovers the hidden face of the normally
off-screen dubbers, rendering visible the effaced labor of a particular cinematic process while revealing the technical supports of neocolonialism. The voices, to go back to the title, are those of Brazil,
but the images and the mentality and the corporate structure behind them are not.

One of Bakhtin's major contributions to the theorization of
language, as we have seen, was his emphasis on its political dimension. Everyday language exchange, for Bakhtin, is a "historical
event, albeit an infinitesimal one." There is no political struggle,
for Bakhtin, that does not also pass through "the word." Language
and power intersect wherever the question of language becomes
involved with asymmetrical power arrangements. As potent symbols of collective identities, natural languages, for example, form
the focus of deep loyalties existing at the very razor's edge of national difference. In South Africa, blacks protest the imposition
of Afrikaans as the official language of education; in the United
States, Hispanics struggle for bilingual education and examination. But even monolingual societies are characterized by heteroglossia; they englobe multiple "languages" or "dialects" that both
reveal and produce social position, each existing in a distinct relation to the hegemonic language. Linguistic performance and competence, Stuart Hall points out, is "socially distributed, not only by
class but also by gender."[30] Patriarchal oppression, as feminist sociolinguists point out, passes through language, as does feminist
resistance to oppression. Issues of race also intersect with questions of language, power, and social stratification. Black English in
the United States was often called "bad English," because linguists
failed to take into account the specific African-historical roots and
the immanent logical structure of black speech.

Although languages as abstract entities do not exist in hierarchies of value, languages as lived entities operate within hierarchies of power. What, then, are the implications of this language/
power intersection for the cinema, simply in terms of polyglossia?

How many of the estimated five thousand languages currently in use around the world are actually spoken in the cinema? Are any major languages completely lacking in cinematic representation? How many languages appear briefly in an ethnographic film and as quickly disappear? How many films are never subtitled, due to insufficient funds, and therefore never distributed internationally? What is the linguistic dimension of an emerging cinema within a situation of "unstable bilingualism" such as that of Quebec? What about anticolonialist films, such as Pontecorvo's *Burn,* which are artificially made to speak a hegemonic language in order to guarantee geographic distribution and economic survival?

Bakhtin is refreshingly unethnocentric when he speaks of polyglossia. In "Epic and Novel," he partially attributes the emergence of the novel to a specific linguistic rupture in the history of European civilization, noting "its emergence from a socially isolated and culturally deaf, semipatriarchal society, and its entrance into international and interlingual contacts and relationships." As a result, Bakhtin writes, "a multitude of different languages, cultures, and times became available to Europe, and this became a decisive factor in its life and thought."[31] Bakhtin, like most contemporary linguistic theorists, tends to see the diverse "natural languages" in an egalitarian manner, as at once irreducibly distinct and radically equal. Yet we know that if all languages are in principle equal, some languages, both within the cinema and outside it, have been made "more equal than others." Inscribed within the play of power, languages as used in films are caught up in hierarchies rooted in cultural hegemonies and political domination. English, for example, has long been the linguistic vehicle for the projection of Anglo-American power, technology, and finance, and Hollywood films, for their part, have at times reflected this power, often betraying a linguistic hubris bred of empire. Presuming to speak of others in its native idiom, Hollywood proposed to tell not only its own stories but also the stories and legends of other nations, and not only to Americans but also to the other nations themselves, and always in English. In Cecil B. De Mille epics, both the ancient Egyptians and the Israelites spoke English, and so, for that matter, did God. In Hollywood, the Greeks of the Odyssey, the Romans of Ben Hur, Cleopatra of Egypt, Madame Bovary of France, Count Vronsky of Russia, Helen of Troy, and Jesus of Nazareth all had as their *lingua franca* the English of Southern California. Hollywood both profited from and itself promoted the world-wide dissemination of the English language, thus contributing indirectly to the subtle erosion of the linguistic autonomy of other cultures. By virtue of its global diffusion, Hollywoodean English became an agent in the spread of first-world cultural hegemony.

In the aftermath of World War II, especially, English became what George Steiner has called the "vulgate" of Anglo-American power. Countless films in the postwar period, as a consequence, reflect the prestige and projection of English and the axiomatic self-confidence of its speakers. The producer Prokosch, in *Contempt,* in this regard, embodies the self-importance and linguistic arrogance of the industrial managers of American cinema; while he is more or less monolingual, his European collaborators move easily from French to German to English and Italian. In *Der Amerikanische Freund* (The American Friend, 1977), Wim Wenders calls attention to this lack of linguistic reciprocity between American and European. The major non-American characters all speak English along with their native language, while the American friend Tom, the "cowboy in Hamburg," speaks only English. Jonathon's last sentence to the Swiss doctor—"It hurts in any language"—echoes another filmic demonstration of linguistic nonreciprocity—Miguel/Michael's response, in *Touch of Evil,* to Quinlan's insistence that he speak English, not Spanish: "I think it will be unpleasant in any language." Like many New German films, *The American Friend* critically foregrounds the widespread dissemination of the English language and of American pop culture, thus illustrating the ways in which "the Yanks," as another Wenders character puts it in *Kings of the Road,* "have colonized our subconscious."

For Bakhtin, language is a social battleground, the place where political struggles are engaged both comprehensively and intimately. Human beings do not simply enter into language as a master code; they participate in it as socially constituted subjects. Where there is no true commonality of interest, the power relations implicit in what Bakhtin calls "tact" determine the conditions of social meeting and linguistic exchange. In the case of colonialism, linguistic reciprocity is simply ruled out of court. The interest of Sembene's *La Noire de . . .* (Black Girl, 1966), in this sense, lies in having the film's female protagonist stand at the point of convergence of multiple oppressions—as colonized, as black, as woman, as maid—and in conveying her oppression specifically through language. Diouana, who the spectator knows is fluent in French, overhears her employer say of her: "She understands French . . . by instinct . . . like an animal." The colonialist, who, according to

Fanon, cannot speak of the colonized without resorting to the bestiary, here transforms the defining human characteristic—the capacity for language—into a sign of animality. The colonialist habit of linguistic nondialogism (Diouana knows their language, but her employers, even though they have lived in Africa for years, have made no effort to learn hers) distinguishes colonial bilingualism from ordinary linguistic dualism. For the colonizer, the language and the culture of the colonized are degraded and unworthy of interest, while for the colonized, mastery of the colonizer's tongue is both a means for survival and a daily humiliation. Possession of two languages is not here a matter of having two tools but rather entails participation in two conflicting psychic and cultural realms.

In *Xala* (1975), Sembene again interarticulates questions of language, culture, and power in ways that are susceptible to a translinguistic analysis. The protagonist, El Hadji, a polygamous Senegalese businessman who becomes afflicted with *xala*—a religiously sanctioned curse of impotence—embodies the neocolonized attitudes of the African elite so vehemently denounced by Fanon. Sembene structures the film around the opposition of Wolof and French as the focal point of conflict. The elite make nationalist speeches in Wolof while wearing African dress, but they speak French among themselves and reveal European suits beneath their African garb. Many of the characterizations revolve on the question of language. El Hadji's first wife, Adja, representing the precolonial African woman, speaks Wolof and wears traditional clothes. His second wife, Oumi, representing the colonized mimic of European fashions, affects French and wears wigs, sunglasses, and low-cut dresses. El Hadji's daughter, Rama, finally, representing the progressive synthesis of Africa and Europe, knows French but insists on speaking Wolof to her Francophile father. Conflicts involving language, then, are made to carry with them a strong charge of social and cultural tension.

For the colonizer, to be human is to speak his language. In countless films, linguistic discrimination and colonialist "tact" go hand in hand with condescending characterization and distorted social portraiture. The Native Americans of Hollywood westerns, denuded of their own idiom, mouth pidgin English, a mark of their inability to master the "civilized" language. One may judge the depth and generosity of a society or a culture, according to Bakhtin, by the respect it accords to the "alien word." In many First World films set in the Third World, the "word of the other" is elided, distorted, or caricatured. In films set in North Africa, for example, Arabic exists as an indecipherable murmur, while the "real" language of communication is the French of Jean Gabin in *Pepe le Moko* or the English of Bogart and Bergman in *Casablanca*. Even in David Lean's *Lawrence of Arabia* (1962), a film that is pretentiously, even ostentatiously, sympathetic to the Arabs, we hear almost no Arabic, but English is spoken in a motley of accents, almost all of which (Omar Sharif's being the exception) have little to do with Arabic.

In the realm of Latin American linguistic sensitivities, a similarly cavalier attitude led to the misattribution of major languages. Mervyn Leroy's *Latin Lovers* (1953), for example, mistakenly suggests that the national language of Brazil is Spanish. Although Carmen Miranda was called the "Brazilian bombshell," the names given her character (such as Rosita Cochellas in *A Date with Judy*, 1948), were more Hispanic than Brazilian. Although she reportedly spoke excellent English, the actress was prodded to speak in her distinctively caricatural manner (the linguistic correlative to her tutti-frutti hat), thus reflecting one of the many ways in which Latins were ridiculed by Hollywood cinema. From within the neocolonized countries, meanwhile, Hollywood became the beacon toward which the Third World looked, the model of "true" cinema. The linguistic corollary of this domination was the assumption that some languages were inherently more "cinematic" than others. The English "I love you," some Brazilian critics argued without irony in the twenties, was intrinsically more beautiful than the Portuguese "eu te amo." In this case, the focus on the phrase "I love you" is highly overdetermined, for not only do these words reflect the lure of a romantic model of cinema projecting glamour and popular stars but they also express an intuitive sense of the erotics of linguistic neocolonialism. In short, the colonizing language exercises a kind of phallic power and attraction.

Against this same backdrop we must understand the linguistic duality of Carlos Diegues's *Bye Bye Brazil* (1980), a film that looks at English, as it were, "through" Portuguese. Precisely because of the widespread dissemination of English, the film was titled in English even in Brazil. The theme song by Chico Buarque features English expressions like "bye bye" and "night and day" and "OK" as an index of the Americanization (and in this case the multinationalization) of a world where Amazonian tribal chiefs wear designer jeans and backwoods rock groups sound like the Bee Gees. Even the name of the traveling entertainment troupe—

"Caravana Rolidei"—a phonetic transcription of the Brazilian pronunciation of the English "holiday"—reflects this linguistic colonization. A typical colonial ambivalence operates: on the one hand, sincere affection for an alien tongue; on the other, the penchant for resentful parody and creative distortion, the refusal to "get it straight."

Even monolingual societies are characterized by heteroglossia; they enclose multiple languages and "dialects" that both reveal and produce social position, each existing in a distinct relation to the hegemonic language. In many British New Wave films from the sixties, upper-class English is brandished like a coat of arms, an instrument of snobbery and exclusion, while working-class speech is carried bitterly, like a stigmata. The protagonist of Clive Donner's *Nothing But the Best* (1964), a rather cynical latter-day reincarnation of Eliza Doolittle, gradually sheds his working-class speech in favor of Oxbridge English as a requisite for scaling the social heights. Just as "the poetic work," for Bakhtin, "is a powerful condenser of unspoken social evaluations,"[32] so the cinematic "word" can be a sensitive barometer of social pressure and dynamics. It can reveal, for example, the stratifications characteristic of any national language, the ways in which variations in accent or syntax reflect different positions in the social hierarchy. It can show individuals speaking in attitudes of authority or powerlessness, as words become instruments of intimidation or abuse, condescension or contempt.

Elsewhere, issues of race intersect with questions of language, power, and social stratification. In Perry Henzel's *The Harder They Come* (1973), the singer-protagonist's lower-class status is marked by his speaking Jamaican "dialect," while the higher-class figures more closely approximate "standard" English, thus positing a homology between class and linguistic hegemony. Since often a "dialect" is nothing more than a "language without an army," or at least without economic or political power, it is often stigmatized as substandard. Black English in the United States was often called "bad" English because linguists failed to take into account the specific African historical roots and imminent logical structure of black speech. Blacks performed what Bakhtin calls "reaccentuation," developing a coded language of resistance. One of the innovations of Melvin Van Peebles's *Sweet Sweetback's Baadasssss Song* (1971), a film whose very title resonates with black intonations, was to abandon Sidney Poitier just-like-white-people middle-class diction in order to get down and talk black.

Two other filmmakers who emphasize the relation between language and oppression are the Brazilian Glauber Rocha and the Chilean Raul Ruiz. (Their sensitivity to the subject was certainly heightened by their condition as Latin Americans in exile, a privileged vantage point for appreciating the mutual illumination of languages and cultures.) The title of Rocha's *Der Leone Have Sept Cabecas* subverts the linguistic positioning of the spectator by mingling five of the languages of Africa's colonizers. Rocha's Brechtian fable animates emblematic figures representing the diverse colonizers, further suggesting an identity of roles among them by having an Italian-accented speaker play the role of the American, a Frenchman play the German, and so forth. Another polyglot fable, Raul Ruiz's *Het Dak Van de Walvis* (The Top of the Whale, 1981), also focuses on the linguistic aspect of oppression. The point of departure for the film was Ruiz's discovery that certain tribes in Chile, due to their traumatic memory of genocide, spoke their own language only among themselves and never in front of a European. The resulting tale concerns a French anthropologist's visit to the last surviving members of an Indian tribe whose language has defied all attempts at interpretation. This exile's film goes in and out of French, English, German, Spanish, Dutch, and the invented lingo of the Patagonian Indians. One passage, it is interesting to note, stages the Bakhtinian idea that "multiplicity of meaning takes shape in actual use." Bakhtin cites Nikolai Y. Marr's theory of a prehistoric language in which one signifier is used to make reference to all the objects viewed as important by a given society. Whether or not Ruiz was aware of the Marr allusion to a pansemiotic sign, he illustrates it by having his anthropologist discover that the mysterious Indian language in fact consists of one phrase; no matter what the anthropologist shows the Indians, they respond "yamas gutan." When the anthropologist later discovers that the Indians change names each month and invent a new language every day, he returns to Europe in despair. In his study of linguistics and anthropology, quoted by Bakhtin, Marr argues that "the greatest obstacle [to the study of aboriginal speech] is caused not by the difficulty of the research itself, nor the lack of solid data, but by our scientific thinking, which is locked into the traditional outlook of philology or the history of culture and has not been nurtured by ethnological and linguistic perception of living speech in its limitlessly free, creative ebb and flow."[33] Ruiz would seem to agree, since he turns a tale about language into a sardonic demystification of the humorlessness of academics and the colonialist hubris of Western anthropology.

The intonation of the same word, Bakhtin argues, differs profoundly between inimical social groups. "You taught me language," Caliban tells Prospero in *The Tempest*, "and my profit on it is, I know how to curse. The red plague rid you for learning me your language." In the social life of the utterance as a concrete social act, Bakhtin constantly reminds us, each word is subject to rival pronunciations, intonations, and allusions. While the discourse of Power strives to officialize a single language, one dialect, into the Language, in fact language is a tension-filled and contradiction-ridden entity, a locus of heteroglossia that is ever open to historical process. Languages can serve not only to oppress and alienate but also to liberate. The "system" of language so dear to the Saussureans, I have tried to suggest, is subject to centripetal and centrifugal forces; it is always susceptible to subversion. By shifting attention away from the abstract system of langue to the concrete heterogeneity of parole, Bakhtin suggests the dialogical nature of language, its constantly changing relationship to power, and thus points to the possibility of reappropriating its dynamism in the world.

Film, Literature, and the Carnivalesque

Bakhtin's ideas concerning carnival are intimately linked to the linguistic ideas developed in *Marxism and the Philosophy of Language*. Indeed, I would argue that it is important to see carnival "within" a larger translinguistic context if one is to avoid its assimilation to other, ultimately less subversive categories such as "comedy" and "play." In the case of "translinguistics," as in carnival theory, we find a common sense of borders transgressed; in both instances, Bakhtin pits decentralizing energies (speech, carnival) against a hegemonic project of centralization (officialdom, the language system). In both cases what was thought to be marginal (popular festivities, vulgar speech) is brought to the center of discussion. Bakhtin's valorization of the anarchizing vitality of parole against the ossified rigidities of langue, in this sense, is isomorphic with his predilection for the subversive force of carnival as opposed to the suffocating decorum of official life and style.

Bakhtin first sketched out his visionary ideas concerning "carnivalization" in *Problems of Dostoevsky's Poetics,* but it was in *Rabelais and His World* (originally entitled "François Rabelais and Popular Culture in the Middle Ages and the Renaissance") that he gave the notion its fullest and richest formulation. The point of departure for the latter book is Bakhtin's conviction that of all European writers, Rabelais was "the least understood and appreciated," precisely because scholars failed to discern his profound links with popular culture, especially popular festivities such as carnival, and failed to appreciate the literary modes associated with carnival—that is, parody and grotesque realism.

Carnival, for Bakhtin, refers to the pre-Lenten revelry whose origins can be traced back to the Dionysian festivities of the Greeks and the Saturnalia of the Romans, but which enjoyed its apogee of both observance and symbolic meaning in the High Middle Ages. In that period, Bakhtin points out, carnival played a central symbolic role in the life of the community. Much more than the mere cessation of productive labor, carnival represented an alternative cosmovision characterized by the ludic undermining of all norms. The carnivalesque principle abolishes hierarchies, levels social classes, and creates another life free from conventional rules and restrictions. In carnival, all that is marginalized and excluded— the mad, the scandalous, the aleatory—takes over the center in a liberating explosion of otherness. The principle of material body— hunger, thirst, defecation, copulation—becomes a positively corrosive force, and festive laughter enjoys a symbolic victory over death, over all that is held sacred, over all that oppresses and restricts.

Bakhtin sees Rabelais as a kind of literary rebel whose vitality derives from his drawing on the taproot of the popular culture of his time. Rabelais transposes into literature the spirit of carnival, which is nothing more than "life itself . . . shaped according to a certain pattern of play." Rabelais' images have an undestroyable nonofficial nature; "no dogma, no authoritarianism, no narrow-minded seriousness can coexist with [them]." Bakhtin enumerates the fundamental forms of carnival culture: ritual spectacles, pageants, festivals; comic and parodic verbal compositions; and the diverse genres of "marketplace speech" (curses, oaths, profanations). Bakhtin inventories the various popular manifestations that went against the grain of the official medieval ecclesiastical and feudal culture: the *festa stultorum* (feast of fools), presided over by "lords of misrule"; the *Coena Cypriani* (Cyprian Suppers), in which the Scriptures were travestied); the *parodia sacra* (in which specific Catholic liturgies were parodied); and the *risus paschalis* (Easter laughter). In all these festive rituals, the Church, one of the most powerful institutions of the period, was mocked and symbolically relativized.

Within carnival, all hierarchical distinctions, all barriers, all norms and prohibitions, are temporarily suspended, while a qualitatively different kind of communication, based on "free and familiar contact," is established. Carnival, for Bakhtin, generates a special kind of universal laughter, a cosmic gaiety that is directed at everyone, including the carnival's participants. For the carnivalesque spirit, laughter has deep philosophical meaning; it constitutes a special perspective on experience, one that is no less profound than seriousness or tears. In Rabelais, laughter becomes the form of a free and critical consciousness that mocks dogmatism and fanaticism. Rabelais' philosophy, for Bakhtin, is not to be found where he seems most serious, but rather where he is laughing most wholeheartedly.

Rabelaisian imagery is also intimately linked to the topos of the banquet, of the feast as a temporary transfer to a utopian world of pleasure and abundance. Banquet imagery plays a primordial role in Rabelais, where virtually every page alludes to food and drink. Pantagruel's first heroic feats, accomplished still in the cradle, have to do with food. *Gargantua* begins with a cattle-slaughtering feast, while the Fourth Book features a carnivalesque war of the sausages, forever a favored carnival image. A chapter is devoted to "Why Monks Love Kitchens," and Panurge's scatological tirade concludes with the exhortation "Let us drink!" The origins of the overwhelming joyfulness of the feast, for Bakhtin, can be traced to the joy of primitive peoples at the conclusion of the hunt or harvest—that is, in moments of celebration of fecundity and abundance, of victory over scarcity and fear, of ritual regeneration within cyclical time. Only later, in the classical symposia, did the image of feasting lose its agricultural overtones and become sublimated into the idea of festive dialogue accompanied by food and drink, where "banqueting liberates speech."

Bakhtin's formulations about "carnival" almost inevitably bring to mind similar formulations by Nietzsche concerning the "Dionysian." As a well-educated multilingual polymath, Bakhtin was familiar with philosophical writing, and indeed makes scattered references to Nietzsche in his writings. As James M. Curtius points out in "Mikhail Bakhtin, Nietzsche, and Russian Pre-Revolutionary Thought," Bakhtin studied with the Polish-born classicist Tadeusz Zelinsky at St. Petersburg University during World War I. Unlike most Russian classicists, Zelinsky hailed *The Birth of Tragedy* as a great work and, Curtius claims, "taught Bakhtin to think in Nietzschean terms."[1] In their biography, Katerina Clark and Michael Holquist also suggest that Bakhtin might have been influenced by Zelinsky's Nietzsche-derived Hellenism.[2] It is of interest, therefore, to clarify the similarities as well as the differences between the Nietzschean and the Bakhtinian conceptions, as well as to speak of other affinities. Both Nietzsche and Bakhtin recognized that carnival was a real cultural practice and not merely a textual entity. In *The Joyful Wisdom,* Nietzsche compares the work of art to that higher art, "the art of festivals":

Formerly, all works of art adorned the great festival mood of humanity, to commemorate high and happy moments. Now one uses works of art to lure aside from the great via dolorosa of humanity those who are wretched, exhausted and sick and to offer them a brief lustful moment—a little intoxication and madness.[3]

In the opening pages of *The Birth of Tragedy,* Nietzsche's account of the nature of the Dionysian recalls, on some levels, Bakhtin's depiction of carnival:

Either under the influence of the narcotic draught, of which the songs of all primitive men and peoples speak, or with the potent coming of spring that penetrates all nature with joy, these Dionysian emotions awake, and as they grow in intensity everything subjective vanishes into complete self-forgetfulness. In the German Middle Ages, too, singing and dancing crowds, ever increasing in number, whirled themselves from place to place under this same Dionysian impulse. In these dancers of St. John and St. Vitus, we rediscover the Bacchic choruses of the Greeks. . . . There are some who, from obtuseness or lack of experience, turn away from such phenomena as "folk diseases," with contempt or pity born of the consciousness of their own "healthy-mindedness." But of course such poor wretches have no idea how corpselike and ghostly their so-called "healthy-mindedness" looks when the glowing life of the Dionysian revelers roars past them.[4]

Dionysian festivity, for Nietzsche, affirms not only the "union between man and man" but also the union of man with a "nature which has become alienated, hostile, or subjugated." Dionysian rites also level social classes and annihilate conventional decorum: "Now the slave is a free man; now all the rigid, hostile barriers that necessity, caprice or 'impudent convention' have fixed between man and man are broken." Dionysianism entails the collapse of the *principium individuationis:* "Now, with the gospel of universal harmony, each one feels himself not only united, reconciled, and fused with his neighbor, but as one with him, as if the veil of maya had been torn aside and were now merely fluttering in tatters before the mysterious primordial unity." Nietzsche also stresses, in terms that anticipate the polyrhythmic frenzy of the Africanized carnivals of Latin America and the Caribbean, the primordial role of music, of the "wave beat of rhythm," inciting the participants to "the greatest exaltation of [their] symbolic faculties," calling the "entire symbolism of the body" into play, and triggering "the whole pantomime of dancing, forcing every member into rhythmic movement." The rhythm, Nietzsche writes in *The Joyful Wisdom,* "produces an unconquerable desire to yield, to join in; not only the step of the foot, but also the soul itself follows the measure."[5]

Bakhtin's carnival and Nietzsche's Dionysian fête have in common their appeal to the primordial concept of a collective rite whose folk origins antedate Christianity, a rite in which mask-wearing revelers become "possessed" and transform themselves (whether through costume, attitude, or musical frenzy) into blissful alterity. Both Bakhtin and Nietzsche contrast a stifling official culture with a vital unofficial one. Nietzsche's recuperation of the Dionysian parallels Bakhtin's recuperation of the forbidden, the repressed, the grotesque, the noncanonical. Both celebrate the body not as a self-contained system delineated by the ego but rather as the site of dispersion and multiplicity; both glorify the excessive body that outstrips its own limits and transgresses the norms of decency. Similarly, the implicit cognitive thrust of "gay relativity" and carnival as a popular mode of knowledge evokes Nietzsche's "fröhliche wissenschaft" as a joyful descent into contradiction. Both thinkers share a belief in *homo ridens,* in the profundity and cognitive value of laughter. Zarathustra pronounces laughter "holy," as the transcendence of guilty self-consciousness and morbid introspection, while Bakhtin celebrates the cheerful ambivalence of carnival hilarity. Nietzsche's polemic against monism, finally, recalls Bakhtin's arguments against monologism, just as the Bakhtinian trope of the "nonfinalizability" of human character and meaning recalls Nietzsche's Dionysus as the embodiment of the eternally creative principle, forever exulting in the transformation of appearances.

Although both Nietzsche and Bakhtin see carnival-style festivities as a respite from socially engendered hypocrisy and fear of the body, Nietzsche tends to blame the Christian religion for this phobia, while Bakhtin is more likely to blame feudal ideology and class hierarchy. And here we touch on a signal difference of emphasis between the two thinkers. What Nietzsche values in the Dionysian experience is the transcendence of the individuating ego, led to feel a euphoric loss of self as it is subsumed into a larger philosophical whole, whereas Bakhtin is more interested in the symbolic overturning of social hierarchies within a kind of orgiastic egalitarianism. Bakhtin's predilection for the "low"—the lower classes, the "lower bodily stratum"—clashes with Nietzsche's affection for the "higher souls" and "finer sensibilities." (This concern has a generic correlative; Nietzsche associates Dionysianism with "high tragic" myth, while Bakhtin associates carnival with the "low," "vulgar" comic genres, with wordplay, parody, and billingsgate.) Nor does Bakhtin share Nietzsche's aversion to what Nietzsche sometimes called "the masses" or "the herd" and what Bakhtin, in a more populist vein, called "the people." Bakhtin does not share, in short, Nietzsche's thoroughgoing elitism. While Nietzsche praised a glorious state of solitude in which the philosophical soul renewed contact with the spirit of Nature, Bakhtin was more interested in the sentiment of community and *gemeinschaft* fostered by the promiscuous interminglings of carnival.

Bakhtin's familiarity with carnivals came not through literature alone, for Soviet carnivals were organized after the revolution, and Bakhtin probably witnessed them. But Bakhtin presumably came into contact with only the relatively "weak" forms of carnival, those coming at the end of the long downward trajectory charted in *Rabelais and His World*. Today, while it is true that European carnivals have generally degenerated into the ossified repetition of perennial rituals, one would be ill informed and ethnocentric to speak of the "end of carnival." Carnival in Latin America and the Caribbean, for example, remains, as we shall see in Chapter 4, a living and vibrant tradition, for there a profoundly mestizo culture—Amerindian, European, Afro-American—has given birth to an immensely creative cultural phenomenon. The kind of ecstatic Dionysian festival for which Nietzsche was so nostalgic—in which "singing and dancing crowds, ever increasing in number, whirled themselves from place to place under [a] Dionysian impulse"—exists in full force in certain parts of the Caribbean and in Brazilian cities like Salvador or Recife.

It would be wrong, furthermore, to think of such carnivals as vestigial reminiscences of an "archaic" culture; in fact, they are dynamically evolving phenomena that incorporate even the contemporary mass media. Indeed, more and more North American and European cities are developing minicarnivals that are linked to the presence of Latin American, Caribbean, and African immigrant communities. Brooklyn's annual Caribbean carnival attracts millions of participants, while the annual Greenwich Village parade for Halloween, that somewhat morbid pagan-Protestant musicless carnival, now combines a profusion of multithemed costumes with the ecstatic polyrhythms of samba percussionists. All these phenomena indicate, I would argue, a kind of latter-day "carnivalization" of North American culture.

Some anatomists of the carnivalesque, unfortunately, reduce carnival to a purely textual entity, forgetting that real-life carnival retains a certain dynamism. In his contribution to the book *Carnival!* Umberto Eco, for example, equates carnival with the "comic," failing to discern either carnival's present-day vitality or its progressive potential.[6] For Eco, carnival, like comedy, is an authorized transgression deeply dependent on a law that it only apparently violates: "the law must be so pervasively and profoundly interjected as to be overwhelmingly present at the moment of its violation." Since carnival is parasitic on the rules it breaks, it must necessarily, for Eco, be defined as brief; an entire year of ritual obedience is necessary to make the ephemeral transgression enjoyable. (Or as Shakespeare put it,

> If all the year were playing holidays
> To sport would be as tedious as to work.

It is wrong, Eco argues, to see carnival as subversive; in fact, the powerful have always used *circenses* to muffle popular rebellion, just as the contemporary mass media, instruments of social control, operate a "continuous carnivalization of life."

Eco's view of carnival is ultimately elitist, Eurocentric, and undialectical. His complacent generalization that "popular cultures are always determined by cultivated cultures" is not only elitist but also flies in the face of everything we know about the never-ending circulation between popular and elite forms. Brazilian carnival, to take just one example, constitutes an intricate crisscross between the erudite and the popular as well as between the European and the African; its festival exuberantly mingles the wigs of the *ancien régime* with *candomblé* beads, Hispanic guitar with African *cuica,* Portuguese *entrudo,* and African *congada.* Eco's analysis is Eurocentric in its assumption that contemporary carnivals exist only in the degraded form of mass-media "carnivalizations." All of Eco's references, furthermore, are European—Aristotelian comedy, Roman circuses, contemporary First World mass media. Eco's refusal to recognize carnival as an ongoing, corporeal, collective practice leads him to reduce it to the generic textual entity of "the comic," but even within his own terms, Eco makes indefensible generalizations, arguing, for example, that comedy is always conservative and "always racist": "only the others, the Barbarians, are supposed to pay." Eco's analysis would allow little place for Brecht's fundamentally comic, antitragic leftist theatre or for Bakhtin's emphasis on the progressive, demystificatory role of parody. Carnival, moreover, as the privileged space of marginality, might be seen as fundamentally *anti*racist rather than racist.

Whereas Eco argues that carnivals are necessarily brief, Bakhtin describes a late-medieval world in which three months of the year are given over to carnival-style activities, a period of time in some ways reproduced by the December-to-March carnival cycle that animates such cities as Salvador, Bahia, in Brazil. Eco's claim that the powerful have always either used or tolerated carnivals also is simplistic. While it is true that official power has at times used carnival to channel energies that might otherwise have fueled popular revolt, it has just as often been the case that carnival itself has been the object of official repression. C. L. Barber documents this repressive process as it took place in Elizabethan England; Peter Stallybrass and Allon White delineate it as it affected England in later periods; and countless Brazilian historians have spoken of the official repression of carnival in Brazil, where the hostility toward carnival has often been linked to antiblack racism and an animus against Afro-Brazilian religious expression. Carnival cannot be equated, furthermore, with the contemporary mass media. We must distinguish, as I will argue later, between authentic, participatory carnivals, on the one hand, and ersatz or degraded carnivals, on the other. The appeal of the mass media derives partially from their capacity for relaying, in a degraded manner, the distant cultural memory (or the vague future hope) of carnival. The mass media thus offer insipid, enervated, co-optable forms of carnival; they capitalize on the frustrated desire for a truly egalitarian society by serving up distorted versions of its utopian promise. As if to compensate for a general loss of communitarian pleasure, the mass media constantly offer the simulacra of carnival-style festivity. But that is hardly the same thing as offering carnival itself, or even of using carnivalesque strategies, for carnival is participatory, joyfully critical, and potentially subversive.

Since carnival, at least since the Dionysian festivals, has been intimately linked to music and dance, the concept is also relevant to the musical comedy. The musical comedy can be seen as a two-dimensional carnival in which the oppressive structures of everyday life are not so much overturned (as in Bakhtin's conception) as they are stylized, choreographed, and mythically transcended.

Richard Dyer's analysis, in "Entertainment and Utopia," of the Hollywood musical as performing an artistic "change of signs" whereby the negatives of social existence are turned into the positives of artistic transmutation strikingly parallels Bakhtin's account of carnival.[7] For Dyer, the musical offers a utopian world characterized by "energy" (for Bakhtin, carnival's gestural freedom and effervescence of dance and movement), "abundance" (in carnival, omnipresent feasting, the fat of Mardi gras), "intensity" (in carnival, the heightened theatricality of an alternative, "second" life), "transparency" (carnival's "free and familiar contact"), and "community" (carnival as loss of self, collective *jouissance*).

For Bakhtin, carnival is not only a living social practice but also a perennial generating fund of popular forms and festive rituals. Bakhtin's "carnival" borders on other related categories, ranging from Mircea Eliade's discussion of archaic transhistorical festivities, to Elias Canetti's analysis of the "feast crowd," to Henri Lefebvre's politicized recuperation of "la fête," to Michel Maffesoli's "orgiasme," to Victor Turner's and Mary Douglas's anthropological anatomies of "liminal rituals" and "communitas."[8] It is useful to break down Bakhtin's notion of carnival, moreover, into a constellation of interrelated tropes and ideas, not all of which are attractive to the same constituencies. Carnival, in this sense, evokes a number of distinct concepts:

1. the valorization of Eros and the life force, an actualization of perennial nature myths (an idea attractive to vitalist currents of left and right);
2. a somewhat more morbid version of (1) emphasizing ritual sacrifice, the concatenation of life and death, Eros and Thanatos, as crystallized by orgiastic sacrifice, a trope picked up by writers such as Bataille and filmmakers like Bunuel (and relentlessly commercialized by the mass media);
3. the notion of bisexuality and the practice of transvestitism as a release from the burden of socially imposed sex roles;
4. a corporeal semiotic celebrating the grotesque, excessive body and the "orifices" and "protuberances," of the "lower bodily stratum" (attractive to those struggling against a puritanical view of the body);
5. the foregrounding of social overturning and the counterhegemonic subversion of established power via the "world upside down" (a strategy especially attractive to the revolutionary left and to oppositional culture generally);

6. the cognate trope of social and political life as a perpetual "crowning and uncrowning," implying the permanence of change as the source of popular hope (emphasized as well by the theory and practice of Brechtian theatre);

7. the topos of carnival as "gay relativity" and Janus-face ambivalence and ambiguity (an idea attractive to relativists of all stripes);

8. the idea of carnival as the locus of oceanic feelings of union with the community (ideas appealing ambiguously to left and right alike);

9. the quasi-religious idea of carnival as the "space of the sacred" and "time in parentheses" of a mystical union with the cosmos;

10. a perspective on language which valorizes the obscene, the nonsensical, and "marketplace speech" as expressive of the linguistic creativity of the common people;

11. a rejection of social decorum entailing a release from oppressive etiquette, politeness, and good manners;

12. the concept of an anticlassical aesthetic emphasizing not harmonious beauty and formal unity but rather asymmetry, heterogeneity, the oxymoron, and the mésalliance; and

13. the view of carnival as participatory spectacle, a "pageant without footlights" which erases the boundaries between spectator and performer (a procedure picked up by the European avant-garde in the twenties and by alternative theatre in the sixties—for example, by the Living Theatre).

In this connection, we might ask, are we not being sentimental and nostalgic when we speak about carnival today? Is a medieval-style carnival even possible when what was once a seasonal ritual taking three months of the year is reduced to a few dispersed weekends and brief holidays? What can carnival mean in an age of the loss of community and "the waning of affect?" What about the political ambiguities of carnival? Carnival is, admittedly, the Bakhtinian category most susceptible to co-optation, at times becoming the pretext for a vacuous ludism that discerns redeeming elements even in the most degraded cultural productions and activities. It would be wrong, for example, to see the carousing of the government elite at California's "Bohemian Grove" as a Bakhtinian celebration of popular culture, since such macho rituals form an integral part of exactly that power structure which a more subversive carnival would symbolically overturn. The boundless libertarianism of carnival, furthermore, takes place "within" the larger principle of dialogism, in resonance with the voices of others. Carnival, in our sense, is more than a party or a festival; it is the oppositional culture of the oppressed, a countermodel of cultural production and desire. It offers a view of the official world as seen from below—not the mere disruption of etiquette but as a symbolic, anticipatory overthrow of oppressive social structures. On the positive side, it is ecstatic collectivity, the joyful affirmation of change, a dress rehearsal for utopia. On the negative, critical side, it is a demystificatory instrument for everything in the social formation which renders collectivity impossible: class hierarchy, sexual repression, patriarchy, dogmatism, and paranoia.

Real-life carnivals are, of course, politically ambiguous affairs that can be egalitarian and emancipatory or oppressive and hierarchical. (Carnival in this sense can be seen, in Jamesonian terms, as a master code in which competing class discourses struggle for ascendancy.) Carnivals seldom turn into revolutions, even though the situationist "Theses on the Commune" called the commune the "greatest carnival of the nineteenth century," and even though journalists invariably describe moments of popular rebellion as accompanied by a "carnival-like atmosphere." Carnivals can constitute a symbolic rebellion *by* the weak or a festive scapegoating *of* the weak, or both at the same time. We must ask who is carnivalizing whom, for what reasons, by which means, and in what circumstances. Historically, carnivals can be seen as misogynistic and masculinist, or as protofeminist, occasions for women in traditional societies to seize moments of noninstrumental eroticism. "Sex without the price of lifelong subordination to one man," three feminists write in *Remaking Love*, "was something glimpsed only at rare events—village holidays, religious festivals, carnivals."[9] At the same time, it would be a mistake, as Stallybrass and White point out, to see carnival, in an essentialist manner, as *intrinsically* radical or, for that matter, intrinsically conservative.[10] Civic festivals have always been the point of convergence of conservative rituals that regenerate the status quo and subversive currents that threaten ossified hierarchies. Actual carnivals form shifting configurations of symbolic practices whose political valence changes with each context and situation. As Emmanuel Le Roy Ladurie observes in *Le Carnaval de Romans*:

Carnival is not only a dualistic, prankish, and *purely momentary* inversion of society, destined in the last analysis to justify in an "objectively" conservative fashion the world as it is. It is rather more an instrument of satiric, lyric, epic knowledge for groups in their complexity; therefore, [it is] an instrument of action, with eventual modifying force, in the direction of social change and possible progress. . . . The feast and social change do not always go in the same direction.[11]

All carnivals must be seen as complex crisscrossings of ideological manipulation and utopian desire. The Bakhtinian view, in this sense, perhaps tends to overestimate the political efficacy of real-life carnivals, as if carnival operated in abstraction from the "institutional sites in which the complex relations of discourse and power are actually negotiated."[12] As "situated utterances," carnivals are inserted into specific historical moments and are inevitably inflected by the hierarchical arrangements of everyday social life.

But the political limitations of real-life carnivals are not necessarily those of carnivalesque strategies in art. Art becomes carnivalized in those texts which productively deploy the traces, whether absorbed directly, indirectly, or through intermediate links, of carnivalistic folk culture. The Bakhtinian conception of the "carnivalesque" as a literary, textual echo of the social practice of carnival has already served as an exploratory device for treating the work of a wide diversity of literary figures: Chaucer, Shakespeare, Cervantes, Molière, Diderot, Joyce, Mann, Brecht, Pynchon, Carpentier, Cabrera Infante, and Raymond Queneau, among others. Six years before the translation of *Rabelais and His World* into English, C. L. Barber performed a similar kind of analysis in his book *Shakespeare's Festive Comedy: A Study of Dramatic Form and Its Relation to Social Custom*. Deploying a slightly modified critical vocabulary—"Aristaphonic" and "Saturnalian" rather than "Menippean" and "carnivalesque"—Barber emphasized the crucial importance of the traditions of popular theatre and holidays for an understanding of Shakespeare's comedies, delineating the "Saturnalian pattern" of the comedies as a kind of festive epistemology moving from Saturnalian release to humorous understanding.[13]

Barber traces this Saturnalian pattern to many sources: the theatrical institution of clowning, the literary cult of fools and folly, and the real-life community observances of feast days, morris dances, wassailings, mummings, masques, and pageants. Shakespeare's casual references to popular festivities—"Come, woo me, woo me! for now I am in a holiday humour and like enough to consent"—are premised on thorough audience familiarity with such cultural phenomena. They illuminate not only those comedies in which Shakespeare drew directly on holiday motifs—*A Midsummer Night's Dream* and *Twelfth Night*—but also those plays in which there is little direct reference to holiday—for instance, *As You Like It* and *Henry IV*. Barber analyzes the textual reminiscences of these practices, in a manner distinctly reminiscent of Bakhtin, as evoking liberation from social decorum through raucous eroticism and "gay relativity."[14] The holiday motif brought with it the artistic and narrative strategies associated with carnival: parody and burlesque in the form of the "low take-off on what the high people were doing." The *Pyramus and Thisby* play-within-the-play in *A Midsummer Night's Dream,* for example, burlesques the loftily tragic death scene in *Romeo and Juliet* in a crude doggerel style. Similarly, specific Shakespearean characters—Falstaff, for example—incorporate the carnival spirit. Falstaff, described as "god Bacchus, god fatback . . . god barrelbelly," constitutes an obese symbol of carnival's orality and cornucopian gluttony. (In *Chimes at Midnight,* Orson Welles lent his rotund, "excessive" body to this Saturnalian figure.) The witty apologist for folly and vice, Falstaff, an example of "life overflowing its bounds by sheer vitality," is associated imagistically with the gay eating and drinking of Shrove Tuesday and other carnival-style holidays.

Bakhtin's ideas concerning carnival are inseparable from his generic analysis of what he calls "the Menippea." In *Problems of Dostoevsky's Poetics,* Bakhtin traces Dostoevsky's "polyphonic" artistic strategies back to earlier seriocomic genres linked to "the carnivalesque perception of the world," genres such as the Socratic dialogue and, especially, the Menippean satire.[15] The latter took its name from the philosopher Menippus of Gadara (third century B.C.), who gave the genre a more definitive form. As examples of the genre, Bakhtin cites the *Satyricon* of Petronius, *The Metamorphoses* (The Golden Ass) of Apuleius, and *De Consolatione Philosophiae* of Boëthius. Menippean satire, for Bakhtin, is profoundly rooted in the Saturnalian tradition and prepares the way for literary "carnivalization." In a concise but evocative passage in his book on Dostoevsky, Bakhtin posits a number of "essential traits" of the Menippea:

1. the constant presence of the comic element;
2. an extraordinary freedom of plot and philosophical invention;
3. an emphasis on the adventures of an idea in its passage through the world;
4. the fusion of the fantastic, the symbolic, and slum naturalism;

5. the foregrounding of philosophical universalism and "ultimate questions";

6. a three-planed structure involving heaven, earth, and hell;

7. a fondness for the experimental and the fantastic;

8. an emphasis on moral-psychological experimentation, split personality, insanity, and abnormal psychic states showing the "unfinalizability of man" and his "noncoincidence with himself";

9. a fondness for scandal and violations of decorum;

10. a love of sharp contrasts and oxymoronic combinations;

11. elements of social utopia;

12. the wide use of inserted genres;

13. a polystylistic language and approach; and

14. overt and hidden polemics with various philosophical, religious, and ideological schools and mockery of "masters of thought."

After such figures as Rabelais and Shakespeare, carnival, at least in Europe, went underground as a social practice but remained as a literary echo in the works of Cervantes and Diderot, and in the "polyphonic" and "Menippean" novels of Dostoevsky. In the modernist period, carnival ceases to be a collective cleansing ritual open to all the people and becomes the instrument of a marginalized caste. The elimination of carnival as a real social practice led to the development of salon carnivals, compensatory Bohemias offering what Allon White calls "liminoid positions" on the margins of polite society. Thus movements such as expressionism and surrealism took over in displaced form much of the grotesque bodily symbolism and playful dislocations—exiled fragments of the "carnivalesque Diaspora" (White)—which had once formed part of European carnival. Carnival, in this modified and somewhat hostile form, is present in the provocations of Dada, the dislocations of surrealism, in the travesty-revolts of Genet's *The Maids,* or *The Blacks,* and indeed in the avant-garde generally. In fact, it is in its formal audacity, not just in its violations of social decorum, that the avant-garde betrays its link to the perennial rituals of carnival. (And carnival itself, conversely, as a counterhegemonic and anti-institutional mode of cultural production, can be seen as proleptic of the avant-garde.) Rabelais remained misunderstood, according to Bakhtin, because of his "nonliterary nature—that is, because of the nonconformity of his images to the norms and canons predominant in the sixteenth century." Marginal and subversive art, with its adversary relationship to power and to official culture, thus reincarnates the spirit of carnival. The linguistic corollary of carnivalization entails the liberation of language from the norms of good sense and etiquette. The rules of grammar are suspended in what Rabelais called a *gramatica jocosa,* in which grammatical categories, cases and verb forms, are ludically undermined.

The "historical avant-gardes" of the late nineteenth and the early twentieth century saw themselves, in a sense, as existing in a parodic relation to all that was self-serious and tragic in the antecedent high-art tradition. Parody, present already in the work of Laforgue and Lautreamont, becomes radicalized in the work of Jarry, Tzara, and Vache, where we find resuscitated the techniques of the profanation and renovation of cultural objects familiar from Rabelais and the carnivalesque tradition. Bakhtin, for his part, while unenthusiastic about what he called the "vaudevillian antics" of the Russian futurists, was in no way antimodernist (unlike, for example, Lukacs) or even anti-avant-garde. But Bakhtin would probably see modernism as less a radical break with the past than a radicalization, in an altered context, of carnivalesque strategies—the violation of bodily taboos, parody, antigrammaticality—already present in Rabelais.

Before moving on to the cinematic manifestations of the carnivalesque and the Menippea, I would like briefly to explore a seminal literary example of what one might call the "modernist carnivalesque"—Alfred Jarry's *Ubu Roi.* In *Rabelais and His World,* Bakhtin speaks of Jarry in the context of the "complex and contradictory" developments of the carnivalesque in the "modernist" line, in contrast with the "realist grotesque" line of Bertolt Brecht and Pablo Neruda.[16] *Ubu Roi* mingles artistic strategies rooted in Menippean satire with a modernist hostility to the bourgeois audience. The carnivalesque strategies of the play begin with its parodic title—*Ubu Roi*—an uneuphonious and mocking echo of *Oedipus Rex.* The play itself devours the high literary tradition and regurgitates it for comic ends, hybridizing genres in a defiant cocktail of tragedy and grand guignol. The opening expletive—"Merdre!" (shittr!)—heralds the play's carnivalesque penchant for the scatological and the "lower bodily stratum." The constant feasting, and Ubu's irrepressible gluttony, reflect the defiant orality of carnival, an orality which borders, at times, on the cannibalistic. Père Ubu, especially, always seems on the brink of unleashing his anthropophagous tendencies. "I'm going to sharpen my teeth," he tells Mere Ubu, "on your shanks."

It is easy to find in *Ubu Roi* most of the essential characteristics of Menippean satire and carnivalesque parody. Here the deep regenerating currents of carnivalesque art work to dissolve the conventions of bourgeois realism. Rather than reconstitute the world in a recognizably bourgeois form, Jarry fabricates a disconcertingly syncretic world whose very decor is oxymoronic, representing both indoors and outdoors—and the tropical, temperate, and arctic zones—all at once. In the dislocated theatrescapes of the original production of *Ubu Roi,* snow fell near palm trees and doors opened onto the sky, and the public was disconcerted by heterogeneous carnival-style costumes that were as "unchronological and as lacking in local color as possible."[17] Mère Ubu begins dressed in a "concierge's outfit," the revenge-hero Bougrelas is dressed as a baby in "a little skirt and bonnet," and Bordure, despite his English accent, sports a Hungarian musician's costume. Throughout, the emphasis is on the heteroclite, the oxymoronic, the scandalous. Even the historical "scene" and the geographical locale of *Ubu*—which is set in Poland, "that is to say, Nowhere"—is oxymoronic. In program notes distributed to the first-night audience, Jarry elaborated: "Nowhere is everywhere, and first of all in the country where one happens to be. That is why Ubu speaks French." The initial setting, then, is simultaneously nowhere (with its etymological overtones of "utopia"), everywhere, and France. Then, in keeping with the spatial freedom and liberty of invention of the Menippea, the play takes us on a whirlwind tour of Europe, to Russia, the Ukraine, Lithuania, and Livonia. The final scene brings us, in the space of a brief, presumably continuous dialogue, from the Baltic, past Germany, past Hamlet's Elsinore, and into the North Sea.

Menippean satire displays a total freedom of philosophical and thematic invention unbounded by historical limits. The dramatic structure of *Ubu* constitutes a protracted *non sequitur*. Although the plot mechanisms are parodically derived from Elizabethan tragedy and the Shakespearean history plays, Jarry suspends the usual laws of motivation at work in those plays. Ubu, the reincarnated Macbeth in Jarry's play, is motivated primarily by the prospect of having an unlimited supply of sausage rather than by any ambition for wealth and power. (Sausages, Bakhtin points out, are a favored carnival motif; Rabelais, for example, portrays the struggle of Protestantism and Catholicism as a war be-

tween King Lent and the sausages inhabiting Savage Island.)
Whereas Shakespearean tragedy inexorably leads to transfigured
moments of anguished lucidity, Jarryesque theatre leads only to
absurd tautologies. Escaping from Poland with his vanquished fel-
lows, Ubu points to Germany and declares that Germany "cannot
compare with Poland. For if there were no Poland, there would be
no Poles."

Parody plays a primordial role in *Ubu*. The play's epigraph
facetiously suggests that the Shakespearean tragedies were in fact
inspired by the exploits of Ubu, and the play itself forms an anthology of parodic Shakespearean references: a central plot modeled on
Macbeth (with Mère Ubu playing the ambitious Lady Macbeth to
the sluggish Ubu), a political conspiracy modeled on *Julius Caesar,*
and a revenge hero ("How sad it is to find oneself alone at fourteen
with a terrible vengeance to pursue!") patterned on *Hamlet.* Apart
from plot borrowings and references, Jarry hyperbolizes the procedures of Elizabethan dramaturgy. Since no decor or props can
represent the "Polish army marching through the Ukraine," Jarry
uses a cardboard horse's head for "the equestrian scenes." As in
Julius Caesar, huge crowds are epitomized in two or three actors,
but Jarry calls attention to the disproportion between the minimal
signifier—a lone actor—and the signified—a huge crowd—by
having Ubu exclaim: "What a mass of people!" Jarry appreciated
what we would now call the carnivalesque side of Shakespeare's
theatre—its bawdy wordplay, its verbal exuberance, its boisterous
heteroglossia.

In the verbal carnival of *Ubu,* language celebrates its freedom
from the usual hierarchies and decorum. The play often works on
the principle of absurd accumulation, whether of past participles
("I'm wounded," moans Père Ubu, "I'm punctured, I'm perforated,
I'm administered, I'm buried") or substantives (Père Ubu threat-
ens Mère Ubu with "twisting of the nose, tearing out of the hair,
penetration of little bits of wood into the ears, extraction of the
brain . . . laceration of the posterior, partial or perhaps even total
suppression of the spinal marrow . . . and finally the grand re-
enacted decollation of John the Baptist, the whole taken from the
very Holy Scriptures"). This last inventory of comic cruelties recalls another feature of the carnivalesque according to Bakhtin—
its tendency to laugh at death and violence. Its blows are only "to
laugh," to be taken no more seriously than a clown's feigned fall or
a puppet's demise. *Ubu* proliferates in comic dismemberments, in
"beheading and [the] twisting of legs," in the "twisting of the nose

and teeth and [the] extraction of the tongue," but it is all, ultimately, *pour rire*.

As a character, Ubu is very much the Anarch figure, the Rei
Momo (like Rabelais' Pichrochole) who reveals in caricatural form
the actual mechanisms of social and political life. A polite summary of Ubu's political philosophy would be: kill the opposition and
steal from everyone. To those who object, Ubu answers, "Dans la
trappe!" (the Ubuesque equivalent of "Off with their heads!"). Jarry reveals that power comes out of the barrel of a gun—or in this
case from the "shittry saber" and "phynancial stick." The economic
motive, the concern with "phynance," is also omnipresent in *Ubu*:
"I'm going to get rich," Ubu promises, "and I won't give up one sou."
His exacerbated lust for property is reflected in an unnatural (for
the French language) stress on possessive adjectives: "I'm going to
make MY list of MY goods. Clerk, read MY list of MY goods." The logic
of power and property is comically simplified, stripped of all idealization and mystification, and rendered in carnivalesque form.

The Parisian opening of *Ubu* was roughly contemporaneous
with the Lumières' first film screenings in the Grand Café, and it is
not difficult to encounter spirits akin to Jarry in the cinema as well.
The films of Luis Bunuel, for example, clearly reflect the spirit of
carnival and the Menippea, as well as the influence of the "modernist" line founded by Jarry. An impassioned admirer of both the artistic work and the personal style of Jarry, Bunuel saw film as a
privileged instrument in his struggle against outmoded social and
artistic conventions. Just as Jarry denounced the "well-made
play," Bunuel attacked the "cinedramas" and the "sentimental in-
fection." Indeed, the view that reduces Bunuel to the quintessential Surrealist filmmaker is, finally, rather superficial. Bunuel's
roots go back, ultimately, to some of the same sources that fed Jarry's work, to Rabelais, Cervantes, and, more broadly, the Menippea. In fact, it is Bunuel, more than any other, who forges a direct
link between the formal and thematic transgressions of the avant-
garde and the medieval heritage of carnivalesque irreverence. As a
child, Bunuel practiced black masses, and as an adolescent, he and
Garcia Lorca would shave closely, powder their faces, and masquerade as nuns to flirt with male passengers on streetcars, a piece
of biographical evidence that merely confirms the omnipresent
anticlericalism of the films. Like medieval carnival, Bunuel's de-
sacralizations depend on Christianity as a source of imagery and
fount of inspiration. In this sense, Bunuel, who often expressed a
fondness for the Middle Ages, which he called, following Huys-

mans, that "exquisite period," and who grew up in what he himself called a "medieval atmosphere," resurrects the jocose impieties of that period.

Within the walls of the festive cloister that is Bunuel's *oeuvre,* then, the echoes of carnival laughter resound. Here blasphemy becomes an aesthetic strategy, a fond method for generating art. The religious travesties so frequent in Bunuel films form the contemporary counterpart of the monkish pranks and *parodia sacra* of the Middle Ages. The parodistic liturgies of *Simon of the Desert,* for example, anachronistically mingle the language and style of fifth-century anchorites with that of contemporary political demagogues, leading the pious monks to inadvertently chant "Down with Christ" and "Long live the heretics." In the same film, Bunuel has his holy protagonist pronounce a benediction over excrement, in a gesture at once scatological and eschatological. The "Last Supper" sequence of *Viridiana,* meanwhile, melds an iconoclastic assault on "high art"—Handel's *Messiah,* the da Vinci painting—with orgiastic sacrilege in the tradition of the medieval "Coena Cypriani," which like this sequence also parodied the Last Supper. Bunuel also deploys the soundtrack to comically undercut Viridiana's prayers, so that each line of the "pater noster" is interrupted by mooing cows, squeaking plows, and the like. Such sacrileges, in Bunuel, constitute a prolongation through film of what Bunuel in his autobiography calls the proud Spanish tradition of blasphemy, in which "extraordinary vulgarities—referring chiefly to the Virgin Mary, the Apostles, God, Christ and the Holy Spirit, not to mention the Pope—are strung end to end in a series of impressive scatological exclamations."[18] Bunuel's attacks on the church, in sum, derive less from "surrealist provocations" than from a proud European countertradition of comic desacralization.

Bunuel's autobiography, *My Last Sigh,* in this regard, elicits a double fascination: first, it offers glimpses of the carnivalesque person behind the persona we project as "Luis Bunuel"; and second, it provides a parallel instance of carnivalesque *écriture*—this time quite literal and graphological—suggesting homologies to the narrative strategies and cinematic devices of the films. The entire text can be seen as an example of carnival's "laughing at death," a hearty giggle in the face of mortality. Death is omnipresent in *My Last Sigh,* but it is always evoked with laughter, in an atmosphere of "gay relativity." The book's title, which might have been better rendered "My Last Breath" or "My Last Gasp," heralds the theme of this debauched pilgrimage toward the shrine of Thanatos. The immediate motivation for the writing of the book, we learn, is Bunuel's awareness of encroaching senility and impending death. The book begins with semicomic anecdotes about his mother's loss of memory and ends with a contemplated deathbed prank: a planned counterfeit deathbed conversion to Catholicism as a provocation for assembled atheist friends. (Bakhtin cites a legend about a similar jest, involving masquerade and a scriptural travesty, on the part of Rabelais himself on the threshold of death.)

The autobiography also confirms the extent to which Bunuel's artistic strategies are rooted in a love of festive play and the comic overturning of hierarchies. Bunuel alludes to "the watering rites of spring," allegedly his own invention, which consist simply of pouring a bucket of water over the head of the first person to come along—a ritual evoked in Fernando Rey's drenching of Carole Bouquet in *That Obscure Object of Desire*. Throughout, Bunuel shows a penchant for mocking the pretensions of high art, reducing the cult of painting, for example, to a mechanical set of ridiculous gestures: "I find it impossible to spend hours in galleries analyzing and gesticulating." His disrespect for the *objet d'art* extends even to his own films: "I imagine a huge pyre in my own little garden, where all my negatives and all the copies of my films go up in flames. It wouldn't make the slightest difference."

My Last Sigh, also exhibits Bunuel's fondness for childlike nonsense and comic enumerations. Many sentences bring together incongruous lists of heteroclite objects in a manner reminiscent of the incongruities of the films: the monstrance in the limousine (*L'Age d'Or*), the carcass and the priest (*Un Chien Andalou*), the bear in the mansion (*The Exterminating Angel*). Bunuel's films can thus be seen as visualizing and objectifying the carnivalesque-surrealist trope of the "absurd list," the stringing together of impossibilia. Think, for example, of the series of symbolic objects—a bishop, a plow, a burning pine tree, a giraffe, the feathers of a pillow—defenestrated by the angry protagonist in *L'Age d'Or*. In a chapter entitled "Pro and Con," similarly, Bunuel enumerates his likes and dislikes. He detests newspaper reporters, but has mixed emotions when it comes to spiders. He likes "punctuality" and also "little tools like pliers and scissors." He dislikes acronyms, but is, on the other hand, "very fond of rats and snakes." In this deliberate mismatching of categories, and in the disruption of the normal rhetoric of subordination and juxtaposition, one hears an echo of surrealist dislocations and the *gramatica jocosa* of Rabelais and Menippean satire, suggesting a kind of playful isomorphism between the literary and cinematic expression of a carnivalesque attitude.

Filmic texts dramatize and enact their relation to social power not only through theme and "image" but also through their critical relation to the structures of discursive authority as mediated by the formal parameters of the text. Bunuel's *L'Age d'Or* in this sense carnivalizes not only the Catholic Church but also etiquette in all its forms—social, amorous, religious, narrative, and cinematic. Here Bunuel regards bourgeois society with a kind of ethnographic distance, decomposing and anatomizing its established hierarchies and rituals. The film performs what anthropologists such as Barbara Babcock call "symbolic inversion," expressive behavior that inverts, contradicts, abrogates, or proposes alternatives to commonly held cultural, linguistic, artistic, religious, political, and social codes.[19] Modot's slap of Lya Lys's mother has the same relation to social decorum that *L'Age d'Or* itself has to religious and artistic decorum. Religious decorum is undermined by the systematic association of religion with death (e.g., through the bishops' skeletons in the second sequence), as well as by the ironic decontextualization of Catholic symbols, dignitaries, and artifacts—the prelate out the window, the divinity at the orgy. The empty discourse of the pompous politician celebrating the founding of imperial Rome is undercut by the sudden intrusion of the "lower bodily principle" in the form of two lovers making noisy love in the mud, a filmic realization of the carnival topos of "redeeming filth." The upper class is quite literally slapped in the face (Lya Lys's mother) or covered with flies (her father).

Cinematic decorum, meanwhile, is undercut in *L'Age d'Or* by a pervasive antigrammaticality that proposes the impossible temporality of the Menippean chronotope. Bunuel has his "Majorcans"—a gallery of humorless figures representing the military, ecclesiastical, and political establishment—lay the first stone for the foundation of "imperial Rome" in the "Year of our Lord, 1930," an oxymoronic ellipsis of over two thousand years. Narrative decorum, finally, is laid low by a perversely purposeless trajectory that leads us from one *non sequitur* to another, and finally to a promising love affair that turns into a frustrating *coitus interruptus*. The final sequence, for its part, forms an outrageously sacreligious *parodia sacra*. We see the survivors of a night of orgies in the Chateau de Selliny—"four well-known and utter scoundrels" knowing "no law but their own depravity." The first of the degenerate scoundrels to appear is dressed like a Hebrew of the first century and bears an unmistakable resemblance to the pictorial Jesus. The implied equation of Christ and Sade forms at once a temporal oxymoron, a surrealist antinomy, and an anticlerical provocation in the tradition of the *risus paschalis*.

We have already spoken of the carnivalesque disruption of language and of "speech genres" in Bunuel's *The Exterminating Angel* (1962), but we have yet to speak of the film's demonstrable links both to the carnivalesque spirit and to its latter-day heir, the theatrical avant-garde. *The Exterminating Angel* offers a more politicized version of the themes that obsessed the "theatre of the absurd": entrapment (one thinks of Sartre's protoabsurdist *Huis Clos*); paralysis (Hamm in his wheelchair and his parents in their dustbin in Beckett's *Endgame*); proliferating chaos (*Rhinoceros*); and the comic devaluation of language (*The Bald Soprano*). The film's central premise—the entrapment of a group of Mexican socialites—is as calculatedly implausible as those of many Beckett or Ionesco plays. The film also shares with absurdist theatre its affinity with burlesque film comedy. *The Exterminating Angel,* like Ionesco's *The Chairs,* is structured on the comic formula of an inexorable descent from normality into anarchy, all performed in Keatonesque deadpan. The bear that wanders into *The Exterminating Angel* descends not only from the bear of Elizabethan entertainments but also from the bear that frightens Père Ubu in Jarry's play and the bear that follows Chaplin along an icy precipice in *The Gold Rush*.

Bunuel radicalizes these burlesque and avant-garde topoi by linking them to the carnivalesque theme of social inversion and the "world upside down." The "Exterminating Angel" in this sense executes a kind of millennial mission of social justice, an apocalyptic laying low of the noble and the powerful. In fact, *The Exterminating Angel* should be paired with another of Bunuel's Mexican films, *Los Olvidados,* in the sense that the logic of the former film is to reduce its upper-class protagonists to the miserable condition of the slum-dwellers of the latter. One of the aristocrats alludes to this irony by complaining that they have been "forgotten" (*olvidados*). Social distinctions are leveled in a spirit of carnivalesque degradation. The subversion of conventional hierarchies begins when the servants abandon the Nobile mansion, the way "rats abandon a sinking ship," an excuse for Bunuel to mock the helplessness of pampered aristocrats when forced by circumstances to take care of their own needs. As the social contract begins to break down, the "castaways of Providence Street" are thrown increasingly into the promiscuous conditions daily lived by "los olvidados." The mansion becomes an overcrowded minislum, without running water, where people sleep on the floor in forced cohabitation with one another and with animals. Stripped of their class advantages, the aristocrats degenerate into distinctly ungenteel behavior. As in a slum, copulation and defecation, expressions of the "lower bodily stratum," shed the privilege of privacy, and bourgeois etiquette and civility disintegrate. The same aristocrats who spilled food as an amusing "theatrical" device are now ravaged by hunger and on the verge, it is suggested, of ritual murder and even cannibalism. In short, as Nobile laments, all that they have hated since childhood—"vulgarity, violence, dirt—have become [their] constant companions."

Another Jarryesque artist is Jean-Luc Godard, a director whose entire career has been strewn with provocations and outrages against Hollywood (*Made in U.S.A.*), the bourgeoisie (*La Chinoise*), the liberal left (*Letter to Jane*), and the Catholic Church (*Hail Mary*). Godard shares with Jarry a penchant for desacralizing canonical texts, from *Carmen* (*Prenom Carmen*), through *King Lear,* to classical opera in *Aria*. (Godard's *Lear,* for example, features a tragic protagonist who exhibits incestuous longings for his daughter, anachronistic references to telexes and an intrauterine action sequence of a sperm fertilizing an egg.) Godard's *Les Carabiniers* (1963) declares an explicit debt to Jarry and *Ubu Roi*. Godard's location of the scene of *Les Carabiniers* as "at once everywhere and nowhere" quite literally echoes Jarry's "in Poland, that is to say, Nowhere." Godard has one of his heroines utter precisely the word that scandalized Jarry's public in 1896—"Merdre!" and has the concluding epigraph with which he "buries" his two heroes—Michelangelo and Ulysses—paraphrase the letter to Madame Rachilde with which Jarry, himself near death, "buried" Père Ubu.[20] But more important than these explicit homages is the fact that *Les Carabiniers* adopts the carnivalesque and Menippean strategies of the Jarry play. If *Ubu Roi* is tragic farce, *Les Carabiniers* is absurdist epic. Just as the title of Jarry's play lexically and syntactically evokes classical tragedy and Shakespearean history play, but this time with a comically degraded protagonist, so *Les Carabiniers* treats the perennial epic subject—war—but through protagonists who present, like Ubu, a precipitate of gluttony, cupidity, and brutality. The motivations of the protagonists in the two texts are equally ignoble. Ubu wants to get rich, eat sausages, and roll around the streets in a carriage. Ulysses and Michelangelo want to rape women, steal Hawaiian guitars, and eat in restaurants without paying their bills. The narratives of the two texts obey the carnivalesque pattern of comic crownings and uncrownings as an intimation of the inevitability of historical change. Ubu overthrows the king, exercises arbitrary power, and is in turn overthrown and exiled. Ulysses and Michelangelo go to war for "the king," win chimerical booty in the form of postcards, which they take to be deeds to property, and are finally betrayed by the very soldiers who recruited their services.

Godard's distanced, often comic treatment of physical violence is also indebted to Jarry, but ultimately derives, of course, from the venerable tradition of carnivalesque comic violence. In Rabelais, puppet theatre, and commedia dell'arte, death is often a comic episode projected onto a "grotesque and clownish plane." The unpitying nature of carnivalesque art is organically connected to its clear conventionality. The reader/spectator perceives the staged violence as if it were occurring to puppets, whose "sufferings" are seen not as the sufferings of real people but in a spirit of carnival and ritual. Murders in *Ubu* are flippant, performed with the nonchalance with which one tosses away a cigarette. Several people die instantly when Père Ubu poisons them with a lavatory brush, but no one reacts with horror, and Ubu's own response is to ask Mère Ubu to pass the cutlets. It was precisely this neutral tone in the face of the most outrageous violence which impressed Godard in Jarry's play. Contemplating the adaptation of *Ubu* for the screen, Godard claimed to see Ubu very much as a gangster with soft hat and raincoat, who says his "merdre" in the tone of "I've missed my train," with the "dialogue very neutral in the Bresson manner."[21]

If Godard's light-hearted approach to violence reflects, on one level, a typically modernist dissociation of horrible events from their distanced recounting, on another it reflects a carnivalesque strategy of radical simplification aimed at the unmasking and ridiculing of the hypocrisies of a Power stripped of all euphemism. Godard's professed goal was to make the logic of war so simple a child could understand it, and if war is anything in the film, it is above all a kind of bellicose consumerism, a pretext for pillage. Godard counterpoints sound and image to highlight the contradictions between the patriotic glorifications of war and the sanguinary realities they mask. The conventional ethical hierarchies of war—massive aerial bombardments are antiseptic and humane;

disemboweling with a knife is evil and barbaric—are leveled and revealed to be prevarications. Such codes are shown to be as absurd as those of Ubu's coconspirators, who, while outraged at the idea of poisoning the king with arsenic, hail a plan to bifurcate him with a sword as "noble and valiant."

Carnivalesque art is uninterested in psychological verisimilitude or conventional audience identification with rounded personalities. (In Rabelais, Bakhtin tells us, "life has absolutely no individual aspect.")[22] Both *Ubu* and *Les Carabiniers* cut off all sentimental participation in the spectacle. Even the grandiosely improbable names of the characters—Michelangelo, Ulysses, Cleopatra, King Ubu—remove them to a realm of parody, quite beyond ordinary identification. Jarry's play renders the most rudimentary empathy (not to mention the classical pity and fear) simply unthinkable. The characters are those of the Menippea, walking demonstrations of "man's non-coincidence with himself," ambulatory oxymorons given to sudden and improbable ethical turnabouts. Mère Ubu, who in her overreaching for Ubu has generally displayed not so much as a soupçon of conscience or concern for justice, abruptly lectures Ubu: "The young Bougrelas will win, because he has justice on his side." Père Ubu, learning that his rival will gain the crown that he himself has coveted and even murdered for, acquiesces with unexpected nonchalance, adding, "I don't envy him his crown."

The critics, responding predictably to Godard's provocations, denounced *Les Carabiniers* as "incoherent" and a "pitiful farce," failing to situate the film within a carnivalesque tradition in which the overturning of hierarchies forms part of a provocative avant-garde aesthetic. This leveling is at once emotional—mass murder and buying groceries are performed with the same dispassion—and "grammatical," in that the film violates the conventions of cinematic grammar. (Witness the gratuitous zooms, the facetious eyeline matches, the blocks of "dead sound.") The confounding of generic conventions and the parodic approach to serious film genres offended the critics, a reaction hardly surprising given the close link between generic and social conventions. The separation of styles, as Auerbach shows in *Mimesis* and as Bourdieu documents in *Distinction: A Social Critique of the Judgement of Taste,* has tended historically to be tied to class hierarchy, and any generic or discursive "leveling" in the realm of art portends, for the conservative critic, an ominous leveling within society itself. In carnivalesque texts like *Ubu* and *Les Carabiniers,* the censoring faculty simply goes on strike in protest against all cultural rigidity. Just as the surrealists praised "la sauvagerie" as an antidote to a stultifying civilization, Jarry and Godard give free reign to their taste for carnival-style nonsense and horseplay. Their "puerile" gags and scatological references reflect the irreverence of artists on raucous holiday from the strictures of official culture. Carnival operates a perpetual decanonization. Rather than high art's sublimation, we are given a strategy of reduction and degradation, which uses obscenity, scatology, burlesque, and caricature to turn upside down all the forms and values by which, in Pierre Bourdieu's words, "the dominant groups project and recognize their sublimity."[23]

The category of carnival, defined in Bakhtinian terms as "concretely sensuous ritual-pageant thoughts," has broad relevance for cinematic expression, potentially applying to a wide gamut of film texts on a spectrum ranging from the literal-historical to the poetic-figurative:

1. films that explicitly thematize contemporary carnival in its literal denotation (from Vigo's *A Propos de Nice* to Marcel Camus' *Black Orpheus*);

2. films that treat carnival as a historical phenomenon (Imamura's *Eijanaika!*);

3. films that adapt carnivalesque or Menippean literary texts (Fellini's *Satyricon,* Pasolini's *Decameron* and *Canterbury Tales,* Welles's *Chimes at Midnight*);

4. films that use humor to anarchize institutional hierarchies (Vigo's *Zero de Conduite,* the Marx Brothers' *Duck Soup*) or direct corrosive laughter at patriarchal authority (Lizzie Borden's *Born in Flames*);

5. films that comically privilege, whether visually or verbally, the "lower bodily stratum" (Makavejev's *Sweet Movie* and *WR: Mysteries of the Organism;* Richard Pryor's "Concert" films);

6. films that aggressively overturn a classical aesthetic based on formal harmony and good taste (John Waters' *Pink Flamingos* and *Polyester;* the "aesthetic of garbage" films from Brazil);

7. films that celebrate social inversions (Alea's *The Last Supper*);

8. films that parody high art or genres (Buster Keaton's *The Three Ages,* Woody Allen's *Love and Death,* Mel Brooks's *History of the World, Part I;*

9. films that foster "antigrammaticality," carnivalizing film on a purely formal level (e.g., the films of the American avant-garde);

10. films or film-related experiences that strive to erase the barriers between spectator and spectacle (the *Rocky Horror Picture Show* phenomenon).

At times we can discern the distorted echoes of carnival even in carnival's negation or degradation. Films such as *Who's Afraid of Virginia Woolf?* or *Don's Party* present aborted carnivals, symposia gone awry, where drunken banqueting, instead of liberating speech, merely fuels obnoxious candor and escalating aggression. Even "slasher" films such as *Halloween* can be seen as offering inverted, dystopian versions of carnival, in which phenomena that had once been the objects of cathartic laughter undergo a kind of sickly mutation, now transformed into morbid and pathological stigmata of merely private terrors.

It is not my purpose here to explore all the films susceptible to carnivalesque analysis; such a task would be both impossible and pointless. Instead, I would like to examine a few examples—some frankly comic, and others more ambivalent and historically informed—of the "carnivalesque" in film. I am not suggesting, I hasten to add, that all the films discussed are "subversive" or "revolutionary"; in some cases, the carnivalesque tradition is deployed in a purely ludic or even a commercialized manner, while elsewhere it becomes more aggressive and at times subversive.[24] The films of Monty Python, for example, can be seen as purely ludic prolongations of some of the traditions of which Bakhtin speaks. Films such as *The Life of Brian* (1979), *The Holy Grail* (1974), and *Monty Python Live at the Hollywood Bowl* not only parody literary and cinematic genres but they also lampoon two vestigial institutions inherited from the Middle Ages—the church and the monarchy—the very institutions mocked by Bakhtin's carnival as well. *Monty Python Live at the Hollywood Bowl* features a sketch in the *Coena Cypriani* tradition of parodies of the *Last Supper*. The Python version has a cantankerous and foul-mouthed pope berate a cockney-accented Michelangelo for painting a *Last Supper* that includes three Christs ("one fat one and two skinny ones"), twenty-eight disciples, and a kangaroo. Another sketch alludes to the "festive symposium" tradition by reducing the history of philosophy to the mouthings of an interminable series of drunks:

Emmanuel Kant was a real pissant
Who was very rarely stable.
Heidegger, Heidegger was a boozy beggar
Who would think you under the table.

David Hume could out-consume
Schopenhauer and Hegel
and Wittgenstein was a beery swine
and just as sloshed as Schlegel. . . .

The Life of Brian mocks religion and the Church by positing a Christlike figure who becomes the Messiah by accident, who performs fraudulent miracles, and who tells his followers not to "Follow Him," but rather to "Fuck off!" While the biblical Christ is crucified in the company of two thieves, Brian is but one of one hundred forty crucifixions on the same day. The Romans in this pseudobiblical epic have comic-phallic names such as Naughtius Maximus and Biggus Dickus, names that recall carnival's penchant for mocking the body's protuberances. *The Life of Brian* carnivalizes the "Sermon on the Mount" as well. A stereotypically Anglo-Christ, wrapped in white robes, addresses the assembled multitude from a mountaintop. The camera brings us back to the periphery of the crowd, where the congregation strains to hear the distant, loudspeakerless Jesus, from which aural vantage point they imagine him to be saying "Blessed are the Greeks" and "Blessed are the cheesemakers." *The Life of Brian* can be seen, then, as a contemporary *parodia sacra,* here updated for the age of mass-mediated culture.

There also exists a home-grown American carnivalesque tradition rooted both in the popular (fairground, vaudeville, burlesque, stand-up comedy) and in the erudite intertext (Mark Twain), a tradition that in the cinema would include, for example, the Keaton parodies of Griffith (*The Three Ages*) and of the western (*Go West*), King Vidor's *Show People,* the more irreverent of the Chaplin films, certain films of the Marx Brothers, and the films of maverick directors like Preston Sturgess. The tradition would include as well certain films inflected by stand-up comedy—for instance, those directed by Stanley Kubrick and Mel Brooks. Certain forms of stand-up comedy, registered in a number of "concert films," also incarnate the carnivalesque spirit. In "Forms of Time and Chronotype in the Novel," Bakhtin speaks of the "time-honored bluntness of the fool's language" and the "exposure of all that is vulgar and falsely stereotyped in human relationships." In the struggle against conventions, Bakhtin argues, masks take on extraordinary significance. The masks of the clown, Bakhtin writes,

grant the right not to understand, the right to confuse, to tease, to hyperbolize life; the right to parody others while talking, the right to not be taken literally, not "to be oneself"... the right to rip off masks, the right to rage at others with a primeval (almost cultic) rage—and finally, the right to betray to the public a personal life, down to its most private and prurient little secrets.[25]

In reading such a passage, it is difficult not to hear anticipations of our contemporary comics—the "cultic rage" of a John Cleese, the "comic spasms" of a John Belushi, the "hyperbolizations" and "prurient little secrets" of a Richard Pryor, and the manic free-association confessions of a Robin Williams—all latter-day echoes of Bakhtin's clown.

In the dominant Hollywood tradition, carnival is at times evoked in its local sense of "fairground, side show, amusement park," historically latter-day (often commercialized) echoes of old-time carnival. The link between carnival and American cinema, in this sense, is both metonymic and metaphoric: metonymic in that cinema grew up, as it were, in the shadow of the side show, as an entertainment quite literally situated near the fairground and the penny arcade; and metaphoric in the sense that countless films cite the regressive pleasures of commercial carnivals—roller coasters, carousels, Ferris wheels—to analogize those of the cinema itself (e.g., the fairground sequence of *Strangers on a Train*). Carnival motifs at times show up in surprising places. In Penny Marshall's *Big,* twelve-year-old Josh Baskin achieves his magical metamorphosis into an adult through the agency of a mechanized "carnival" fortuneteller who grants his wish. But quite apart from the "carnival" setting, his boy-man status resuscitates the perennial carnival trope of the *puer-rex* (boy-king) and *puer-senex* (child-man), even though the character's sense of play does not form part of a robust communal celebration but is largely limited to the enjoyment (and even the invention and promotion) of commercially distributed toys. In other cases, a film's diegesis might take place against the backdrop of "real" carnival. The destination of Captain America and Billy, in Peter Fonda's *Easy Rider* (1969), is New Orleans's Mardi gras, which becomes the scene, in the film, of a series of inversions of the sacred and the profane: the church becomes a brothel; the Virgin Mary, a whore; and the Eucharist, LSD.[26]

The political valence of carnivalesque strategies in American film is constantly shifting. In *The Theatre and Its Double,* Antonin Artaud paid tribute to the "boiling anarchy" animating *Animal Crackers* and *Monkey Business,* leading to "an essential disintegration of the real by poetry." The conclusion of *Monkey Busi-*

ness, for Artaud, was a "hymn to anarchy and wholehearted revolt."[27] The Marx Brothers' films combine an antiauthoritarian
stance toward certain institutions—the law, opera, racetrack pro-
prietors—with a cinematic and linguistic *gramatica jocosa,* which
involves, in Patricia Mellenkamp's words, the "derailment of logic
and of grammar's proprietary laws," and the "breaking and entering [of] the narrative as well as houses, constantly shattering any
imposed cause-effect logic."[28]

The films of the Marx Brothers have been sufficiently analyzed for us not to linger on them here, except to point up a feature
that is especially emblematic of the American comic tradition—
their subversion of "good manners." In a political culture, and a
commercial film industry, where radical alternatives have been
more or less ruled "out of bounds," it is not surprising that "subversion" often takes the apparently apolitical form of comic aggressions that violate respectable decorum and decent standards of
bodily behavior. "Good education," Bakhtin writes in *Rabelais and
His World,* "demands: not to place the elbows on the table, to walk
without protruding the shoulder blades or swinging the hips, to
hold in the abdomen, to eat without loud chewing, not to snort and
pant, to keep the mouth shut . . . in other words, to close up and
limit the body's confines and to smooth the bulges." Good manners,
as Norbert Elias demonstrates, are never simply good manners;
the social control of bodily functions such as eating, yawning, spit-
ting, and touching serves to repress "socially undesirable impulses
or inclinations."[29] Societies, Pierre Bourdieu points out, set great
store on the "seemingly most insignificant details of dress, bearing,
physical and verbal manners" because they entrust to the body
"the fundamental principles of the arbitrary content of the culture." The concessions of politeness, he adds, always involve "political concessions."[30] And John Murray Cuddihy, in *The Ordeal of
Civility: Freud, Marx, Lèvi-Strauss, and the Jewish Struggle with
Modernity,* shows how those three thinkers, each in his own way,
struggled against the bourgeois Christian norm of "civility," which
they saw as a hypocritical mask for cruel and criminal kinds of
behavior.

Another filmmaker working out of the carnivalesque tradition, Mel Brooks, in *History of the World, Part I,* combines an attack on bourgeois civility with a carnivalized history from a marginalized and distinctly Jewish perspective. The Inquisition
sequence of the Brooks film, as Ella Shohat points out, melds an
ironic carnivalesque atmosphere with a parodic evocation of the

history film and the Busby Berkeley musical, in order to mock official sadomasochistic rituals and Christian anti-Semitism.[31] The liturgy of the Catholic mass is superimposed on the cries of tortured people as a tortured Jew asks in Yiddish-accented English, "Is it polite? Is it considerate? To make my private parts a public game?" The projection of bourgeois codes of etiquette onto an inquisition context exposes their underlying hypocrisy, since it was in the name of a civilizing mission that Europe committed acts of barbarism against its internal and external "others." The episode, as Shohat further points out, prolongs a specifically Jewish carnivalesque tradition, that of Purim, the celebration of the prevention of genocide through Esther's dissembling. Here the redemptive sexuality of the biblical Esther is transformed into the kitsch eroticism of Esther Williams, as Brooks himself dresses up as the Grand Inquisitor, in homage to the Purimspiel tradition of satirically dressing up as Haman, the biblical oppressor of the Jews.[32] At the same time, the film imagistically associates the order and regimentation of Busby Berkeley musicals with the medieval order of Catholic hierarchy. Brooks adopts a similar strategy in the "Springtime for Hitler" sequence of *The Producers* by featuring goose-stepping Nazis in a Rockettes-style chorus line, and by having Berkeley-style aerial shots sweep over chorines festooned with black eagles and pretzels, in such a way as to suggest a subliminal link between Nazi spectacle and Hollywood entertainment, and even implying, through the structural analogies between the "Inquisition" and the "Springtime for Hitler" production numbers, a historical connection between the Inquisition and the Third Reich.

A number of filmmakers, I would argue, have been misunderstood or misappreciated because their work has been judged by the canons of "good taste" or "political correctness" rather than as prolongations of a perennial carnivalesque tradition. Italian culture, for example, with its mingled origins in Roman Saturnalia and Catholic religiosity, is especially rich in carnivalesque reminiscences. We find echoes of carnival in Fellini's adaptation of the classic Menippean text—*The Satyricon*—in the comic anticlericalism of *8½* and even in the banquetlike, sausage-stuffed aesthetic of *Fred and Ginger,* which constantly draws parallels, and contrasts, between perennial Saturnalia and the contemporary mass media. Pier Paolo Pasolini, similarly, in his "trilogy of life," adopts a series of clearly carnivalesque literary texts—*The Decameron, The Canterbury Tales, The Arabian Nights*—privileging the "lower bodily stratum," "marketplace speech" and the ironic encounters triggered by social heteroglossia. In keeping with Bakhtin's emphasis on the medieval and Renaissance marketplace as the site of social heteroglossia and liberated speech, Joel Kanoff points out, each of the trilogy films begins in a marketplace setting that is subsequently exploited as diegetic focal point.[33] The carnivalesque references are at times quite explicit and close to the surface. In both *The Decameron* and *The Canterbury Tales,* for example, Pasolini experiments with staged reconstructions of carnivalesque Brueghel canvases, most notably *The Battle between Carnival and Lent.* In their stress on urination, defecation, copulation, and the unmasking of official and priestly authority figures, these films forge something like the cinematic equivalent of what Bakhtin calls "grotesque realism."

The notion of carnival is also pertinent to the work of Lina Wertmuller. Much of the harsh criticism of Wertmuller's work has been grounded in a kind of "genre mistake" by which the carnivalesque origins of her art have gone unrecognized. Bruno Bettelheim, shocked at Wertmuller's farcical treatment of the Holocaust in *Seven Beauties,* excoriated the film as "completely untrue to the reality of the camps," and feminists denounced the "exploitation" of Elena Fiore's obesity in *The Seduction of Mimi.* But as William and Joan Magretta point out, the fatness of Wertmuller's women does not signify misogyny "any more than Walt Disney's dimwitted Goofy signifies a contempt for dogs."[34] The Magrettas go on to explore the roots of Wertmuller's work in the carnivalesque rituals of Italian folk culture, in commedia dell'arte, in opera buffa, and in the Italian puppet theatre, forms of expression that ultimately go back to the Menippea discussed in *Problems of Dostoevsky's Poetics* and to the carnivalesque art anatomized in *Rabelais and His World.*

The supposed "cynicism" of Italian film comedies, Jurij Lotman points out, derives from the language of the puppet theatre and commedia dell'arte, where death can be a comic episode and a murder a parody. The violence is perceived by the audience "not as the death or suffering of real people, but in a spirit of carnival and ritual."[35] In Wertmuller's case, the link to this tradition was quite direct, since she had worked with the puppet troupe of Maria Signorelli, noted for its use of grotesque stylization and carnivalesque language. The Magrettas trace a number of elements of grotesque stylization, typical of the carnivalesque, in Wertmuller's *oeuvre:*

1. the use of stock characters who hyperbolize well-known social and comic types (the macho Sicilian worker, the Mafia Don, the Sicilian Mama, the liberated woman from the North, the whorehouse madame) and plots (e.g., the traditional farce of cuckoldry in *The Seduction of Mimi*);

2. carnivalesque language liberated from the norms of decency and etiquette, as in the boisterous whorehouse dinner in *Love and Anarchy* or the ritual exchange of insults between Rafaella and Gennarino in *Swept Away;*

3. antimimetic stylization, whether through intrusive musical commentary (e.g., the operatic underlining of farcical sequences, as in the deployment of *La Traviata,* to foil Mimi's courtship of Fiore); and

4. *lazzi*—the bits of comic business typical of commedia dell'arte (e.g., the mimed trial of Pasqualino in *Seven Beauties*).

In sum, to ignore Wertmuller's roots in the tradition of Italian popular carnivalesque comedy is inevitably to fail to understand her work. Spectators are not obliged to "like" or even to respect Wertmuller's work, but they are asked to withhold judgment until that work has been conceptualized within the appropriate framework.

A number of films treat carnival in its literal denotation, whether as contemporary event or historical phenomenon. The "narrative" of Jean Vigo's satirical documentary *A Propos de Nice,* for example, revolves on the titular city's real-life carnival. Vigo's ironic film documents the acting-out of the vestigial movements of a once vital carnival. Vigo catches carnival at the end of the parabola of decline charted in *Rabelais and His World,* and that trajectory takes us from a truly popular and deeply utopian festival to a relatively ossified and elitist one. The familiar iconography and activities—abundant food, extravagant costumes, festive decorations, masquerades, pranks, and dances—are present, but they have been somewhat drained of emotional force and social rebellion. Instead of the free play of carnival and the erasure of boundaries between spectator and performer, we find fireworks as spectator sport and institutionalized "games of chance."

Linked by family and ideology to the anarchist movement and by aspiration to the surrealists, Vigo promotes a critical vision of carnival as a "situated utterance," celebrating what is subversive in carnival while demystifying the social elite of the city that is its site. Rather than glorify Nice in the manner of the conventional documentary or "city film," Vigo exposes its class contradictions, ripping the mask off its superficially festive surface to reveal the class oppression underneath. The elegance of the richest neighborhoods, for example, is foiled by the poverty of the "other Nice," the Nice of those who build the puppets and work in the factories, and who have neither time nor money for the roulette table. But more important than the film's profilmic carnival is the manner in which Vigo himself carnivalizes both the bourgeois society of Nice and the canonical documentary genre, whose formal decorum he consistently undermines through a kind of cinematic *gramatica jocosa*. Vigo's camera literalizes the carnival trope of the "world askew" and the "logic of the turnabout" by favoring arch off-balance shooting angles and unusual camera movements. Repeatedly, Vigo's montage metaphorically links "les bons bourgeois" with animals: an aristocratic grand dame on the "Promenade des Anglais" is compared to a poodle; another wealthy woman is ironically juxtaposed, by the editing, with an ostrich; and a venerable gentleman, presumably of the finest pedigree, is symbolically equated with a horse. While Vigo does not celebrate the social prestige of Nice, he does celebrate certain aspects of its popular carnival. Recurrent shots, filmed at a low and slaked angle, show women dancing in escalatingly erotic frenzy, evoking a kind of collective and exuberant sexuality. The "sensual body" of this writhing crowd quite simply ignores the implied censure of religious officialdom, a representative of which (a priest) is made, via the montage, to leer voyeuristically at the women enjoying their dance.

Shohei Imamura's *Eijanaika!* (1981), meanwhile, can be regarded as a historical study of both the revolutionary potential and the real political limitations of carnival. The film is set in the city of Edo in 1866 during the events that led to Japan's Meiji revolution, which was not a revolution in the conventional sense of an overturning from below—the lower classes were not involved in the shift in power—but was rather a kind of palace coup occurring strictly within the ranks of the elite Samurai class. The film takes its title from an unusual phenomenon witnessed during the turbulent months preceding the "revolution." *Eijanaika* means something like "Who cares!" or "Why not?" or "What the hell!" and refers to the chant uttered by swirling, gyrating crowds of drunken, naked people who periodically charged into the streets, dancing and chanting "Eijanaika!" The film offers a vivid and colorful image of the "glowing life of Dionysian revelers" in the form of a chaotic and irreverent multitude, propelled by music and rhythm, whirling from place to place in frenzied exuberance. The film proliferates in images of the grotesque body and the sounds of "marketplace speech." Prostitutes shout clever curses and ordinary women lift their skirts and laughingly urinate as a provocation to the soldiers recruited to defend the imperial order.

What interests Imamura is the fact that although the people were living in poverty, inflation was rampant, and social and political institutions were crumbling, the "people" could still participate in a utopian festival whose very slogan seemed to celebrate the fact that everything was possible. The film renders the utopian aspect of carnival—the fact that the people, from the heart of their misery, can express a happiness that is irrational yet real, anticipatory or reminiscent of some happier state—as if to suggest that by merely dramatizing happiness, one might elicit a cause for happiness. Carnival is revealed, then, as a transgressive space, more or less tolerated by the law, in which class resentments and utopian aspirations are acted out in ritual and symbolic form. At the same time, the film shows the political limitations of carnival. The dancing crowds, inspired by the mad logic of "Why not?" and convinced that everything is possible, take increasingly greater risks, eventually deciding to take over the palace. For a moment, the authorities and the soldiers seem to retreat, but the illusion is shattered by bursts of gunfire, and the festive crowd is massacred without mercy, as if only guns could discipline a people whose dreams were running wild. We are reminded of Emmanuel Le Roy Ladurie's remarks, in *Carnival at Flanders,* concerning the crucial place occupied by rites of inversion in restoring order in the face of popular revolt. Just as the people pushed the license of carnival to the absolute stretching point of anarchy and open revolt, so the world was turned right side up again with a savage repression of the revolt. But despite the real-life limitations on the carnivalesque actions in the diegesis, the film itself can be seen, on another level, as expressing solidarity with the revelers, for it recounts the events not from the point of view of the Samurai, who were the real power wielders and the makers of history, but from the point of view of those who were dancing in the streets as their history was being made by others. In this sense, the film, like carnival itself, offers a people's view of history as seen "from below."

The culture of real laughter (as opposed to canned or forced laughter) is absolutely central to Bakhtin's conception of carnival: enormous, creative, derisive, renewing laughter that grasps phenomena in the process of change and transition, finding in every victory a defeat and in every defeat a potential victory. Laughter for Bakhtin has cognitive value. It is the goal as well as the means of knowledge: "Laughter demolishes fear and piety before an object . . . thus clearing the ground for an absolutely free investigation."[36] Carnivalesque laughter can be raucous, subversive, even angry, a laughter that erases old differences and installs new, unstable ones. Laughter is profound, communitarian, erotic, a current passing from self to self in a free and familiar atmosphere. It is the adult memory of the cascading giggles of children, who laugh not necessarily at specific localizable "jokes" but as part of a collective contagion. Bataille, in this same vein, speaks of the "radiant spell of laughter," the remorseless laughter of children who laugh even though adults tell them that "there is nothing to laugh at," the "communicable spell" of an intoxication that "gives onto a world of flagrant joy."[37]

Bakhtin's theory of laughter accords very well with what Ruby Rich calls "Medusan" feminist films. Rich takes the term from Cixous's "Laugh of the Medusa," where the French theorist celebrates the potential of feminist texts to "blow up the law, to break up 'the truth' with laughter."[38] Lizzie Borden's *Born in Flames,* Nelly Kaplan's *A Very Curious Girl,* and Ana Carolina's *Sea of Roses* can all be seen as Medusan films that direct satirical laughter against what Luce Iragaray calls "l'esprit de sérieux" of phallocentrism. There is a touch of the Medusan in the laughter that explodes in Marleen Gooris's film *A Question of Silence.* The film revolves on the legal proceedings against three women, of different classes and unknown to each other, who have killed a boutique proprietor who was about to arrest a woman for shoplifting.

From a Bakhtinian perspective, the film is of interest on a number of levels. First, the film proliferates in sexual reversals— here it is the men's behavior that is shown to be irrational; here is it the men who are the butt of the jokes, both for the women in the diegesis and for the film itself. Avoiding a discourse of victimization, the film shows active women who respond to sexist statements, who investigate, struggle, shoplift, and even murder, or who, like Frau Jongman, use silence as an act of resistance. Second, the issue is framed not as one of the three women's guilt—the women are universally acknowledged to have committed the murder—but of their sanity. Janine, the court-appointed psychiatrist in the film, defends the women's action as constituting, within the context of their lives, a quite reasonable response to patriarchal oppression. The film is obviously informed by feminist discussions of female "madness"—the "madwoman in the attic"—both as a patriarchal construct and as an incipient form of revolt. Citing Edwin Ardener and Elaine Showalter, Linda Williams sees the accused women as inhabiting a "wild zone" or "no-man's land" of women's culture cut off to men.[39] In a Bakhtinian perspective, this realm recalls the notion of carnival "madness" as representing an alternative "second life" of the oppressed. After the murder, interestingly, all three women perpetrators perform a slightly unorthodox action with carnivalesque overtones. Christine takes her child on a ride on a "carnival" fairground roller coaster. Anne, the café worker, has an elegant meal—the equivalent of the carnival "banquet." And Andrea, the secretary, goes out and has sex with a stranger on her terms, a contemporary translation not only of carnival's sexual license but also of the implicitly feminist trope of "the disorderly woman" and the "woman on top."

In keeping with Bakhtin's description of official rituals, the trial in the film is static, formal, hierarchical, and predetermined in outcome. When the woman lawyer, Janine, insists that the court consider the murder as the accountable act of three women against a man, the prosecuting counsel protests that the question of gender makes absolutely no difference to him, that he would try the case in exactly the same manner if the three women had killed another woman, or if three men had killed a woman. At this point, one of the women, Frau Jongman, responds to the statement with irrepressible laughter. The camera pans over the witnesses, who one by one start to laugh, after which the other murderers join in, as does, finally, Janine. The counsel's denial of difference provokes the mocking laughter of the differentiated, as if in response to Iragaray's rhetorical question: "Isn't laughter the first form of liberation from secular oppression? Isn't the phallic tantamount to the seriousness of the meaning?" Laughter, Bakhtin writes, "only unites; it cannot divide." He speaks of "the social, choral nature of laughter, its striving to pervade all peoples and the entire world."[40] *A Question of Silence* exhibits what Mary Russo in another context calls "the conflictual laughter of social subjects in a classist, racist, ageist, sexist society . . . the laughter we have now."[41] At the same time, the court, echoing with the derisive laughter of the women, provides a powerful audiovisual realization of an anticipatory utopia of laughter, showing laughter's unifying force, its subversive refusal of ready-made definitions, its choral intimation of nascent revolutionary collectivities.

Of Cannibals and Carnivals

Bakhtin gives the name "carnival" to the decentralizing (centrifugal) forces that militate against official power and ideology. But parallel to this opposition between carnival and officialdom "within" a culture there is an opposition "between" cultures—namely, that which contrasts "closed," self-sufficient, "deaf" cultures, on the one hand, with "open," permeable, and "hearing" cultures, on the other. What Bakhtin calls "decentering" occurs when a national culture loses its sealed-off and self-sufficient character and becomes conscious of itself as only one among many cultures. The Renaissance, for Bakhtin, was a moment of passage from a closed to an open culture not only across the frontiers of Europe but also between Europe and its "others": Africa, Asia, and the New World of the Americas. Similarly, as Bakhtin suggests in *The Formal Method,* European modernism constituted a moment in which non-European cultures became the catalysts for the supersession, within Europe, of a retrograde culture-bound verism, in which Africa, Asia, and the Americas provided the stimulus for generating alternative forms and attitudes. In this chapter, I will attempt to demonstrate the pertinence of Bakhtin's ideas concerning carnival, parody, and intertextual dialogism to a Latin American culture that is both marginal and "open" in Bakhtin's sense, in hopes of "fleshing out" Bakhtin's theories by extending them to a national tradition about which he never spoke, but for which his categories have the utmost relevance.

Bakhtin's theories of carnival arose not only out of his literary studies but also out of a vital, oral Russian culture that was in some respects marginal to mainstream "metropolitan" European culture. In this sense the Russian cultural situation bears comparison to that of Latin America. In both instances, we find the pervasive sense of spatial marginality and temporal retard that characterizes "liminal" societies existing at the far edges of Europe. In both instances, we find a kind of insecure or tremulous nationalism in societies dominated by foreign-influenced elites; in both we find highly politicized artists, ever aware of the pressures of censorship and the real possibility of repression, and in both the repressive context generates an array of double-voiced, allegorical, and parodic strategies.

Although Bakhtin himself rarely referred to Latin American culture, many Latin American intellectuals have found in his notion of the carnivalesque the key to the specificity of Latin American cultural production.[1] Since Latin America has been economically, politically, and culturally marginalized, critics such as Emir Rodriguez Monegal and Haroldo de Campos argue, its best artists have made this marginalization, this ironic sense of belonging to two cultures—one's own and that of the metropolitan centers of power—absolutely central to their work.[2] As necessarily bicultural and often tricultural people, Latin American artists and intellectuals inhabit a peculiar realm of irony where words and images are seldom taken at face value, whence the paradigmatic importance of parody and carnivalization as "ambivalent" solutions within a situation of cultural asymmetry. Latin American art is necessarily parodic, caught in specular games of doubling and redoubling, an art for which, as René Menil said in a West Indian context, "naïveté is forbidden."[3]

Deploying Bakhtinian categories, Latin American critics have found carnivalesque reminiscences and strategies in the Rabelaisian gigantism of Garcia Márquez's *A Hundred Years of Solitude* and in the parodic intertextuality of Guillermo Cabrera Infante's *Tres Tristes Tigres,* as well as in the less "obviously" carnivalesque works of writers like Jorge Luis Borges and Machado de Assis. Borges, at first glance a patrician writer, Emir Monegal argues, carnivalizes European literary classics, turning Dante's *Divine Comedy,* for example, into a "trivial" love story in *El Aleph,* while Machado de Assis crowds *Dom Casmurro,* his novel about male jealousy, with parodic echoes of Shakespeare's *Othello.* The ironic sense of European or North American ideas reencountered "fora de lugar" (out of place), in Roberto Schwartz's expression, pervades Latin American literature. The novels of Manuel Puig offer a literary/cinematic version of this out-of-placeness by constantly reminding us of the ubiquitous presence of Hollywood films in Latin America as a kind of cultural *lingua franca*. Puig shows us a Latin America metaphorically "betrayed by Rita Hayworth," in the sense that First World cultural domination has engendered a feeling that real life is somehow "elsewhere," in the cultural "centers" of Europe and North America, and not on the "periphery" of Argentina or Brazil.

In the 1920s, the Brazilian "modernists" (whose only "crime" against prestige was to have written in Portuguese) responded to this situation by calling for cultural "anthropophagy," a devouring of the techniques and information of the superdeveloped countries undertaken in an effort to struggle against colonialist domination. Just as the aboriginal Tupinamba Indians of Brazil devoured their enemies in order to appropriate their force, the modernists argued, Brazilian artists and intellectuals should digest imported cultural products and exploit them as raw material for a new synthesis, thus turning the imposed culture back, transformed, against the colonizer. The modernists called for the "de-Vespucciazation" of the Americas—the reference is to Amerigo Vespucci—and the "de-Cabralization" of Brazil—referring to Pedro Cabral, Brazil's Portuguese "discoverer." These satiric allusions formed part of a strong anticolonialist impulse. The *Revista de Antropofagia* (Cannibalist Review) describes colonialism as a "descent into slavery" and laments that Brazilians, even after modernism, continue to be "slaves of the Occident . . . and of a rotting European culture." They denounce "import culture" and the "importers of canned consciousness" and the "colonial mentality." Against this servile mentality, the modernists propose "the unification of all efficacious revolts tending in a human direction." At times close to anarchism, they argue that "all legislation is dangerous" and offer as their own counterutopia the model of an indigenous matriarchal society, without armies, police, or social hierarchy, a culture characterized by "sensibility learned in harmony with the earth."[4]

For the modernists, cannibalism was an authentic native tradition as well as a key metaphor for cultural independence. "Only cannibalism unites us," modernist Oswald de Andrade proclaimed. "Tupi or not Tupi, that is the question." Oswald dated his *Cannibal Manifesto* 374—"the year Bishop Sardinha was swallowed" (a reference to the historical deglutition by Brazilian Indians of their first Portuguese-supplied bishop). Cannibalism as metaphor, then, was not only a way for Brazilian "redskin" artists to thumb their noses at their own Europeanized literary "pale-faces," but it was also a carnivalized response to cultural colonialism. By comically underlining the cannibalistic nature of all processes of cultural assimilation, the modernists desacralized not only European models, as Monegal points out, but also their own cultural activities.[5] Within this new formulation, parody takes on a new and strategic role. "Anthropophagy" assumes the inevitability of cultural interchange between Latin America and the First World's metropolitan centers and the consequent impossibility of any nostalgic return to an originary purity. Since there can be no unproblematic recovery of national origins undefiled by alien influences, the artist in the dominated culture should not try to ignore the foreign presence but should rather swallow it, carnivalize it, recycle it for national ends. "Anthropophagy," in this sense, can be seen as another name for Kristeva's "intertextuality" or Bakhtin's "dialogism" and "carnivalization," but this time in a context of neocolonial cultural domination. Indeed, it is striking that one of the traditions to be sympathetically devoured, for the modernists, was precisely the Menippean tradition of which Bakhtin speaks. Oswald de Andrade speaks of a "culture of laughter" which drew inspiration from antiquity and generated the "genial scriblings of Erasmus," the "satire and fantasy" of Rabelais, and the "mordant novelty" of Jarry, "the magnificent author of *Ubu Roi.*"[6]

Cannibalism as metaphor has a long history. Within the Western tradition, cannibalism has often been the "name of the other," the ultimate marker of difference in a coded opposition of light/dark, rational/irrational, civilized/savage. But even within the European tradition, many writers have turned the cannibalist trope against Europe. Montaigne, in "Des Cannibales" (based, ironically, on interviews with Brazilian Indians), argued that civilized Europeans were ultimately more barbarous than cannibals, since cannibals ate the flesh of the dead only to appropriate the strength of their enemies, while Europeans tortured and slaughtered in the name of a religion of love. Herman Melville echoed Montaigne by asking, "Which of us is not a cannibal?" With the European avant-garde, the metaphor took on renewed vigor. Alfred Jarry, in "Anthropophagie" (1902), spoke of that "branche trop négligée de l'anthropophagie," and in "L'Almanach du Père Ubu" addressed himself to "amateur cannibals."[7] The Dadaists entitled one of their organs *Cannibale,* and in 1920 Francis Picabia issued the "Manifeste Cannibale Dada." The vogue of "primitivism" in Europe made it quite natural for the cannibalist metaphor to enter avant-gardist language. But the cannibalist metaphor in Europe, as Brazilian critic Augusto de Campos points out, never led to the constitution of a cultural movement, never defined an ideology, and never enjoyed such profound resonances within the ambient culture as it did in Brazil. The nihilism of Dada had little to do with what de Campos calls the "generous ideological utopia" of Brazilian anthropophagy. Only in Brazil did anthropophagy become a key trope in a cultural movement that was to prolong itself over many decades, ranging from the first *Cannibalistic Review* in the twenties, with its various "dentitions," through Oswald de Andrade's speculations in the fifties concerning anthropophagy as "the philosophy of the technicized primitive," to the pop recyclings of the metaphor in the tropicalist movement of the late sixties.

The "cannibalist" and "carnivalist" metaphors have certain features in common. Both refer to "oral" rituals of resistance, one literal, the other figurative. Both evoke a kind of dissolving of the boundaries of self through the physical or spiritual commingling of self and other. Both reject the ideal of what Oswald de Andrade, in common with Bakhtin, called "canonical" beauty: "Against canonical beauty, natural beauty—ugly, brute, barbarous, illogical."[8] Both call for the "cordial mastication" and critical recycling of foreign culture. Modernist cannibalism argues for the critical "devouring" of the scientific technique and artistic information of the superdeveloped metropolitan countries in order to reelaborate them with autonomy, while parodic carnivalism defended the absorption of metropolitan culture, but in an ironic, "double-voiced" mode.

But before returning to the cannibalist metaphor, we must first explore the other senses in which Latin America is "carnivalesque." The carnivalism of Latin America is, on a certain level, quite literal and concrete. For while European carnivals have become pale memories of Rabelaisian frenzies of yore, carnival in Latin America—especially in those countries impregnated by the African cultures brought by slaves—remains a vibrant and protean expression of a polyphonic culture. Brazilian carnival, for example, combines ecstatic polyrhythmic percussion and "orgiastic" behavior with the elaborate "folk opera" of the samba schools and the spontaneous street theatre of revelers mingling in "free and familiar contact." It was in part contact with such festivals that led the Cuban writer Alejo Carpentier to formulate his concept of the "real maravilloso americano" and to contrast Europe's labored attempts to resuscitate the marvelous with the quotidian magic of Latin American life.[9] Octavio Paz writes of the Mexican calendar, similarly, that it is "peopled with fiestas" that represent the "advent of the unexpected" in an "enchanted world" existing in "another time."[10] What was remote and metaphoric for European modernists—magic, carnival, anthropophagy—was more familiar and quasi-literal for Latin Americans. The heterogeneous cultures that made up Latin America had engendered a new historical reality that subverted the conventional patterns of occidental rationalism. "The primitivism that appeared in France as exoticism," wrote Oswald de Andrade, "was for us in Brazil real primitivism."[11] As a result, writes Brazilian critic Antonio Candido, the "provocations of a Picasso, a Brancusi, a Max Jacob, a Tristan Tzara, were, in the end, more coherent with *our* cultural heritage than with theirs."[12]

There was, of course, a good deal of concrete interanimation between the Brazilian and European avant-gardes. Blaise Cendrars, Le Corbusier, Marinetti, and Benjamin Peret all went to Brazil, just as Oswald de Andrade, Sergio Milliet, Paulo Prado, and other key figures in the Brazilian modernist movement made frequent trips to Europe. Oswald de Andrade saluted surrealism, in a self-mockingly patronizing manner, as one of the richest "preanthropophagic" movements. Anthropophagy, added Oswald, always sets its face against the Occident, but warmly embraces "the discontented European, the European nauseated by the farce of Europe."[13] But the exotic metaphors of the European avant-garde had a strange way of "taking flesh" in the Latin American context, resulting in a kind of ironic echo effect between European and Latin American modernism. The Parisian avant-garde of the twenties, as we know, was fascinated by the art and culture of Africa and the Americas. Léger, Cendrars, and Milhaud based their staging of "La Création du Monde" on African cosmogony; Bataille wrote about pre-Colombian art and Aztec sacrifices; Artaud fled France for the Mexico of the Tarahumara Indians; and the avant-garde generally cultivated the mystique of voodoo and African art. But when "re-invoiced" in such countries as Brazil, all this became quite concrete and literal. Thus Jarry's "too neglected branch of anthropophagy" came to refer in Brazil to the putatively "real" cannibalism of the Tupinamba, and surrealist "trance" writing became the collective trance of Afro-Brazilian religion. Latin Americans' familiarity with the "madness" of carnival, with African-derived trance religions, with folkloric poetry, thus made it easy for them to assimilate artistic procedures that in Europe had represented a more dramatic rupture with ambient values and spiritual traditions.[14]

While European anatomists of carnival tend to reduce it, as we have seen, to a merely textual phenomenon, Brazilian analysts are inevitably aware of carnival in its living, breathing, permeating reality. Indeed, a number of Brazilian scholars have developed Bakhtinian-style analyses both of carnival itself and of its erudite prolongations in literature, music, and the cinema. These analyses have been largely based on the brief sections on carnival and Menippean satire in *Problems of Dostoevsky's Poetics,* published in Brazil in 1981, or on a reading, in French, English, or Russian, of *Rabelais and His World.* (Since the book on Rabelais has only recently been translated into Portuguese, Brazil offers the anomalous situation in which a book is published *after* its central ideas have been disseminated.) Brazilian literary critics such as Affonso Romano de Sant'Anna, Boris Schnaiderman, Flavio Kothe, Suzana Camargo, and Haroldo de Campos have performed Bakhtinian analyses not only of Brazilian modernism (Oswald de Andrade's *Serafim Ponte Grande*, Mario de Andrade's *Macunaima,* and Jorge Amado's *Pais do Carnaval*) but also of the work of more classical writers (Machado de Assis, Gregorio de Matos) as well as of popular "folk" literature (e.g., the "cord literature" of the Northeast). On occasion, in fact, Bakhtin becomes a reference not only for critics but also for the artist-producers themselves. São Paulo theatre director Antunes Filho, for example, based his recent production of *Xica da Silva,* a play about an eighteenth-century black slavewoman who became a virtual empress of the richest region of Brazil, on the Bakhtinian notion of carnivalization. "The idea that a black slave might become an empress even during slavery is an idea that has everything to do with carnival," said the director, "and the only appropriate aesthetic for such a play is one based on carnivalization." He describes *Xica da Silva* as a "tragedy that provokes laughter, reminiscent of those popular festivities which incorporate the idea of renewal through laughter."[15]

The special relevance of Bakhtin's notion of the carnivalesque for Brazil goes beyond literary analysis and production, however, for in Brazil the idea of carnival has formed an integral part of the very *theorization* of national identity and culture. In *Carnavais, Malandros e Herois* (Carnivals, Hustlers, and Heroes, 1980), in an attempt to elucidate what he calls the "Brazilian dilemma"—that is, the coexistence in Brazil and within the Brazilian personality of one side that is festive, "cordial," and democratic, and of another that is censorious, hierarchical, and authoritarian—Brazilian anthropologist Roberto da Matta deploys carnival as a kind of anthropological key to the national lifestyle.[16] Philosopher José Guilherme Merquior, similarly, in *Saudades do Carnaval* (Nostalgia for Carnival, 1972), argues that the cultural substratum of Brazil is "orgiastic," since Brazil "entered into modern culture vaccinated against its anticarnivalism."[17] (Charles de Gaulle inadvertently echoed Merquior's judgment, but on a negative register, in his famous remark on visiting Brazil: "Ce n'est pas un pays sérieux.") Oswald de Andrade, in his "Brazil-Wood Manifesto" calls carnival the "religious ritual of the Brazil-wood race," where "Wagner is submerged by carnival revelers."[18] Writer-composer Jorge Mautner evokes Nietzsche in his description of Bahia's carnival as the locus of "savage anthropophagy," a place where a "marvelous multitude [is] completely given over to Dionysus, a Bacchic delirium of the tearing apart of the mysterious god of Thrace," a "black chaos to challenge future Homers," which exists side by side with "an Apollonian playfulness," a "Dionysian pageant, where the god of death encounters to god of life, in an illumination of ecstasy and intoxication which pale and sophisticated populations try to reproduce through diverse forms of mysticism."[19] Countless Brazilian writers, from historian Sergio Buarque de Holanda, who spoke of the Brazilian as the "homem cordial" (cordial man), through Antonio Candido, with his "dialectics of *malandragen* [playful quick-wittedness]" have found in the notion of carnival a kind of "open sesame" to the Brazilian character.

Roberto da Matta describes Brazilian carnival in terms that are strikingly reminiscent of Bakhtin's account of medieval carnival as a time of festive laughter and gay relativity. Carnival, for da Matta, is a collective celebration and ritual that gives voice to a symbolic resistance, on the part of the marginalized majority of Brazilians, to internal hegemonies of class, race, and gender. Working out of the anthropological tradition of Victor Turner and Max Gluckman, da Matta describes carnival as the place where the oppressive quotidian hierarchies of Brazilian life are momentarily dissolved. As the "privileged locus of inversion," carnival allows all those who have been socially marginalized to take over, for a brief period, the symbolic center of national life. The business district, usually synonymous with serious productive labor, becomes the irradiating center of playfulness, and night changes places with day.

Liberatory mechanisms such as the donning of costumes and masks divorce individuals from their ordinary positions within the social formation and project them into a playful *communitas*. Black *favelados* dress up as kings and queens, adults as children, while men dress as women, and women, less frequently, as men. Carnival thus dramatizes certain utopian aspirations of Brazilian culture—freedom, equality, the mingling of races. In its symbolic thrust, at least, carnival translates a profoundly democratic and egalitarian impulse. As a moment of collective catharsis, a profoundly social and interactive form of *jouissance,* carnival offers a transindividual taste of freedom in which costumed revelers play out imaginary roles corresponding to their deepest desires.

But carnivalesque egalitarianism represents only one pole of the phenomenon. To illustrate the "Brazilian dilemma," da Matta draws an exemplary contrast between carnival and the September 7 Brazilian Independence Day military parade. While carnival is celebrated by all the people, including the powerless, the military parade is performed only by official members of the powerful armed forces. While carnival turns night into day, the parade invariably occurs during the day. If carnival is antihierarchical, the military parade is strictly ordered according to the military chain of command. While carnival blurs the line between performer and audience—the entire populace *becomes* the carnival—the military parade enforces separation of the marchers from the observers, whose role it is to remain passive and merely applaud. While carnival costumes, suggestively called *fantasias* in Portuguese, constitute a means for expressing freedom and fantasy, military dress remains uniform (hence the name) and subordinated to rank. While carnival costumes heighten discontinuity with everyday life—one dresses as that which one is *not* in everyday life—the military parade emphasizes professional continuity—one is a colonel in the parade and in real life. While carnival dance displays gestural freedom and exuberance, the military march exhibits rigidly controlled movements. The sexual license of carnival, meanwhile, contrasts with the parade's atmosphere of sexual repression. Whereas carnival promotes creativity, the parade virtually forbids it; creativity is regarded as a mistake, an error. And while carnival is performed in a spirit of childlike play, the military parade is a deadly serious exercise.

If there is a problem in da Matta's analysis, it is his failure, at times also displayed by Bakhtin himself, to adequately theorize the political ambiguities of carnival. Whatever its utopian symbolic thrust, carnival as a "situated utterance"—as lived, for example, in a contemporary Third World capitalist society like Brazil—is inevitably inflected by hierarchical social arrangements. Da Matta's analysis of carnival, in this sense, fails to take into account the extent to which black and white, rich and poor, men and women, heterosexual and homosexual, live distinct carnivals. The *favelado* who cannot afford rum to celebrate, the *mulata* maid who is mistreated all year and then erotically exalted during carnival, the transvestite who comes into ephemeral glory—all these come to carnival from a different and more marginal position than those who enjoy power all year long and therefore have less need to symbolically overturn it.

In the wake of da Matta's seminal analysis, other anthropologists and commentators have nuanced or criticized his views. Carnival is infinitely more varied, argues anthropologist Peter Fry, than da Matta's analysis suggests, not only in terms of region and city, but also in terms of class, ethnic group, and historical period.[20] The practice of carnival, furthermore, often diverges sharply from its theory. While the rhetoric of carnival, like that of populist politics, annuls or inverts the social inequalities of everyday life, the practice of carnival at times dramatizes these inequalities. Antonio Riserio, in *Carnaval Ijexa,* an account of the role of blacks in the Bahian carnival, gives evidence to buttress Fry's critique. The carnival "blocos," he points out, tend to divide themselves in terms of class and race; the whites tend to parade in "blocos de barão" (baronial groups) and dress up as European nobles, while the blacks and mulattoes tend to dress up as Africans or indigenous Brazilians. Rather than manifest a logic of inversion and ethnic crossover, then, the Bahian carnival dramatizes ethnic allegiance.[21] As a "situated utterance," carnival cannot evade social tension and the realities of power, but it can poetically amplify, critique, or point to the possible transcendence of these tensions. Carnival in Brazil, as elsewhere, constitutes both a release for popular resentment *and* a locus of popular resistance; it is the constant site of struggle between the two tendencies, between official power and popular imagination, hegemony and resistance, co-optation and subversion.

Our interest here, in any case, is less in literal carnival than in its artistic prolongations. The point of this summary of carnival is simply to suggest that a consciousness of carnival permeates all of Brazilian life and art. Just as Rabelais' work was deeply imbued with the awareness of the popular festivities of the time, so the Brazilian artist is inevitably aware of the cultural universe of car-

nival as an ever-present repertoire of gestures, symbols, and metaphors, a fund of knowledge that is at once popular and erudite, a
set of artistic strategies that potentially can be mobilized to crystallize popular irreverence. Brazilian popular music, for example,
often deploys carnival imagery and motifs to allegorize, if not revolution, at least an end to dictatorship. Chico Buarque de Holanda's
samba "Apesar de Voce" (Despite You), composed at the height of
the military dictatorship, evokes a popular, carnival-like celebration at the fall of an unnamed "you" who was widely understood to
represent Medici, Brazil's dictator. And Buarque's 1984 samba
"Vai Passar" (It Will Pass) alludes—through its lyrics, its instrumentation, and its rhythms—to the annual samba school pageant
in such a way as to call for the end of the military regime. Some of
the lyrics go as follows:

> Vai passar nesta avenida um samba popular
> Cada paralelepípedo da velha cidade
> Essa noite vai se arrepiar
> Ao lembrar
> Que aqui passaram sambas imortais
> Que aqui sangraram pelos nossos pés
> Que aqui sambaram nossos ancestrais . . .
>
> . . . E um dia
> Afinal
> Timha direito a uma alegria fugaz
> Uma ofegante epidemia
> Que se chamama carnaval
> O carnaval, o carnaval (vai passar)
>
> A popular samba is coming down the avenue
> All the cobble stones of the old city
> Will thrill tonight
> When they recall
> The immortal sambas that passed this way
> That they bled about our feet
> That our ancestors danced samba here . . .
>
> . . . And one day
> Finally
> They had the right to an ephemeral joy
> A breathless contagion called carnival
> Oh carnival, oh carnival (it will pass)

As Charles Perrone points out, the song, within the style of the *samba-enredo* (samba-plot) genre, proliferates in carnival references such as the passing of the parade, the veneration of samba school ancestors, the exclamations of excitement in the streets, and the singing and dancing till dawn. At the same time, the song offers a metaphorical vision of recent Brazilian history, moving from past repression ("an unhappy page of history") to the joyful announcement that this too will pass.[22]

Another excellent example of the relevance of Bakhtinian categories for the comprehension of Brazilian cultural production is Mario de Andrade's brilliant modernist novel *Macunaíma* (1928), a book that seems in retrospect almost expressly designed to elicit a Bakhtinian exegesis.[23] Here we encounter virtually all the Bakhtinian themes: carnivalesque inversions, double-voiced parodic discourse, social and artistic heteroglossia, cultural and textual polyphony. An anthropologist and musicologist as well as poet and novelist, Mario de Andrade compiled Amerindian, Luso-Brazilian, and African legends to create *Macunaíma*. He called his text a "rhapsody" both in the musical sense of a "free fantasy on an epic, heroic, or national theme" and in the etymological sense of "stitcher" since the novel "stitches" tales to form a kind of artistic crazy quilt. In what amounts to an anthology of Brazilian folklore, de Andrade combines oaths, nursery rhymes, proverbs, and elements of popular as well as erudite literature with the indigenous legends collected by German anthologist Theodor Koch-Grunberg in the headwaters of the Orinoco between 1911 and 1913 and published in his two-volume *Vom Roroima zum Orinoco: Ergebnisse einer Reise in Nord Bresilien und Venezuela in den Jahren 1911–1913* in 1923.[24]

Like *Gargantua and Pantagruel, Macunaíma* conflates two carnivalesque traditions: the erudite, literary tradition and the popular tradition of carnival as praxis. On the erudite side of its intertext, *Macunaíma* is indebted to epic (the novel was called the "Brazilian *Odyssey*") and more precisely to comic epic, to Rabelais, to the Brazilian "Indianist" novelists such as José de Alencar, as well as to de Andrade's fellow Brazilian modernists. The book is indebted as well to the European avant-garde and especially to the surrealists, some of whom were the author's friends and whom he "invited" into the book as characters. (Significantly, the novel refers to the surrealists as *macumbeiros*—that is, practitioners of Afro-Brazilian trance religion, thus highlighting once again the Brazilian literalization of the avant-garde's metaphors.) If *Mac-*

unaíma is a Brazilian epic, it is clearly an ironic one. Bakhtin, we may recall, was hostile to epic, which he regarded as a fixed, monoglossic genre, composed in a fetishized, artificially preserved language allowing no contact between the world evoked—eternally petrified in an untouchable past—and the present community of writers and readers. He was enthusiastic, however, about the comic-parodic epic of Rabelais and Cervantes, which exists at the very source of the modern dialogical tradition in the novel. *Macunaíma* is in this sense clearly antiepic. The language of *Macunaíma* does not convey a petrified past; rather, it is defiantly *contemporary,* constantly evoking present-day debates, events, and idiom. And if the authentic epic hero is all *sapientia et fortitudo,* Macunaíma is but intermittently brave and not infrequently stupid. His most characteristic phrase, equivalent to Gargantua's "A Boire!," is "Ai! Que preguiça!" (What laziness!); laziness, in fact, serves as an epic retarding device in *Macunaíma.* While occasionally crafty and courageous like Ulysses, Macunaíma is more often dumb and egocentric like Ubu. He utters his epic challenges by telephone, and the telephone, symptomatically, is almost always busy.

Mario de Andrade himself repeatedly claimed that he innovated nothing and that he was merely writing in the tradition of Apuleius, Petronius, Rabelais, and Lazarillo de Tormes—in short, in the tradition of Bakhtin's "Menippean satire." Indeed, as Suzana Camargo has pointed out, *Macunaíma* can easily be shown to demonstrate all of Bakhtin's "essential characteristics" of the Menippea.[25] To linger on just a few of those characteristics, the novel flaunts the freedom from historical limits and the liberty of philosophical invention that are typical of Menippean satire by having its "scene" bound improbably and without transition from the Amazon to the backlands of São Paulo in an impossible zigzag. (This passion for spatial and temporal expanses, Bakhtin points out, was also typical of Rabelais.) The novel also proliferates in magical transformations, characters changing color or coming back to life, and animals turning into buildings or telephones. De Andrade also anachronistically mingles historical periods, facilitating what Bakhtin calls "the dialogue of the dead with the living," so that seventeenth-century characters, for example, rub elbows with contemporary ones. This freedom of invention, in the novel, derives from a double source—first from the Menippea, but also from the Amazonian legends themselves, with their heritage of totemic and animistic imagery. "Fish used to be people just like us," Macunaíma tells his brothers. Indeed, in the world of this novel, characters literally turn into stars, as they do in Amerindian legends, becoming constellations to be deciphered by those who remain on earth.

Rabelais' grotesque realism, for Bakhtin, is a means of evoking the voice of the people: "The material bodily principle is contained not in the biological individual, not in the bourgeois ego, but in the people, a people who are continually growing and renewed. This is why all that is bodily becomes grandiose, exaggerated, immeasurable."[26] Mario de Andrade's oxymoronic protagonist, similarly, is a larger-than-life composite character, a summa of Brazil, who epitomizes the ethnic roots as well as the qualities and defects of an entire people. A composite of several heroes found in the Amerindian source-legends, his very name is oxymoronic, composed of the root *maku* (bad) and the suffix *-ima* (great). Macunaíma, "the hero without any character," as the novel's subtitle has it, not only lacks character in the conventional moral sense but also lacks the psychological coherence of the autonomous ego and the sociological coherence of the verisimilar character. Ethnically, he is at once black, white, and Indian, and morally he is by turns selfish, generous, cruel, sensual, and tender. As a representative of "the grotesque body of the people" rather than a rounded personage, his character consists, as Mario de Andrade explained in a letter to Manuel Bandeira, in "not having any character and his logic . . . in not having any logic."[27]

The "autographed literature" of personal authorship, according to Bakhtin, is merely a drop in an ocean of anonymous folk literature. In *Macunaíma,* Mario de Andrade exploits the antimimetic logic of folktales, which never pretend to be realistic but rather tend toward spatial and temporal indeterminacy. The characters of folktales, as Vladimir Propp points out, tend to lack psychological depth. They are "functions," instruments of action rather than interior revelation. *Macunaíma,* in a significant coincidence, was published the same year as Propp's *Morphology of the Folk Tale,* in which Propp analyzes Russian folktales into thirty-one "functions" or interchangeable incidents. Brazilian poet-critic Haroldo de Campos, in fact, has written a "Morphology" of *Macunaíma,* in which he applies the Proppian categories to the de Andrade novel.[28] The logic of *Macunaíma,* he argues, is the logic of folktales—not the logic of individual tales, but the logic of the processes by which the folk imagination constructs tales. Mario de Andrade exploits folklore as a way of generating stories, not by mechanistically compiling tales, but rather by "interbreeding them"; the characters from one body of legend (e.g., Amerindian) perform actions taken from another body of legend (e.g., African), and thus the two traditions cross-fertilize each other. In *Macunaíma,* folktales become part of a productive combinatoire by which the collective language of the tribe is transformed into literary parole.

In still another significant coincidence, both Bakhtin and Mario de Andrade were developing theories of "polyphony" in the middle and late twenties. Both writers were well informed in musical matters. Mario de Andrade was a professional musicologist and amateur composer, while Bakhtin, as is well known, was inordinately fond of analytical terms drawn from music: *voice, accent, orchestration, counterpoint, polyphony*. In *Problems of Dostoevsky's Poetics,* Bakhtin credits the Russian author with creating the "polyphonic novel," suggesting the orchestration of a textual plurality of unmerged voices and consciousnesses. Mario de Andrade, in *A Escrava que Não é Isaura* (The Slave Who Is Not Isaura, 1925), speaks of *polifonismo,* here with regard to modernist poetry, as referring to the "theorization of certain procedures employed by certain modernist poets." De Andrade defines "poetic polyphony" as "the simultaneous artistic union of two or more melodies whose temporary effects of sonorous conflict collaborate to create a total final effect," a definition that is not too distant from Bakhtin's.[29]

The language of *Macunaíma* also has a composite, polyphonic, collective character. Constituting what Mario de Andrade himself called a "veritable esperanto," a linguistic nowhere borrowed from all regions of Brazil and ranging from the archaic to the neologistic, it exploits to the maximum the rich potentialities of Brazilian Portuguese, weaving rhymed maxims ("Eat shit but never bet"), gnomic wisdom ("The whole marsh doesn't mourn when one crab dies"), and popular superstitions into a splendid linguistic tapestry. *Macunaíma* taps the linguistic genius of the Brazilian people by fusing its jokes, legends, songs, nursery rhymes, and slang, its Indianisms and Africanisms, into a panfolkloric saga. By embracing what he calls the "age-old inheritance of the people's errors"—here again we find the privileging of the noncanonical—de Andrade sounds a barbaric yawp of protest against a double colonization, first by colonialist Europe and second by the European-dominated cultural elite within Brazil. The novel captures the aphoristic cynicism of the people ("Every Man for Himself and God Against Everyone!" and "God gives nuts to people without teeth") as well as popular culture's gift for nonsense ("Our hero closed his

eyes so as not to see himself being eaten"). *Macunaíma* carnivalizes language by comically exploiting linguistic incongruities.
Mario de Andrade has his presumably illiterate protagonist learn
Latin and Greek (in order to collect "dirty words") and compose a
parodic letter in the chaste Portuguese of the epic poet Camoes. In
the world of *Macunaíma,* even monkeys speak Latin.

Carnivalesque art, since it sees its characters not as flesh-
and-blood people but as abstract puppetlike figures, laughs at
beatings, dismemberment, and even death. The cannibalism that
pervades *Macunaíma,* like that which pervades *Gargantua and
Pantagruel*—where at one point Gargantua swallows six pilgrims
with his salad, washing them down with a gulp of white wine—is
ultimately "pour rire." The comic tradition of the Menippea, for
Bakhtin, favors "ritual (cultic) indecency," in an atmosphere of
"cheerful death . . . surrounded by food, drink, sexual indecencies
and symbols of conception and fertility."[30] *Macunaíma* is full of
macabre humor and comic mutilations. Just as Rabelais is fond of
the image of the "cheerfully dying man" (e.g., the poet Ramin-
agrobis), and lists a series of "deaths from laughing," *Macunaíma*
has the protagonist's mother drop dead out of literal respect for the
proverb "caiu dente, é morte de parente" (a tooth falls, a relative
dies).

By focusing on the shared physiological processes of bodily
life—copulation, birth, eating, drinking, defecation—the carnivalesque aesthetic offers a temporary suspension of hierarchy and
prohibition. The carnivalesque, for Bakhtin, is designed to transfer all that is spiritual, ideal, and abstract to the material level, to
the sphere of earth and the body. Excrement, as a literal expression of the "lower bodily stratum," forms part of the fecund imagery
of the grotesque. Old-time carnivals in Europe featured the festive
slinging of cow dung ("le jeu de la merde"), a penchant that was later sublimated into more refined forms of slapstick (throwing tal-
cum or water balloons, for example) and other amiable aggressions. Within the excremental vision of *Macunaíma,* feces enjoy
great prestige. Macunaíma is recurrently shat on by vultures and
geese and all manner of fowl. Urine, too, carries great dignity within the carnivalesque aesthetic. Gargantua urinates on the multitude, just as the child Macunaíma "pisses hot on his old mother,
frightening the mosquitoes." (We will return to *Macunaíma* when
we speak of the 1969 film adaptation.)

The carnivalesque, I have said, forms an especially apt instrument for the investigation of Brazilian cultural production,

whether literature, painting, music, or the cinema. Brazilian cinema, especially, has always been deeply impregnated by the cultural values associated with carnival. The forms of this carnivalesque presence range from the profilmic incorporation of actual carnival activities—a feature of the first "views" at the turn of the century, as of some of the most recent films—through more diffuse allusions via music or costume, to the use of strategies of travesty and inversion unaccompanied by any direct reference to carnival. The very word *carnival* figures prominently in the titles of a disproportionate number of Brazilian films, from early views such as *O Carnaval de 1908* (1908 Carnival), through sound-era "chanchadas" such as *Alô Alô Carnaval* (1936), to post-Cinema Novo productions such as *Quando o Carnaval Chegar* (When Carnival Comes, 1971). The "chanchadas," musical comedies that were popular throughout the thirties, forties, and fifties, not only were released at carnival time but also were intended to promote the annual repertory of carnival songs and were designated, as if in anticipation of Bakhtinian analysis, *filmes carnavalescos*—"carnivalesque films."

The mere profilmic foregrounding of carnival itself, it should be pointed out, does not of itself make a film "carnivalesque." The Franco-Brazilian production *Black Orpheus,* for example, registers the phenomenal surface of carnival—dance, rhythm, music, color, laughter—but does so ultimately in the service of a stereotypical and Eurocentric vision. Its Brazilian characters play out the archetypal patterns provided by European myth against the photogenic backdrop of Rio's beauty, in a film that prettifies the city's favelas and isolates carnival from its social and cultural context. While the carnivalesque proposes a dialectical critique of everyday life, *Black Orpheus* hints at a metaphysical transcendence within an idealized décor.

More interesting than the visual display of carnival is the use of carnivalesque strategies. Such strategies must be seen within the context of neocolonial hegemony—that is, in the light of the central reality of a political and economic dependency that conditions all Brazilian cultural production. According to the perspective adopted by "dependency analysis," a world capitalist system locks countries such as Brazil into a kind of negative dialectic that simultaneously generates development at the center and underdevelopment on the periphery.[31] The consequences of hegemony are particularly visible within the film industry, where the Hollywood film has been a strong presence virtually since the beginnings of Brazilian cinema. After a brief period of control of its internal market, known to Brazilian film historians as the "Bela Epoca" or "Golden Age," Brazil lost that control to Hollywood, which consolidated its domination during and after World War I. Slowly the cinema came to be equated with one of its specific modes; the "dialect" of Hollywood film came to be seen as the universal language, internalized to some extent by filmmakers, exhibitors, and spectators alike.

In the face of foreign domination, the visible presence of Brazilian cinema was guaranteed in the postsound era only by the incessant production of "chanchadas," the most popular genre ever produced in Brazil. A derogatory epithet created by hostile mainstream critics, "chanchada" refers to a body of films (first made in the early thirties, and continuing in modified form up to the present) featuring predominantly comic plots interspersed with musical numbers. The chanchada was from its inception intimately linked to the world of carnival. The "Alô, Alô" in the titles of early chanchadas such as *Alô Alô Brasil* (1935) and *Alô Alô Carnaval* (1936)—the latter featuring an already-famous Carmen Miranda—alludes to the common salutation by radio announcers to carnival revelers. But even the chanchadas that are not marked by the diegetic presence of carnival are still linked to the larger universe of carnival in that they incorporate the social inversions that are typical of carnival and develop, like carnival itself, an implicit social critique. Many thirties chanchadas, for example, aim satirical barbs at the political life and administration of Rio de Janeiro. And this at a time when carnival itself tended to constitute a collective revenge, on the part of Cariocas, for the lack of water, light, and public transport and a pretext for satirically lambasting the city establishment.

It was in a chanchada studio—Cinedia—that Orson Welles, in 1942, worked on his own never-to-be-completed film about carnival—a semidocumentary that was to be entitled "It's All True" and that was ultimately undone through an unfortunate combination of circumstances that included the hostility of a new management team at RKO, the fatal accident of one of the film's leading participants, and, it is now becoming clear, racism on the part of American studio executives, politicians, and the Brazilian elite.[32] The Rio de Janeiro sequence of the film, most of which was actually filmed, was conceived as an enthusiastic homage to the gregarious spirit and protean energy of Rio's carnival. According to the accounts of those who were close to Welles, the director became deeply involved in the cultural universe of samba and carnival. Vinicius de Morais, author of the source-play of *Black Orpheus,* described Welles as a "master of our carnival . . . familiar with its mannerisms, rhythms, instruments."[33] In his presentation of the film, Welles describes Brazil's carnival very much along Bakhtinian lines, as a privileged moment of "free and familiar contact" in which individuals, according to Welles, "set aside their self-consciousness and timidity and reticence." Carnival's "hilarious congestion," Welles writes, "exists in the very hottest latitudes of human hilarity," and as yet remains "uncharted and unexplored."[34]

Despite Robert Wise's (reported) judgment that Welles's carnival footage was "simply a jumble of what was essentially travelogue stuff," it is not so difficult, on the basis of the material available for screening as well as the notes of Welles and his collaborators, to discern a coherent overall intention in the carnival sequence.[35] The goal was to create a kind of pan-American fictive-documentary-musical without Hollywood stars and without conventional story. The goal was to initiate the spectator into carnival, to leave "the audience as open-mouthed and google-eyed as we were who shot the action." The film was to document the process by which the periphery (the poor blacks from the favellas surrounding Rio) takes over the center (the business and government district). It would show the people singing, dancing, and beating samba rhythms in buses and trolley cars, for example, turning what is ordinarily an annoyance—overcrowded public transport—into transfigured moments of collective creativity.

At the same time, Welles recognized that carnival is a many-languaged phenomenon, lived differently depending on one's race and class. The film was to explore the differences between the popular street carnival and the fashionable balls, showing the diverse locations where carnivals were celebrated and the kinds of people who frequented them. Welles also planned to emphasize what Bakhtin would call the "erasure of the boundaries between spectator and spectacle." In carnival, Welles wrote, the "people entertain themselves and others almost without let-up." He planned microsequences to convey the cheerful rituals and atmosphere of carnival, foregrounding not so much spectacle per se as carnival's myriad forms of human interplay: that between performing musicians and responding audience, between groups of revelers throwing confetti and streamers, between lovers and lovers-to-be. What mattered always was the interplay generated by what Bakhtin would call the "in-between" of carnival's "gay relativity"—not its activities per se, but its contagiously ludic, raucously dialogic quality.[36]

Although Welles's carnival film was never completed, hundreds of Brazilian carnivalesque films were produced by such studios as Cinedia and Atlantida. And in the chanchadas of the fifties, especially, parody became a crucial strategy within the "filmes carnavalescos." The parodic strategies that one frequently finds in the chanchadas are premised on North American hegemony; they assume that the audience, given the asymmetrical nature of the informational exchange between North and South America, has already been inundated by North American cultural products. But the parodic response is almost always ambivalent, mingling assertive national self-pride with idealization of the foreign, internalized as "ideal ego." The *rapports de force* between idealization and critique varies from film to film. In some films, Brazilian cinema itself becomes the object of attack, the scapegoat for the incapacity of an underdeveloped country to copy the powerful technological efficiency of American films, while in others, parody becomes a means to subvert canonized codes. Thus parody stands at the point of convergence of multiple contradictions, at times serving a negative aesthetic based on the servile self-derision of "colonial mimicry" and at other times becoming an instrument of carnivalized revolt against hegemony.

Brazilian scholar-critic João Luiz Vieira cites one chanchada in particular as an encapsulation of these ambiguities.[37] In 1952, amidst much negative criticism of the chanchada and its major producer Atlantida, a film appropriately entitled *Carnaval Atlantida* responded to such charges by proposing a model of cinema based on sublime debauchery and carnivalesque irony. The subject of *Carnaval Atlantida* is filmmaking itself and, more specifically, the inappropriateness of the Hollywood model for Brazil. The film director within the film, Cecilio B. De Milho (Cecil B. De Corn), abandons his plan for an epic superproduction of the story of Helen of Troy, implicitly recognizing that the conditions of national cinema are not propitious for a serious film on a grand scale. The Hollywood-dictated standards for the genre—ostentatious sets and the proverbial cast of thousands—simply were not feasible in an underdeveloped country. Against the overreaching De Milho, other characters argue for a more popular, less lofty adaptation of the story, recommending that the director discard the proposed epic in favor of a carnival film. De Milho cedes to popular pressure, but insists on the right to make the epic version "later"—that is, when Brazilian cinema will have acquired the technical means and financial resources to produce such films. For the present, however, Helen of Troy can appear only in carnivalesque guise.

One sequence, in which De Milho explains his conception of the proposed *Helen of Troy,* demonstrates the Brazilian internalization of Hollywood standards: the set, a precariously constructed Greek palace, is heavy and artificial, and the actors' gestures are theatrical. The producer's elitist vision is then contrasted with the point of view of two studio janitors, interpreted by black actors Colé and Grande Otelo. Through their eyes we move from De Milho's "scene" to the scene as they imagine it. The black singer Blecaute (Blackout) appears dressed in Greek costume singing "Dona Cegonha," a carnival song written for that year's celebration, accompanied by Grande Otelo tripping over his toga. Serious European themes, then, had to be relocated within the context of Brazilian carnival. *"Helen of Troy* won't work," De Milho is told, "the people want to dance and move." *Carnaval Atlantida* thus traces the fecund interrelationships between parody, chanchada, and carnival, suggesting a compensatory mechanism that guarantees popular success in a foreign-dominated market.

Vieira discusses two other chanchada parodies from the early fifties: Carlos Manga's *Nem Sansão nem Dalila* (Neither Samson nor Delilah, 1954) and *Matar ou Correr* (To Kill or to Run, 1954). The former film parodies the Cecil B. De Mille blockbuster, an enormous financial success in Brazil in the early fifties. As Vieira points out, the film allegorizes the relation between American and Brazilian cinema, and the mediating role of parody, in the form of a prop. In contrast to the original, where the strength of Samson (Victor Mature) derives from his natural hair, in the parody it derives from a wig. The Brazilian parody, it is implied, is to Hollywood superproductions as a cheap wig is to the natural hair of the American star. The "natural" strength of the hair metaphorizes the power of a developed film industry linked to the internal mechanisms of a powerful economy, in opposition to the simulated strength of an accessory, derivative, dominated cinema. At the same time, the wig, as one of the favored costume devices of carnival revelers, evokes an organic element within the language of Brazilian carnival.

Carlos Manga's other parody, *Matar ou Correr,* spoofs Fred Zinneman's *High Noon* (1952), which in Portuguese bore the title *Matar ou Morrer* (To Kill or to Die). *Matar ou Correr* respects the integrity of its model, locating its parody exclusively in the comic chanchada figures of Grande Otelo and Oscarito, treated as two ridiculous but sympathetic Brazilians lost in the heroic world of the western. All the other characters—the ingénue, the saloon singer, the villain—act according to the conventional pattern; only the "Brazilian" characters, visitors from the carnivalesque world of the chanchada, refuse to conform to the conventions of generic representation. The character impersonated by Grande Otelo, Ciscocada (in Portuguese a play on "Cisco Kid" and "coconut candy"), is made instantly laughable in his overlarge furry calfskin pants, which are visibly disproportionate to his modest stature. The figure of Oscarito, as Kid Bolha (Kid Bubble), the appointed sheriff of "City Down," lacks the courage and dignity of his prototype, the Gary Cooper figure in *High Noon*. After a career as a charlatan, he is appointed sheriff by mere chance rather than through legitimate strength or intelligence. He is a complete tabula rasa in the survival codes of the western—fighting, shooting, and even mounting a horse. When he learns that the villain is arriving on the two o'clock train, he collapses in fear and invokes the aid of his departed mother. And in the climactic duel, he is unable to draw his pistols and ultimately hits the villain through sheer chance.

Apart from the characterological parody of comic epic, *Matar ou Correr* also introduces other deconstructive devices. The film's initial intertitles, for example, alert us to imminent anachronisms, a sharp departure from the affectation of historical realism of the conventional western. A text, superimposed over a simplified drawing of Rio's celebrated cityscape, reads:

This picture was shot at a certain place in the West, at an unspecified time. In order to make our work easier, and to facilitate the work of the actors and the public's understanding, the language spoken in the film is doubtless Portuguese. We have maintained, however, the local expression *Waltzung,* meaning everything is fine, OK, wonderful.

This Jarryesque foregrounding of the linguistic improbability of the text anticipates other reflexive devices in the film, the most telling of which is Kid Bolha's desperate attempt to delay "high noon" by pulling back the hands of the clock. This direct citation of a distinctive feature of the original—its posited equivalence between fictional (story) time and screen (discourse) time—mocks the model's narrative strategies and deconstructs the spatiotemporal coordinates of mimetic representation.

There is no place here to review all the parodic films examined by Vieira in his excellent study. They include *A Banana Mecanica* (The Mechanical Banana, 1973), a partial parody that took commercial advantage of the furor created by the anticipated Brazilian censorship of Kubrik's *Clockwork Orange*; *Nos Tempos da Vasolina* (Back in the Time of Vaseline, 1979), a parody of *Grease* (called in Portuguese "Back in the Time of Brilhantine"); *Bacalhau* (Codfish, 1976), a parody of *Jaws*; *O Jeca Contra o Capeta* (The Country Bumpkin against the Devil, 1926), a parody of *The Exorcist*; *Costinha e o King-Mong* (Costinha and King Mong, 1977), a parody of Dino de Laurentis's *King Kong*; and *E.Teia a Mulher do Extraterrestre em Sua Aventura no Rio de Janeiro* (Mrs. E.T., the Wife of the Extraterrestrial, and Her Adventure in Rio de Janeiro, 1984), a parody of Spielberg's *E.T.* Most of these recent parodies, symptomatically, take as their object Hollywood "high-tech" superspectacles. Unlike other arts such as literature or painting, which are only indirectly affected by neocolonial hegemony, cinema by its very nature entails direct involvement with an advanced technology that is usually monopolized by the metropolitan countries. The fascination that these exhibitions of omnipotent technology exert on Brazilians is reflected in the fact that other successful Hollywood films that happened not to be superproductions were not parodied. The aim of the high-tech parodies, in any case, is to seize the box-office leftovers of dominant cinema, which places them in a parasitic and shadowy relation to their prototypes. At the same time, they direct cathartic laughter against dominant cinema, resulting in a kind of purifying practice or aesthetic exorcism similar to that achieved by the rituals of inversion studied by anthropologists. Generally, the high-tech parodies missed their chance to critique the aesthetics and politics of Hollywood and thus renovate film language while forming a new audience that would be able to deconstruct and critically rework the canonized forms of spectatorial fascination.

Commercial Brazilian films, while perhaps marginal in relation to Hollywood, constituted the mainstream, at least through the fifties, within Brazil itself. In the early sixties, the Cinema Novo movement declared its opposition both to the dominant foreign model and to commercial Brazilian cinema. Seeing itself as the avant-gardist voice of Third World alterity, Cinema Novo discarded the carnivalesque good humor of the chanchada in favor of a didactic practice that attempted to transform a negative condition—peripheral underdevelopment—into a positive source of signification. Instead of the pleasurable indulgences of carnival, Cinema Novo proposed an "aesthetic of hunger" and a kind of pedagogic displeasure in the service of political consciousness. In its wish to make a definitive break with Hollywood alienation, however, Cinema Novo at times threw out the baby of pleasure with the bathwater of imperialism and thus lost contact with its public.

Only in its "cannibal-tropicalist" phase in the late sixties did Brazilian cinema rediscover carnival and parody. The cultural movement called tropicalism, which emerged in the late sixties, drew inspiration from the Brazilian modernist movement of the twenties—a modernism that, unlike its European counterpart, fused political nationalism with aesthetic internationalism—and especially from Oswald de Andrade's notion of "anthropophagy" as metaphorically applied to cultural products. The twenties "anthropophagy," as consumed and recycled for the sixties, implied a transcendence of Cinema Novo's Manichean opposition between "authentic Brazilian cinema" and "Hollywood alienation." Tropicalism, as it was expressed in the theatre, music, and cinema, aggressively mingled the folkloric and the industrial, the native and the foreign. Its favored technique was what Bakhtin would have called "textual polyphony"—that is, the aggressive collage of discourses, the result of an anthropophagic devouring of all cultural stimuli in all their heterogeneity.

As exploited by the Brazilian modernists, the cannibalist metaphor had a positive and negative pole. The positive pole posited aboriginal matriarchy and communalism as utopian model. "The Indian," Oswald de Andrade wrote, "had no police, no repression, no nervous disorders, no shame at being nude, no class struggle, no slavery."[38] Synthesizing insights from Montaigne, Nietzsche, Marx, and Freud, Oswald de Andrade saw indigenous society as offering a more adequate model of social behavior, especially in terms of the full enjoyment of leisure. Playing with the Portuguese word *negocio* (business), but literally with *neg-ocio,* or the negation of leisure, de Andrade offered a proto-Marcusean encomium to leisurely pleasure that was rooted in his knowledge and theorization of indigenous society.[39] Here again we find the literalization, in Brazil, of the metaphors of the European avant-garde. While the Dadaists called for "progressive unemployment," and Breton's surrealist "rules" forbade regular work, Brazilian artist-intellectuals could point to existing indigenous societies that were quite free from work, in the occidental sense, and from coercive power.[40] The negative pole of the cannibalist metaphor, meanwhile, made cannibalism a critical instrument for exposing the exploitative social Darwinism of bourgeois society. The two poles complement each other, of course, in the sense that the cannibalism-as-critique motif contemplates the melancholy distance separating contemporary society from the imagined ideal communitas of the Amerindian. "At the heart of every utopia," Oswald de Andrade wrote, "there is not only a dream but also a protest."[41]

Of the two poles of the cannibalist metaphor, Joaquim Pedro de Andrade's 1969 adaptation of *Macunaíma* clearly emphasizes the negative pole. Fusing what he knew of Oswald de Andrade's anthropophagical movement with the theme of cannibalism that runs through the Mario de Andrade novel, the director turns the theme of cannibalism into a springboard for a critique of repressive military rule and of the predatory capitalist model of the short-lived Brazilian "economic miracle." In a preface written to accompany the film at the Venice Film Festival, the director offered a kind of cannibalistic hermeneutic to help spectators decode the Rabelaisian "parole gelées" of the film:

Cannibalism is an exemplary mode of consumerism adopted by under-developed peoples. . . . The traditionally dominant, conservative social classes continue their control of the power structure—and we rediscover cannibalism. . . . The present work relationships, as well as the relationships between people—social, political, and economic—are still, basically, cannibalistic. Those who can, "eat" others through their consumption of products, or even more directly in sexual relationships. Cannibalism has merely institutionalized and cleverly disguised itself. . . . Meanwhile, voraciously, nations devour their people. *Macunaíma* . . . is the story of a Brazilian devoured by Brazil.

The cannibalist theme is treated in all its variations: people so hungry they eat themselves; an ogre who offers Macunaíma a piece of his leg; the urban guerrilla who devours him sexually; the cannibal-giant-capitalist Pietro Pietra with his anthropophagous soup; the capitalist's wife, who wants to eat him alive; and finally the man-eating siren who lures him to his death. We see the rich devouring the poor, and the poor, in desperation, devouring each other. The left, meanwhile, while being devoured by the right, purifies itself by eating itself, a practice that Joaquim Pedro de Andrade calls the "cannibalism of the weak."[42]

Despite the grim underlying message of its allegory, in terms of aesthetic strategy *Macunaíma* renewed Brazilian cinema's contact with the world of carnival and the chanchada. This renewed contact takes many forms in the film, most notably through the casting of key chanchada actors like Grande Otelo and Zeze Macedo, but also through the inclusion of songs that were popular in the chanchada period. The socially conscious recycling of chanchada strategies enabled *Macunaíma* to realize a goal that had long been inaccessible to Cinema Novo directors—the reconciliation of political and aesthetic avant-gardism with popular appeal. But the film rejected the implicitly rosy social vision of the chanchada by refusing the shallow utopianism of the chanchada's conventional happy ending. In *Macunaíma,* the ideal of the hustler-trickster-hero typical of the chanchada is revealed to be empty, a social dead end.

Like its source-novel, *Macunaíma* offers many of the features that are associated with carnivalization and Menippean satire. The first narrated words (in both film and novel)—"In the depths of the virgin forest was born Macunaíma, hero of his people"—signal entry into the carnivalized world of comic epic. The images convey what Bakhtin calls "the grotesque body of the people." We see an improbably old white woman (played by a man) stand and grunt until she/he deposits a wailing fifty-year-old black "baby" on the ground. The expression on the "mother's" face recalls Bakhtin's description of the grotesque body in Rabelais: "The gaping mouth, the protruding eyes, sweat, trembling, suffocation, the swollen face— all these are typical symptoms of the grotesque life of the body: here they have the meaning of the act of birth."[43] The hero is virtually shat into existence, rather like Gargantua, born during a maternal bout of severe diarrhea, since his mother had eaten "too much tripe." Here we find as well the "violent contrasts" of the Menippea: the man/woman "mother" (reminiscent of Bakhtin's favored image the "pregnant hag"), the adult "baby," the black/white "family." The birth itself, at once prodigious and grotesque, encapsulates what Bakhtin sees as a privileged carnival image: the old, near death, giving birth to the new.

The décor and costumes, meanwhile, are oxymoronic and syncretic. The hut that serves as maternity ward is half-backlander and half-Indian, while the manner of giving birth, in a standing position to take advantage of gravity, is Indian. The names are Indian, but the family itself is at once black, Indian, and European. At the same time, the institution of the family is desentimentalized and comically degraded. Instead of the usual exclamations at the newborn's "cuteness," the family reacts to the hero's birth with "How ugly!" and "He stinks!" The film further underlines the surrealist nature of this family by having the same actor (Paulo José) play both the original "mother" of Macunaíma and Macunaíma himself (in his later, white incarnation), while another actor (Grande Otelo) plays both the first and the second black Macunaíma. Thus the white Macunaíma gives birth to the black Macunaíma who is magically transformed into the white Macunaíma who marries Ci the guerrilla and thus fathers the original black Macunaíma.

The logic of carnival is that of the world turned upside down, in which the powerful are mocked and ridiculous kings are enthroned and then dethroned in an atmosphere of gay relativity. The film proliferates in the sexual inversions that are common in carnivalesque literature and in carnival itself: Paulo José in drag giving birth to the protagonist; Macunaíma costumed as a French divorcée to trick the cannibal-giant; and the giant himself in the kind of Hollywood bubble bath usually reserved for starlets. The Ubuesque industrial magnate and people-eater Pietro Pietra is the most powerful figure in *Macunaíma,* and he too is dethroned. In his purple smoking jacket, with green boxer shorts covering his padded buttocks, he looks very much like the "Rei Momo," the burlesque Lord of the Revels in Brazil's carnival. Graced with multinational names and an Italian accent, the figure of Pietro Pietra refers in the novel to the Italian *nouveau riche* families of the twenties and in the film to the dependent national bourgeoisie with its secondhand American technology. Pietro lives in the hybrid vulgarity of a kitsch palace where rococo clocks and breathing mannequins cohabit with Egyptian sphinxes. He struggles with Macunaíma over an amulet—an amulet whose traditional folkloric role was to guarantee fishing and hunting (i.e., prosperity). As a millionaire who wants to eat Macunaíma, the hero of his people, the figure of Pietro alludes to all the "multinational" economic giants who want to devour Brazil and its resources. But even Macunaíma, though he defeats Pietro and wins the amulet, is enthroned and then dethroned. After feeling the "immense satisfaction" of defeating the giant, he dissipates his advantage by returning to the jungle with the useless electronic bric-a-brac of consumer civilization.

The "cheerful death" of Menippean satire, Bakhtin claims, is "always surrounded by food, drink, sexual indecencies and symbols of conception and fertility."[44] Two sequences in *Macunaíma* especially encapsulate the spirit of what Bakhtin calls "cultic indecency." One is the sumptuous banquet-wake for Macunaíma's mother. As the family gorges itself and wails for the departed mother, we see Macunaíma being "consoled" by Sofara, his brother's girlfriend, whose ass the "child" begins to stroke lustily, thus illustrating what Bakhtin calls the "tight matrix of death with laughter, with food, with drink, with sexual indecency."[45] The other sequence features a party given by Pietro Pietra in celebration of his daughter's wedding, for which the cannibalistically inclined Pietra has devised a festive game, a lottery in which the winners are thrown into a pool of fragmented bodies and voracious piranha fish. A close look at the pool reveals it to be an anthropophagic *feijoada* (the Brazilian national dish, invented during slavery, consisting of sauce, black beans, and sausage), in which human blood and limbs stand in for sauce and sausage. Macunaíma tricks Pietro into falling in, and as he is being devoured, the cheerfully dying giant shouts that the feijoada needs more salt.

Macunaíma was predictably censured by some critics for its "bad taste," an irrelevant category for a carnivalesque aesthetic since it invokes exactly what is being derided. The director himself said that the film was intended to be in "execrable taste . . . innocently filthy like the jokes of children." But however grotesque or fantastic, the carnivalesque aesthetic retains a commitment to a certain realism that addresses everyday life and contemporary events. Menippean satire, as the "journalistic" genre of antiquity, was forever engaging in contemporary polemics. The novel *Macunaíma* mocks São Paulo's politicians and *nouveau riche,* as well as the literary pretensions of the Brazilian "Parnassians," while the film lampoons a host of satirical targets: the political repression triggered by the 1968 "coup-within-the-coup" ("Suspicious attitude," explains the plainclothesman as he arrests Macunaíma); structural racism (explaining why the black brother Jigue was a singled out for arrest, the white Manaape reminds him that "a white man running is a champion; a black man running is a thief"); and the rampant consumerism inherent in the Brazilian economic model, the absurdity of which is emphasized by its uselessness in the Amazon jungle.

As Randal Johnson points out in his illuminating study of *Macunaíma,* Joaquim Pedro de Andrade consistently "actualizes" and "cinematizes" the source-novel.[46] The character Ci, an Amazonian warrior in the novel—who, having sampled Macunaíma's "play," cannot stop making love—is transformed by the film into a sexual activist and urban guerrilla equipped with all the requisite paraphernalia: a ditto machine for leaflets; material for making bombs; and money, presumably the booty from the bank robberies then practiced by the far left. The film also "cinematizes" the parodic elements of the novel, transferring them to a filmic-intertextual level. When the black Macunaíma enters a magic fountain that turns him white, the soundtrack plays the Portuguese version of "By a Waterfall," taken from the Lloyd Bacon musical *Footlight Parade* (1933), a film whose musical numbers were directed by Busby Berkeley. The choice seems especially apt when we recall that the original diegetic inspiration for the "By a Waterfall" number was black children playing with the water spurting from a Harlem hydrant, a sight that suggests to the James Cagney character the spectacular possibilities of waterfalls splashing on white bodies. The allusion is richly suggestive, evoking not only a complex play of black and white but also the relation between the American musical comedy and Brazil's carnivalized imitations of them in the chanchada, the genre in which Grande Otelo, the black actor who plays Macunaíma, was the most famous star.[47]

Macunaíma appealed to the anarchistic sentiments of the Brazilian people, nourishing feelings of revolt through satirical festivity even at the height of the political repression. The film established a tangential relation with the tropicalist movement—through its anthropophagic theme and technique, in its emphasis on camp and the lack of national character, and in its mélange of high-art tradition and mass-mediated culture—but its ultimate allegiance was with the allegorical strategies of Cinema Novo, with its desire to make a broadly metaphorical critique of the Brazilian situation, but performed here with an oblique humor and cunning that caught even the censors off guard.

Other filmmakers were more aggressive. At the same time that Cinema Novo entered its "tropicalist" phase, an alternative underground cinema emerged. While Brazilian commercial cinema was by definition on the margins of hegemonic cinema, and while Cinema Novo was on the margins of commercial cinema, the underground cinema was, as it were, on the outskirts of the margins. Not only were these films made in a "marginal" area of the city—the low-life district of São Paulo known as "Boca do Lixo" (mouth of garbage)—but they also featured marginal characters. As Cinema Novo moved toward relatively big-budget, "quality" films, the underground rejected well-made cinema in favor of a "dirty screen" and "garbage aesthetics." The "garbage" metaphor, as Brazilian critic Ismail Xavier points out, expressed an aggressive sense of marginality, the sense of a marginal culture condemned to recycle the materials of a dominant one.[48] A "garbage style" for the underground was the style most appropriate to a Third World country picking through the mass-mediated leavings of an international system dominated by First World monopoly capitalism.

Underground cinema practiced what Aimé Cesaire, in another context, called a "neologistic" cultural politics—that is, an improvisational collage strategy that called attention to an "existence among fragments" and that mingled local performances with foreign media and symbols. Parodic intertextuality played a key role in many of the underground films. I will discuss here only a few representative examples. Rogerio Sganzerla's *Bandido da Luz Vermelha* (Red-Light Bandit, 1968), a seminal independent production, outlines the rise and fall of a famous outlaw mythologized by the mass media. Sganzerla shows an anthropophagic openness to all intertextual influences, including those of Hollywood and the mass media. Rejecting what he sees as Cinema Novo's purism, Sganzerla deploys Hollywood against Hollywood through tactics of generic conflation and discursive collage in a manner that would later be called "postmodern." Sganzerla himself was quite explicit about this tactic, in interviews, calling the film a "film-summa, a western, a musical documentary, detective story, chanchada, and science fiction." Such an improbable collage of incompatible genres turns the film into a polyphonic compilation of pastiches, a kind of cinematic writing in quotation marks that is akin to Bakhtin's "mutual illumination of languages."

Bandido da Luz Vermelha posits a homology, as Ismail Xavier points out, between a red-light district in a Third World country as a "realm of garbage" and the text itself as a collection of film and mass-media refuse. The garbage-as-random-assortment-collage principle works both "horizontally," through the forced contiguity of heterogeneous and mutually relativizing discourses, and "vertically," through the superimposition, at the same syntagmatic point, of multiple elements—for example, through the overlaying of voice-over narration with multiple sources of music playing simultaneously. Typifying this strategy, the film's soundtrack literalizes polyphony by mixing a wide range of musical materials: Hollywood program music, classical compositions, symphonic pieces, Brazilian and American camp materials. Beethoven's Fifth Symphony coincides with the Brazilian folksong "Asa Branca" in a provocative leveling of high-classical and "low"-folkloric art. This leveling is but one of the many ways in which *Bandido da Luz Vermelha* modifies and transforms one of the favored aesthetic procedures of Cinema Novo—the erudite elaboration of popular culture—by promiscuously mingling, in a chaotic heteroglossia, the languages of city and country, metropole and periphery, and thus causing a carnivalesque overturning of hierarchies, a condensation of modes of discourse that are usually thought to be separate.

Artur Omar's *Triste Tropico* (1974), a kind of parodic anthropological "fictive documentary"—which antedates Woody Allen's comparable generic amalgam, *Zelig,* by almost a decade—plays with the idea of marginality in a different way. Its title, transparently inspired by Lèvi-Strauss's ethnographic memoir about Brazil, triggers an evocative chain of cultural associations. While Lèvi-Strauss went from Europe to Brazil only to discover the ethnocentric prejudices of Europe, the human subject of *Triste Tropico* goes to Europe—and here his trajectory parallels that of innumerable Brazilian artists and intellectuals—only to discover Brazil. Thus the film inserts itself into the perennial discussion of Brazil's problematic relationship to Europe (its colonizing mother), a discussion that is ever undergoing changes of etiquette: "nationalism," "modernism," "tropicalism." *Triste Tropico* is not a tropicalist film, however; it is rather a distanced reflection on the whole notion of the "tropics" as Europe's other, as something "exotic."

Triste Tropics touches on the two tropes—"carnivalism" and "cannibalism"—orienting our discussion. Its opening shots—traffic in São Paulo, old photographs, carnival in Rio—make us expect a fairly innocuous documentary. An off-screen narrator, speaking in the confident tone and stilted language to which documentaries have accustomed us, tells us that the film concerns a certain Arthur Alvaro de Noronha, known as Dr. Arthur, who returned from studies in Paris to practice medicine in Brazil. In Paris, we are told, the doctor became friendly with André Breton, Paul Eluard, and Max Ernst, our first clue that a truly surrealist biography awaits us. As the film continues, the narration becomes progressively more improbable and hallucinatory. The doctor becomes involved with Indians, compiles an almanac of herbal panaceas, becomes an indigenous Messiah, and finally degenerates into a practitioner of sodomy (an exclamatory intertitle underlines the horror!) and cannibalism. At the same time, the images progressively detach themselves from the narration, becoming less and less illustrative and more and more chaotic and apocalyptic. We begin to suspect that we have been the dupes of an immense joke, as if Borges had slyly rewritten Conrad's *Heart of Darkness,* and that the illustrious Dr. Arthur is merely the figment of the imagination of the director, whose name, we recall, also is Arthur.

The central procedure of *Triste Tropico* is to superimpose an impeccably linear (albeit absurd) narration on extremely discontinuous sonorous and imagistic materials—a chaotic anthology of Brazilian, American, Argentinian, and Cuban music superimposed on amateur movies from the twenties, contemporary footage from Europe, shots of Rio's carnival, staged scenes, archival material, clips from other fiction films, engravings, almanac illustrations. Within this audiovisual *bricolage* we encounter certain Lèvi-Straussian binary oppositions—some specifically cinematic (black/white versus color, old footage versus new), some broadly cultural (coast versus interior, "raw" Brazil versus "cooked" Europe, classical Apollonian order versus Dionysian carnivalesque frenzy, *la pensée sauvage* versus *la pensée civilisee*).

The same method of ironic hybridization serves equally well in Julio Bressane's *Tabu* (Taboo, 1982), a film that continues the author's project, initiated in his earlier films, of "transvaluating" the codes of the chanchada. Bressane posits a hypothetical meeting between popular twenties composer Lamartine Babo and modernist Oswald de Andrade, played by Colé, the chanchada veteran familiar to us from *Carnaval Atlantida*. Lamartine Babo here invokes the spirit of popular culture and carnival (a point underlined by the casting of popular singer-composer Caetano Veloso to incarnate the role), while de Andrade embodies the erudite avant-garde theorization and elaboration of popular culture. This suggestive structural mechanism allows Bressane to place in correlation, through a kind of retrospective rapprochement or Bakhtinian "dialogue of the dead," the popular carnival music of Rio and the erudite literary vanguardism of São Paulo. At the same time, the film elegiacally celebrates the Rio of the thirties as a utopian tropical paradise by associating it with interpolated footage from Murnau's *Tabu*. One remarkable audiovisual montage superimposes a carnival song about the daily chores of fishermen, delivered by chanchada star Emilinha Borba, on Murnau's images of natives dancing in Tahiti. By spreading the spirit of carnival to the South Pacific, in a kind of joyful heterotopian contamination, Bressane demonstrates, once again, the inexhaustible suggestiveness of a tradition that is rooted in anthropophagic modernism and its latter-day incarnation, tropicalism.

The seventies and eighties have witnessed a kind of "recarnivalization" of Brazilian cinema, not only as a key trope orienting the filmmakers' conception of their own production, but also as a means of renewing contact with the popular audience. Carnival, and Rio's "samba schools," form a quite literal presence in Walter Lima Jr.'s *Lira do Delirio* (Delicious Lyre, 1978), Vera Figueredo's *Samba da Criação do Mundo* (Samba of the Creation of the World, 1979), and Glauber Rocha's *Idade da Terra* (Age of the Earth, 1980). Paulo Cesar Saraceni's *Natal de Portella* (1988) chronicles the career of one of the historic founders of one of Rio's samba schools. In other cases, carnival forms part of the wider circulation of popular and erudite culture. The stories of Diegues's *Xica da Silva* (1976) and Walter Lima Jr.'s *Chico Rei* (1982), for example, were first presented as samba-school pageants for Rio's carnival. Indeed, Diegues has said that he conceived both *Xica da Silva* and *Quilombo* (1984) as *samba-enredos* (samba-narratives)—that is, as analogous in their procedures to the collections of songs, dances, costumes, and lyrics that form part of the popular narrative form known as a samba-school presentation. Fernando Cony Campos's *Ladrões de Cinema* (Cinema Thieves, 1977), meanwhile, foregrounds this analogy by having his marginalized *favelado* protagonists steal filmmaking equipment from American tourists visiting Rio's carnival. The *favelados* conceive the film they plan to make—concerning an abortive Brazilian revolt against Portuguese colonialism—as a kind of samba-school narration.

In the films of the seventies and eighties, carnival becomes a kind of emblem of national identity, a culturally rooted master trope crystallizing a richly syncretic culture that still has a place for an orgiastic ritual that is at once sacred and profane. For the Cinema Novo veterans, the reaffirmation of carnival signifies a retreat from the old puritanical-leftist equation of party/festivity with escapist alienation, a tendency found, for example, in *Cinco Vezes Favela* (Five Times Favela, 1962), where the popular classes were exhorted to abandon the samba in favor of union militancy. But this "rediscovery" of carnival has its own ambiguities. At its best, this strategy leads to a popular yet didactic cinema that fuses social critique with carnival-style joy. At its most innocuous, it turns into the complacent affirmation of presumed Brazilian traits, eliding real conflicts in favor of the celebration of the "cordiality" of the fun-loving Brazilian. At its worst, its superficial view of carnival celebrates the Brazilian capacity for political conciliation, mocked by Glauber Rocha as the historical tendency for the now repentant right to hold hands again with the now well behaved left while "tudo acaba em samba" (everything ends in the samba). For Bakhtin, carnival is conflictual; while festive, it can also be angry. But in the apolitical Brazilian carnival films, the happy togetherness of the party forms the utopian horizon of a cinema that has one eye on the samba and the other on the box office.

We have examined a historically evolving constellation of possible strategies—cannibalistic and carnivalistic—for a marginalized cinema—in this case the Brazilian—in search of a language at once accessible, innovative, and deconstructive. The challenge for such filmmakers is, while acknowledging the scarcity of means generated by economic underdevelopment, to offer an aesthetic strategy that is appropriate to this reality and congenial with the culture, so as to make the work a critical response to, rather than merely a symptom of, underdevelopment. Virtually all the films discussed here can be seen as comic versions of what Ismail Xavier calls "allegories of underdevelopment." The chanchada parodies, for example, allegorize a cruel proportion of power: Oscarito's wig to Victor Mature's hair (in *Nem Sansão nem Dalila*), Carlos Manga's parodic cat (in the logo preceding *Matar ou Correr*) to MGM's lion; Cape Carnival (in Victor Lima's *Os Cosmonautas*) to Cape Canaveral; cruzeiro to dollar (in "The Six Million Cruzeiro Man"); and codfish to shark (in *Bacalhau*). At their best, the parodies challenge this proportion as neither inevitable nor eternal but historical.

The avant-garde films, meanwhile, also take as their point of departure the widespread penetration of dominant cinema within Brazil. They orchestrate their orgies of clashing allusions and citations not in a spirit of reverential homage but in an impulse of creative disrespect and irreverence. Their hybridization of incompatible materials produces a textual heterotopia in which antagonistic generic strands mutually critique and relativize one another. Within this textual polyglossia, to return to Bakhtin's term, the dominant cinema is made to war against itself, while the Brazilian magister ludi stands aside and ironizes. The double-consciousness of these artists, their awareness that life on the periphery passes both "here" and "elsewhere," generates a double-voiced discourse. This double-voicedness is implicit in the modernist trope of anthropophagy, of devouring the foreign, the alien word, in order to affirm the national. At the same time, these artists do not portray a situation of cultural passivity. They are deeply aware of the resistance culture that is rooted in "lo real maravilloso americano." Indeed, many of the critical phrases associated with the contemporary Renaissance within Latin American art—"magical realism," "quotidian surreality"—not only assert an alternative culture but also suggest the inadequacy of the high-mimetic European tradition for the expressive needs of an oppressed but polyphonic culture.

Parody, Hegel argued, emerges when artists outgrow conventions and are ready to dissociate themselves from the past. For Marx, history itself is susceptible to parodic repetition, as he suggests in his celebrated aphorism that history repeats itself, the first time as tragedy and the second time as farce. Or, to take the Bakhtinian formulation, parody is "humanity saying goodbye to the dead past with a laugh." To the temporal historicizing critique inherent in parody, Latin American artists add a spatial, even geographical, dimension emphasizing the inappropriateness, the out-of-placeness of metropolitan models that are nonetheless omnipresent. (The trope of marginality, in the end, is a Eurocentric misnomer, since life is lived centrally wherever there are human subjects.) Brazilian cinema, for its part, has often been most effective when it has been most outrageous, when it has drawn on the deep traditions of carnival's "gay relativity" and thus managed to touch something deep in the Brazilian cultural unconscious.

The kinds of films we have been discussing here have historically been the object of a multiplicity of superimposed prejudices—against comedy as an "inferior" form (a prejudice traceable at least as far back as Aristotle); against parody (seen as parasitic and derivative); against punning (as the "lowest form of humor"); against generic impurity and leveling (seen by the conservative critic as portending an ominous leveling within society itself); against physicality and what Bakhtin calls the "material bodily stratum"; against sexuality (seen as animalistic and degrading); and, more subtly, against the lower-class popular audience. These prejudices have in common the notion of higher/lower, superior/inferior, a complex set of homologies linking parallel hierarchizations traversing issues of corporality, class, and genre. In this sense, our argument has itself been carnivalesque, operating a dislocation in the analysis away from what had been considered paradigmatic in favor of marginal or critically devalued forms. Thus, in a typically Bakhtinian gesture, we have relegated the established center to the margins of our concern and enthroned what was regarded as marginal, making it the critical center.

The Grotesque Body and Cinematic Eroticism

In *Rabelais and His World,* Bakhtin developed his view of the "grotesque body" and "the material bodily lower stratum." For Rabelais, Bakhtin argues, the key elements of the body are those points at which it outgrows itself and transgresses its own limits, those places where "the confines between bodies and between the body and the world are overcome," where "there is an interchange and an interorientation":

Eating, drinking, defecation and other elimination (sweating, blowing of the nose, sneezing), as well as copulation, pregnancy, dismemberment, swallowing up by another body—all these acts are performed on the confines of the body and the outer world, or on the confines of the old and new body. In all these events the beginning and end of life are closely linked and interwoven.[1]

The aspects of the Rabelaisian body that Bakhtin emphasizes, then, have in common the fact that it is within them that the somatic membrane separating self from self and self from world becomes permeable. Bakhtin stresses the free interplay between the body and the world, as, for example, in the ingestion or expulsion of food. For Bakhtin, the body is a festival of becoming, a plurality, not a closed system but a perpetual experiment. (That Bakhtin spent much of his life as a cripple lends a special poignancy to his enthusiasm.) Bakhtin is fascinated by the unfinished body, the elastic, malleable body, the body that outgrows itself, that reaches beyond its own limits and conceives new bodies. He praises the body in movement, the body of Rabelais' Gargamelle, whose labor pains are indistinguishable from her bowel movements. He extols the active body, the sweating, farting, lubricating, defecating body, the body overcome by tragicomic seizures like sneezes and orgasms. He celebrates all the body's secretions, against a polite tradition for which the only mentionable secretions, as Stephen Greenblatt points out, were tears, and where even they were tolerated only in women.[2] Bakhtin's vision exalts the "base" products of the body: feces, urine, sperm, menstrual flow—in sum, all that has been banned from respectable representation because official decorum remains chained to a Manichean notion of the body's fundamental uncleanliness.

The view of the body developed by Bakhtin in *Rabelais and His World,* it goes without saying, was not designed to please the Soviet authorities. Originally presented as a dissertation, the text divided the Moscow scholarly community, and the State Accreditation Bureau ultimately denied Bakhtin his doctorate. Bakhtin's thesis, as Clark and Holquist point out, can be seen as a subtle Aesopian attack on the puritanical rigidities of Stalinism, its conservative aesthetic tastes, its fondness for "order and hierarchy." Bakhtin's dissertation carnivalized not only the ruling order but also the canonized forms of dissertation writing, usually designed to flatter the academic avatars of a repressive state educational apparatus. The very focus on Rabelais, the rhapsode of the delights of endless gluttony, creative obscenity, and indefatigable sexuality, already conveys a clear oppositional message. Rabelais' anticlericalism, within Bakhtin's hermeneutic allegory, was deployed as a weapon against Stalinist orthodoxy. With immense cunning, Bakhtin took officially consecrated Stalinist themes—the "people," "folk art," the oppressiveness of the church—and made them boomerang against Soviet officialdom. He deployed the same strategy of subversive co-optation or the "anthropophagic" devouring of dominant discourses that we have encountered elsewhere. In an atmosphere where the body was surrounded by interdiction, where all explicitly sexual or corporeal representation was dismissed as "naturalism" or "zoologism," Bakhtin dared to sing the body electric in all its glorious obscenity. In a superegoish climate where nonmainstream sexual practices were denounced as deviant manifestations of "bourgeois decadence," Bakhtin applauded human sexuality and the right to difference.

Against the static, classic, finished beauty of antique sculpture, Bakhtin counterposed the mutable body, the "passing of one form into another," reflecting the "ever incompleted character of being."[3] The body's central principle (like that of language) is growth and change; by exceeding its limits, the body expresses its essence. The grotesque body is not a rigid *langue,* but a *parole* in constant semiosis. As a shifting series of vortexes of energy, the site of unanchored polysemy and radical differentiality, the grotesque body is given to excess, and thus to the gigantism and hyperbole of its artistic forms—its outsized noses and swollen buttocks, and the masks that emphasize metamorphosis and the "violation of natural boundaries."[4] Bakhtin's view of the body is democratic and antihierarchical in terms of the relationship both between and within bodies. By calling attention to the paradoxical attractiveness of the grotesque body, Bakhtin rejects what might be called the "fascism of beauty," the construction of an ideal type or language of beauty in relation to which other types are seen as inferior "dialectal" variations.

The Bakhtinian view of the body is antihierarchical, furthermore, even in an intracorporeal sense. Bakhtin's leveling undoes binarisms and overturns hierarchies. He celebrates, for example, the inner body of the bowels, the intestines, and the blood as well as the outer body of "apertures and convexities," with its "various ramifications and offshoots: the open mouth, the genital organs, the breasts, the phallus, the potbelly, the nose."[5] Bakhtin also implicitly dehierarchizes the senses. While a strongly rooted and ideologically informed hierarchy places the "noble" sense of sight (etymologically linked to wisdom in innumerable languages) "over" the more "vulgar" senses of smell and taste (more obviously bodily and physical and thus more closely linked to the body and sexual pleasure), Bakhtin sees *all* the senses as equally noble and "positively" grotesque. In its undercutting of the hegemony of the visible, Bakhtin's thought accords very well with the feminism of Luce Iregaray, who argues that more than the other senses, the eye "objectifies and masters": "It sets at a distance, maintains the distance. In our culture, the predominance of the look over smell, taste, touch, hearing, has brought an impoverishment of bodily relations." Male sexuality, for Iregaray, contributes to the "disembodiment" and "dematerialization" of eroticism. Male sexuality becomes privileged both because it operates visually and because the male sex organ is visible.[6]

The life of the grotesque body, for Bakhtin, is marked by "three crucial moments of spasm": the spasms of birth, the spasms of orgasm, and the spasms of death. Traditional popular comic gestures and tricks, Bakhtin points out, recapitulate the three main acts in the life of the grotesque body: sexual intercourse, death throes (in their comic presentation—hanging tongue, expressionless popping eyes, suffocation, death rattle), and the act of birth. Frequently these three acts are transformed or merged into each other insofar as their exterior symptoms and expressions coincide (spasms, tensions, popping eyes, sweat, convulsions of arms and legs).[7]

What interests me here, apart from the rich artistic tradition invoked, is that Bakhtin always posits the life of the body, and especially sexuality, *in relation to something beyond itself,* here to the entire trajectory of human life. It is as if Bakhtin is incapable of mentioning any bodily process without immediately bringing in all the other bodily processes, in a "neighboring" that is at once spatial and temporal. "To concern oneself with the lower stratum of the body," he writes, with "the life of the belly and the reproductive organs . . . relates to acts of defecation and copulation, conception, pregnancy, and birth."[8] Or again, the body exceeds its own limits "in copulation, pregnancy, childbirth, the throes of death, eating, drinking, and defecation."[9] Bakhtin's emphasis on the ceaseless metamorphoses of death and renewal as a shared collective human reality has the further advantage, from a feminist perspective, of refusing to project male fear of death onto the imago of woman, of refusing the masculinist *non sequitur* of scapegoating women for a universal process.

Bakhtin found his concept of the grotesque embodied in the laughing pregnant old hags of the Kerch terra-cotta figurines, which "combine senile, decaying, and deformed flesh with the flesh of new life, conceived but as yet unformed." Such an image, as Mary Russo points out, is necessarily ambivalent for a feminist reader, since it comes with "the connotations of fear and loathing associated with the biological processes of reproduction and of aging."[10] At the same time, as Russo goes on to point out, Bakhtin's "description of these ancient crones is at least exuberant" and bathed in "communal hilarity" and points, by implication at least, to a new kind of cultural politics.

Bakhtin's attitude toward sexuality is inseparable from his attitude toward the body in general. Bakhtin rarely spoke of sexuality per se, but his attitudes can easily be inferred from his writings. He quotes with approval, for example, Montaigne's protest against puritanical prohibitions on sexual representations:

What harm has the genital act, so natural, so necessary, and so lawful, done to humanity, that we dare not speak of it without shame, and exclude it from serious and orderly conversation? We boldly utter the words *kill, rob, betray:* and the other we only dare mutter under our breath.[11]

But Bakhtin goes farther than Montaigne in linking the "genital act" to history and to the life of the larger social "body." Within class society, Bakhtin argues in "Forms of Time and Chronotope in the Novel," food, drink, and copulation "lose their ancient 'pathos' (their link, their unity with the laboring life of the social whole); they become a petty private matter; they seem to exhaust all their significance within the boundaries of individual life."[12] Bakhtin denounces, then, what might be called the "monadization" or "diadization" of eroticism. Nor is he especially interested in a hyper-refined and idealized "romantic love." When artistic fiction becomes preoccupied with "individual life-sequences," he suggests, it tends to develop the central motif of love as "the sublimated form of the sexual act and of fertility."[13]

Extrapolating from Bakhtin, we might see our contemporary views of love and sexuality as a kind of palimpsest, in which traces of archaic folk culture coexist with romantic, Victorian, and modern hygienic-functionalist formulations. Bakhtin never develops a sexualist discourse. Indeed, his refusal to speak of sex per se is itself significant and productive, having less to do with Stalinist censoriousness than with something central to Bakhtin's vision. Bakhtin's view of sexuality is above all paratactic; in his prose, all the nouns and verbs associated with the grotesque body and the lower stratum interfecundate along the same syntagmatic axis. The word *copulation,* for example, almost invariably comes accompanied by its close cousins—*defecation, urination, perspiration,* not to mention *pregnancy, childbirth, and death*. For Bakhtin, sexuality always exists in relation—in relation to the general existence of the body, in relation to other persons, and in relation to the "laboring life of the social whole." Rather than envision sexuality exclusively as a "genital act," as a series of isolating close-ups of body parts, Bakhtin sees sexuality as a broad, multi-centered canvas, a crowded Brueghelesque space teeming with the vital activities of the people. Sexuality per se is relativized and relationalized.

In "Freedom of Interpretation: Bakhtin and the Challenge of Feminist Criticism," Wayne Booth discourses on the relation between Rabelais' work, flawed as it is by a certain sexism, and Bakhtin's response to that work. Bakhtin, we may recall, claims that Rabelais is not hostile to women but rather shares with the "popular comic tradition" an "ambivalent attitude" toward women as representing the "material bodily lower stratum" that "degrades and regenerates simultaneously."[14] The problem, according to Booth, is that Bakhtin, like Rabelais, addresses himself largely to men; he assumes an exclusively male audience. What is still more problematic, Booth continues, is that Rabelais never even tries to imagine a woman's point of view or to incorporate women into a dialogue: "Nowhere in Bakhtin," Booth argues, "does one discover any suggestion that he sees the importance of this kind of monologue, not even when he discusses Rabelais' attitude toward women."[15]

I have no quarrel with the essential thrust of Booth's argument—despite a certain smug paternalism in its formulation—and I agree with Mary Russo's observation that Bakhtin "failed to incorporate the social relations of gender in his semiotic model of the body politic." Nevertheless, my emphasis here will be somewhat different. If we shift our focus from Rabelais per se to Rabelais *as seen by* Bakhtin, it strikes me that we encounter much that is, if not feminist, at least eminently compatible with feminism. Rather than privilege sexual difference *between* bodies, with the phallus as ultimate signifier, Bakhtin discerns difference *within* the body. (The body in its entirety, to use Freudian terminology, becomes an object of cathexis.) For Bakhtin, all bodies are self-differentiating; every body is a constantly expanding and contracting universe (a view that anticipates Cixous's "body without beginning and without end"). There is no privileging of the male term over the female, no positing of lack, no dynamism contrasted with atrophy, no exalted protuberance that lays down the law for all the lesser contours, no "triumphant contempt" for "mutilated creatures."

Bakhtin's view of the body is not phallocentric or even cephalocentric. He throws down, in this sense, the tyranny of head and phallus. Bakhtin privileges not only the genitals but also the bowels, the swallowing, devouring belly, the "gaping mouth" and the anus, corporeal zones quite neutral from the standpoint of sexual difference, zones where the male-female binary opposition becomes quite simply nonpertinent. By emphasizing the active body, Bakhtin by-passes the question of possession, of who has and who does not have. And by emphasizing the "inner body," Bakhtin stresses that which is common to both genders. Even his repeatedly paired terms *orifices* and *protuberances* disallow sexual monopoly or binary contrast, since both men and women have "orifices and protuberances." Here too the contrast with Lacan is striking. While for Lacan, object *A* is always "bound to the orifices of the body," something which the subject, "in order to constitute itself, has separated itself off as organ" and which "serves as a symbol of the lack," Bakhtin sees orifices not as symbols of lack but as openings, channels of communication.[16] Bakhtin's emphasis is on commonalities on the margins; his view of the body, like his view of the social formation, is, to put it oxymoronically, marginocentric.

Against a patriarchal ideology of innate difference, Bakhtin implicitly exalts the blurring and shifting of gender distinctions, a release from the boundaries of socially imposed sex roles. Bakhtin lauds the androgynous body of carnival representation. He cites, for example, the emblem gracing Gargantua's hat, portraying a body with two heads, four arms, a pair of asses, and a brace of sex organs, male and female. Bakhtin's account, in these terms, has certain affinities with Cixous's positing of the ideal of bisexuality, of a bisexual subject open to the circulation of multiple drives and desires, a bisexuality that does not annul differences but rather stirs them up and pursues them.

A corollary to the exaltation of androgyny, in Bakhtin's carnival, is the practice of transvestitism, of men dressing as women and women as men. Transvestitism per se is not necessarily progressive or feminist. It can be seen, as Mary Russo points out, as an ambivalent "acting out of the dilemmas of femininity."[17] On the one hand, transvestitism can be motivated by dreams of androgyny, parodying patriarchal dress, or operating what Kaja Silverman calls "male divestiture," the symbolic stripping away of masculine privilege. On the other, transvestitism can easily degenerate into misogynistic caricature. The point I would like to emphasize here, however, has to do with the relation between transvestitism and the historical evolution of codes of dress. J. C. Flugel, in *The Psychology of Clothes,* speaks of what he calls the "Great Masculine Renunciation," whereby male clothing underwent a kind of visual purification:

Men gave up their right to all the brighter, gayer, more elaborate, and more varied forms of ornamentation, leaving these entirely to the use of women, and thereby making their own tailoring the most austere and ascetic of arts. . . . Man abandoned his claim to be considered beautiful. He henceforth aimed at being only useful.[18]

Men's clothing, then, came to symbolize male devotion to the principles of duty, renunciation, and self-control. The "complement" of this masculine renunciation, as Kaja Silverman points out, was the specularization of women, the exclusive association of women with narcissism, ornament, and playfulness in clothing.[19] Carnival, in this sense, brings back the sartorial exuberance of an earlier, more festive time which allowed for the decorative, narcissistic, ludic aspects of male dress. Carnival gleefully specularizes *all* its celebrants, male and female, in a festivity that authorizes a general exhibitionism in the name of a common pleasure.

Now I in no way wish to conflate Bakhtin's views with those of recent theoretical feminists, nor am I unaware of the dangers of what Andrew Ross calls "libertine fantasies of mobility," of going beyond gender, fantasies whose utopian claims are ultimately premised on male power and privilege.[20] One might object, for example, that by calling attention to the shared processes of the inner body and to the commonalities between men and women, Bakhtin simply *elides* real differences within a false, implicitly masculinist universalization, refusing to acknowledge that even the inner body is lived differently by men than by women. (Quite apart from the overlay of ideological constructions that symbolically oppress women, the biological facts of menstruation, pregnancy, childbirth, and nursing, along with the social realities of patriarchal medicine and differential contraception, imply an inner-bodily life that is distinct.) My interest here, however, is less in theoretical positions on sexual difference than in affinities of sensibility and possibilities of rapprochement between Bakhtin and feminist, as well as feminine, discourses. A perusal of erotic writing by women—from the more high-brow work of Anais Nin to popular collections such as *Pleasures: Women Write Erotica* and *Erotic Interludes*—reveals certain intriguing coincidences of language and emphasis between Bakhtin's account of the grotesque body and the erotic body written about by women. Both Bakhtin and the women writers stress a kind of libidinal multiplicity and decentering; the geography of pleasure, for both, is seen as ranging over and within the entire body. Both are highly synesthetic in approach; just as Bakhtin dehierarchizes the senses, the women writers implicitly overthrow the primacy of sight (and thus of voyeurism), frequently appealing to the relatively neglected senses of smell, taste, touch, and hearing. Like Bakhtin, they stress the inner body, the "surge of blood," the "silent whorl" resonating through the body, the "subtle movements" of the corporeal "dance." The metaphors emphasize liquidity ("eddying currents," "melting away," "flesh streaming away," "passion flooding into pelvis") or electrical energy (buzzing current, radiating heat, "flutters of energy").

A number of the writers stress the dissolution of the very distinction between inner and outer; there is no longer inside and outside, but only a kind of mutual invagination. The emphasis, as in Bakhtin, is on the breaking down of walls ("she felt herself breaking apart . . . her body shattering, falling away, all of it cracking and falling away") or the transcendence of self ("I felt myself expand beyond the limits of my body") or on fusion ("melting together," "orgasmic blending," "there seemed to be no separation," and "they couldn't tell where her body stopped and his body began"). It was precisely this fear of loss of identity, Klaus Theweleit argues in *Male Fantasies,* that inspired the proto-Nazi "Freikorps" movement's pathological fear of women, seen as associated with a menacing liquidity, as flowing substance, as vaginal swamp and boiling flood. In "Strangers in the Universe," Signe Hammer describes this erotic blurring of borders:

I felt an opening outward begin, he was inside me but we were both inside the same skin, a great, mysterious cave, and then we were floating together in a vastness that rolled out to infinity. . . . We didn't know who was inside whom; we were both inside and there was no outside, we occupied all infinity and rolled together in it, our two heads like one planet orbiting a great sun that was somewhere inside the universe of our bodies.[21]

Although the language here is somewhat more haloed and rarefied than that favored by Bakhtin, certain secret complicities link the two discourses. Both Bakhtin and the women erotic writers stress what Bakhtin would call the "in-between" of persons, the dissolving of the walls of skin, "the melting of blood into a single, bright, liquid flame," the fire that consumes and destroys borders, the mutual ingestion of lovers, the "eroding flesh," the trespassing of boundaries, the "flowing out of the soul through the tongue." The writers speak of the erotic contagion, the impression that the erotic feeling would leak "out into the atmosphere and [make] people around us as happy as we were." Susan Griffin, in an eminently Bakhtinian phrase, speaks of the "radiance" and electricity in the "tiny invisible place between our bodies."[22] And Susan Block speaks of lovemaking as "breathing life into something between us that was somehow different from our cranky, lonely male and female selves . . . something utterly out of control."[23] Bakhtin and the women writers share, finally, a view of sexuality as "situated," an "ecological" sense of the importance of the environment of eroticism.

Although Bakhtin rarely spoke of eroticism per se and never, to my knowledge, spoke about the cinema, Bakhtin's thought, I would suggest, has a contribution to make to the contemporary debate surrounding cinematic eroticism and pornography. Imagining cinematic eroticism through Bakhtin can help us partially reframe a debate that too often lapses into the formulaic repetition of Manichean binarisms: bad porn versus good erotica; bad censorship versus good freedom; bad repression versus good hedonism. Bakhtin's categories can be enlisted in the service of a nonmoralistic critique of establishment pornography, a critique that does not invoke the retrograde and repressive notions of "good taste" and "seemly behavior." I would like to explore, then, in a necessarily speculative fashion, the relevance of Bakhtin's vision of the "grotesque body," and of "carnival" and the "carnivalesque," for erotic representations. What is the relevance of Bakhtinian "translinguistics" to the semiotics of sexuality and sexual discourse? How can Bakhtinian categories point to viable strategies for the critique—and more important the transvaluation—of cinematic eroticism?

One possible approach would be to retrospectively enlist Bakhtin in the defense of pornography as it is presently constituted. One taking such a position might argue that pornography constitutes a contemporary version of Bakhtin's "carnival," overthrowing puritanical taboos, fostering carnival's "free and familiar contact" and the promiscuous "intermingling of bodies." Within this perspective, the close-up attention to male and female genitalia shows carnival's predilection for the body's "lower bodily stratum." Zoom-ins to spread-eagled actresses pay homage to the "protuberances and orifices" of the body, and the privileging of male ejaculation, multiplied to surrealistic dissemination via optical tricks in films such as *Behind the Green Door,* provides a modernday equivalent to ancient seasonal rituals of fecundity.

Such an analysis, it goes without saying, does not convince even for a second. The analyst scrutinizing pornography within a Bakhtinian perspective is likely to say, "No, that is not what Bakhtin meant, not what he meant at all." A Bakhtinian defense of pornography in its dominant forms would be truly grotesque, and not in Bakhtin's positive sense of that word. While porn does level its characters to their sexual common denominator, this leveling hardly constitutes a carnivalesque overturning. Porn often seems more premised on puritanical taboos than antithetical to them; it has a vested interest in the prohibitions it purports to fight. Porn's "celebration" of the body usually amounts to little more than the dreary *mise en scène* of male partialism—that is, the anxious fore-grounding of fragmented body parts manifesting sexual difference. The veneration of the ejaculating penis, often center-frame and gi-ganticized by wide-angle lenses, rather than an homage to fecun-dity, is a salute to the phallus, which synecdochically "stands in," as it were, for the absent male spectator. While Bakhtin's carnival is inclusive—the party to which everyone is invited—porn tends to be exclusive, its delights, as Pascal Bruckner and Alain Finkelraut point out, being three times limited—to the eye, to the genitalia, and to men.[24] In Bakhtinian terms, most porn is "monologic" in that it subordinates everything to the masculine imagination. Even when porn purports to be "dialogic" by incorporating the sex-ual practices of the other—for example, by offering lesbian scenes—it is generally only a case of monologism masquerading as dialogism, since lesbian scenes are almost invariably staged in view of the imperious needs of the straight male spectator, under his watchful eye. ("No possibility of sexual staging escapes him," writes Luce Iragaray; "so long as he is the organizer, anything goes.")[25] Even porn's temporalities and rhythms are distinctly male. In narrative and aesthetic terms, porn orchestrates what Nabokov in *Lolita* calls "the copulation of clichés" aimed at stimu-lating a "tepid lust." Canonical porn, in sum, constitutes not carni-val's banquet but rather the junk food of the erotic imagination.

At the same time, we cannot regard porn as uniformly retro-grade, nor would we want to throw the baby of consensual eroti-cism out with the bathwater of machismo. The problem with what Ellen Willis calls "establishment porn" is not that it is sexually arousing—stimulating desire is as worthy an artistic goal as stim-ulating social anger or aesthetic admiration—but that it is sex-ist.[26] The problem is not that porn is vulgar but that it is monologic. The notion that the vulgarity of porn can be "transmogrified" into a more classy "erotica" redeemed by more plausible plots and believ-able characters, more artsy angles, and out-of-focus shots under-scored by Chopin on the soundtrack is a bourgeois prejudice ulti-mately quite alien to a Bakhtinian perspective. We should not scapegoat porn, furthermore, for the general ambient sexism that pervades government, the corporations, the workplace, the home, and the media; porn is only one extreme on a continuum. The syn-ecdochic denunciations of porn which take the violent part for the erotic whole miss the point that porn often appeals, as Ann Kaplan and others have pointed out, not to a desire for woman's debasement but rather to a desire for her desire, especially in a vestigially Victorian society where desire in women is still censured, stigmatized, driven underground.[27]

We cannot be essentialist about the porn experience. In fact, porn has no single audience. Instead, different communities approach porn from what Bakhtin would call "diverse dialogical angles." Tom Waugh and others have spoken eloquently of the salutary role of porn within the cultural life of the gay male subculture, its assuaging of solitudes in asserting: "You are not alone. Others do what you fantasize." There is no unitary spectator, then, but a multitude of spectatorial positions. Porn seen in a red-light district by men on their way to the local bordellos is not the same as porn shared by a couple or a group of friends. Any sexual representation gains its "intonation," and "social accent," to use Bakhtin's terminology, only within the larger dialogue with the spectator, with other texts, and with the ambient social and political context.

Nor can we view porn itself as a monolith. Within the apparently unified language of porn, we might easily posit a number of sublanguages or dialects. By-passing the subliminally class-based binarism of "porn" and "erotica" (in which "porn" simply becomes the eroticism of the lower-class other), we can posit a wide taxonomic spectrum of (partially overlapping) varieties of porn:

1. what Eileen O'Neill calls "noxious porn" (films that violate all respect for personhood, e.g., snuff films);

2. sadistic-phallocratic porn (which explicitly fosters the degradation of women);

3. "canonical" or "establishment" porn (porn that merely relays the ambient sexual mores, a ghettoized emancipation that leaves power structures untouched);

4. "ludic" porn (which presents sex as a self-purposeful, playful activity);

5. "obscene" porn (which violates social customs and mores);

6. sublime, "visionary" porn (which links sexuality to mystical transcendence);

7. "subversive" or "transgressive" porn (which links the violation of sexual taboos to a broader attack on socially established hierarchies and the dominant order);

8. Brechtian metaporn (which metalinguistically dismantles pornographic discourse).

An exhaustive study would have to touch on the positive variety of erotic-pornographic films and erotic moments in films—the ludic bisexual romps of James Broughton's films (*The Bed, The Golden Positions*), the sordid sexual-comic situations of Warhol's films (*Heat, Trash, Blue Movie*), films made "with" rather than "about" homosexuality (Kenneth Anger's *Fireworks,* Jean Genet's *Chant d'Amour*) or lesbianism (Constance Beeson's *Holding*). My purpose here, however, is not to be exhaustive but rather to explore, within a Bakhtinian perspective, a number of viable strategies for the critique and transvaluation of porn through the liberating deployment of sexuality, obscenity, and the grotesque. Some of those strategies include: the grotesque body, transgressive writing, parodic carnivalization, metapornographic reflexivity, performer/spectator dialogism, and the translinguistic analysis of sexual communication.

In *Rabelais and His World,* Bakhtin described late medieval carnival as a utopian festival favoring "free and familiar contact" and the "intermingling of bodies," a "second life" offering ephemeral entrance into a sphere of freedom. It is useful to regard porn, I think, as an "ersatz" or "degraded" carnival, one that capitalizes on the repressed desire for carnival-style eroticism by serving up the simulacrum of its utopian promise. Commercial porn, in this sense, can be envisaged as a torn shred of carnival, the detritus of a once robust and irreverent tradition. Porn offers the simulacrum of a panerotic world where sex is always available, where women are infinitely pliable and always desirous, where sex lurks in every office, street, and home, sex without amorous prelude and gloriously free of consequence and responsibility. Once the link of carnival to "essential aspects of being" and to "the organic system of popular festive images" has been broken, Bakhtin argues in *Rabelais and His World,* obscenity "becomes narrowly sexual, isolated, individual" (p. 109). Some contemporary porn, remarkably, fits Bakhtin's description, in "Forms of Time and of the Chronotope in the Novel," of an ancient literary genre, which he calls "the adventure novel of everyday life." Citing Apuleius's *Golden Ass,* Bakhtin offers the following account:

At its center is obscenity, that is, the seamier side of sexual love, love alienated from reproduction, from a progression of generations, from the structures of the family and the clan. Here everyday life is priapic, its logic is the logic of obscenity.[28]

In the contemporary period, the priapic nature of porn serves an important social and ideological function. As real life becomes more repressed and puritanical, sexual imagery, paradoxically, becomes more debauched, as if in compensation for a lost sexual playfulness. The media daily offer us what Arthur Kroker and Michael Dorland designate the "theatrics of sado-masochism in the simulacrum . . . [the postmodern body] doubled in an endless labyrinth of media images."[29] In the age of what Karen Jaehne calls the "Great Detumescence," the on-screen display of sexual abundance plays a role analogous to that of the gild-and-glitter musicals of the Great Depression. Porn, in this sense, is a diversionary gratification, an attempt to recoup in the domain of sexual fantasy what has been lost in real festivity. Although carnival embraces and welcomes eroticism, mere orgasm is not its telos; its goal is playfulness in the broadest sense, a collective *jouissance,* a felt unity with the community and the cosmos. Carnival is gregarious, participatory, and public, while porn is passive and usually monadic, whether consumed by an aggregation of vaguely guilty solitudes in the porn theater ghettos or in the privatized space of the self-entertaining monad. While carnival comes for free, porn is paid for with cash, check, or money order. Rather than carnival's "free and familiar contact," establishment porn offers the anxious commerce of bodies performing ritualized exertions. On the actresses' faces we read, usually, the simulation of desire, and on the man's, grim duty, aerobic perseverance, the solitude of the long-distance comer.

Rinse Dream's *Café Flesh,* while it does betray some of the phallocentrism that seems to be porn's congenital vice, in other ways provides clues to a possible transvaluation of porn. The film is set in a postnuclear cabaret, entertainment center of a world where the vast majority of earthlings have been rendered incapable of performing sexual activity. In this mutant universe, the survivors break down into those who can and those who cannot, and where the majority that cannot, watch the majority that can. The "positives" perform, but the "negatives" can only observe. The majority desires love, but the mere touch of any other renders them violently ill. The film's premise can be seen as triply allegorical. On one level, its division into sex positives and sex negatives can be seen as allegorizing the Social Darwinist division of society into haves and have-nots, with the property, in this case, being sexual capacity itself. On another level, the film allegorizes the "no touch" sexual relationship between porn and its audience, between the sex positives who perform on the stage/screen and the zombie-like sex negatives sitting in the theater. On a third level, finally, one might see the film as proleptically allegorizing the world of AIDS panic, where people want to make love but cannot do it without becoming violently sick, and where the enemy is invisible, invisible like radiation and invisible like AIDS (comparable in their quiet devastation).

In this connection, we might ask: What can an erotic carnival mean in the era of what Arthur Kroker calls "panic sex," of "panic penises" and "panic ovaries"? What can the Bakhtinian celebration of the body and its fluids mean in the age of "sex without secretions"? What can carnivalesque fecundity mean in the age of surrogate mothers and gene retreading? What can "free and familiar contact" and "the intermingling of bodies" mean in the age of video porn and computerized phone eroticism? But especially, what can it mean in the age of AIDS, when the spirit of Thanatos presides over the ecstasies of Eros, and all our orgies come wrapped in the aroma of mortality? The contemporary era seems to have fallen victim to a number of melancholy literalizations. The venerable *liebestod* trope, as innumerable commentators have pointed out, has been rendered excruciatingly literal by the AIDS virus. (*Café Flesh* presciently crystallized this feeling in what amounts to a proleptic elegy for the lost possibilities of sexuality.) Bakhtin's favored carnival image of old age giving birth to vibrant new life, similarly, becomes morbidly horrible in the context of AIDS-infected mothers giving birth to AIDS-infected babies. But even late-medieval carnival, we are reminded, took place against the backdrop of real plague and imagined apocalypse. It is this backdrop which explains the skeletons, the candlelight processions, and the at times macabre imagery of medieval feasts. An indispensable accessory of carnival was a set called "Hell," which was mock-solemnly burned in a joyful bonfire at the height of the festivities. The historical event of the plague, inspiring "cosmic terror" and "eschatological images," Bakhtin points out, served as the starting point for Rabelais' novel. For medieval popular culture, according to Bakhtin, gout and gonhorrea were "gay diseases" essentially connected to the material bodily lower stratum, and many of Rabelais' most ribald jokes revolved on the "merry disease" of syphilis. Carnival is the feast enjoyed *after* staring death in the face; it is, for Bakhtin, a symbolic victory over fear and paranoia. Carnival is not a cure for AIDS, nor can it substitute for political action or medical research, but the spirit of carnival can nourish the principle of hope and the possibilities of community in an age tending toward private defeatism and apocalyptic despair.

Our concern, in any case, is not with literal carnival but rather with carnival as a fund of comic-festive imagery, a perennial constellation of artistic strategies and symbolic practices. In this sense, Rosa von Praunheim's *Ein Virus Kennt Keine Moral* (A Virus Knows No Morals, 1985) is a brilliant example of a "carnivalesque" approach to the unlikely topic of AIDS. This extraordinarily literate film, in fact, is explicitly linked to the Menippean tradition going back to Aristophanes—alluding, for example, to the "cloud-cuckoo land" of Aristophanes' *The Birds*—precisely the tradition of which Bakhtin speaks in *Problems of Dostoevsky's Poetics*. The film was collectively scripted by von Praunheim and leading members of his cast—the collaborative process of production thus matches the collective feeling and politics of the film—and revolves around Rudiger, the irresponsible proprietor of a gay sauna and his naïve lover, a church choir singer named Christian. Rudiger lures his customers with "safe sex" pornos from the United States but ends up getting AIDS himself. The film's other satirical vignettes include: a woman who tries to seduce a bisexual, saying she wants a baby by a gay man "before they die out"; a sinister researcher named Doctor Blood, who attempts to trace the epidemic to a parodically caricatural Africa; transvestites staging a contemporary version of Poe's (vestigially carnivalesque) "Masque of the Red Death"; and a "liberal" government promoting a death camp-amusement park called "Hellgayland." Portrayed as a kind of dystopian amusement park, Hellgayland is, in fact, a quarantine center equipped with housing and medical and recreational facilities, and conducted according to an AIDS-dictated calendar. (Given the limited life expectancy of the inmates, for example, Christmas is observed once a month.) The action is repeatedly interrupted by the sung commentaries of a parodic "chorus" of transvestites. Avoiding the pitfalls of both nihilistic frivolity and puritanical moralism, the film deploys gallows humor not only to alert the audience to dangers but also to point to possible solutions. (New York screenings of the film were coordinated with concrete efforts to provide information, organize benefits, and press political demands.) The film's Brechtian refrain, sung by the transvestite chorus, sums up the activist stance of the film. To the tune of "He's Got the Whole World in His Hands," the chorus sings directly to the audience: "You've got your own fate / in your hands!" Fatalistic religiosity gives way to activist politics. What moves us in the film, finally, is the power of its anger and the audacity of its humor. Von Praunheim combines the evocation of the beauty of gay sexuality with a full and vivid apprehension of the AIDS danger, aiming carni-valesque ridicule at the platitudes of demagogic politicians and the puritanical nostrums of the "just say no" proponents of the "New Sobriety." The fantasy of sexual liberation and the principle of po-litical utopianism, in this film, are indissolubly wed.

In Bakhtin's view, as we have seen, carnival is more than a mere festivity; it is the oppositional culture of the oppressed, the symbolic, anticipatory overthrow of oppressive social structures. Carnivalesque egalitarianism crowns and uncrowns, pulling gro-tesque monarchs off their thrones and installing comic lords of misrule in their place. We can see an inkling of the contemporary possibilities of this kind of comic crowning and uncrowning in the early seventies film *Tricia's Wedding*. Made and performed by the "Cockettes," a gay transvestite group from San Francisco, the film revolves around a mock restaging of Tricia Nixon's wedding recep-tion on the White House lawn. A gay anarchist laces the punch with LSD, and the result is a comic return of the repressed and the symbolic comeuppance of the powerful. In the climactic scene, the Richard Nixon character, portrayed up to that point as a homo-phobic macho obsessed with his virility, makes a homoerotic pass at a Mick Jagger look-alike. Bourgeois decorum, political hypoc-risy, and homophobia are simultaneously mocked within a gro-tesque hyperbolic camp style. The perennial tropes of carnival—transvestitism, madness, crownings and uncrownings, indecent behavior—are deployed in an irreverent attack on sexual and po-litical repression.

Parody, for Bakhtin, is the privileged mode of artistic carni-valization. By appropriating an existing discourse but introducing into it an orientation oblique or even diametrically opposed to that of the original, parody, as we have already suggested, is especially well suited to the needs of oppositional culture, precisely because it deploys the force of the dominant discourse against itself. A Bra-zilian film by Joaquim Pedro de Andrade is a striking example of this strategy. At the height of the military dictatorship in the six-ties and seventies, Brazil witnessed the emergence of a genre called the "pornochanchada," vapid soft-core erotic comedies with titles like *A Bra for Daddy, The Secretaries Who Do . . . Everything!* and *The Virgin and the Macho*. The military regime, phenome-nally alert to the slightest violations of "morality" and "decency" in the films of Cinema Novo directors, hypocritically tolerated and even encouraged the pornochanchadas. In 1980, de Andrade sati-rized the genre in his "metapornochanchada" *Vereda Tropical*

(American title, "Tropical Fruit"). In de Andrade's film, the object of desire takes the form of a watermelon. That is to say, the protagonist of the film literally loves watermelons. *Tropical Fruit* demystifies the pornochanchada by according to the watermelon the function usually accorded the woman in such films. The protagonist seduces the watermelon as if it were a frightened virgin, deflowers it ritualistically, and subjects it to sadomasochistic perversities. A series of shots even achieves what has remained inaccessible to more conventional, nonvegetative pornography— shots from inside the pink wetness of the watermelon itself. Thus the film mocks the spectator's desire to see—and only see—everything. The film mocks the self-defeating nature of pornography's Pyrrhic victories over visual taboos. After conquering the contours of the female body, then the pudenda and the vulva, the phallic camera finally penetrates the last fortress in a fantastic voyage to the very center, the holy of holies. Yet the victory is in every sense a hollow one, revealing little more than the covert totalitarianism of masculinist pleasure.

Tropical Fruit also switches the terms of secondary identification of the pornochanchada. The woman—usually cast as the coy sex object—is here the spectator's delegate, asking the protagonist precisely those questions we would like to ask. Nor does she ever undress for the spectator. The watermelon-loving protagonist, meanwhile, is scarcely an ideal figure for male projection. While pornochanchada protagonists were generally playboys driving the latest sports cars and living in luxurious apartments, the protagonist of *Tropical Fruit* is physically unattractive and professionally incompetent. Hardly the macho sexual athlete of the pornochanchada, he suffers from premature ejaculation even with his watermelons. In sum, *Tropical Fruit* answers the male voyeur's implicit request for a female sex object by offering an ironically reified, vegetative example of pure alterity. (The Brazilian military government, sensing the insult to machismo in a film completely devoid of nudity and heterosexual or homosexual lovemaking, banned the film, while tolerating the much more explicit pornochanchadas *Tropical Fruit* so acerbically mocked.)

Sauve Qui Peut/(la Vie) (Every Man for Himself, 1980), coauthored by Jean-Luc Godard and Anne-Marie Miéville, also deploys corrosive comedy in order to illuminate the nature of pornography and masculine desire. The film concretizes scenarios of desire in distanced, often grotesque forms designed less to flatter the spectator than to make the spectator see him- or herself as comic object. The most effective example of this strategy involves a listless four-person "orgy" featuring a businessman, a secretary, a prostitute, and a male assistant. Godard and Mieville stage the sexual fantasies of the businessman, which take the form of a technocrat's wet-dream—the Taylorization of sexual production. In this utilitarian fantasy, in which Jeremy Bentham meets Wilhelm Reich, sex is programmed and disciplined under the panoptic eye of management. The boss plans the work and sets the procedures. Like a filmmaker, he assigns precise movements, attitudes, and postures to his "actors." The image taken care of, he transfers his attention to the soundtrack. Each participant is assigned a diphthong ("ai!" "ei!")—presumably the signifier of rampant desire—which he or she is to repeat at regular intervals. The orgy participants, like assembly-line workers, are reduced to well-defined jerks, twists, and quivers. Alphavillean sex is displayed as a well-oiled machine, the libido disciplined by the logic of profit and alienation. The sex workers are desensitized, emotionless. The boss exercises his patriarchal prerogatives, yet ultimately he cannot enjoy his power. The character Isabelle reads his face and finds "dark pride, terminal despair, arrogance, and fear." All this, it goes without saying, is highly anti-erotic. We are shown the ritual performance of a sexual paradigm. There are no writhing bodies; there is only the empty multiplication of sexual signifiers in a kind of caricatural formula of an orgy, an orgy rendered as parodic sign.

Another strategy for the progressive deployment of eroticism in the cinema is what might be called transgressive *écriture,* literary or cinematic, in which the violation of sexual taboos is linked to the violation of discursive norms. The filmmaker Bunuel and the writer Bataille have in common this penchant for the association of formal with sexual/social transgression. Not only were the two personally and artistically close, but they share undeniable affinities with Bakhtin. Bataille's account of ritual transgressions mingling intense pleasure (at the transcendence of boundaries) with intense anguish (at the realization of the force of norms) evokes a slightly more morbid version of Bakhtin's carnival. Both Bataille and Bunuel develop a kind of sublime or transcendental pornography whereby saint meets voluptuary in a world which celebrates all that introduces a note of "excess" into the orderly round of respectable activity: childbirth, copulation, defecation, regenerating filth, and orgiastic excess (e.g., the scatological eroticism of *Story of the Eye,* or the Sadean sacrilege of "Christ's orgy" at the finale of *L'Age d'Or*).

More important for our purposes, both Bunuel and Bataille deploy eroticism as a crucial strategy in a deeply transgressive *écriture* that displays a kind of isomorphism between the violation of sexual taboos and the violation of discursive norms, a subject explored by Susan Sontag in "The Pornographic Imagination," and by Susan Suleiman in "Pornography and the Avant-Garde."[30] For both Sontag and Suleiman, the transgressive thrust of Bataille's work, especially his pornographic fictions, must be read as a metaphor for the transgressive use of language. The sexually scandalous scenes of *The Story of the Eye,* they argue somewhat too strongly, signify Bataille's scandalous verbal violations, not vice versa. In Bunuel's case, as we have seen, formal cinematic and narrative transgressions—what Bakhtin would call *grammatica jocosa*—are linked to the ludic-erotic interrogation of all social decorums. And with both Bunuel and Bataille, sexuality is wielded not gratuitously but in relation, for its primordial power of scandal.

In his films, Bunuel constantly transgresses the normative modes of sexual expression in such a way as to intimate excess, violation, and social critique. Bunuel's exalted vision of love-death, almost utopian in its aspiration, at times recalls the sublime pornography of Bataille's *Story of the Eye.* Both capture the oxymoronic nature of love's healing cataclysms, in which "orgasms ravage faces with sobs and horrible shrieks"; for them, eroticism is apocalyptic and danger is an aphrodisiac. For the narrator of *The Story of the Eye,* death is the logical outcome of erection, and the goal of sexual licentiousness is a "geometric incandescence . . . the coinciding point of life and death, being and nothingness."[31] Bunuel's *L'Age d'Or* achieves the fulgurating cinematic equivalent of Bataille's vision by having Modot, his face bloodied, ardently embrace Lya Lys as he murmurs, "Mon amour, mon amour." In *The Exterminating Angel,* similarly, Beatriz and Eduardo, with a corpse at their side for inspiration, make soft-focus *l'amour fou,* invoking the language of death ("the rictus . . . horrible . . . my love . . . my death!") while in the throes of orgasm. We are clearly in the presence of a latter-day version of carnival's linkage of the spasms of love with those of death, but without the third spasm, that of childbirth, and its metaphorical corollary, fecundity.

What saves Bunuel from being just one more morbid executioner of the occidental *liebestod* motif is the acerbic humor he brings to his theme. Bunuel consistently uses corrosive laughter to undercut the seriousness of the sexual proceedings. In *Chien An-*

dalou, L'Age d'Or, and *That Obscure Object of Desire,* love becomes a tragicomic obstacle course leading only to protracted frustration. Modot and Lya Lys's clumsy attempts at lovemaking in *L'Age d'Or* are in this sense paradigmatic. The obstacles, in this case, are both external—the policemen, the nuns, the priests who separate the two lovers—and internal. Burlesque comedy and high tragedy meet as the two stumble over chairs, bang their heads on flower-pots, are interrupted by music, and become fetishistically distracted by the feet of statues. ("I defy any art lover," wrote Bataille, "to love a painting as much as a fetishist loves a shoe.")[32] The Wagnerian music, meanwhile (appropriately from the "Liebestod"), at once aptly and incongruously evokes a constantly swelling, unfulfilled desire, a perpetual tumescence that never reaches climax.

For Bunuel, as for Bataille, transgression does not negate an interdiction; it transcends and completes it. Taboos exist only to be violated. Thus Bunuel plays a kind of erotic "trick" on religion by using it as a kind of aphrodisiac. Dialectically negating the negation, Bunuel exploits religious prohibitions in order to intensify what the prohibitions are designed to combat—desire itself. Sexual pleasure, for Bunuel, exists only in a religious context: "It is an exciting, dark, sinful, diabolical experience."[33] Bunuel cites with approval Thomas Aquinas's idea that sex, even in marriage, is a venial sin: "Sin multiplies the possibilities of desire."[34] Thus religion becomes a trampoline for desire. Innumerable passages in Bunuel films fuse religious law and sexual transgression in a kind of transcendental pornography. Francisco becomes enamored of Gloria's feet during mass; the blasphemous debauch of *L'Age d'Or* is conducted by a Jesus Christ look-alike; the orgy and the rape of *Viridiana* take place to the sounds of the "Hallelujah Chorus."[35]

All of the artists here discussed fit into the Bakhtinian conceptualization of sexuality "in relation" to the general life of the body. No conceptual hierarchy places copulation, or orgasm, at the summit of importance. Bakhtinian thought, in this sense, stands somewhat outside what Stephen Heath calls "the sexual fix," the modern hypostasization of sexuality as the imperious raison d'être of human existence.[36] Copulation for Bakhtin is inseparable from defecation and urination and other semicomic reminders of the body's delectable grotesquery. Bakhtin's comprehensive vision illuminates, if only by contrast, what is so oppressive about most pornography—its relentless single-mindedness, its humorlessness, its obsessive sexualist teleology manifested cinematically by the inexorable zoom-ins to the fuck, the cock, the cunt, its endless repetition of what Luce Iragaray calls "the law of the same." And it is this single-mindedness which generates porn's inevitable loss of aura and mystery. Although sex is autotelic and self-justifying, when it is focused on exclusively it seems to lose its quality and to implode. For Bakhtin, sexuality exists only in relation—in relation to the general existence of the body, to other persons, and to the common social life.

Another way of viewing sexuality "in relation" is to see it as a discursive reality, to foreground its nature as a "language" and a "discourse." Within a Bakhtinian perspective, language, including cinematic language, is not only the material but also the object of representation. Artistic texts do not so much "call up" a world as "translate" and "re-present," in a reflexive manner, the languages and discourses of the world. The "metapornography" practiced by Jean-Luc Godard has precisely this quality of exposing cinematic eroticism, especially, as a discursive and linguistic construct. From his first films in the late fifties through the films coauthored with Anne-Marie Miéville in the seventies and eighties, Godard has conducted what Bakhtin would call a "submerged polemic" with pornography, a kind of metatextual dialogue with porn as a preexisting body of texts. Time and again Godard returns to the scene of pornography, to the sexual fascination of its images and the frustration implicit in its lure. Godard approaches the subject of porn's built-in trajectory of disenchantment in *Tout Va Bien*. We see Susan (Jane Fonda) showing Jacques (Yves Montand) a photograph of a penis being fondled by a woman's hand. The image fills the screen for what seems an unnaturally long time, as Susan's off-screen voice comments: "Admit that this image satisfies you less than it did three years ago." On one level, she is referring to the declining satisfactions of their own relationship, but on another she is referring to the law of diminishing returns in the exploitation of sexual imagery in the cinema. Canonical pornography manufactures its own satiation as each new mystery is exhausted; the pornographee becomes apathetic and virtually unexcitable. The cinematic images become, as Sartre says of photographs in *Le Nausée,* like aphrodisiacs that have lost their potency. In still another sense, Susan's comment might have been addressed to the exaggerated hopes of the erotic visionaries who saw the mere portrayal of sexual coupling as "wonderfully dangerous" in its "heavenly power."[37] The routinization of such images seems to have deprived them of their power of scandal and utopia. They can regain that power, I would suggest again, only in relation to alternative structures of feeling, to alternative models of cinema and human relating, and to what Bakhtin calls "the collective life of the clan."

Despite the relative sexual audacity of his films, Godard's work is generally marked by a *pudeur* that derives not from a puritanical distrust of sexuality but rather from a sensitivity to the generally exploitative nature of such images within dominant cinema. In his "submerged polemic" with porn, Godard constantly highlights the constructed nature of its discourse, always short-circuiting the incipient titillation of the imagery so as to make the spectator conscious of his or her investment in cinematic voyeurism. The subversion of a certain kind of pleasure, however, can itself be intensely pleasurable. A kind of aesthetic jubilation transports us from the privatized space of individual fantasy to the broader social space of discourse in which we see our own desires as strangely comic. (Self-directed laughter is still laughter, and carnival laughter is directed even toward its own participants.) The porn-film sequence of *Masculin, Féminin,* for example, provides a kind of object lesson in pornography and the spectator's relation to it. The cited film—which is said to parody Bergman's *The Silence* because it is Swedish and involves impersonal sexual encounters in an unidentified land—is prefaced by an ironic intertitle in ersatz Scandinavian: "4X: Ein Sensitiv und Rapid Film." (The "4X" refers simultaneously to a grade of film stock, to "X" as in "X-rated," to "x" as in the four-star system of journalistic evaluation, and to an index of quality fabrication in French condoms; the "sensitiv" and "rapid" refer both to the "sensibility" and quick pace of the film and to the light-"sensitivity" of the film stock.) The film-within-the-film mirrors *Masculin, Féminin* as a whole: both concern relations between the sexes, although the porn film offers a particularly reductionist version in which communication is limited to the paralinguistics of grunts and the proxemics of lust, the crudity of which is heightened by a distorting mirror that turns the male figure, especially, into a kind of monster. While aware of the film's gross stupidity, Paul and his friends are unable to leave: "We control our thoughts," says Paul's interior monologue, "but not our emotions, which are everything." Paul's commentary speaks of the role of the desiring spectator, of our emotional demands on films: "Marilyn Monroe had aged terribly. It made us sad. It wasn't the film we dreamed of . . . the total film we carried within ourselves . . . that we wanted to make . . . or more secretly that we wanted to live." Paul's off-screen words coincide with the close-up of the woman in the porn film. Her face moves down screen, presumably in the direction of the man's penis. The implied off-screen fellatio, as an act of unilateral homage to the phallus, metaphorizes the porn film's relation to the male spectator; he remains passive while being serviced by a competent sexual/cinematic technician in a nonreciprocated *onanisme à deux.* The juxtaposition of Paul's lament with the pornographic images, meanwhile, suggests a kind of proportion: a quick blow-job among strangers is to our dreams of love what pornography is to true cinema.

The advantage of Bakhtinian categories, I have already implied, is that they almost always apply equally to art and to life. Thus *carnival* refers both to a real-world social practice and to a textual manifestation. *Heteroglossia,* similarly, can designate a social, a linguistic, or a textual reality. *Polyphony* can characterize a poem, a novel, or even an entire culture. Within this perspective, it is possible to take a "translinguistic" approach to the theme of eroticism and sexuality. The trope of sex as *fait langagier* is of course not new; it is implicit in the very idea of love as the "universal language." In *A Lover's Discourse,* Roland Barthes speaks of the "language-nature of the amorous sentiment" and "the endlessly glossed form of the amorous relation."[38] Barthes compares language to a skin that we rub against others: "It is as if I had words instead of fingers, or fingers at the tip of my words." Not only is eroticism linguistic, but language is erotic. The eroticism of language and the language of eroticism, then, mutually implicate each other, while metalanguage leads to auto-erotic *jouissance*: "language experiences orgasm upon touching itself."[39]

But let us explore further what light translinguistics can shed on both two-dimensional and three-dimensional eroticism. We will begin, as Bakhtin would, with the axiomatic omnipresence of language in all human life and culture, including erotic life and discourse. Language penetrates eroticism and sexuality in countless ways. It structures, as analysts as diverse as Lacan and feminist sociolinguists have pointed out, our very thinking about sexual difference. Quite apart from the woman's obligatory assumption of the "nom du père," different languages "see" gender differently. Some languages, such as English, minimize gender difference, while others, such as Hebrew and Arabic, oblige women and men to use distinct *morphological* forms. (From the Hebrew title of the film *I Love You Rosa* [Ani ohev otach], for example, the Hebrew speaker knows that the person speaking is a man and the person loved is a woman, a point marked in English only by the presence of the feminine proper name Rosa). Each language also deploys structuring tropes that subliminally orient or accent sexual activity. Many languages metaphorically link sex with eating (*comer* in Portuguese), a trope realized in countless films that intermingle what Bakhtin would call the "food series" with the "sex series"—one thinks of the "banquet sexuality" of *Tom Jones* or the erotic passing of egg yolks from mouth to mouth in *Tampopo*. Other languages link sexuality with cognition (the biblical "to know"), or with agriculture and plowing (the etymological root of the English verb "to fuck"). The metaphors can be reciprocal or gender specific. (In Portuguese, for example, the woman "gives" sexually, while the man "eats.")

Language informs sexuality at every point—in the eroticizing power of the spoken word, in the erotic effect of reading (the libidinal "pleasure of the text"), in the conversations that lead to or accompany sex, in the "paralinguistic" groans, moans, and sighs that provide its soundtrack, in the remembered voices (personal, familial, institutional, mass-mediated) that reverberate in our minds during lovemaking, and in the discourses (ecclesiastical, medical, from the pope to Dr. Ruth) that surround sex as a socio-ideological phenomenon embedded in language-inflected representations. The word is present in every erotic encounter, even silent ones, if only in the form of "inner speech." Even masturbation is accompanied by inner speech, by remembered or anticipated verbal fragments; its monologues, like those of Dostoevsky's characters, can be oriented to the other, to a hoped-for or remembered "responsive understanding."

Moreover, just as language constantly permeates sex, sex itself can be regarded as a kind of language. If we take seriously Bakhtin's idea that all human acts, including nonverbal ones, are "potential texts" understandable in the "dialogical context of their time," we begin to glimpse the possibilities of a translinguistics of sexuality, in both intra- and intercorporeal terms. Within the body, transmitters speed across synapses, neurons signal, and messages race from the erogenous zones to the brain and back again. Even corporeal secretions are communicative, constituting transmissions from the inner self to the outer body and to the other. The body in arousal exhibits indexical signs of desire; it sweats, stretches, reaches out, opens up, lubricates, thereby making way for erotic dialogue.

Eroticism, like the cinema, is "multitrack." The erotic gesture can take verbal, tactile, olfactory, or visual form. An utterance performed on one track (e.g., a verbal gesture such as a loving word) can be "answered" by an utterance performed on another track (e.g., the tactile "utterance" of a caress). Or the response to a caress can be linguistic (a caressing word) or paralinguistic (a moan or a sigh). The body can make utterances that are susceptible to verbal translation and vice versa. It can speak in the monologue of masturbation, the dialogue of the couple, or the polylogue of the orgy. The body can speak with inaudible commands, invitations, warnings. Sex at its worst is an exercise in power, a clash of languages and mistranslations of linguistic, gestural, and proxemic codes, an epidermal juxtaposition of monologues, dialogue gone awry. Sex at its best is an "ideal speech situation," a communicative utopia, a microcarnival (just as carnival is macro-*jouissance*) characterized by "free and familiar contact" and transindividual fusion. The sexual utterance, like any utterance, needs the other for completion. From a Bakhtinian perspective, erotic interlocution is an exchange of other-oriented utterances, a dialogue dominated by responsive understanding, a mutual coauthoring, a mingling of voices, not only in the irreducible act of intercourse, but also as part of a larger, more open-ended encounter.

The "language of love" is not unitary, and there is no standard language of sex. Writers like Anais Nin, Luce Iragaray, and Helene Cixous all speak of the inadequacy of the male discourse of sexuality, suggesting that the language of sex has "yet to be invented." The erotic dialogue is a "situated utterance" that is subject to the "ensemble of codes governing discursive interaction." The concepts of "tact" and "intonation," as implied earlier, allow for the possibility of a politically informed analysis of concrete social exchanges, including, I would suggest, erotic exchanges. Erotic dialogue in a sexist society is inevitably shadowed by the realities of gender inequality. (Sadomasochism, in this sense, might be viewed as the "theatrical" acting out of the implicit "tact" of sexual exchange.) In a misogynistic culture, male culture especially becomes codified with notions of conquest, and the sexual act becomes, in the words of the authors of *Remaking Love,* a "microdrama of male dominance and female passivity."[40] Women's amorous discourse has traditionally been coded as silent, as consisting in gestures, facial expressions, and other paraverbal communication, while men, as George Steiner points out in *After Babel,* use speech to conceal the sexually aggressive function of their lips and tongues: "Women know the change in a man's voice, the crowding of cadence, the heightened fluency triggered by sexual excitement . . . the flattened speech and dulled intonations after orgasm."[41]

Erotic exchanges in film, similarly, could easily be examined in terms of "tact," seen as the product of the relations between all the interlocutors (on and off screen), the concrete situation of the "conversation," and the "aggregate of social relationships and ideological horizons informing the discourse." At the center of any erotic film, we find the dialogical or nondialogical interplay of sexually speaking (or listening) subjects, persons engaged in literal or metaphorical dialogue. In the wings, meanwhile, there are unheard and unseen participants—the filmmakers and technicians manipulating the technology and the producers hoping for a profit. In commercial theaters, we find public settings controlled, formally as well as informally, by men. And both in the theater and at home, we find the audience, with which the film also dialogues, an audience traversed by contradictions involving gender, class, sexual preference, race, age, and politics. Erotic "tact," in film as in life, would be determined, in a Bakhtinian view, by the aggregate of environing social relationships (e.g., the ambient realities of patriarchy and homophobia), the ideological horizons of the erotic interlocutors (e.g., the interiorized myths and ideologies animating the participants), and the concrete situation enveloping the interlocutors (e.g., two gay lovers in a situation of discrimination, boss and secretary in a context of sexual harassment, etc.).

All political struggle, according to Bakhtin, passes through the word. Patriarchal oppression, for example, as feminist sociolinguists have pointed out, is exercised through language, as is feminist resistance to that oppression. Godard and Miéville's *Sauve Qui Peut/(la Vie)* especially highlights the nonreciprocity of linguistic exchange between men and women. In the film the prostitute Isabelle calls her clients "monsieur"; they do not call her "madame." The boss, exercising his male prerogative as arbiter of female beauty, obliges his secretary to say: "My tits are not beautiful." She lacks the social power to oblige him to say: "My pot belly is unattractive." Isabelle's pimps spank her (a quintessential gesture of paternalistic infantilization) and force her to admit that no woman, be she duchess, secretary, or tennis champion, can be truly independent. One of the businessmen who rents Isabelle's body is named, significantly, "Monsieur Personne." The john, the man with the cash, is a person, a subject, while the prostitute is differentially defined as nonperson, object. Yet in the end the designation reverberates ironically, since *personne,* in French, can also mean "no one." It is the john who is no one, who is demeaned, reduced to the actantial function of the paying customer (the trickster "tricked"); it is he who depersonalizes himself.[42]

Lying on the border of the verbal and the nonverbal, what Bakhtin calls "intonation" constitutes a subtle fashioner and reflector of social relations. Intonation serves as a kind of barometer of alterations in the social atmosphere. *Sauve Qui Peut/(la Vie)* can be analyzed in terms of social and sexual "tact" and "intonation." The film features, for example, a kind of temporal experiment in the form of fifteen step-printed saccadic "skids"—variations of stop-action or slow-motion movement—that interrupt the more conventional twenty-four-frames-per-second defilement of the rest of the film. A striking proportion of the slowed segments have to do with relations between men and women. Godard and Miéville especially pinpoint the epidermal abrasiveness of contemporary sexual relations. At times this abrasiveness is explicitly violent— Isabelle getting knocked around by her pimps—and at times it is more subtle and indirect. We see Paul advance toward Isabelle in pulsingly retarded movements, gradually occupying her space. As she watches warily, we seem to witness a phallic incursion, a slow-motion minirape. Later Paul embraces, or better falls upon, Denise in a noisy, slow-motion collision, crystallizing a situation in which lovers find it difficult to touch without bruising. The film, in such moments, dissects what Foucault would call the "capillary" forms of power, the ways in which relations of domination seep into the grain of everyday life and penetrate even the smallest gestures. Or, to switch to semiotic language, the film analyzes sexual proxemics, the codes regulating interpersonal touching within the context of a phallocratic "tact" and misogynistic "intonation." One imagines the possibility of another kind of erotic film, one that explores the subtle differences in erotic proxemics and verbal intonation between mother and daughter, father and daughter, father and son, mother and son, sister and brother, between heterosexual lovers, between homosexual lovers.

Films such as *Sauve Qui Peut/(la Vie)* evoke the possibilities of films that might advance the semiotic analysis of the tact of everyday erotic life. One envisions, for example, an entire film devoted to a brief kiss or an act of love, analyzed into an infinitude of tiny utterances, minifoci of resistance, collaboration, aggression, and incomprehension, or of generosity, anticipation, sharing, and wit. The vast expressive resources of the cinema, in this sense, despite the general obsession with sexuality, have barely been tapped.

One thinks of film's resources for the *mise en scène* of discursive-erotic situations, its capacity to juxtapose multiple images portraying a variety of sexualities (something Godard begins to do in *Numero Deux*), the possibilities opened up by its multitrack nature for ironic contextualizations (e.g., the sounds of roller-derby violence superimposed on lovemaking in Wexler's *Medium Cool*), the potentialities of montage and superimposition for conveying the power of desire (e.g., the poignant sequence in *L'Atalante* where the separated lovers express their longing for each other by caressing themselves), and the capacities of split-screen and subtitles for conveying the ironies of misfired erotic communication.

The notion of "tact," as we have seen before, applies not only to verbal or erotic exchanges within films (or in life) but also figuratively to the "tact" involved in the metaphorical dialogue that takes place between film and spectator. What might be the implicit tact of the relationship between erotic films and their audiences? What address is implied? What kind of interlocution does porn promote, and can one imagine an alternative form? Might sexually explicit films develop a different kind of tact, one that goes beyond the capitalized circulation of the bodies of women? David James has suggested one answer in his essay "Hardcore: Resistance(?) in the Postmodern."[43] James speaks of California Erotic Video Circles, where couples, in order to share and intensify the customary pleasure of coupling, tape themselves making love and invite similar taped responses from other couples. Here, James argues, there is no commercial motivation; all that is expected is a responding videotape. While establishment porn tends to efface the apparatus, here the performers acknowledge the camera and often observe themselves on monitors. In porn, the performers' pleasure is subordinated to the instrumentality of commodity production; the rhythm of sexual activity is disrupted by the industrial requirements of conventional shooting procedures. But with the Video Circles tapes the participants' pleasure is paramount and largely determines the textual organization. The tapes lack fetishistic close-ups and intrasequential editing; there is no montage of genital contact and no ritual obeisance to the most ubiquitous trope of porn—the close-up of the male's ejaculation. Rather than pornography's "rendezvous *manqué*" between exhibitionist and voyeur, premised on the impossibility of real contact between performer and spectator, these videotapes open up the possibility of actual contact and even propose what James calls a "social network of desire" beyond the realm of commodity relations and the control of the Mafia and the corporations. While it would be naïve to idealize such experiments, as if they could be conducted outside of patriarchy, homophobia, and the "aggregate of social relationships," they do suggest at least the *theoretical* possibility, within a radically reordered society, of persons, couples, and groups nourishing an eroticism founded not on the individual gaze but on a shared experience, the possibility of desire experienced not as the pursuit of a fading object but as a communal current passing between persons. In such a society, sexual play, itself a kind of conversation, would be dialogically amplified within a community of erotic aspirations.

An erotic "translinguistics," then, would propose at once a sensual and reciprocal communicative model of sexual interlocution. It would "get to the bottom" of the old metaphor of sexuality as a *lingua franca,* much as Metz tried to get to the bottom of the old metaphor of "film language." A Bakhtinian model would draw its metaphors not from the domains of conquest ("penetration"), hygienics ("healthy relationships"), labor ("working at sex"), economics ("rewards," "investments," and "dividends"), or property ("my" wife), but rather from the metalanguage of self-aware communication. A Bakhtinian "translinguistics" of eroticism would destroy the double myth of a single language of eroticism and a unified language. It would speak of carnal polyphony, of sexual heteroglossia and the "many-languagedness" of sexual pleasure and practice, what Cixous calls the "thousands of tongues" of eroticism. It would look for "dialogism" on every level (interpersonal, intertextual, interspectatorial), and it would combat the persecutory power of an array of monologisms (patriarchy, heterosexism, puritanism). Its emphasis would be not on unilateral desire, lure, and misrecognition, but on what Bakhtin would call the "in between" of erotic interlocution.

■■■■■■ From Dialogism
to *Zelig*

Of overarching importance in Bakhtin's thought and method is the notion of "dialogism." With the question of dialogism, Bakhtin writes in "The Problem of the Text," "we are approaching the frontier of the philosophy of language and of thinking in the human sciences in general."[1] "To be," he writes in *Problems of Dostoevsky's Poetics,* "means to communicate dialogically. When dialogue ends, everything ends."[2] In "The Problem of Speech Genres," Bakhtin offers a clear formulation of this dialogism of the utterance:

Utterances are not indifferent to one another, and are not self-sufficient; they are aware of and mutually reflect one another. . . . Each utterance is filled with echoes and reverberations of other utterances to which it is related by the communality of the sphere of speech communication. . . . Each utterance refutes, affirms, supplements, and relies on the others, presupposes them to be known, and somehow takes them into account.[3]

Dialogism consists not in the mere encounter of two voices, then, but in the fact that every utterance is emitted in anticipation of the discourse of an interlocutor. In all his writings, Bakhtin tirelessly reiterates this idea of the dialogical or relational nature of the utterance. Bakhtinian dialogism, Dana Polan suggests, can be seen as a "rewriting" of the Saussurean view of language as the diacritical play of difference, this time recast as the play of difference between the text and *all its others:* author, intertext, real and imagined addressees, and the communicative context.[4] Polan's interpretation is confirmed by the move, in the following passage in "Discourse in the Novel," from the "merely" linguistic to the social and semantic: "The linguistic significance of an utterance," Bakhtin writes, "is understood against the background of language, while its actual meaning is understood against the background of other concrete utterances on the same theme, a background made up of contradictory opinions, points of view, value judgements."[5]

Bakhtin is not always consistent in his views on dialogism, however. At times he describes it as an inherent characteristic of language itself, but elsewhere he posits it as a liberatory praxis exclusive to the novel as a multivocal genre. Even within the novel, Bakhtin at times contrasts essentially monologic writers such as Tolstoy with the "dialogical" Dostoevsky, yet at other times he cites Tolstoy as an example of dialogism. At times, Bakhtin appears not to draw the full potential consequences from his own theory, as in his recurrent declarations that dialogism functions fully only in the novel, and not in the theatre or poetry. In such cases, we are obliged to follow Bakhtin's ideas where they lead, ignoring the somewhat arbitrary limits that he himself placed on them.

Nor is Bakhtin completely clear on the relation between "dialogics" and "dialectics." Recurrently, he emphasizes dialectics as a kind of abstraction from dialogics, a residue of the dialogical process, what is left after all that is personal and vital has been taken out. His emphasis tends to be on the "lacks" of dialectics and the plenitudes of dialogics; he describes dialectics as lacking personalized voices, lacking the separation and interaction of voices, devoid of "intonations" and "valuations." Some of Bakhtin's emphases doubtless have to do with a submerged polemic against Stalinism, yet at the same time we can regret that Bakhtin never completely developed his ideas on the relation between interpersonal communication and larger arrangements of power and modes of production. In this sense, his analysis lacks a theory of "mediations." At the same time, one might see dialogism as potentially dialectical. Having revealed the dialogical nature of language and communication, Bakhtin encloses them in a schema that seems to exclude dialectics, but he does so without ever explaining his point of view in detail. Indeed, one might see dialogism as a more embracing dialectic, and Bakhtin's vision of a world in which voices echo and cross and reverberate across the social totality "needs" the dialectical vision of "competing class discourses" (Jameson) just as dialectics "needs" dialogics for its humanization, personalization, and aestheticization. In this sense, however, Bakhtin's work is full of zigzags, at times seeming idealist and at times Marxist, and it is up to us to forge the synthesis rather than look for it in the texts.

The word *dialogism* in Bakhtin's writings progressively accretes meanings and connotations without ever losing this central idea of "the relation between the utterance and other utterances." Although Bakhtin often refers to dialogue in the literal sense to provide examples of the dialogic, the dialogic cannot in any way be equated with dialogue itself. Nor can dialogue and monologue be seen as in absolute opposition, since a monologue can also be dialogic, given the fact that every utterance, including the solitary utterance, has its "others" and exists against the backdrop of other utterances. Even a hermit, for Bakhtin, does not "own his words." The word always comes, as Bakhtin puts it repeatedly, "from the mouth of another." The word, he writes in "Discourse in the Novel," is half someone else's. It becomes "one's own only when the speaker populates it with his own intention, his own accent, when he appropriates the word, adapting it to his own semantic and expressive intention."[6] The word, then, is a shared patrimony:

The word (or in general any sign) is interindividual. Everything that is said, expressed, is located outside the "soul" of the speaker and does not belong to him. The word cannot be assigned to a single speaker. The author (speaker) has his own inalienable right to the word, but the listener also has his rights, and those whose voices are heard in the word before the author comes upon it also have their rights.[7]

The novel, for Bakhtin, is the preeminent dialogical genre, just as Dostoevsky is the preeminent modern dialogical writer. The novel is dialogic because it represents fictive subjects within a dynamic field of heteroglot discourse. It reflects, refracts, symbolically enacts, and even engenders dialogism and heteroglossia. Dostoevsky in his fictions points to the inner dialogism of all discourse, even that which on the surface is solitary and monologic, thus demonstrating the ontological impossibility of real aloneness. In the face of a capitalist individualism that "produces" the lonely alienation of such figures as the "underground man," Dostoevsky affirms the illusory nature of solitude. The psyche, for Bakhtin, is an "extraterritorial part of the organism." The individual is not master of a sovereign interior territory, but rather exists on the frontiers. "To be" signifies being "for" and "through" others. Even looking inside ourselves, as in confessional literature, we look in and through the eyes of others. Thanks to Dostoevsky, Bakhtin writes, we discover the complexity of the apparently simple acts of writing in one's diary or looking in the mirror. In both cases, we encounter a crossing of perspectives, the intersection of multiple consciousnesses.

Dialogism, as we have seen, refers in the broadest sense to the infinite and open-ended possibilities generated by all the discursive practices of a culture, the matrix of communicative utterances that "reach" the text not only through recognizable citations but also through a subtle process of dissemination. Dialogism in this broad sense is central not only to the canonical texts of the literary and philosophical tradition of the Western world—one thinks of the Socratic dialogues, the medieval *débats* and *défis,* not to mention the errant dialogue of Don Quixote and Sancho Panza in Cervantes' novel or the "moi" and "lui" in Diderot's *Le Neveu de Rameau*—but also to noncanonical texts. It is central, furthermore, even to those utterances which are not conventionally thought of as "texts." The idea of "intertextuality," after all, is in one sense a truism, known to Montaigne, who wrote that "more books have been written about other books than any other subject," and to T. S. Eliot, whose idea of the relation between "tradition" and "individual talent" might be seen as a conservatively formulated prolepsis of "intertextuality," one that assumes the "integrity" of both the tradition and the individual talent.

Bakhtinian dialogism, however, is far more radical, in that it appeals simultaneously to everyday speech and to literary and artistic tradition. Bakhtinian dialogism is concerned with all the "series" that enter into a text, be that text verbal or nonverbal, erudite or popular. The popular, furthermore, enters into the erudite, and vice versa. The "semantic treasures Shakespeare embedded in his works," Bakhtin writes,

were created and collected through the centuries and even millennia: they lay hidden in the language, and not only in the literary language, but also in those strata of the popular language that before Shakespeare's time had not entered literature, in the diverse genres and forms of speech communication, in the forms of a mighty national culture (primarily carnival forms) that were shaped through millennia, in theatre-spectacle genres (mystery plays, farces, and so forth), in plots whose roots go back to prehistoric antiquity, and, finally, in forms of thinking.[8]

The Bakhtinian reformulation of the problem of intertextuality must be seen as an "answer" not only to the purely intrinsic formalist and structuralist paradigms of linguistic theory and literary criticism, but also to the vulgar Marxist paradigms of extrinsic class-biographical and extrinsic ideological determinations. Bakhtin attacks the limitation of the literary scholar-critic's interest exclusively to the "literary series." The notion of dialogism goes far beyond the literary-historical tradition of tracing "sources" and "influences." Bakhtin is interested in a more diffuse dissemination of ideas as they penetrate and interanimate *all* the "series," literary and nonliterary, as they are generated by what he calls the "powerful deep currents of culture." Literary scholarship, he argues, should establish closer links with the history of culture: "Literature is an inseparable part of culture and it cannot be understood outside the total context of the entire culture of a given epoch."9

The artistic text, then, must be understood within what Bakhtin calls the "differentiated unity of the epoch's entire culture."10 Dialogism operates within all cultural production, whether it be literate or nonliterate, verbal or nonverbal, highbrow or lowbrow. In the films of a Godard or a Ruiz, the artist becomes the orchestrator, the amplifier of the ambient messages thrown up by all the series—literary, painterly, musical, cinematic, publicitary, and so on. But the same basic dialogical mechanisms also operate within what is known as "popular culture." (Bakhtin rejects, we may recall, the formalist hierarchization of "poetic" over "practical" speech.) Take, for example, the phenomenon of "hip-hop"— that is, the interrelated cultural universes of rapping, graffiti, and break dance. The practice of rap, the form of popular music that combines turntable pyrotechnics with aggressive talking—the very word *rap* means "to dialogue"—can be seen as a street-smart embodiment of Bakhtin's theories of dialogism and intertextuality. Largely the creation of black and Hispanic working-class teenagers, rap, like gospel and other forms of black music, is ultimately based on African call-and-response patterns, on a kind of interanimation of performer and listener that is clearly reminiscent of Bakhtin's interactive, performance-centered theory of language. The multiple strands that were woven into rap, as David Toop inventories them, include disco, street funk, radio disk jockeys, be-bop singers, Cab Calloway, tap dancers, stand-up comics, the Last Poets, Gil Scott Heron, Muhammed Ali, doo-wop groups, ring games, skip-rope rhymes, prison and army songs, signifying, and "the dozens," traditions going all the way "back to the griots of Nigeria and Gambia."11 On another level, rapping can be seen as a rhythmed extension of what Bakhtin calls "everyday speech genres," since the broad genre of rap is subdivided into local subgenres called "insult raps," "message raps," "party raps," "advice raps," "news raps" and so on. Rap's free-wheeling raid on the intertext, furthermore, by-passes the bourgeois laws of copyright. Bits of text drawn from other songs, political speeches, and advertisements are placed in ironic relationships for purposes of mutual relativization. "Quoting" is marshaled in the service of a gamut of attitudes, from violating to joking to reverential homage (e.g., to James Brown). Rap musicians recycled the voices of black martyrs such as Malcolm X and Martin Luther King. By such recycling and "versioning"—or as Bakhtin would put it, "re-invoicing"—the rappers "set up a direct line to their culture heroes, to the Afro-American intertext."[12]

In an illuminating essay—"Why Is It Fresh? Rap Music and Bakhtin"—Elizabeth Wheeler explicitly applies Bakhtinian categories to the world of hip-hop, demonstrating the extent to which rap is intensely, even exuberantly, dialogic.[13] The hip-hop musician, Wheeler argues, dialogically uses ready-made materials as a matter of inner-city expediency, since records are cheaper than instruments and music lessons. Rap quite literally emerges, she points out, from a dialogical process, from the conversations of members of a crew who stand close together, look each other in the eye, trade rhymes, homages or insults, and generally "feed on each other's intensity." Performing close textual analyses of specific rap songs such as "The Message" and "La-Di-Da-Di," Wheeler finds numerous instances of Bakhtinian dialogism: "polyphonic discourse," "hidden internal polemic," "polemically colored autobiography," "confession," "discourse with a sideward glance," and "sarcastic rejoinder."

For Bakhtin, as we have seen, entire genres, languages, and even cultures are susceptible to "mutual illumination." His insight takes on special relevance in a contemporary world where communication is "global," where cultural circulation, if in many respects asymmetrical, is still multivoiced, and where it is becoming more and more difficult to corral human diversity into the old categories of independent cultures and nations. Third World culture, as I suggested earlier, is by definition a multivoiced field of intercultural discourse, and some would argue that it is the proleptic site of postmodern collage culture. In a brilliant song-poem appropriately titled "Lingua" (language), Brazilian popular singer-composer Caetano Veloso offers an eminently dialogical text, at once literary and musical, which fosters the mutual illumination of languages, (musical) genres, and even entire cultures within the context of contemporary popular culture. In doing so, he takes off from a common quality in Brazilian popular music and art generally, its tendency, in a land of multiple cultural traditions, to "play off" one tradition or genre against another—Portuguese fado against samba (e.g., Chico Buarque's "Fado Tropical"), samba against rock, reggae against bolero, hillbilly music against calypso, and so on. The lyrics of "Lingua" are, in part, as follows:

> Gosto de sentir a minha lingua rocçr
> A lingua de Luis de Camões
> Gosto de ser e de estar
> E quero me dedicar
> A criar confusões de prosodia
> E uma profusão de parodias
> Que encurtem dores
> E furtem cores como camalões
> Gosto do Pessoa na pessoa
> Da Rosa no Rosa
> E sei que a poesia está para a prosa
> Assim como o amor esta para a amizade
> E quem há de negar que está lhe é superior
> E deixa os portugais morreram à mingua
> "Minha patria é minha lingua"
> Fala Mangueira!
> Fala!

> I like to feel my tongue brush up against
> The tongue/language of Luis de Camões
> I like the verb "ser" [to be] and "estar" [state of being]
> And I want to dedicate myself
> To creating confusions of prosody
> And profusions of parody
> Mitigate delicious sadnesses
> And switch colors like chameleons
> I like the Pessoa in the person
> And the Rosa in the Rose
> And I know that poetry is to prose
> As love is to friendship
> And who would dare deny that the latter is superior
> And let the Portugals die abandoned
> "My homeland is my language"
> Speak Mangueira!
> Speak!

This poem, apart from being more or less untranslatable, is also vertiginously rich in dialogical resonances. The self-designated genre of the song, first of all, is "samba-rap"—that is, a neologistic synthesis of Brazilian samba with precisely the kind of rap music analyzed by Elizabeth Wheeler. The underlying rhythm is that of rap music, and the acoustic effects include raplike record scratching and synthesizer and rhythm-machine effects. Caetano, usually a supremely gentle singer, here adopts the tongue-in-cheek bravado style of rap, the style appropriate to the proudly ironic recounting of sexual prowess and physical courage, but rendered here in praise of the poetic capacities of the Portuguese language. The opening stanzas are replete with homages to both "noble" and popular poets: to the seventeenth-century Portuguese epic poet Luis de Camões, author of *Os Lusíados;* to the Portuguese modernist poet Fernando Pessoa ("I like the Pessoa in the person"); and, ambiguously, to erudite quasi-Joycean writer Guimaraes Rosa and/or popular composer Noel Rosa ("And [I like] the Rosa in the Rose"). The quotation "Minha patria é minha lingua" ("My homeland is my language") is itself a citation of a famous Fernando Pessoa poem. The national plural "Portugals" derives from French anthropologist Roger Bastide's theories concerning the diverse "Brazils." The exhortation "Speak Mangueira!" meanwhile, refers to the traditional shout that marks the beginning of the movement into the carnival procession of one of Rio's most famous "samba schools," and its performance, too, is seen as speech, performance, parole. (Indeed, the Saussurean concept of "parole" is often translated, in Portuguese, as "fala.")
"Lingua" concludes:

A lingua é minha patria
Eu não tenho patria: tenho matria
Eu quero fratria
Poesia concreta e prosa caotica

Otica futura
Tá craude bro voce e tu lhe amo
Que queu te faço, nego?
Bote ligeiro
Samba-rap, chic-left com banana
Será que ele está no Pao de Acucar
Nos canto-falamos como quem inveja negros
Que sofrem horrores no Gueto do Harlem
Livros, discos, videos à mancheia
E deixa que digam, que pensem, que falem.

Language is my fatherland
I have no fatherland; I have a Motherland
And I want a brotherland
Concrete poetry and chaotic prose

Future vision
It's crowded, bro', you and you all love him
What can I do you, my soul man?
Put on a light
Samba-rap, the chic-left with banana
Might he be hiding on Sugar Loaf Mountain?
We sing-talk like those who envy blacks
Suffering horrors in the Harlem ghetto
Books, records, videos by the handful,
And let them say what they like, think what they like, speak what
they like.

Here again we find the collage of citations and the pluralization of
discourses drawn from all the "series," from the language of Rio's
surfers to that of the most sophisticated São Paulo poets. The passage begins with the (now) correct citation of the Fernando Pessoa
poem. "Poesia Concreta" refers to a sophisticated post-World War
II school of poetry that emphasized wordplay and the concrete
sound qualities of words, a school that was a strong influence on
Caetano himself. "Craude" (English "crowd") is derived from the
slang of Rio's surfers. "Might he be hiding on Sugar Loaf Mountain?" alludes to a character invented by avant-garde musician Ar-
rio Barnabe—Clara Crocodilo—the joke being that Sugar Loaf
Mountain is hardly an ideal place to hide. The reference to books by
the handful comes from a poem by the nineteenth-century romantic poet Castro Alves (like Caetano, a Bahian), but has been updated here to include records and videos.

It is only in the eyes of another culture, Bakhtin writes, "that
a foreign culture reveals itself fully and profoundly." But this dialogical encounter of two cultures does not result in the loss of
identity of each culture; instead, "each retains its own unity and
open totality, but they are mutually enriched." The Caetano song-
poem wonderfully illustrates this mutual enrichment, simultaneously operating the reciprocal familiarization and the mutual defamiliarization of two cultures. The song fundamentally combines
two song traditions—the African-derived "talking samba" (the last
line of the poem quotes one of the most famous) and North American rap, itself deeply rooted in a number of African and North

American traditions (call-and-response, blues, "signifying," and so on). Thus the Third World poet-singer posits a certain cultural unity between Brazil and the United States based on the common Africanized resistance culture of both countries. The song proliferates in allusions to Afro-Brazilian and black American culture: "bro" is a shortened form of "brother" as in "soul brother," and "nego" is a common Brazilian term of endearment that literally means "negro" but is used to apply to any intimate friend. "Samba-rap" is the song's self-designation as a cross-cultural hybrid. "Chicleft com banana" is a translingual piece of wordplay that combines a reference to a well-known Gilberto Gil song entitled "Chicklets with Banana" ("the two comestibles being synecdochic, respectively, for Brazilian and North American music) with "chic-left," an allusion to Tom Wolfe's famous phrase "radical chic." In such a rhythmed song-poem, dialogisms are superimposed in a ludic spirit.

Within cinema studies, the notion of dialogism is rich in analytic potential for a wide range of film authors and film texts. Here, however, I would like to look at the work of just one filmmaker, Woody Allen, through Bakhtin's conceptual categories, touching briefly on *Stardust Memories* before moving on to a more extended analysis of *Zelig*. The first film participates in what Bakhtin, in reference to the novel, calls "the autocriticism of discourse," in which artistic discourse is tested in its relationship to social reality. Within this "line," Bakhtin cites two types. The first type concentrates the critique and trial of literary discourse around the hero—a "literary man"—who tries to live according to the rules of literature. (*Don Quixote* and *Madame Bovary* are two obvious examples.) The second type introduces an author in the process of writing the novel, not as a character but as the real author of the given work. (Bakhtin cites *Tristram Shandy*.) "Alongside the apparent novel there are fragments of a 'novel about the novel.'" Of the two types, *Stardust Memories* corresponds more closely to the second type. Like Fellini's *8½*, Stardust Memories is about a filmmaker, in emotional and intellectual crisis, in the process of making a film. Allen casts himself as Sandy Bates, a celebrity director who reluctantly attends a retrospective in his own honor, where he is obliged to listen to the fawning praise of his fans and the inane censure of his critics. Allen places in the mouth of various characters all the conceivable charges that might be leveled against Allen's *oeuvre* in general and against *Stardust Memories* in particular. The strategy recalls that of Dostoevskyean characters, such as the Underground Man, who practice a policy of anticipatory self-depreciation. (Indeed, the Woody Allen stand-up-comic persona has much to do with the Dostoevskyean figures that Allen must have encountered in his early reading.) Bakhtin calls this strategy "loophole discourse," whereby its practitioner wards off all finalization and self-definition. "A loophole," Bakhtin writes in *Problems of Dostoevsky's Poetics,* "is the retention for oneself of the possibility for altering the ultimate, final meaning of one's own words" (p. 233). In *Stardust Memories,* the filmmaker's "loophole" consists in demonstrating his advance knowledge of all possible criticisms of himself and his work. The "loophole word" repudiates itself in advance in anticipation of the hostile word of the other. Thus Allen, only partially conflatable with the filmmaker in the film, has the studio executives find the clips from Bates's "Suppression" (the film within the film) "horrible," "a disgrace," and" pretentious." Indeed, most of the charges that were in fact leveled at *Stardust Memories* were pronounced in advance by characters in the film: "His filming style is too fancy." "His insights are shallow and morbid." "He tries to document his suffering and fob it off as art." "What does he have to suffer about?" "Why do all comedians turn out to be sentimental bores?"

In loophole discourse, for Bakhtin, each statement anticipates a series of reactions and answers them in advance; indeed, each answers the imagined responses to the answers. In the case of *Stardust Memories,* the critics, apparently lacking any sense of irony, proceeded to make all the mistaken interpretative moves anticipated by the film itself, while dismissing the film's satire on the critics as a neurotic defense mechanism on Allen's part. Like Bates's critics in the film, they found *Stardust Memories* derivative, self-indulgent, and unfunny. The theme of derivativeness was evoked even by the titles of many of the journalistic reviews—"Woody Doesn't Rhyme with Federico" (Sarris), "Inferiors Woody Allen Hides Behind Fellini" (Schiff), and "Woody's 8 Wrongs" (Shalit)—a charge that seems especially ironic in the context of a film calling such explicit attention to its dialogical relation to the Fellini film. The opening sequence, for example, constitutes a kind of parodic degradation of its prototype, the initial tunnel sequence from $8^{1}/_{2}$. In both, the male protagonists are trapped within vehicles in a nightmarish world, but in *Stardust Memories* Woody Allen's owlish face substitutes for Marcello Mastroianni's handsome one, an old train replaces a new car, and a Jersey dump takes the place of the Mediterranean seashore. The charge of derivativeness, in any case, misses the point. Allen has always focused attention on the filmic intertext, a fact rendered transparent in his titles: *Play It Again, Sam* evokes Michael Curtiz and Humphrey Bogart; *A Midsummer Night's Sex Comedy* renders homage to Shakespeare and Bergman, and so on. When asked if the mad-scientist routine in one of the films within the film was an homage to Vincent Price, the Tony Roberts character answers: "No, we just stole it outright." Woody Allen does not obscure his borrowings; rather, he suggests that such dialogical pilfering is a fundamental part of the process of creation.

Allen takes this process further in *Zelig* (1983), a film that conveniently recapitulates and exemplifies a number of our themes—dialogism, intertextuality, polyphony, and the mutual illumination of languages and cultures. When first released, the film was regarded, in terms more appropriate to its protagonist than to the film, as a kind of brilliant "freak" or well-executed "gimmick." Overwhelmed by the apparent audacity of the film's premise, critics ignored the film's deep roots in a dense literary and philosophical intertext and downplayed the multileveled suggestiveness of its chameleon parable. What follows is a kind of playful Bakhtinian meditation on *Zelig* which attempts to disengage the genres and traditions with which it dialogues and which explores the variegated strata of its allegorical palimpsest: film as chameleon, the artist as chameleon, the Jewish experience as chameleon, and the self as chameleon.[14]

Far from being a "freak" or a "gimmick," as a provincial critique of the film would have it, *Zelig* can be seen as giving cinematic expression to a perennial literary mode—namely, the Menippean satire anatomized by Bakhtin as a seriocomic genre linked to the carnivalesque perception of the world. A hasty review of the fourteen traits that Bakhtin posits as distinctive of the genre reveals that *Zelig* features a remarkably high proportion: "freedom from historical limits" (the film's unlikely neighboring of a contemporary actor with long-deceased public figures); "total liberty of thematic and philosophical invention" (the central anecdotal nucleus concerning a lizard-man and his metamorphoses); "philosophical universalism" (the thematic of chameleonism as global metaphor); "overt and hidden polemics with various philosophical, religious, and ideological schools" (the satire on various establishment discourses); the debate with "masters of thought" (here contemporary-culture heroes Susan Sontag, Saul Bellow, and Irving Howe); "a fondness for inserted genres" (here documentary, Hol-

lywood melodrama, cinema *verité*); and "a concern with topical issues" (the multileveled discussion of such issues as racism, assimilation, and the culture industry). The very premise of the film—a
chameleon-like protagonist who comes physically to resemble all
those with whom he comes in contact—finds an antecedent in the
metamorphoses that typify the Menippea (the transformation of
human characters, for example, into pumpkins and donkeys). As a
veritable summa of ethnic personalities and social categories (Indian, black, Chinese, Protestant, Catholic, and Jew), Zelig also in-
carnates the "oxymoronic protagonist" of the Menippea. And as a
one-man polyphony of possible human comportments, Zelig embodies what Bakhtin calls, in reference to the Menippea, "human
nonfinalizability" and "a man's noncoincidence with himself."
He also typifies the Menippean fondness for "abnormal psychic
states" in which man has a "dialogical relationship with himself"
and where "being is fraught with the possibility of split personality."

One consequence of Bakhtin's attitude toward both literary
author and human beings generally as living on "interindividual
territory" is a revised attitude toward artistic "originality." Since
all words, including literary words, always come from "the mouth
of another," artistic creation is never *ex nihilo;* rather, it is premised on antecedent texts. Despite the perennial comparisons that
are made of the artist to a kind of god, demiurge, creator, progeni-
tor, or unacknowledged legislator of mankind, the artist's real role,
for Bakhtin, is more modest and is caught up in more typically human interactions. The individual (artist), for Bakhtin, cannot
be the sole proprietor of an utterance, since any verbal or nonverbal performance "inevitably orients itself with respect to previous
performances in the same sphere, both those by the same author
and those of other authors."[15] The artistic image or word is always
what Bakhtin calls a "hybrid construction" mingling one's own
word with the other's word. Complete originality, as a consequence, is neither possible nor even desirable. In this sense, the
Bakhtinian attitude recalls the medieval indifference to "originality" as an important issue in the evaluation of art. It was only
after the advent of Renaissance individualist humanism that such
inordinate value was placed on individual works of art. Gothic ca-
thedrals, not to mention formulaic romances or folktales, as has often been noted, admitted of no individual "author." Bakhtin would
presumably agree with the view expressed by Northrop Frye in
The Anatomy of Criticism:

The possession of originality cannot make an artist unconventional; it drives him further into convention, obeying the law of the art itself, which seeks constantly to reshape itself from its own depths, and which works through geniuses for its metamorphoses, as it works through minor talents for mutation.[16]

Zelig, I will argue here, is a case of creative nonoriginality, of narrative reshaping itself from its own depths, where the chameleonic theme is perfectly matched to the film's discursive procedures.

   Zelig not only thematizes chameleonism through its protagonist's "uncanny" ability to take on the accent, profession, and ethnicity of his interlocutors, but it also practices chameleonism on a discursive level.[17] In *Zelig,* chameleonism comes to metaphorize intertextuality itself, as the film, like its protagonist, assumes the coloration of its interlocutory texts. Through intertextual mimicry, fiction and documentary, the two genres subtending the film, come to resemble each other in a kind of specular mimesis. Allen creates a "hybrid construction," an oxymoronic genre—the "fictive documentary"—which breaks down the customarily inviolate boundaries separating the two orders of discourse, replacing the usual wall with a permeable membrane. It transcends the traditional separation between the two, not by merely juxtaposing them (à la Makavejev's *WR*), but rather by enlisting documentary's habitual procedures of enunciation and narration to serve what is clearly a sham and parabolic tale, pointing to the truth of Metz's boutade that "all films are fiction films," as well as to its obverse, that all films, even fiction films, are also documentaries.

   This breaking down of borders between what is factual document and what is fictive creation is a familiar one within the Bakhtinian universe. The "journalistic" multigeneric approach that is common to Menippean satire and the Dostoevskyean novel necessarily subverts such boundaries, as does Bakhtin's contention that literary texts, no matter what their genre, represent not reality but the languages and discourses of the world. As an invented story masquerading as true history, *Zelig* constitutes, to paraphrase Hayden White, "pseudohistorical text as filmic artifact." Indeed, *Zelig* can be regarded as a witty gloss on the thesis of White's *Metahistory:* It matters little whether the world that is conveyed to the reader/spectator is conceived to be real or imagined; the manner of making discursive sense of it is identical.[18] On the surface, however, *Zelig* appears to be a conventional documentary in which the portrait of a historical figure is set against the backdrop of the portrait of an age (here the fads of the twenties and thirties), buttressed by the testimony of "witnesses" who recount their memories or advance their interpretations in direct-to-camera interviews.

Throughout, *Zelig* speaks in the double-voiced discourse of parody, the privileged mode of artistic carnivalization. The film lampoons all the hackneyed rhetorical procedures of the canonical documentary: its "authorative," ponderously knowing male narrators; its ritualistic "talking heads"; its quasi-comic redundancies (the image of Eudora writing in her diary is accompanied by the comment "Eudora writes in her diary"); its frequent implausibilities (through what legerdemain did the documentarist manage to witness the eminently private act of Eudora writing in her diary?); its suspect manipulation of stock footage (the commentary "Eudora goes to Europe" is superimposed on a stock shot of an ocean liner—her liner? that trip?); and finally, its penchant for synecdochic music ("Horst Wessel" stands in for the Nazis, the "International" evokes the Communist movement, and "America the Beautiful" substitutes for the United States). The film mocks the official seriousness of all these formulaic procedures, subjecting them to corrosive laughter to the point that it becomes retrospectively difficult to take them seriously again.

There are innumerable ways, Bakhtin argues, of "quoting" an "alien word." The "alien words," in the case of *Zelig,* are the archival shots in the film, drawn from what was originally 150 hours of material. Here the notions of "prior textualization" (Jameson), the "already said" (Bakhtin), and a "mosaic of citations" (Kristeva) take on an oddly physical connotation as we are confronted not with an abstract verbal dissemination but with material strips of celluloid drawn from stock footage, home movies, and old newsreels. Allen resuscitates, as it were, "dead" stock footage, as if in illustration of Bakhtin's dictum that "nothing is absolutely dead: every meaning will have its homecoming festival." Allen then "populates" these alien word-images with his own intentions. Each citation leads to a double-voiced reading: first in relation to its text, and time, of origin; and second as it is incorporated into the new totality of *Zelig.* Allen takes alien "words," framed in another intention, and gives them a new ironic orientation, here exploiting the compelling immediacy of "evidence" to discredit the very idea of evidence.

When *Zelig* is not archival, it is pseudoarchival. (When it is not borrowing "alien words," in Bakhtinian terminology, it is "mimicking" them.) Thanks to Gordon Willis's artful replication of the look and texture and even the technical inadequacies of earlier cinematography, archaic period footage and freshly staged material become virtually indistinguishable. In this sense, *Zelig* celebrates the chameleonic potentialities of the film medium itself as a multitrack sensorial composite offering opportunities for chameleonism denied to single-track media such as literature.[19] Thus Allen is inserted into period photographs, or is made to slither into celebrity home-movies featuring William Randolph Hearst and Carole Lombard, or is simply matted into archival footage, rather like a lizard blending into a new habitat. Through the chameleonism of the laboratory, the film stock itself assumes the tonalities of another epoch. New footage is artificially aged and scratched and made to flicker and look grainy, while saccadic movement simulates actuality footage from the period. Mimetic lighting matches new shots to old material, while the dialogue, registered by twenties-style microphones, imitates the low-fidelity recording of a bygone era.

The promiscuous mingling of recorded historical "truth" with staged fictive "lies" is a crucial strategy in *Zelig*. The initial shots, for example, superimpose Susan Sontag's voice on archival images of a ticker-tape parade. We then see Susan Sontag, and titles reassure us that it is indeed Susan Sontag that we are seeing. The style and drift of her discourse closely conform to our expectations concerning the cultural figure named Susan Sontag, while her persuasive sincerity is here recruited in support of a "lie," that there was a man named Zelig and that she knew of him. Sontag calls Zelig the "phenomenon of the century" and compares him to Charles Lindbergh, thus fostering an illusory sense of a historical continuum, as if the reality of both figures were of a piece. (The allusion to Lindbergh becomes even more ironic when Zelig, following what Bakhtin calls the "logic of the turnabout," performs Lindbergh's feat in a doubly reverse sense—in the opposite direction across the Atlantic and upside down.) Another instance of this blurring of boundaries between the true and the false occurs later, in an interview with the putative "editors" of the defunct *Daily Mirror*, Mike Geibell and Ted Birbauer. They speak convincingly of the journalistic appeal of the Zelig phenomenon, but their words, like those of the Cretan liar, paradoxically raise suspicions about their *own* credibility: "In those days, you got a story, you jazzed it up a little bit, you exaggerated, and you even played with the truth, to sell more papers. But with him, the truth was enough—it never happened before!" The technique is reminiscent of Cervantes' calling into question the veracity of his own sources in *Don Quixote;* the spectator is teased into cognitive antinomies and a dizzying feeling of epistemological vertigo.

The figures interviewed in *Zelig* vary substantially in their fictive status. Susan Sontag, Irving Howe, Bruno Bettelheim, and Saul Bellow, for example, enact their own personae under their own names, making plausible comments reflecting what we know to be their real-life preoccupations. Howe, the author of *World of Our Fathers,* a book about the Jewish immigrant experience on New York's Lower East Side, predictably interprets Zelig as a quintessential exemplum of the transformations involved in assimilation. (Howe thus illustrates the function of the critic, as envisioned by Bakhtin—to make the word of the text his own, to mingle the two "words.") Susan Sontag, again quite plausibly, emphasizes Zelig's "aesthetic instincts" as well as the assertive role of the woman psychoanalyst, seen as a rebel and a maverick within psychoanalytic discourse much as Sontag herself once represented the rebel within art and literary criticism. (The author of *Against Interpretation,* ironically, is entirely willing to interpret.) Saul Bellow, similarly, stresses two motifs common in his fiction: ambiguity (that Zelig's cowardly chameleonism made him a hero) and individuality-versus-conformism (that Zelig's flirtation with fascism had to do with a desire to merge into the masses.)

In the case of the other interviewees, the coefficient of fiction is somewhat higher. Professor Morton Blum plays himself, yet is credited, in a Borges-like "erroneous attribution," as the author of a clearly fraudulent work, *Interpreting Zelig.* The interviews, in fact, steadily escalate in implausibility, just as the narrative events become more improbable and hallucinatory. The relative veracity of the initial interviews, in which intellectuals do at least play themselves, prods us into the illusory expectation that other interviewees also are playing themselves, that Eudora's older sister (played by Elizabeth Rothchild) is in some sense authentic, or even that the interviewed Nazi, whose name, Oswald Pohl, refers to one of Himmler's deputies who was condemned to death at Nuremberg, is in fact a former S.S. *Obergruppenführer.* Perhaps disoriented by Allen's blend of fact and fiction, Richard Grenier somewhat sanctimoniously lamented in the pages of *Commentary* the fact that Woody Allen would find "hilarious" a man who supervised the melting down of gold teeth taken from the bodies of the victims of Hitler's gas chambers.[20] Grenier's reaction, apart from exemplifying the very literal-mindedness mocked by the film, misses the point on a number of levels: first, the real Pohl was executed for his crimes and *therefore* can be made a figure of fun; second, "hilarity" can also entail anger, critique, and even profundity (one should look for Rabelais' profundity, Bakhtin argues, when he is laughing most heartily); and third, the "joke" here, as in Purim and in Carnival, is "on the tyrant." The sequence mocks, finally, the amoral and apolitical "leveling" that characterizes documentaries that give "equal time" to amiable Nazis and progressive intellectuals, all equated in their status as commentators.

To call *Zelig* a "fictive documentary" is on one level to remain somewhat schematic, for in fact the film intertwines *diverse* strands of documentary and *diverse* strands of fiction. Quite apart from mixed-mode antecedents such as Welles's *F for Fake* or the found-footage films of Bruce Conner, *Zelig*'s specifically documentary intertext includes:

1. television compilation films, such as those forming part of the series *Twentieth Century* and *Victory at Sea,* which portrayed historical figures against a period backdrop (*Twentieth Century,* interestingly, at one point considered using a *Zelig*-like procedure called "blue-backing" in order to insert Walter Cronkite into preexisting actuality footage);

2. newsreels (the venerable "Voice of God" narration underlined by bombastic music, for example, recalls the "March of Time" newsreels already parodied in *Citizen Kane*);

3. the contemporary "witness" documentary in which aging interviewees reminisce about their experiences decades before;

4. the contemporary mass-media traditions of television reportage and cinema *verité;* and

5. the television news "quickie" biographies of unknowns (e.g., anonymous assassins) who suddenly emerge into public notoriety, presented by producers who rely on hastily gathered materials such as family albums and group photos of the newly minted "celebrity."

In sum, the film calls on precisely those rhetorical formulae which are most often associated with mass-media veracity to serve as ironic authenticating devices for a preposterous tale about a lizard-man. The heavy artillery of verisimilitude explodes into a narrative void.

Within the general intertextual framework of ersatz documentary, Allen renders ironic homage to the traditional Hollywood black-and-white melodrama. Conjured from the same narrative materials—the life of Zelig—the melodrama offers a metafictive gloss on *Zelig*'s documentary façade. The voice-over and the superimposed titles identify the "quoted" melodrama as *The Changing Man,* a 1935 Warner Brothers production, thus reproducing the common documentary practice of incorporating clips of fiction films. Diverse stylistic stratagems re-create the ambience of a thirties melodrama: a *mise en scène* replicating a low-budget Warner Brothers production (*Zelig* is a Warner production as well); stylized performances by glamorous "stars"; and saccharine music and melodramatic dialogue highlighting Eudora's passion and self-abnegation in curing Zelig. One of the quoted sequences from *The Changing Man* is set in Nazi Germany. We see Zelig (Allen) in long shot behind the haranguing *Führer* as we hear the voice-over: "Like a man emerging from a dream, Zelig notices her." A shot of Zelig waving to Eudora (Mia Farrow) in recognition is followed by a shot-reaction shot between the Doctor, Eudora, and the Zelig (Brown) of *The Changing Man.* The alternating syntagma of fiction film and "documentary," stitched together by an impossible eyeline match between a putatively real and a putatively fictive character, underlines the moment of mutual recognition, culminating in the parodically formulaic finale of the fiction—a close shot of the couple's prolonged kiss accompanied by romantic music swelling to a climax. The double-voiced discourse of *The Changing Man* exposes the textual mechanisms of Hollywood dramatic representation, and specifically the process by which the Hollywood biography brings to the surface a story's latent emotional appeal while editing out its historical contextualization. At the same time, Allen's parodic strategy casts comic light on the central premise of all illusionistic narrative—the presupposition of a preexisting anecdotal substratum from which key blocks have been extracted—by having Zelig complain that Hollywood, when it bought the rights to his life story, took all the best parts and left him with only his sleeping hours.

Zelig takes advantage of the documentary's presumed higher coefficient of veracity in order to undermine the truth claims of *both* documentary and fiction. After the first citation, the narrator claims that *The Changing Man* told the truth, while after the second citation, the by-now elderly Eudora objects that the real story was "nothing like the movie." The film then gives us the true portrayal of the flight from Germany, as recorded by a German newsreel. While a shaky camera records Zelig's escape, a hysterical German narrator denounces Zelig in a string of epithets: "judische, amerikanische, dumkopf." The choice of guarantor of truth is doubly ironic, since Third Reich newsreels were notoriously mendacious and in any case never would have emphasized an incident that turned a "traitor" into a hero and the Nazis into schlemiels.

Like its protagonist, *Zelig* forms a shifting mosaic of creative borrowings. (Plagiarism, symptomatically, is one of the crimes of which our hero is accused.) Within this mosaic, *Zelig* evokes the multiple narrators and investigative style of *Citizen Kane,* while also spoofing Warren Beatty's *Reds,* the filmic reconstruction of the life and loves of John Reed. Set in the same historical period, *Zelig* pilfers a key device from *Reds*—interviews with contemporaries about the events portrayed—but with what Bakhtin would call a "sideways glance." The Allen version mocks the *Reds* device of marshaling real-life witnesses to buttress illusionism by transferring the comments of the interviewees to a chimerical and ludicrous figure, an elusive protean entity in constant metamorphosis, a "hero without any character," a personality perpetually "sous rature."

Zelig's lack of substance, his there's-no-there-there essencelessness, implicitly questions classical notions of character and even suggests a proximity to theoretical reconceptualizations of the literary personage. The narratological analyses of Vladimir Propp, which were contemporaneous with Bakhtin's early writings, posit a "hero" without psychological depth or biographical density, as opposed to the traditional view of character as a "rounded" figure endowed with personal singularity and psychological coherence. Zelig, in this sense, lacks the old-fashioned repertory of attributes associated with the "old stable ego." He resembles, rather, Todorov's "agent of narrative," whose significance is purely virtual, who is little more than a textual marker of blank form awaiting "predication." The very emptiness of Zelig's expression, even in close-up, betokens a kind of cipher, a tabula rasa awaiting inscription. And although the film ultimately retreats from the more radical implications of its fable, the "decentered" character of its protagonist does implicitly, at least, cast suspicion on the classical humanist view of character.

On still another intertextual level, *Zelig* mockingly reinvoices the genre of the "psychological case study"—encapsulated in films like *Spellbound* and *Marnie*—in which the central enigma focuses on the traumatic origins of adult neurosis. Eudora searches for the trauma at the root of Zelig's chameleonism, much as Mark, in *Marnie,* searches for the cause of Marnie's frigidity, or as Constance, in *Spellbound,* explores the etiology of John Ballantine's amnesia. In all three cases, psychoanalytically inclined investigators become erotically involved with the objects of their investigation. In *Zelig,* as in *Spellbound,* the woman psychoanalyst, initially portrayed as coolly rational, pursues her fascination with an identityless patient (later lover) despite the hostility of a patriarchalized psychoanalytic establishment, ultimately shedding her façade of dispassionate scientific rationality in favor of passionate romance. In both films, the analyst's love, as much as her professional competence, catalyzes the recovery of the man's "true self." *Zelig*'s portrayal of the psychoanalytic dialogue, furthermore, is pregnant with comic inversions. Here we see the "chameleon chameleonized," as Zelig loses his bearings in the face of the analyst's feigned insecurity. (Analyst and analysand are both susceptible of falling into the in-between of reciprocal transference.) Then, in another reversal, a hypnotized Zelig progresses from relating traumatic childhood experiences to analyzing his psychoanalyst. The analytic "voyeuse" is herself "vue," as the unconscious Zelig makes the hyperconscious Eudora realize what has long been obvious to the spectator: that she is "all mixed up and nervous" and attracted to Zelig.

Like *Stardust Memories, Zelig* incorporates its own hermeneutic mechanism within the text itself. The intellectuals' interpretative glosses shuttle us between diegetic event and extradiegetic interpretation. The filmic equivalent of literary "pauses" (Genette), in which narrative discursive time is greater than story time, these critical interludes are employed not in the nineteenth-century mode of particularizing space and action (Balzac) but rather in the reflexive "dialogical" manner of the eighteenth-century novel (Fielding). The pauses call attention to the diverse critical and institutional discourses—aesthetic, philosophical, psychoanalytic, sociological, literary, journalistic—that might inflect our reading. The film *Zelig,* like the Zelig phenomenon, becomes an object-text of critical discourse and of cultural and psychoanalytic speculation. Within a kind of hermeneutic ludism, both film and character become a text open to diverse interpretative grids. Zelig himself, Morton Blum points out, was all things to all people: a figure of infamy to Catholics; the symbol of self-improvement for Americans; and for the Freudians, absolutely anything and everything. The commentaries both encourage and channel the free play of interpretation, while provoking laughter at the disparity between the comic image of the human chameleon and the seriousness of his intellectualized presentation.

Zelig's intertext is not merely filmic; it is literary and philosophical as well. *Zelig* alludes, for example, to Melville's *Moby Dick* at four specific points: first, when the hypnotized Zelig confesses that he never finished it (Zelig's first self-splitting arises from his shame in admitting, in front of "very bright people," that he had not read the novel, a token, perhaps, of the power of intimidation of literary intellectuals); second, when Eudora uses *Moby Dick* to construct a persona to which "Doctor" Zelig is supposed to react; third, when Professor Blum describes Zelig as a man who "preferred baseball to reading *Moby Dick*"; and fourth, when the concluding titles inform us that Zelig's only regret as he lay dying was that he "had just begun reading *Moby Dick* and wanted to know how it came out." These apparently whimsical references to the Melville novel point reflexively to certain features of the Allen film, since *Zelig*'s own generic tapestry recalls the dense textual interweave of *Moby Dick*, which, like *Zelig*, might be called a "fictive documentary," and which also manipulates preexisting documents and "alien words": dictionary quotations (on the etymology of *leviathan*); bona fide correspondence (Uno von Troil's letters); conversations (Ekerman with Goethe); biblical (Jonah), philosophical (Plato, Hobbes), and literary (*Hamlet*) quotations; and the encyclopedic material on whaling that is interspersed throughout the fiction, all mobilized in the service of what is, after all, an awesomely improbable story about a chameleonic and ambiguously symbolic whale.

Zelig rings the changes on a theme—chameleonism—that is rich in literary resonance and philosophical association. Just as Shakespeare, for Bakhtin, was shaped by millennia of development of diverse genres and forms of speech communication, by theatre spectacle, and by plots whose roots go back to prehistoric antiquity, so a film like *Zelig* is shaped by an extremely dense cultural and artistic intertext (which is not to equate Woody Allen with Shakespeare, but simply to say that all texts of any complexity are inevitably molded by centuries of narrative and generic tradition). In the broader sense of intertextual dialogism, *Zelig* might be profitably placed in relation not only with Menippean satire and Melvillean "anatomy" but also with Renaissance cosmovision, romantic poetry, and Sartrean existentialism. Lingering briefly on a few of these relations, we are reminded that the Renaissance saw the world in terms of similitude and correspondences. *Zelig* most clearly embodies Renaissance *simpatia,* a kind of limitless identification through which every fragment of reality is attracted to every other fragment, all difference being dissolved in an erotic play of universal attraction. (That *Zelig* does not ever transform himself into a woman, that the boundary of sexual difference is the one line that he dares not cross, suggests, perhaps, the phallocentric limits of Allen-Zelig's *simpatia.*) At the same time, *Zelig* evokes the romantic preoccupation with "self" and "world." "I am part of all that I have met," asserts the narrator of Tennyson's *Ulysses,* while Walt Whitman's capacious soul comes to resemble all it encounters. Keats called the poet "chameleon," without identity. Borges glosses Keats's phrase in his *ficcion* "Everything and Nothing," where he compares Shakespeare to God in their shared multiplicity of identity. *Zelig,* as a kind of peripatetic miracle of neo-Kantian *einfühlung,* offers a seriocomic demonstration of the chameleonic powers of "negative capability," here in the form of a passively empathetic penchant for assimilation to other selves.

The spectator also is "everything and nothing," everywhere and nowhere, everyone and no one. Nietzsche's remarks, in *Nietzsche against Wagner,* about the play of identification in the theatre might easily be extended to the cinema:

In the theatre, one becomes a commoner, herd, woman, Pharisee, electoral mob, lord of patronage, idiot—Wagnerian; there even the most personal conscience succumbs to the leveling magic of the "greatest number"; there the neighbor reigns, indeed there one becomes one's neighbor.[21]

In this sense, Zelig's mutations recall the plural self, the "sujet mutant" (Schefer) fashioned not only by the theatrical but also, even especially, by the cinematic experience.[22] Like the "imaginary" self of Lacanian theory, the cinematic subject defines itself by identifying with "l'image d'autrui" in a veritable bric-a-brac of identifications. Already "doubled" through primary identification with the apparatus, at once in the movie theater and with the camera/projector/screen, the spectator is further dispersed through the multiplicity of perspectives provided by even the most conventional montage. Through cinematic dialogism, the spectator becomes mutable, occupying a plurality of subject positions; he is everywhere, to paraphrase Lacan, "à sa place." Cinema's "polymorphous projection-identifications" (Edgar Morin) allow for ephemeral identifications that transcend ambient morality and social milieu.[23] In the cinema, one becomes one's own neighbor, identifying with sameness and al-

terity, with cop and robber, with cowboy and Indian. Zelig's transformations, in this sense, can be seen as literalizing the psychic
chameleonism of spectatorship, whereby ordinary social positions,
as in carnival, are bracketed, and where the poor fleetingly con-
found themselves with the rich, the black with the white, the woman with the man, and so on.

Zelig can also be seen as allegorizing another kind of "negative capability," that of the actor, and his transmutations evoke
both the acting profession and Sartre's phenomenological updating of the *theatrum mundi* trope.[24] According to this perennial figure, the human personality "wears" ambient lifestyles as if they
were theatrical costumes. One plays roles in life, not only for others, but also for oneself. Clothes are worn as disguise, and facial
expression constitutes a mask. The human personality on stage is
eminently malleable; there are no longer human beings, only roles.
Zelig has the polymorphic anonymity of the character actor, whose
capacity for both self-negation and self-transformation, in some
ways reminiscent of mediumistic trance, makes him capable of extraordinary transfigurations. Zelig not only is seen in the company
of actors but he also becomes a "performing freak" in Martin Geist's
exploitative side show. One of Zelig's wives, espoused during one of
his metamorphoses, claims to have known him when he was "pre-
tending to be an actor" (a paradoxical formulation, since "pre-
tending" is what actors do); and the chameleon-actor analogy is
reinforced when we learn that Zelig's father practiced the same
profession in a Brooklyn theatre, playing the role of Puck in what
seems like an oxymoronic production—the orthodox Yiddish version of *A Midsummer Night's Dream*.

The reference to Yiddish theatre points to still another intertext in which *Zelig* is embedded—that of Yiddish theatre and Borsch
Belt stand-up comedy (the explicit subject of Allen's *Broadway Danny
Rose*). The theatre that "fathered" Zelig was a theatre full of transformations and boisterous polyglossia, fond of oxymoronic protagonists such as the *schlemil*-saint and the *luftmensch*-visionary. The
immigrant experience familiarized Jewish actors and entertain-
ers with a wide variety of ethnic accents and intonations. Indeed,
Zelig exemplifies as well the comic "universe-changing," the
sometimes caricatural ethnic switchabouts that are typical of
Yiddish-derived theatricality, of Fanny Brice performing "I'm an
Indian" or Al Jolson in blackface belting out "Manny," or of Mel
Brooks's Yiddish-speaking Indian in *Blazing Saddles*. Even the
Menippean-style anachronisms of *Zelig,* whereby contemporary

players are made to neighbor with deceased celebrities from the twenties, have everything to do with the anachronic humor of Mel Brooks's "2,000 Year Old Man," or with "Getting Even," Allen's own tale about a Hassidic Rabbi who applies cabalistic numerology to the daily double.

If all human beings, as the *theatrum mundi* trope would have it, are actors, some human beings have been more attuned to acting than others. Oppressed people, one might contend, are necessarily actors prone to double-voiced discourse and obliged to perform diverse "performance styles." The force of historical experience, it has been argued, has made Jews especially sensitive to the theatrical dimension of social life. George Simmel, Helmut Plessner, and Hannah Arendt (not to mention Nietzsche and Marcel Proust) have all spoken of this heightened Jewish sensitivity to the theatrical. Hannah Arendt describes the "exceptional Jews" who were admitted into the philo-Semitic salons of *fin de siècle* Paris under the tacit condition that they would not reveal their status as Jews, a situation that made each of them an experienced actor in a theatre whose curtain never closed. Life became theatrical to the point that the actors themselves, not unlike Zelig, no longer knew who they were.[25] In "The Problem of the Actor," in *Joyful Wisdom,* Nietzsche calls Jews "the adaptable people par excellence," and the Jewish experience and milieu the ideal place for the "rearing of actors" blessed with "histrionic capacity."[26] As someone who wants to "assimilate like crazy" (as Irving Howe describes him), Zelig personifies the internal contradictions of one who is confronted with the "theatrical" challenge of shuttling, as it were, between the performance styles of sharply contrasting social worlds.

Zelig makes a number of references to anti-Semitism. One partisan of Christian purity denounces Zelig as a polygamist and recommends "lynching the little Hebe." In street fights with anti-Semites, Zelig complains, his parents always sided with the anti-Semites. Under hypnosis, Zelig reveals that he chameleonizes because "it's safe." One meaning of dialogism, Paul de Man points out—rather ironically, in light of recent revelations—is "double-talk, the necessary obliqueness of any persecuted speech that cannot, at the risk of survival, openly say what it means to say."[27] Historically, Jews have reacted diversely to the persecutory discourse of anti-Semitism and the temptation, and at times the decree, of assimilation. Some preferred death to forced conversion, while others chose the path of a self-preserving mimetism, thus obeying the religious principle of respect for the sacred character of life, while

Spinoza, in his *Tractatus Theologico-Politicus,* lamented the fate of the *marranos,* who fused so well with the Spaniards that soon thereafter nothing remained of them, not even a memory.[28] Ever since Esther, Jews have often been obliged to play a convoluted game of cultural hide-and-seek in order to avoid victimization by the blindest kind of violence, and it is for this challenge that Zelig, with his singular capacity for metamorphosis, is especially well equipped.

Jews formed Europe's internal other, Todorov points out in *The Conquest of America,* before the colonized peoples became its external other.[29] The Spanish Inquisition, designed to punish Jews and Muslims whose religious metamorphoses were deemed "insincere," coincided with the invasion of the New World, and we can even discern a partial congruency between the stereotypical representations projected onto both the internal "enemy" and the external "savage": "blood drinkers," "cannibals," "sorcerers," "devils."[30] The Jew, like Zelig, was seen as a mask-wearer, a diabolically fascinating shape-shifter. Zelig, in this sense, can be seen as "condensing" a number of the favored themes of anti-Semitism. His "reptilian" nature, for example, recalls Constantine Schuabe, the Jewish villain of the anti-Semitic British best-seller *When It Was Dark,* who displayed the "sinister and troubled regard one sees in a reptile's eyes." More important, Zelig reflects the enforced plurality of the Jewish experience, the long historical apprenticeship in cultural mimicry, and the syncretic incorporation of ambient cultures. Indeed, this plurality often excited the passions of anti-Semites. The notion of a suspect plurality of identities runs like a leitmotif through anti-Semitic discourse—in Houston Stewart Chamberlain's idea of the "mongrel race," for example, or in Hitler's idea that Jews were "hiding" their otherness behind fluent German. "They change nationalities like shirts," ran the litany, and the term *cosmopolitan,* with its connotations of a fluid multicultural identity, became in Stalinist jargon a code word for "Jew." It is Zelig's multiple otherness that provokes the special hatred of the Ku Klux Klan: "As Jew, black, and Indian," the voice-over tells us, "the Ku Klux Klan saw Zelig as a triple threat." In his metamorphoses, Zelig sums up the polymorphic nature of the Jewish experience and even the reality of Jews as a transracial people who literally range in appearance from blonde Hollywood actresses to the black Falashas of Ethiopia.

The psychopathology of assimilation has at times led to extremes of self-degradation, as in the case of the notorious Jewish anti-Semite Otto Weininger, whose claim that "Judaism is the radical evil" supplied ideological ammunition for the enemies of the

Jews.[31] The anti-Semite, to amend Sartre, creates not the Jew but the Jewish anti-Semite, a possibility powerfully imaged by Zelig's ephemeral transformation into a Nazi.[32] (Self-hatred, Arthur Koestler once remarked, is a peculiarly Jewish form of patriotism.) In his flight from ghettoization, in his personal "ordeal of civility" (Cuddihy), Zelig demonstrates a weakness for upward mobility and a fascination with the possibility of moving freely across borders and gaining access to the real centers of gentile power. He gains a certain mobility and even wins access to the Vatican and the Third Reich, but his mimicry, like that of the assimilated Jew who lapses under pressure into "Judendeutsch," is always incomplete, always producing what Homi Bhabha calls "its slippage, its excess, its difference."[33] As a result, Zelig is ejected from the papal balcony and from the Third Reich rostrum.

Occupying a position of maximum social exposure, and open to multifarious influences, Zelig represents the outsider as quasi-insider. From this position, his chameleonism can take him in virtually any direction. Zelig's metamorphoses give physical expression to what George Steiner in "The Homeland as Text" calls the "ontological foreignness" of the Diaspora Jew as a person always in transit, a person with a permanent visa to a messianic other homeland, drawing a kind of anguished vitality from dispersal and from the adaptive demands made by mobility. In another sense, however, Zelig's situation is emblematic of a more general condition. Zelig stands at the end of the historical process (traced by Stephen Greenblatt in *Renaissance Self-Fashioning*) whereby human beings become more and more self-conscious about the fashioning of human identity as a manipulable, artful process, leading to a malleable, cosmopolitan sense of self.[34] For Bakhtin, the process of constructing the self has a linguistic as well as a psychological dimension. It has to do with hearing and assimilating the words of others (mother, father, relatives, friends, representatives of religious, educational, and political institutions, the mass media, etc.), all of which are processed dialogically so that in a sense they become half "one's own words." In Bakhtinian terminology, the assimilated word of the other transforms itself into "internally persuasive discourse."

Such discourse is of decisive significance in the evolution of an individual consciousness: consciousness awakens to independent ideological life precisely in the world of [the] alien discourses surrounding it, and from which it cannot initially separate itself; the process of distinguishing between one's own and another's discourse, between one's own and another's thought, is activated rather late in development. When thought begins to work in an independent, experimenting and discriminating way, what first occurs is a separation between internally persuasive discourse and authoritarian enforced discourse, along with a rejection of those congeries of discourses that do not matter to us, that do not touch us.[35]

According to Bakhtin, one becomes a self through a process of linguistic hybridization (the metaphor is one of Bakhtin's favorites), by acquiring ambient languages and finally forging a kind of personal synthesis. The self lives and breathes any number of languages—familial, bureaucratic, the language of the streets, the language of the mass media—which intersect with one another and which are not mutually exclusive. Zelig exemplifies the contemporary condition of what Lawrence Grossberg calls "nomadic subjectivity." The self, in this sense, forms a kind of shifting hybrid sum of its discursive practices. Internally persuasive discourse is affirmed, for Bakhtin, through "assimilation," through a tight interweaving of the words of others "with one's own word." Zelig, in his constant metamorphoses, represents the person who has lost all capacity to distinguish between his own and the alien word.

Zelig's extreme ideological mobility points to the political ambiguities of chameleonism. A person's ideological development, Bakhtin argues, is an "intense struggle within us for hegemony among various available verbal and ideological points of view, approaches, directions and values."[36] Alien voices, Bakhtin writes, "enter into the struggle for influence within an individual's consciousness (just as they struggle with one another in surrounding social reality)."[37] Zelig, like everyone else, has the choice of trying to chameleonize "vertically" to the powerful, or "horizontally" to the analogously oppressed. (In short, one can "make it" to the top like Norman Podhoretz or struggle sideways like Emma Goldman and Abbie Hoffman.) Zelig, for his part, plays both pariah and parvenu; he is at once the aristocrat chatting on the lawn and the commoner speaking with the kitchen help.

Under hypnosis, Zelig admits to dialogically chameleonizing with another group of "hyphenated Americans." Entering a bar on Saint Patrick's Day, he relates: "I told them I was Irish. My hair turned red. My nose turned up. I spoke about the great potato famine." In *The Ordeal of Civility,* John Murray Cuddihy explores the analogies between the Irish and the Jewish immigrant communities as "latecomers to modernity." While the Irish were the product of the famines of the 1840s, which killed a million Irish and drove them into the world of Anglo-American Protestantism, the Jews were the product of the Russian pogroms, which killed thousands of East European Jews and drove them too into the world of the New World goyim. Both groups had a precarious grasp on political power, and both had a nostalgia for the Old World convivium.[38] Irving Howe describes the relation between the two groups within Tammany Hall as "generally amiable, seldom close, and far more complicated than either side realized."[39]

The point of this excursus is that each of Zelig's transformations has its own peculiar rationale, and while critics have emphasized the bizarre aspects of the transformations, they have tended to ignore the deeper social, cultural, and historical logic that generates and structures them. It makes perfect sense, for example, that Zelig would chameleonize, more or less "horizontally," not only to his Irish fellow-swimmers in the melting pot, but also to the more obviously oppressed minorities—Indians, blacks, Chinese, Mexicans. Each particular transformation bears its particular burden of historical reverberation. Zelig's transformation into the Native American "Indian"—another quintessential marginalized insider—forges a link between Europe's external and internal "others." Similarly, Zelig's recurrent chameleonizing to blackness is deeply rooted in the Jewish experience in Europe. Medieval European iconography contrasted the black image of the synagogue with the white image of the church, an iconography that transmuted itself in the nineteenth century into the image of the "black Jew" common in end-of-the-century racist tracts. Hermann Wegener called Jews "white Negroes," and Julius Streicher, one of the most notorious anti-Semites of both the Weimar Republic and the Third Reich, argued in 1928 for the identity of language between Jew and black: "The swollen lips remind us again of the close relationship between the Jews and the Blacks. Speech takes place with a racially determined intonation."[40]

In the United States, meanwhile, Jewish entertainers took over the preexisting tradition of blackface, endowing it with their own accent and intonation. Al Jolson made blackface recital the foundation of his success, while Sophie Tucker was billed as the "World-renowned Coon Shouter" and Eddie Cantor played Salome in blackface and in drag. In *The Jazz Singer,* Jolson melded Yiddish schmaltz and blackface tradition. The Jewish fondness for blackface, Irving Howe suggests, involves not only shrewd opportunism but also an intuition of deeper affinities: "Black became a mask for Jewish expressiveness, with one woe speaking through the voice of another."⁴¹ What Ronald Sanders calls "ethnic pastiche" is a propensity of peoples who live in culturally bilingual situations. Blackface, Howe suggests, paradoxically enabled Jewish performers to reach "a spontaneity and assertiveness in the declaration of their Jewish selves."⁴² In such a situation, cultural syncretism was inevitable. Irving Berlin mingled Yiddishisms with "coon song" conventions, Isaac Goldberg found musical affinities between black "blue notes" and the "blue note" of Hassidic chant, and Gershwin blended Yiddish folktunes with black melodies. And it was all part of a general movement of American history, a movement by which indigenous, Afro-American, and local-immigrant experiences flowed into the broader "nonfinalized" polyphony of a constantly evolving national culture susceptible to "Judaization," "Africanization," "Latinization," and so on.

In still another sense, Zelig can be seen as exemplifying the Bakhtinian view of the self as a kind of echo chamber of socially orchestrated voices. Zelig's chameleonism, we must remember, is also linguistic. Zelig speaks a variety of languages, apparently without accent, and adopts diverse social "dialects" and "intonations." (The experience of the children of Jewish immigrants was necessarily at least bilingual, involving contact with at least two languages, Yiddish and English, while being "haunted," as it were, by the memory of the sacred language, Hebrew. The result of this creolized situation is what Bakhtin calls the "hybridization" and "assimilation" of the other's word). As a walking polyphony of ethnic personalities, Zelig mimics the appearance and impersonates the voices of the diverse synecdochic cultural figures with whom he comes in contact, representatives of the various ethnic communities of New York City and its environs. Zelig has "lines out," to borrow a metaphor from Melville's Pequod, to everyone else on the social "ship." His metamorphoses, in this sense, simply render visible and palpable what is usually invisible—the constant process of synchresis that occurs when ethnicities brush against and rub off on one another in a context of cultural "many-languagedness."

Zelig would seem, at first glance, to have a happy ending. Zelig's anarchic pluralities are exorcized and domesticated as he discovers his "true self" and settles into monogamous normality. On the surface, the conclusion suggests the endorsement of the complacent American version of Sartrean "authenticity" expressed in the anticonformist discourse of fifties liberalism: the formerly "outer directed" Zelig is now "inner directed." Paradoxically, however, Zelig is never more conformist than when he starts to "be himself." In the end, he acquiesces in middle-class values and speaks in the clichés of ego psychology and the self-help manual. "Be yourself," he tells admiring young people. "You have to be your own man." (Ironically, no one would be soliciting his opinion if he had not "dared" to be a chameleon.) In short, he has become a bland All-American, an acritical parrot of the reigning ideology, with no individuating traits more striking than being a "life-long Democrat" and "loving baseball."

The inane pronouncements generated by Zelig's culminating epiphany generate a certain skepticism that undermines the classical harmony of the film's "happy end." In fact, *Zelig* highlights the curious doubleness of chameleonism, its possession of positive and negative poles. On the one hand, the film presents Zelig's condition as pathological, a neurosis to be cured, a disease whose symptoms include passivity, conformism, and, potentially, fascism. The aleatory blank-check quality of Zelig's chameleonism makes him anxious to assimilate to *any* other, even to that of his enemies. His random cannibalization of the personalities of others turns his own into an aggregation of pastiches, a blank postmodern collage of available styles.[43] In this sense, Zelig lives out one pole of the possibilities pointed out by Bakhtin in terms of self/other relations: acritical absorption *by* the other, the loss of knowledge of which word is the other's and which is one's own.

At the same time, it is possible to tease out a latent utopia stirring within the negativity of Zelig (whose name does, after all, mean "blessed" as well as "silly"), a utopia both hinted at and repressed by what in some ways remains a recalcitrant text.[44] In an oppositional, "anticipatory" reading, *Zelig* can be seen as pointing to the positive potentialities of chameleonism: creative adaptability, artistic transformation, and the vision of a possible communitas of reciprocally empathetic selves. This inkling of a possible life beyond the monad, transcending fixed social poles and ethnic positions, this possibility of an exhilarating indeterminacy (and what is carnival if not exhilarating indeterminacy?), is hinted at (awkwardly) by a man interviewed in a barbershop: "I wish I could be Leonard Zelig, the changing man, for then I could be many different people and some day my wish might come true." It is significant that a man of the people, not a celebrity, articulates this collective fantasy. The man imagines, in short, a Bakhtinian self, a self that is not locked in, that can cross the border to imagine the other as subject and himself as object.[45] ("By objectifying myself," Bakhtin writes, "I gain the opportunity to have an authentically dialogic relation with myself.") The man in the barbershop sees Zelig as a man who "wears" other selves like carnival costumes, whose experience intimates a transindividual taste of freedom.

Zelig offers intriguing glimpses of possibilities not fully realized in the text itself. It intimates a view of the text, and the self, as a partial creation of the other. Biological life, Bakhtin points out, depends on the capacity to respond to environmental stimuli; a living organism resists total fusion, but if completely torn from its environment, it dies. Jacques Derrida, in his essay on apartheid, makes the same point on a linguistic register: "How does one learn the other's language without renouncing one's own?"[46] What is most suggestive in Zelig is the implicit parallelism that links the film's view of both text and self as cultural artifacts. A Bakhtinian reading might discern in Zelig a breaking down of the frontiers of self as well as the frontiers of genre. The somatic membrane separating self from self, like that separating text from text and genre from genre, is more permeable than was once thought; no ontological segregation, no rigid apartness, is possible. The self, in a context of cultural polyphony, is necessarily syncretic. Zelig renders this syncretism visible by offering us a figure who is at once recognizably Woody Allen and black, Indian, and Chinese. Woody Allen does not become Chinese, it is important to note; he becomes a Chinese Woody Allen. The dialogical encounter, Bakhtin insists, is never a complete merging. One cannot become the other, but one can meet the other part way. Within the Bakhtinian "in-between," the self needs the collaboration of others in order to author and define itself, just as the film-text Zelig literally derives its existence from preexisting texts. (Whatever does not come from the tradition, Bunuel was fond of saying, is plagiarism). Zelig's originality, paradoxically, lies in the audacity of its imitation, quotation, and absorption of other texts. Its ironic hybridization of traditionally opposed discourses undermines the monologic truth of generic purity and thus implicitly subverts, perhaps even against its own will, the very idea of "originality" and, by extension, the idea of the truly autonomous self. While Zelig at times seems to fall back into a mystification of self and romance, its chameleonist intertextual strategies point to what Bakhtin would call "the interpersonal definition and fabrication of the world's meaning."

◼️◼️ Envoi: Bakhtin and Mass-Media Critique

In this final "envoi," I would like to explore the pertinence of Bakhtinian conceptualizations to another problematic Bakhtin himself never directly addressed: the cultural politics of the mass media. The left, it seems, has often displayed a schizophrenic attitude toward mass-mediated culture, oscillating between melancholy and euphoria. As the "children of Marx and Coca-Cola," Godard has his character put it in *Masculin, Féminin,* leftists participate in a mass culture they often theoretically condemn. But even apart from this split between personal habits and political stance, the left has shown theoretical ambivalence about the *political* role of the mass media. On the one hand, a certain left (Herbert Schiller, Armand Mattelart, and in a different way, Theodor Adorno and Max Horkheimer), excoriates the mass media as the voice of bourgeois hegemony, the instrument of capitalist reification, an overwhelming apparatus or "influencing machine" broaching little resistance. In this more pessimistic phase, the left laments the media's "total manipulation" of the "false needs" and "false desires" of its narcoleptic audience, and practices, as a didactic corollary, a kind of pedagogy of displeasure, thus ceding a crucial area to the enemy. Another left, in contrast, salutes the revolutionizing impact of modern reproduction techniques (Benjamin) or the mass-mediated subversion of the traditional class privileges of the literary elite (Enzensberger). This left detects progressive potential in mass-mediated cultural products, finding inklings of empowerment in the working-class anger of a

Bruce Springsteen or evidence of emancipatory desire in the collective enthusiasm for superstar concert-telethons for Farm Aid and Amnesty International. At its most optimistic, it finds the germ of subversion in Pee Wee Herman, music video, and even soap opera.

A number of analysts, fortunately, have sought to go beyond this ideological manic-depression by stressing the gaps, fissures, and contradictions lurking just below the apparently unperturbed surface of the mass media. In 1970, in "Constituents of a Theory of the Media," Hans Magnus Enzensberger spoke of television as a "leaky medium," corporately controlled but pressured by popular desire and dependent on "politically unreliable" creative talent to satisfy its inexhaustible appetite for programming.[1] Enzensberger took exception to the manipulation-theory view of the media as engaging in mass deception, emphasizing instead their focus on "real needs" and "real desires." Picking up this utopian strain, writers such as Fredric Jameson, Richard Dyer, and Dick Hebdige highlighted mass culture as a response to what Jameson called the "elemental power of deep social needs." Two excellent recent collections—Tania Modleski's *Studies in Entertainment* and Colin MacCabe's *High Theory/Low Culture*—continue to negotiate between what Meeghan Morris calls the "cheerleaders" and the "prophets of doom" by proposing a dialectical synthesis that eschews both the elitist pessimism of manipulation theory and the naïve affirmative celebrations of the uncritical apologists for mass-mediated culture.[2] Few of these analysts, however, take full advantage of a theorist who might further buttress and animate this more dialectical view—Mikhail Bakhtin.

Mass-Media Heteroglossia

Bakhtin's "historical poetics," I suggested earlier, avoids the twin traps of a vacuous, apolitical formalism and a deterministic version of Marxism that would relegate the world of signs and ideology to a "superstructural" roof on an economic base. Within a Bakhtinian perspective, the mass media can be conceptualized as a "complex network of ideological signs" situated within multiple environments—the generating mass-media environment, the broader generating ideological environment, and the generating socioeconomic environment—each with its own specificities. Television, in this sense, constitutes an electronic microcosm, a contemporary version of Bakhtin's omnivorous "novel," which reflects and relays, distorts and amplifies, the ambient heteroglossia.[3] Television's heteroglossia is of course in some ways severely compromised, truncated; many social voices are never heard or are severely distorted. But as a matrix in which centripetal-dominant and centrifugal-oppositional discourses do battle, the mass media can never completely reduce the antagonistic dialogue of class voices to what Jameson calls the "reassuring hum of bourgeois hegemony." There are patterns of ownership, and clear ideological tendencies, but domination is never complete, for not only is television its owners and its industrial managers; it is also its creative participants, its workers, and its audience, which can resist, pressure, and decode.

Within a Bakhtinian approach, there is no unitary text, no unitary producer, and no unitary spectator; rather, there is a conflictual heteroglossia pervading producer, text, context, and reader/viewer. Each category is traversed by the centripetal and the centrifugal, the hegemonic and the oppositional. The proportion might vary, of course, with category and situation. In contemporary American television, for instance, the owner-producer category is likely to incline toward the hegemonic, yet even here a rift is possible between those who control the apparatus and those who produce for it. The process is conflictual, involving an orchestration of the diverse "voices" responsible for assembling the text, a process that leaves traces and discordances in the text itself. The texts produced, given the conflictual nature of the creative process as well as the socially generated needs of the audience, are likely to feature a certain proportion of resistant messages or at least to make possible resistant readings. The role of a radical hermeneutics of the mass media would be to heighten awareness of all the voices relayed by the mass media, to point both to the "off screen" voices of hegemony and to the contestatory voices that are muffled or suppressed. The goal would be to discern the often distorted undertones of utopia in mass media, while pointing to the real structural obstacles that make utopia less realizable and at times even less imaginable. A Bakhtinian approach would combat the selectivity of hearing promoted by mass culture. It would recuperate the critical and utopian potential of mass-mediated texts, even when this potential is half-denied or repressed within the text itself. The issue is not to impose an interpretation but rather to bring out the text's muffled voices, much as the sound-studio mixer reelaborates a recording to tease out the bass, or clarify the treble, or amplify the instrumentation. A Bakhtinian approach would see television programming as "situated utterance." As "utterance," it is by definition fraught with the communicative possibilities of dialogism, but as "situated," it is contingent, historical, penetrated by both hegemony and resistance. Rather than career schizophrenically between optimism and despair, then, the left should adopt a complex attitude toward the mass media, one involving a whole spectrum of moods and attitudes and strategies.

The Tact of Television Programming

The analysis of televisual heteroglossia needs to incorporate Bakhtin's view of "tact"—that is, the ways in which power inflects televisual "dialogues" and shapes their "representation." The tact of American television, in this perspective, might easily be analyzed in Bakhtinian terms as a product of the relations between the interlocutors (on and off screen), the concrete situation of the "conversation," and the aggregate of social relationships and the ideological horizons informing the discourse. Take, for example, the television "talk show." At the center of such shows, we find the pivotal Bakhtinian trope of the dialogical interplay of speaking subjects, persons in literal or metaphorical dialogue. Waiting in the wings, meanwhile, are the unheard participants in the dialogue: the network managers and the corporate sponsors who "speak" only through commercial messages. And facing the celebrities in the literal space of the studio is the in-the-flesh surrogate audience, an ideally participatory version of the invisible audience at home, with whom host and guest also dialogue, an audience which is itself a cross-section of a populace traversed by contradictions of class, gender, race, age, and politics.

What might emerge from such an analysis would be a profoundly mixed situation, mingling the crassest kind of manipulation with subliminally utopian appeals and modestly progressive gestures. (Indeed, the left badly needs analytical categories, such as those of Bakhtin, which allow for the fact that a given utterance or discourse can be progressive and regressive *at the same time*.) Take, for example, the "Oprah Winfrey Show." Its star constitutes the very model of an articulate and expressive facilitator presiding over an important network program, a black woman whose dynamic presence challenges the patriarchal and ethnic hegemonies of the Phil Donahues and Johnny Carsons. The Oprah programs themselves, furthermore, tend to foreground female discontent with male attitudes and behavior, issues discussed in an atmosphere of spontaneity, identification, and communitarian solidarity. At the same time, if we look at the program as a "situated utterance," we can view Oprah's capacity for what Bakhtin would call "responsive understanding" as a marketable commodity that attracts viewers, in a show whose ultimate *telos*, at least in the eyes of its corporate managers, is to attract an audience to be sold to sponsors.

In the world of the talk show, the corporate sponsors wield the ultimate discursive power; they have the right to suspend or even terminate the conversation. A cold-cash nexus, as well as an ideological filter, severely compromises what appears to be the warm exchange of an "ideal speech situation" (Habermas) based on "free and familiar contact." (The "joke," in Martin Scorcese's *The King of Comedy*, consists in having its protagonist try to "collect" on the implicit promise of television's talk-show "warmth"; Rupert Pupkin literally believes that the talk-show host Jerry Langford, modeled on Johnny Carson, is his "friend.") The communicative utopia is compromised, furthermore, not only by corporate getting and spending but also by the obsession with ratings, by the search for ever more sensational victims (Donahue) or ever more reflexive inanities (David Letterman), by the peripheralization of any truly alternative discourse, and by the insistent success trope that underlies the shows and fosters vicarious identification with the ephemeral triumphs of "stars." The discourse is further marred by other hidden and not-so-hidden agenda having to do with the promotion of books, films, and shows. The conversation, in sum, is neither free nor disinterested; the discourse is bound by the innumerable restraints of corporate and social "tact."

Local "Eyewitness News" programs are susceptible to a similar kind of analysis. Here the conversation is not between guests but between newscasters, and between the newscasters and ourselves. The "show" is framed as what appears to be dialogue: the newscasters address us directly, in the second person, and tell us "Good evening" and "See you tomorrow." Here the tact of the program is clearly integrative, engendering what I have called elsewhere a "regime of the fictive we." In the world of the newsroom, chummy guys and affable gals impersonate ideal good-time neighbors, collectively forming the image of a lively and caring "news family." ("From Our Family to Yours" is a typical eyewitness news slogan). One is struck by the almost surreal discontinuity between the morbidity of most of the news items—the daily harvest of rapes and murders, abandoned babies, child molestation—and the cheerful familial atmosphere surrounding the newscasters. The impression is that the world "out there" is nasty and brutish, but that life "in here"—that is, in the mirroring domains of television studio and home—is comfortable and permeated by trust. This contrast of cold world and warm hearth electronically updates the old, ideologically determined Victorian dichotomy of "home" (the domain of "feminine" feeling) and the street (the locus of "masculine" action). Indeed, television has often been metaphorized as the "electronic hearth." In the studio, a contrived atmosphere of self-conscious informality fosters the impression that we all belong to a harmonious family-community that is sufficiently at ease to kid and joke. Here too, however, many icy calculations form part of the fabrication of "warmth," since we know that the happiness of the news team is a construct favored by news consultants preoccupied with improving ratings.[4]

"Eyewitness News" exemplifies the insight, developed by Hans Magnus Enzensberger, Richard Dyer, and Fredric Jameson, among others, that to explain the public's attraction to a medium, one must look not only for ideological manipulation but also for the kernel of utopian fantasy whereby the medium constitutes itself as a projected fulfillment of what is desired and absent within the status quo. "Eyewitness News" takes the dystopian realities of contemporary urban life under late capitalism, and through an artistic "change of signs" turns them into the simulacrum of a playful and egalitarian communitas, a world characterized by communicative transparency and "free and familiar contact." For what could be more utopian than this newsroom world of ludic productivity, where professionals seem to be having the time of their lives, and where work, as in a musical comedy, is incessantly transformed into play. Within this electronic representation, benign father figures preside over a multiethnic symbolic family where synecdochic figures "represent" the community at large. Whereas ethnic groups might be at each other's throats in the streets, and even in the filmed reports shown on the news, the newscasters themselves live in a racial utopia that suggests an ideal image of the community itself.

The Simulacrum of Carnival

Bakhtin's name for the utopian impulse was, of course, "carnival," and in this sense "Eyewitness News" illustrates a crucial feature of contemporary American television—its tendency to constantly serve up the simulacrum of carnival-style festivity as hyperreal paliatives for an enervated society. Celebrity roasts, in this perspective, can be seen as updated versions of Bakhtin's "festive symposia," in which revelers play the game of "excessive praise and blame." Television's canned laughter becomes the magnetic substitute for real laughter, which is possible only in an ambience of community. Programs like "Fantasy Island" and "Love Boat," meanwhile, as Horace Newcombe and Paul Hirsch point out, offer "liminal" utopias, happy offshore social microcosms.[5] Television also implicitly offers the possibility of universal Andy-Warhol-style stardom, an updating of carnival's erasure of the line between the spectator and the spectacle. The spectator might get a call from a talk-show host, be thanked on a telethon, get interviewed by the "Eyewitness News" team, ask a question on the "Phil Donahue Show," be mocked by a superimposed title on "Saturday Night Live," sing a song on the "Johnny Carson Show," appear on "Dating Game" or "People's Court," or even—and here we approach real stardom—perform on "Star Search." In all these instances, as Elayne Rapping puts it, the people literally "make a spectacle of themselves," thus abolishing, à la carnival, the barrier between performer and audience.

Bakhtin's notion of carnival has considerable explanatory power in accounting for the popular appeal of mass spectacle. American popular culture often reverberates ambiguously with textual echoes of carnival. The analysis of Hollywood musical comedy as a two-dimensional carnival in which the negatives of social existence are turned into the positives of artistic transmutation can easily be extended to account for the appeal of contemporary music videos. Donna Summer's "She Works Hard for the Money" choreographs diverse kinds of womens' drudge work into a joyous celebration of feminine solidarity. Eddie Grant's "Dance Party" (not to mention Dr. Pepper and Pepsi commercials) draws on the old carnival trope of "the people dancing in the streets." And literal echoes of Caribbean carnival can be heard in Lionel Ritchie's "All Night Long," a music video whose music, lyrics, and visuals celebrate a multiethnic and multistyled utopia in which day changes place with night and even policemen forsake authoritarianism to twirl their batons and to break dance in a choreographed takeover of public space.

As I suggested earlier, it is useful to distinguish between "bottom up" carnival as communitarian festivity and adversary culture, on the one hand, and top-down "ersatz" or "degraded" carnivals, on the other. (A Nazi rally, as a dystopian ritual based on the annihilation of difference, a sadomasochistic ritual of submission to a charismatic leader, constitutes a liturgical insertion *into* hierarchy rather than a liberation *from* it, and thus might be seen as the ultimate degraded carnival.) The possessive individualism that has become the norm in many contemporary societies obviously renders a truly communitarian carnival more remote and inaccessible. The three months of the year that were once spent reveling in the people's "second life," are now reduced to yearly holidays that more and more resemble the work period from which they are supposed to offer relief (this ironic resemblance forms the explicit topic of Jacques Tati's "holiday" films). Carnival for the working class has become the weekly "Thank God It's Friday" ritual, which serves merely to renew the body for resumption of work on Monday. For the relatively leisured, it has become Caribbean "carnival" cruises, whose distance from authentic carnival is marked in the envy-preoccupied refrain of the commercial's theme song: "If my friends could see me now!" Bakhtin's boisterously vulgar marketplace, in the postmodern era, has become the musakized consumerist utopia of the shopping mall. The effervescent play of carnival has become the aerobics workout (dance as grim duty), and even parties have become laborious forms of "networking."

In this sense, we can account for the appeal of many mass-mediated products as relaying, in a compromised manner, the distant cultural memory and imagery of authentic carnival. The American mass media are fond of weak or truncated forms of carnival that capitalize on the frustrated desire for a truly egalitarian society by serving up distorted versions of carnival's utopian promise: Fourth of July commercial pageantry, jingoistic sing-alongs, authoritarian rock concerts, festive soft-drink commercials. Any euphoric evaluation that regards television as authentically "carnivalesque" must moderate its euphoria with an awareness of the political constraints involved in any "situated utterance." And this complexity virtually obliges one, in such analyses, to call on the rhetorical figure of the oxymoron: the ersatz carnival, the degenerate utopia, the censored forum. For it is too easy to equate carnival with the mere surface manifestations of carnival imagery and strategies. John Fiske's fascinating reflections on the carnival-like aspects of television wrestling demonstrate both the immense exegetical power and the ultimate limitations of a certain kind of carnivalesque analysis. Fiske correctly traces the origins of a program like "Rock-'n'-Wrestling" to the stylized comic violence of commedia dell'arte and notes with approval the "excessive bodies" of the wrestlers, the parodic elements of their costumes, the mockingly ritualized and stylized nature of their combat, as well as the active nature of the crowd, whose participation ranges from the physical (raining blows on a wrestler), to the verbal (shouting abuse, holding up placards), to the symbolic (waving mannequin dolls of one's favorite wrestler), in such a way that "the categorical distinction between spectacle and spectator is abolished, [and] all participate spectacularly in this inverted, parodic world."[6]

Fiske's highly suggestive analysis rightly cuts through the kind of class snobbery that would applaud the more cerebral, "hip" intertextuality of the "David Letterman Show" while deploring the palpable and gross physicality of "Rock-'n'-Wrestling." At the same time, the celebration of the "grotesque" realism of such a spectacle strikes me as somewhat premature, and calls for a heightened sense of nuance. For while on one level such spectacles are perhaps a tribute to the strength and endurance of popular, disruptive forces, on another level we must remember that strategies that have once been effectively carnivalesque, because they belonged to an oppositional community, will inevitably alter their valence in an age of "failed communities." To what extent, we must ask, is the televisual spectacle of wrestling the product of the *oppositional* culture of the oppressed and to what extent is it a bread-and-circuses show managed from above for purposes of profit? To what extent does such a spectacle merely provide an arena for the acting-out of the ambient aggressivity of late-capitalist culture? Carnival does not exist only in surface appearances or in an inventory of strategies; it has to do with questions of situational thrust. What is the utopia, the model of better social relations, implied by television wrestling? Does it carry what Bloch calls "anticipatory consciousness"? Does it loosen up progressive social energies, release emerging forces, question gender definitions? To what extent does it involve truly "free and familiar contact," as opposed to the simulacrum of such relations? Does it offer a prototype of "the people's second life," or does it merely colonize and exploit the popular imaginary?

Media Jujitsu and the Left

The category of carnival not only accounts for the mass-media channeling of utopian desires but it also has relevance for the political strategies of the left. Bakhtin portrays parodic "carnivalization" as the privileged arm of the weak and dispossessed. Because parody appropriates an existing discourse for its own ends, it is particularly well suited to the needs of the powerless precisely because it *assumes* the force of the dominant discourse only to deploy that force, through a kind of artistic jujitsu, *against* domination. Such an "excorporation" steals elements of the dominant culture and redeploys them in the interests of oppositional praxis. Since the American left has been historically placed in a disadvantaged and defensive position, it is virtually obliged to deploy the dominant discourse, as in the martial arts, against the dominant. The electoral campaign that pitted Ronald Reagan against Walter Mondale provides an excellent example of a missed opportunity for "excorporation." The Republican candidate spoke simplistically of "morning in America," appealing to a kind of nostalgic utopianism couched in the language of community, religion, and spirituality. Exploiting the language of "fraudulent hope" (Ernst Bloch), Reagan thus commandeered the attention of many people who on social and economic grounds should have been repelled by his programs. Reagan and his public-relations managers shrewdly exploited the desire for community while promoting policies that ultimately shatter community. They deployed, furthermore, precise narrative and imagistic strategies: clear scenarios, Manichean characterizations, fast-paced action, and minimal thought—in short, the conventional panoply of devices of the Hollywood fiction film with which Reagan had been associated in the forties. (Grenada, for example, was cast as the damsel in distress, the Cubans as villains, and the United States as hero, in an imperialist rescue fantasy whose "happy ending" was as meaningless as the traditional Hollywood clincher.) In generic terms, Reagan drew on the technological utopianism of science fiction ("Star Wars"), the Manichean moralism of melodrama (the "evil empire," the saintly crusade against drugs and terrorism), and the gaiety of the musical comedy (Liberty Weekend, the Inaugural Ball), all as a cover for the gangster-style cynicism of film noir.

The Democrats, meanwhile, played the earnest Griersonian documentary to Reagan's slick fiction film. They lamented the fate of the country in sanctimonious voice-overs superimposed on images of deprivation and despair, thus playing into the hands of Reagan, who predictably portrayed them as "prophets of gloom." While the "good news" president restricted himself to cheery platitudes, the Democrats brought the bad news of domestic deficits and foreign debacles. To the charms of fiction and entertainment, they counterposed the reality principle and the politics of guilt. By an associational boomerang, they were associated with what they were denouncing. My point is not that the Democrats and the left (overlapping but hardly identical categories) should have emulated the mendacity of the Reagan campaign, but rather that the Democrats have often been paralyzed by an excess of "respect." Intimidated by Reagan's "popularity," they saw that popularity as an invincible essence rather than as a mediated construct, and thus failed to confront Reagan on his favored terrain—the terrain of mass-mediated language and symbol manipulation. Rather than pit their enfeebled charisma against that of the Great Communicator, the Democrats should have deployed audiovisual messages in conjunction with the voice and image of the president in order to forge a link between image and reality, policy and consequence. Such a strategy, relying largely on the president himself, would have constituted a self-indictment more powerful than any verbal attack by a Democratic candidate. In a double operation, the Democrats should have proposed their own counterutopia while "carnivalizing" Reagan. Just as carnival revelers used grotesque realism to deprive the king of the symbols of his power in order to reveal him as a ridiculous figure, so the Democrats should have comically exposed the vacuity of Reagan's ideas and the puppetlike quality of his pronouncements, stripping him of his cue cards and teleprompters and tearing the mask off his cruelty.[7]

Cultural and Political Polyphony

Another category of potential efficacy in media analysis is Bakhtin's notion of "polyphony." This music-derived trope, originally formulated in reference to the complex play of ideological voices in the work of Dostoevsky, refers, although from a distinct angle, to the same phenomenon designated by the terms *dialogism* and *heteroglossia*. The concept of "polyphony" calls attention to the coexistence, in any textual or extratextual situation, of a plurality of voices that do not fuse into a single consciousness but exist on different registers, generating dialogical dynamism among themselves. Both heteroglossia and polyphony point not to mere heterogeneity as such but rather to the dialogical angle at which voices are juxtaposed and counterposed so as to generate something beyond themselves. I would like to speak here of only one dimension of polyphony—the cultural—and of its political consequences. While all cultures are polyphonic in the sense that they include distinct genders, professions, and age groups, some cultures are striking in being *ethnically* polyphonic. Bakhtin's multiethnic source-culture, existing at the crossroads of Europe and Asia, provided innumerable exemplars of cultural and ethnic polyphony.

The New World countries of the Americas similarly deploy myriad cultural voices—that of the indigenous peoples (no matter how suppressed that voice may be), that of the Afro-American (however distorted), that of the Jewish, Italian, Hispanic, and Asiatic communities—each of which condenses, in turn, a multiplicity of social accents having to do with gender, class, and locale—all flowing into a broader, nonfinalized polyphony of cultures.

Much of the potential force and audacity of the national cinemas of the Americas derives from their capacity to stage the conflicts and complementarities of polyphonic culture. The people of Brazil, for example, as the product of ethnic and cultural *mesticaje,* represent a multitude of exiles and diasporas—indigenous people made alien in their own land, blacks brought by force from Africa, immigrants from Europe, Asia, and the Middle East—and much of the force and originality of Brazilian art, as we have seen in *Macunaima,* derives from its polyphonic orchestration of cultural figures and references. Similarly, the culture of the United States is borne under the sign of plurality and syncretism. A city like New York provides a boisterously fractured and conflictual model of heteroglossia whose very language is syncretic, consisting of Yiddishized English, Anglicized Spanish, and the like. When Rupert Pupkin (in *The King of Comedy*) calls Masha "el schmucko supremo," he is offering a typical example of the hybridized language of the city. In films such as *Zelig,* or Alan Parker's *Fame* and Mazursky's *Moscow on the Hudson,* a New York setting helps generate a rich weave of ethnic voices. A Bakhtinian analysis of such films would point both to their polyphonic potential and to the political myopia undermining that potential. In *Fame,* youthful representatives of diverse communities—black, Puerto Rican, Jewish, gay—collaborate within a kind of utopia of artistic expression. In *Moscow on the Hudson,* the Robin Williams character interacts dialogically with a similar gallery of synecdochic ethnic figures—a black security guard, an Italian sales clerk, a Korean taxi-driver, a Cuban lawyer, a Chinese anchorwoman. Each dialogue is inflected by the specific accents of a culturally defined interlocutor. And Zelig's capacity to take on the accent and ethnicity of those with whom he interacts, as we have seen, turns him into a one-man polyphony of cultural voices. The self, in a context of polyphony, is necessarily syncretic, especially when that polyphony is amplified by the media.

While these films evoke the play of ethnic and cultural polyphony, they fail to reveal the political obstacles to true polyphony and equality, much as political liberalism speaks of dialogue but fails to speak of the ways in which hegemonic power blocks and limits dialogue. Rather than subvert the existing power relations between the diverse communities, they tend to orchestrate superficially defined ethnic "types." *Fame* ultimately subordinates polyphony to a "making it" ethos that is less dedicated to transpersonal community than to individual "Fame!" *Moscow on the Hudson* begins by criticizing both the political repression in the Soviet Union and the laissez-faire cruelty in the United States, but it finally degenerates into just another sentimental immigrant saga. And *Zelig,* as we have seen, ultimately retreats from the utopian implications of its fable by having its protagonist rediscover his "true self" and acquiesce in suburban middle-class values, while offering precious little indication of the limitations of its protagonist's vision. A Bakhtinian approach to such films, in any case, would tease out, in an "anticipatory" reading, the latent utopias stirring within such texts, while unmasking the ways in which they repress their utopian potential and fail to signal the real social and political impediments to community.

Each cultural voice, for Bakhtin, exists in dialogue with other voices: "Utterances are not indifferent to one another, and are not self-sufficient; they are aware of and mutually reflect one another."[8] Social diversity is fundamental to *every* utterance, even to that utterance which on the surface ignores or excludes the groups with which it is in relation. All utterances take place against the background of the possible responding utterances of other social points of view. Even the most devout believer and practitioner of apartheid cannot, ultimately, separate himself from the echoing black response to white supremacism. This profoundly *relational* vision differentiates Bakhtin's thought from an innocuous liberal pluralism in several senses. First, Bakhtin sees all utterance and discourse in relation to the deforming effects of power. Second, Bakhtin does not preach a pseudoequality of viewpoints; his sympathies are clearly with the nonofficial viewpoint, with the marginalized, the oppressed, the peripheralized. Third, whereas pluralism is accretive and "tolerant"—it "allows" another voice to add itself to a preexisting core—Bakhtin's view is polyphonic, celebratory, reciprocal, and displacing. Any act of verbal or cultural exchange, for Bakhtin, leaves both interlocutors changed. The historical interlocution of blacks and whites in North America, for example, has profoundly changed both parties. All whites, for example, have been touched by black culture; their speech, music, and body language bear traces of black influence. In the eighties, the majority of white popular singers work within a black-inflected musical idiom. Virtually all the participants, black and white, in the music-video "We Are the World," for example, sing in a melismatic, soulful, improvisational gospel style, thus rendering homage to black musicality in a project that is at the same time concretely linked to relief for Africa.

Emilio de Antonio's satirical documentary about Richard Nixon, *Milhouse: A White Comedy,* offers particularly striking instances of interethnic, relational polyphony. One sound-image montage plays the voice of Nixon extolling "law and order" against a black voice giving an account of what transpired in the black community during the Republican convention: "While Richard Milhouse Nixon and his gang were eating steak and lobster, this is what happened." The ensuing images then "decode" Nixon's grand phrases about "order," showing what they really meant—that is, the repression of any hint of black rebellion. Another sound-image montage plays off Nixon's innocuous "I See a Day" speech against Martin Luther King's stirring "I Have a Dream" oration—the rhetoric and syntax of which Nixon clearly pilfers—showing transparent sympathy for the emotional force and political commitment of the latter while mocking the petit-bourgeois mediocrity of the former. Nixon's voice, promulgating the myth of "equal opportunity," is gradually made to give way to the resonant authority of the voice of King, who, in the powerful accents of the black southern preacher, denounces the barriers to equality while articulating a distant-yet-imaginable promised land of racial harmony. The two voices, in Bakhtinian terminology, are counterposed at a "dialogical" angle, generating a social message that transcends the individual content of the two discourses.

A Bakhtinian analysis would be aware of the dangers of "pseudopolyphonic" discourse, one that marginalizes and disempowers certain voices, and then "dialogues" with a puppetlike entity that has already been forced to make crucial compromises. The notion of polyphony, with its overtones of harmonious simultaneity, must be completed by the notion of heteroglossia, with its undertones of social conflict rooted not in random individual dissonances but in the deep structural cleavages of social life. The film or television commercial in which every eighth face is black, for example, has more to do with the demographics of market research or the bad conscience of liberalism than with authentic polyphony, since the black voice, in such instances, is usually shorn of its soul and deprived of its color and intonation. What John Fiske calls "market-motivated heteroglossia" merely exploits subcultural differences as a marketing strategy for incorporating ethnic and minority audiences. Polyphony consists not in the mere appearance of a representative of a given group but rather in the fostering of a textual setting where that group's voice can be heard with its full force and resonance. The question is not one of pluralism but one of multivocality, one that would abolish social inequalities while heightening and even cultivating cultural difference. Here too a Bakhtinian approach would think "from the margins," seeing blacks and women, for example, not as "interest groups" to be "added on" to a preexisting unity but rather as having been at the dynamic, generating sources of the American experience from the beginning, as groups with their own invaluable "dialogical angle" on the national experience.

In political terms, cultural polyphony would go beyond pluralism to a multiplication of mutually enriching emancipatory discourses. Discourses, for Bakhtin, do not exclude each other but rather intersect. Beyond the mere coexistence of voices, polyphony implies the possibility of the multivoicedness even of individual voices, a capacity on the part of the individual voice to adopt the accents and evaluations of another voice, much as the members of a versatile jazz group might exchange instruments from time to time and play an "alien" part. In political terms this would imply the development of what Charlotte Bunch has called "one-person coalitions"—that is, a situation in which not only blacks but whites too would address issues of racism, where men as well as women would address issues of gender, where heterosexuals would speak about homophobia, the able-bodied about the disabled, and so on. It would not be an issue of speaking "for" the other, but rather of speaking up for the other, alongside the other.[9]

Bakhtin's potential contribution to left cultural and political analysis is immense. Bakhtinian categories, as we have seen, demonstrate a consistent sympathy for all that is marginal—the margins of the body, the margins of the social organism, the margins of language—and an intrinsic identification with difference and alterity, a feature which makes them especially appropriate for the analysis of "minoritarian" discourses. Bakhtin does not directly address Third World issues, for example, but his categories are eminently well suited to them. In this sense, his thought offers a corrective to certain Eurocentric prejudices within Marxism itself. In his writings on India, Marx denounced the "sea of woes" brought by imperialism, but also spoke of England as "history's agent," whose task was "the annihilation of Asian society" and the laying of "the material foundations of Western society in Asia."[10] Engels, similarly, lauded the French conquest of Algeria as a progressive step. Marxism's ambiguous endorsement of the destruction of indigenous New World societies in the name of the forward movement of productive forces entails an unconscionable erasure of difference. In cultural terms, similarly, Marxists have sometimes been indirectly complicitous in the stigmatization of difference. One thinks, for example, of Frankfurt School analyses of popular culture, of Adorno's notorious (and uncharacteristically stupid) remarks about jazz. Even Ernst Bloch, such an acute scanner of the landscape of hope, was deaf to the note of polyphony and utopia in Afro-American music, claiming, in *The Principle of Hope,* that there is "nothing coarser, nastier, more stupid" than jazz dances since the thirties, which are nothing more than "imbecility gone wild"[11]— remarks that disappointingly reflect a deeply rooted ethnocentric prejudice toward African-derived music and dance. In contrast, in *The Formal Method in Literary Scholarship,* Bakhtin speaks of non-European cultures as the catalysts for European modernism's surpassing of a retrograde culture-bound verism. And Bakhtin's oxymoronic carnival aesthetic, in which everything is pregnant with its opposite, implies an alternative logic of nonexclusive opposites and permanent contradiction which transgresses the monologic true-or-false thinking that is typical of Western rationalism.

Unlike many theoretical grids, Bakhtinian methodology does not have to be "stretched" to make room for the marginalized and the excluded; it is perfectly suited to them. Rather than "tolerate" difference in a condescending spirit, the Bakhtinian approach respects and celebrates difference. Rather than expand the center to include the margins, it interrogates and shifts the center from the margins. Bakhtin's thought, properly used, does not represent a retreat from radicalism; rather, it calls attention to all oppressive hierarchies of power, not only those derived from class but also those generated by gender, race, and age. A Bakhtinian textual politics would favor, one would hope, a more open, reciprocal, decentered negotiation of specificity and difference; it would not advise feminist, black, or gay struggles to "wait their turn" while the class struggle achieves its ends.

Bakhtin's thought, I would suggest also, has a good deal to say about the contemporary postmodernism debate as it concerns questions of "center" and "periphery." A certain postmodern social theory dismisses the possibility of meaningful social conflict, arguing that the traditional privileges of Western patriarchal culture have been annulled, that within the global village of transnational capitalism, all cultures are caught up in the meaningless whirl of mass-mediated simulacra. Baudrillard's account of the implosive collapse of boundaries in a mass-mediated global society is exhilaratingly apt in its rendering of the "feel" of life in the simulacral world of the postmodern—indeed, his breathtaking analogies make him a kind of metaphysical poet of the *fin de millénium*—yet his conceptions are painfully inadequate to the experience of the peripheralized. The neutralization of the radical difference of the marginalized, as George Yudice points out, elides the fact that some groups cannot help seeing the world through their own irreducible marginality:

The member of an oppressed marginal group cannot escape the repercussions attached by a society to his/her skin, sex, speech, and other marginalizing marks of distinction: a black in a white world, a woman in a patriarchal culture, an unskilled worker in a (post)industrial economy.[12]

Much of postmodern theory constitutes a very sophisticated example of what Anwar Abdul Malek calls the "hegemonism of possessing minorities," in that its denial of the reality of marginalization is a luxury only those who are not marginalized can afford. Thus the center proclaims the end of its privileges just when the periphery begins to lay claim to them. "Surely it is no coincidence," writes Elizabeth Fox-Genovese, "that the Western white male elite proclaimed the death of the subject at precisely the moment at which it might have had to share that status with the women and peoples of other races and classes who were beginning to challenge its supremacy."[13] Thus thinkers from the center, blithely confident in national power and international projection, denounce peripheral nationalism as atavistic and passé. Thus metropolitan writers announce the "death of the author" just when peripheral writers begin to win an international audience. Disseminated and metropolitan filmmakers call for the *fin de cinema* just as Third World filmmakers begin to create viable industries.

All these "divestitures" are a privilege available only to the West, for the proclamation of the end of margins does not short-circuit the mechanisms that effectively disappropriate peoples of their culture or nations of their power. All the theoretical collapsing of boundaries does not, to put it with brutal materiality, turn

Third World monies into viable currencies or guarantee peripheral writers the international hearing they would take for granted were they from the center. The postmodern collapsing of center and margin does contain, admittedly, a grain of truth: the margins form an integral part of the contemporary scene; they are not behind the center, but live the same historical moment. Power no longer radiates, as in the old RKO logo, from discrete centers, and it is more and more difficult, as James Clifford points out, to find a cultural position "outside" the center from which to attack it.[14] Yet a Bakhtinian formulation would see the center as still operating as a center, even if that center were more dispersed and diffuse. To speak of centrifugal and centripetal forces within the social whole, as Bakhtin does, is not to erase the differences between center and margin but rather to dynamize and dialectize them. The same process, in this perspective, generates *both* center and margins. Contradictions take place within a conflictual unity, but the contradictions are real nevertheless. The center, though claiming to be in disintegration, still operates as a center—as Nelly Richard puts it, "filing away any divergencies into a system of codes whose meanings, both semantically and territorially, it continues to administer by exclusive right."[15] If postmodernism has spread the telematic feel of First World consumerism around the globe, it has hardly deconstructed the relations of power which continue to marginalize countries and their cultures.

Bakhtin's broad view, embracing many cultures and millennia of artistic productions, also has the potential of deprovincializing a film-critical discourse that remains too rigidly tied to nineteenth-century conventions of verisimilitude. In its fondness for intertextual parody and formal aggressions, the Bakhtinian aesthetic is quite reconcilable with modernist reflexivity and even with a certain avant-garde, but it is not reconcilable with an empty formalism. Bakhtin retains a certain allegiance to realism, not in the sense of mimetic reproduction of the real, but in the quasi-Brechtian sense of revealing the "causal network" of events, of communicating the profound sociality and historicity of human behavior. Bakhtin speaks of "grotesque realism"—that is, an anti-illusionistic style which remains physical, carnal, and material, which tells social truths, but does so in stylized, parodic, and hyperbolic rather than naturalistic form. His thought shares with the avant-garde a common impulse toward social, formal, and libidinal rebellion, but the rebellion is here allied with, rather than hostile to, popular adversary culture.

Bakhtin points the way to transcending some of the felt insufficiencies of other theoretical grids. His concept of dialogism, of language and discourse as "shared territory," inoculates us from the individualist assumptions undergirding romantic theories of art while still allowing us to be attuned to the specific ways in which artists orchestrate diverse social voices. His emphasis on a boundless context that constantly interacts with and modifies the text helps us avoid the formalist fetishization of the autonomous art object. His emphasis on the "situated utterance" and the "interpersonal generation of meaning" helps us avoid the static ahistoricism of an apolitical, "value free" semiotics. The notion of heteroglossia, finally, proposes a fundamentally nonunitary, constantly shifting cultural field in which the most varied discourses exist in shifting, multivalenced oppositional relationships. Heteroglossia, after all, can be seen as another name for the social and even the psychic contradictions that constitute the subject, like the media, as the site of conflicting discourses and competing voices. Bakhtin would reject the idea of a unitary political subject: *the* bourgeois, *the* proletarian. A Bakhtinian perspective would be attuned to the voice of the proletarian in the bourgeois and the voice of the bourgeois in the proletarian, without denying that social class remains a meaningful, even indispensable, category. For Bakhtin, the self is a matrix of discursive forms, the site of multiple identities and identifications, a subject traversed by multiple discourses—which in no way denies the realities of class, gender, and nation but only complicates them. A Bakhtinian view might agree with Morley that "the same man may be simultaneously a productive worker, a trade union member, a supporter of the Social Democratic party, a consumer, a racist, a home owner, a wife beater and a Christian,"[16] but it would go even further to suggest that *within* each category there also exists heterogeneity. Thus, within the worker-racist there is also an antiracist (just as within the academic antiracist there might lurk a racist). The Bakhtinian view of the self as discursively, and therefore politically, discontinuous suggests a kind of gap; the same person, within a given area, might be crossed by what Ernst Bloch calls "forward-dreaming" discourses and backward-looking "vestigial" holdovers. Political attitudes, in this perspective, are multiform, even schizophrenic, the point being not that these "contradictions" provide some sort of solace for the victims of oppression but only that the struggle against oppression must take heterogeneity into account.

The left, we noted at the start, has often displayed a schizophrenic attitude toward mass-mediated culture, at times endorsing entertainment uncritically and at times lamenting the delight that mass audiences take in alienated spectacles. Too often a puritanical Marxism throws out the baby of pleasure with the bathwater of ideology. This refusal of pleasure has at times created an immense gap between left cultural criticism and the people it purports to serve. Indeed, the political consequences of left puritanism have been enormous. An austere, superegoish left that addresses its audience in moralistic terms—while advertising and mass culture speak to its deepest desires and fantasies—is theoretically and pragmatically handicapped. The broad American hostility to socialism has as much to do with the widespread misconception that socialist societies are necessarily "gray," "dreary," and "anti-erotic" as with any conviction that socialist economics are unsound or socialist analysis is incorrect. A Bakhtinian approach, it seems to me, would appreciate rather than deplore the fact of mass-mediated pleasure, embracing it as a potential friend while critiquing its alienation. The point, as Enzensberger and others have shown, is that the consciousness industry and capitalism cannot ultimately satisfy the real needs they exploit. Thus the left, deploying "anticipatory" readings, must treat mass-media texts as inadvertently predictive of possible future states of social life.

A Bakhtinian analytic of popular and mass culture would think through the social logic of our personal and collective desires, while demystifying the political and ideological structures that channel those desires in oppressive directions. It would appeal to deeply rooted but socially frustrated aspirations—for new, pleasurable forms of work, for solidarity, for festivity, for community. It would restore the notion of collective pleasure—of which carnival is but one form—to its rightful place within left thought. It would remind us of the collective pleasure, for example, of acting in concert for a passionately shared social goal, and would restore parodic, dialogical, and carnivalesque strategies to their deserved place in left artistic and critical practice. Aware of the double play of ideology and utopia, it would propose a double movement of celebration and critique. Aware of the inert weight of system and power, it would also see openings for their subversion. Even truncated, crippled dreams, as Bloch has shown, retain a kernel of hope. In this sense, Bakhtin synthesizes what Ernst Bloch calls Marxism's "cold current" (the disabused analysis of economic oppression and social alienation) with its "warm current" (its intoxicating glimpses of collective freedom). In dialogue with a nonfinalizing Marxism and an open-ended feminism—both of which it needs for its own dialogical self-completion—Bakhtinian thought can point the way to a transcendence of sterile dichotomies and exhausted paradigms. Most important, Bakhtin's conceptualizations suggest the possibility of a radical cultural critique, applicable to the mass media, which might crystallize the thrust of collective desire while being aware of its degraded expression, a cultural critique precluding neither laughter, pleasure, nor subversion.

Notes

Introduction

1. See, for example, Julia Kristeva, "Word, Dialogue, and Novel," in *Desire in Language: A Semiotic Approach to Literature and Art* (New York: Columbia University Press, 1980). For more on the relation between Bakhtin and poststructuralism, see Robert Young, "Back to Bakhtin," *Cultural Critique*, no. 2 (Winter 1985–86); and Allon White, "The Struggle over Bakhtin: Fraternal Reply to Robert Young, *Cultural Critique*, no. 8 (Winter 1987–88).

2. White, "The Struggle over Bakhtin." p. 218.

3. Ibid.

4. Quoted in Boris Schnaiderman, *Turbilhão e Semente* (São Paulo: Duas Cidades, 1983), p. 108.

5. See Jessica Benjamin, *The Bonds of Love* (New York: Pantheon, 1988).

6. Unpublished essay given to me by the author.

7. Paul de Man, "Dialogue and Dialogism," *Poetics Today* 4, no. 1 (1983): 99–107.

8. V. N. Voloshinov, *Marxism and the Philosophy of Language,* trans. Ladislav Matejka and I. R. Titunik (Cambridge, Mass.: Harvard University Press, 1986), p. 95.

9. Ibid.

10. Graham Pechey compares the battle over what he calls "Bakhtin's theoretical and political legacy" to the contention over Walter Benjamin that pitted the proponents of a thoroughgoing secularism with the adherents of highly traditionalist religious discourses.

11. For left readings, see Fredric Jameson, *The Political Unconscious: Narrative as a Socially Symbolic Act* (Ithaca: Cornell University Press, 1981); Terry Eagleton, *Against the Grain* (London: Verso, 1986); Tony Bennett, *Formalism and Marxism* (London: Methuen, 1979); Ken Hirschkop, "A Response to the Forum on Mikhail Bakhtin," in *Bakhtin: Essays and Dialogues on His Work,* ed. Gary Saul Morson (Chicago: University of Chicago Press, 1986); and

Peter Stallybrass and Allon White, *The Politics and Poetics of Transgression* (Ithaca: Cornell University Press, 1986). For liberal readings, see Katerina Clark and Michael Holquist, *Mikhail Bakhtin* (Cambridge, Mass.: Harvard University Press, 1984); Gary Saul Morson, "Who Speaks for Bakhtin?" in *Bakhtin,* ed. Morson; and Wayne Booth's "Introduction" to Mikhail Bakhtin, *Problems of Dostoevsky's Poetics,* trans. Caryl Emerson (Minneapolis: University of Minnesota Press, 1984).

12. M. M. Bakhtin, "The Problem of the Text in Linguistics, Philology, and the Human Sciences: An Experiment in Philosophical Analysis" (hereafter cited as "The Problem of the Text"), in *Speech Genres and Other Late Essays,* trans. Vern W. McGee, ed. Caryl Emerson and Michael Holquist (Austin: University of Texas Press, 1986), p. 103.

13. See Walter Ong, *The Presence of the Word* (New Haven: Yale University Press, 1967) and *Interfaces of the Word* (Ithaca: Cornell University Press, 1977); Frances Yates, *The Art of Memory* (Chicago: University of Chicago Press, 1966); Johannes Fabian, *Time and the Other: How Anthropology Makes Its Object* (New York: Columbia University Press, 1983); and James Clifford and George Marcus, eds., *Writing Culture: The Poetics and Politics of Ethnography* (Berkeley and Los Angeles: University of California Press, 1986).

14. See George Yudice, "Bakhtin and the Subject of Postmodernism," in *Bakhtin: Radical Perspectives*, forthcoming from University of Minnesota Press.

15. M. M. Bakhtin, "Discourse in the Novel," in *The Dialogical Imagination,* trans. Caryl Emerson and Michael Holquist (Austin: University of Texas Press, 1981), p. 259.

16. Ibid.

17. M. M. Bakhtin, "The Problem of Speech Genres," in *Speech Genres and Other Late Essays,* p. 95.

18. For just a few examples of reader-oriented television analysis, see Robert C. Allen, *Speaking of Soap Operas* (Chapel Hill: University of North Carolina Press, 1985); Ien Ang, *Watching Dallas: Soap Opera and the Melodramatic Imagination* (London: Methuen, 1985); Charlotte Brunsdon, *"Crossroads:* Notes on Soap Opera," *Screen* 22, no. 4 (1981); Tania Modleski, *Loving with a Vengeance: Mass-Produced Fantasies for Women* (New York: Methuen, 1984); David Morley, *The Nationwide Audience* (London: BFI, 1980); Stuart Hall, "Encoding/Decoding," in *Culture, Media, Language,* ed. D. Hobson, S. Hall, A. Lowe, and P. Willis (London: Hutchinson, 1980); and John Fiske, "British Cultural Studies and Television," in *Channels of Discourse,* ed. Robert C. Allen (Chapel Hill: University of North Carolina Press, 1987). Much of the recent work on television reception was brought to bear in a symposium held in Blaubeuren, West Germany, entitled "Rethinking the Audience: New Tendencies in Television Research."

19. Dale Bauer, *Feminist Dialogics: A Theory of Failed Community* (Albany: State University of New York Press, 1988), p. xiii.

Chapter 1. Translinguistics and Semiotics

1. Language-related citations from Canudo and Delluc can be found in a number of classical anthologies: Marcel Lapierre, *Anthologie du Cinéma* (Paris: La

Nouvelle Edition, 1946); Marcel L'Herbier, *Intelligence du Cinématographe* (Paris: Edition Correa, 1946); and Pierre L'Herminier, *L'Art du Cinéma* (Paris: Seghers, 1960).

2. See, for example, Bela Balazs, *Theory of the Film: Character and Growth of a New Art* (New York: Arno Press, 1972).

3. For an English version, see Herbert Eagle, ed., *Russian Formalist Film Theory* (Ann Arbor: Michigan Slavic Publications, 1981).

4. V. N. Voloshinov, *Marxism and the Philosophy of Language,* trans. Ladislav Matejka and I. R. Titunik (Cambridge, Mass.: Harvard University Press, 1986), p. 78.

5. R. Barton Palmer, "Metz's Model of Film Syntagmatics: A Text Grammar Critique" (Paper presented at the annual meeting of the Society for Cinema Studies, New Orleans, 1986).

6. Voloshinov, *Marxism and the Philosophy of Language,* p. 69.

7. M. M. Bakhtin and P. M. Medvedev, *The Formal Method in Literary Scholarship: A Critical Introduction to Sociological Poetics* (hereafter cited as *The Formal Method*), trans. Albert J. Wehrle (Cambridge, Mass.: Harvard University Press, 1985), p. 15.

8. Voloshinov, *Marxism and the Philosophy of Language,* p. 24.

9. Bakhtin and Medvedev, *The Formal Method,* p. 27.

10. Voloshinov, *Marxism and the Philosophy of Language,* p. 110.

11. See M. M. Bakhtin, "The Problem of Speech Genres," in *Speech Genres and Other Late Essays,* trans. Vern W. McGee, ed. Caryl Emerson and Michael Holquist (Austin: University of Texas Press, 1986). Bakhtin's "move" from "sentence" to "utterance" anticipates, of course, the later thought of Foucault, for whom the sentence corresponds to *langue,* while the utterance is the mode of existence of language in "discourse," and of Benveniste, with his concern for the role of the subject within signification, and, speaking more generally, the overall shift within linguistics from the study of small, abstract units to the examination of rhetoric, pragmatics, and discourse analysis.

12. Viktor Shklovsky, "Art as Technique," in L. T. Lemon and M. J. Reis, eds., *Russian Formalist Criticism: Four Essays* (Lincoln: University of Nebraska Press, 1965), p. 12.

13. Christian Metz, *Language and Cinema,* trans. Donna J. Umiker-Sebeok (The Hague: Mouton, 1974). This egregiously inept translation turned Metz's somewhat arid text into an unreadable monstrosity. Two of Metz's key terms—*langue* and *langage*—were more or less systematically mistranslated into their opposites, which transformed much of the book into nonsense.

14. M. M. Bakhtin, "The Problem of the Text," in *Speech Genres and Other Late Essays,* p. 122.

15. Bakhtin, "The Problem of Speech Genres," p. 71.

16. Gary Saul Morson, ed., *Literature and History: Theoretical Problems and Russian Case Studies* (Stanford: Stanford University Press, 1986), p. 265.

17. Christian Metz, "The Imaginary Signifier," in *The Imaginary Signifier,* trans. Ben Brewster et al. (Bloomington: Indiana University Press, 1982).

18. M. M. Bakhtin, "Discourse in the Novel," in *The Dialogical Imagination,* trans. Caryl Emerson and Michael Holquist (Austin: University of Texas Press, 1981), p. 259.

19. V. N. Voloshinov [M. M. Bakhtin], "Discourse in Life and Discourse in Poetry: Questions of Sociological Poetics," in *Bakhtin School Papers,* trans.

Noel Owen and Joe Andrew, ed. Ann Shukman, Russian Poetics in Translation, vol. 10 (Oxford: RPT Publications, 1983), p. 18.

20. Bakhtin and Medvedev, *The Formal Method,* pp. 95–96.

21. For a semiotic analysis of television news, see Robert Stam, "Television News and Its Spectator," in *Regarding Television,* ed. E. Ann Kaplan (Frederick, Md.: University Publications of America, 1983).

22. Metz, *Language and Cinema,* p. 103.

23. Bakhtin, "Discourse in the Novel," p. 416.

24. M. M. Bakhtin, "From Notes Made in 1970–71," in *Speech Genres and Other Late Essays,* p. 147.

25. Viktor Shklovsky is quoted by Graham Pechey in "Bakhtin, Marxism, and Post-Structuralism," in *Literature, Politics, and Theory: Papers from the Essex Conference, 1976–84,* ed. Francis Barker, Peter Hulme, Margaret Iverson, and Diana Loxley (London: Methuen, 1986), pp. 113–14. (Shklovsky made the comparison in *Rozanov* [1921] and *Theory of Prose* [1925].) For Tynyanov's interpretation, see J. Tynyanov, "Problems in the Study of Literature and Language," in *Readings in Russian Poetics,* trans. and ed. Ladislav Matejka and Krystyna Pomorska (Cambridge, Mass.: MIT Press, 1971), p. 79.

26. See Pechey, "Bakhtin, Marxism, and Post-Structuralism."

27. See Michael Rifaterre, "The Referential Illusion," *Columbia Review* 57, no. 2 (Winter 1978).

28. M. M. Bakhtin, "From the Prehistory of Novelistic Discourse," in *The Dialogical Imagination,* p. 49.

29. Bakhtin, "Discourse in the Novel," p. 292.

30. Christian Metz, *Film Language,* trans. Michael Taylor (New York: Oxford University Press, 1974), p. 95.

31. Christian Metz, "The Fiction Film and Its Spectator," in *The Imaginary Signifier,* pp. 135–36.

32. See Bakhtin and Medvedev, *The Formal Method,* especially the final chapter.

Chapter 2. Language, Difference, and Power

1. Some material in this chapter was first presented in Robert Stam and Ella Shohat, "The Cinema after Babel: Language, Difference, and Power," *Screen* 26, nos. 3–4 (May-August 1985). I would like to thank Ella Shohat, for generously allowing me to include passages from the "shared territory" of that essay.

2. M. M. Bakhtin, "The Problem of the Text," in *Speech Genres and Other Late Essays,* trans. Vern W. McGee, ed. Caryl Emerson and Michael Holquist (Austin: University of Texas Press, 1986), p. 118.

3. M. M. Bakhtin, "The Problem of Speech Genres," in *Speech Genres and Other Late Essays,* p. 60.

4. V. N. Voloshinov, *Marxism and the Philosophy of Language,* trans. Ladislav Matejka and I. R. Titunik (Cambridge, Mass.: Harvard University Press, 1986), p. 15.

5. Bakhtin, "The Problem of the Text," p. 118.

6. Even the perceptual cognitive processes of understanding films are engaged, I would argue, with verbal activities, in the sense that it is language that largely mediates between perception, cognition, and affect. These processes, in Bakhtinian terminology, are "bathed in language," even if they can-

not be entirely *reduced* to language. The processes of picking up narrative cues, applying schemata, grasping the relations between shots and between characters, of which David Bordwell speaks so usefully in *Narration in the Fiction Film* (Madison: University of Wisconsin Press, 1985), can in no way be entirely divorced from speech. These processes are all verbally inflected, even if they are not always verbally anchored.

7. M. M. Bakhtin, "From the Prehistory of Novelistic Discourse," in *The Dialogical Imagination,* trans. Caryl Emerson and Michael Holquist (Austin: University of Texas Press, 1981), p. 68.

8. Bakhtin, "The Problem of the Text," p. 106.

9. V. N. Voloshinov [M. M. Bakhtin], "Literary Stylistics," in *Bakhtin School Papers,* trans. Noel Owen and Joe Andrew, ed. Ann Shukman, Russian Poetics in Translation, vol. 10 (Oxford: RPT Publications, 1983), p. 117.

10. See Roland Barthes, "Rhetoric of the Image," in Roland Barthes, *Image/Music/Text,* ed. Stephen Heath (New York: Hill & Wang, 1977).

11. Voloshinov, *Marxism and the Philosophy of Language,* p. 15.

12. See J. J. Nattiez, *Fondements d'une Sémiologie de la Musique* (Paris: Union Generale d'Editions, 1975).

13. David Bordwell, in *Narration in the Fiction Film* (Madison: University of Wisconsin Press, 1985), argues for downplaying the role of verbal activity in film comprehension since it "is by no means clearly established that human perception and cognition are fundamentally determined by the processes of natural language; indeed, much psycholinguistic evidence runs the other way" (p. 130). But while Bordwell is right to argue against procrustean approaches to film/language analogy, it is important to distinguish between a number of distinct issues: (1) the question of analogy, i.e., whether film is language or at least languagelike; (2) the question of the role of verbal language in film; and (3) the role of verbal activity in understanding film. In regard to this last issue, no one is claiming that the processes of language fundamentally *determine* perception and cognition, but only that language, perception, and cognition act in concert; while distinguishable, they operate in a kind of symbiosis. It is difficult to imagine how all the hypothesis testing and narrative comprehension, about which Bordwell speaks so illuminatingly, could possibly take place entirely apart from verbal activity.

14. Boris Eikhenbaum, "Problems of Film Stylistics," *Screen* 15, no.3 (Autumn 1974), pp. 7–32.

15. Noel Carroll, working from a very different perspective, speaks of cases where visual images have a structured origin in particular clichés, proverbs (in the manner of Flemish painting), or metaphors. See his "Language and Cinema: Preliminary Notes for a Theory of Verbal Images," *Millennium,* nos. 7–9 (Fall/Winter 1980/81).

16. Voloshinov, *Marxism and the Philosophy of Language,* p. 15.

17. Voloshinov [Bakhtin], "Literary Stylistics," p. 104.

18. See Eikhenbaum, "Problems of Film Stylistics."

19. See Christian Metz, "Le Perçu et le Nommé," in *Essais Semiotiques* (Paris: Klincksieck, 1977).

20. For more on "inner speech," see L. S. Vygotsky, *Thought and Language* (Cambridge, Mass.: MIT Press, 1962); S. M. Eisenstein, *Film Form* (New York: Harcourt, Brace & Co., 1949); and Stephen Heath, "Language, Sight, and Sound," *Questions of Cinema* (London: Macmillan & Co., 1980). See also Paul

Willemen's "Reflections on Eikhenbaum's Concept of Internal Speech in the Cinema," *Screen* 15, no. 4 (Winter 1974/75); "Notes on Subjectivity," *Screen* 19, no. 1 (Spring 1978); and "Cinematic Discourse: The Problem of Inner Speech," *Screen* 22, no. 3 (Fall 1981). The notion of inner speech has philosophical antecedents in such thinkers as Herder, Humboldt, Thomas Aquinas, and Plato. See James Stam, *Inquiries into the Origin of Language* (New York: Harper & Row, 1976).

21. V. N. Voloshinov [M. M. Bakhtin], "Discourse in Life and Discourse in Poetry: Questions of Sociological Poetics," in *Bakhtin School Papers*, p. 27.

22. See David Black, "Narrative Film and the Synoptic Tendency" (Ph.D. diss., Cinema Studies Department, New York University).

23. M. M. Bakhtin, "From Notes Made in 1970–71," in *Speech Genres and Other Late Essays*, p. 143.

24. Fredric Jameson, *The Prisonhouse of Language: A Critical Account of Structuralism and Russian Formalism* (Princeton: Princeton University Press, 1972), pp. viii, ix.

25. Jean-Pierre Gorin, quoted in *New Yorker Films* (rental catalogue, 1983–84), p. 68.

26. M. M. Bakhtin, "Toward a Methodology for the Human Sciences," in *Speech Genres and Other Late Essays*, p. 169.

27. Vivian Sobchack, "Sixteen Ways to Pronounce 'Potato': Authority and Authorship in *Poto and Cabengo*," *Journal of Film and Video* 36, no. 4 (Fall 1984), p. 21.

28. M. M. Bakhtin, "Epic and Novel," in *The Dialogical Imagination*, p. 12.

29. Bakhtin, "From the Prehistory of Novelistic Discourse," p. 61.

30. Quoted in W. Rowland and B. Watkins, eds., *Interpreting Television: Current Research Perspectives* (Beverly Hills: Sage, 1984).

31. Bakhtin, "Epic and Novel," p. 11.

32. Voloshinov [Bakhtin], "Discourse in Life and Discourse in Poetry," p. 19.

33. N. J. Marr, *Po etapam jafetskoj teorii* (Through the Stages of the Japhetic Theory, 1926), p. 269, quoted in Voloshinov, *Marxism and the Philosophy of Language*, p. 72.

Chapter 3. Film, Literature, and the Carnivalesque

1. See Bernice G. Rosenthal, ed., *Nietzsche in Russia* (Princeton: Princeton University Press, 1986).

2. Katerina Clark and Michael Holquist, *Mikhail Bakhtin* (Cambridge, Mass.: Harvard University Press, 1984), pp. 30–31.

3. See Friedrich Nietzsche, *Joyful Wisdom*, trans. Kurt F. Reinhardt (New York: Ungar, 1960).

4. Friedrich Nietzsche, *The Birth of Tragedy and The Case of Wagner* (New York: Random House, 1967), p. 37.

5. Nietzsche, *The Joyful Wisdom*, p. 117.

6. See Umberto Eco, V. V. Ivanov, and Monica Rector, *Carnival!* ed. Thomas A. Sebeok (New York: Mouton, 1984).

7. Richard Dyer, "Entertainment and Utopia," in *Genre: The Musical*, ed. Rick Altman (London: Routledge & Kegan Paul, 1981).

8. See Mircea Eliade, *The Myth of the Eternal Return* (New York: Pantheon Books, 1954); Elias Canetti, *Crowds and Power* (New York: Continuum, 1960); Henri Lefebvre, *La Vie Quotidienne dans le Monde Moderne* (Paris: Gallimard, 1968); Michel Maffesoli, *L'Ombre de Dionysos* (Paris: Kilnksieck, 1982); and Victor Turner, *The Ritual Process* (Ithaca: Cornell University Press, 1969).

9. See Barbara Ehrenreich, Elizabeth Hess, and Gloria Jacobs, *Remaking Love* (New York: Anchor Press, 1987), p. 199.

10. See Peter Stallybrass and Allon White, *The Politics and Poetics of Transgression* (Ithaca: Cornell University Press, 1986).

11. Emmanuel Le Roy Ladurie, *Le Carnaval de Romans* (Paris: 1979), pp. 349–50.

12. Graham Pechey, "On the Borders of Bakhtin: Dialogization, Decolonization," *Oxford Literary Review* 9 (1988): 76.

13. See C. L. Barber, *Shakespeare's Festive Comedy: A Study of Dramatic Form and Its Relation to Social Custom* (Princeton: Princeton University Press, 1959).

14. Barber's analysis of Shakespeare is in some ways more "Bakhtinian" than Bakhtin's; Bakhtin's infrequent remarks concerning Shakespeare's work are rather disappointing. In *Problems of Dostoevsky's Poetics,* for example, Bakhtin discerns "early buddings of polyphony" in Shakespeare's dramas but only across the entire *oeuvre.* See M. M. Bakhtin, *Problems of Dostoevsky's Poetics,* trans. Caryl Emerson (Minneapolis: University of Minnesota Press, 1984), pp. 33–34.

15. Bakhtin, *Problems of Dostoevsky's Poetics,* pp. 112–22.

16. M. M. Bakhtin, *Rabelais and His World,* trans. Helene Iswolsky (Cambridge, Mass.: MIT Press, 1968), p. 46.

17. Alfred Jarry, "Lettres à Lugné-Poe," *Tout Ubu* (Paris: Librairie Generale Française, 1962), p. 133.

18. Luis Bunuel, *My Last Sigh* (New York: Alfred A. Knopf, 1983), p. 159.

19. For more on the concept of symbolic inversion, see Barbara Babcock, ed., *The Reversible World* (Ithaca: Cornell University Press, 1976).

20. The letter to Madame Rachilde reads as follows: "With this Père Ubu, who has earned his rest, is going to sleep. He believes that the brain, during decomposition, continues to function after death, and that its dreams are our paradise." The Godard version substitutes the "two brothers" for "Père Ubu": "And with that, the two brothers went to sleep for eternity, believing that the brain, during decomposition, functions after death, and that its dreams are our Paradise." Jarry's letter is quoted in Roger Shattuck, *The Banquet Years* (New York: Vintage, 1955), p. 220.

21. Jean-Luc Godard, *Godard on Godard* (London: Secker & Warburg, 1972), p. 190.

22. M. M. Bakhtin, "Forms of Time and Chronotope in the Novel," in *The Dialogical Imagination,* trans. Caryl Emerson and Michael Holquist (Austin: University of Texas Press, 1981), p. 239.

23. Pierre Bourdieu, *Distinction: A Social Critique of the Judgement of Taste,* trans. Richard Nice (Cambridge, Mass.: Harvard University Press, 1984), p. 491.

24. I develop these distinctions in relation to literary and cinematic reflexivity in *Reflexivity in Film and Literature: From Don Quixote to Jean-Luc God-*

ard (Ann Arbor: UMI Research Press, 1985). There I argue that reflexivity comes with no preattached political valence; it can be grounded in art-for-art's-sake aestheticism or in dialectical materialism. It is useful to distinguish, I argue, between three perennial modes of reflexive fiction: (1) ludic (e.g., the playful self-referentiality of a Borges novella or a Keaton film); (2) aggressive (e.g., the modernist "dehumanization" of *L'Age d'Or*); and (3) didactic (the materialist fictions of Brecht, Vertov, Godard).

25. Bakhtin, "Forms of Time and Chronotope in the Novel," p. 163.

26. For more on *Easy Rider* and sacred/profane inversions, see Barbara Babcock, "Liberty's a Whore": Inversions, Marginalia, and Picaresque Narrative," in Babcock, *The Reversible World*.

27. Antonin Artaud, *Le Théâtre et son Double* (Paris: Gallimard, 1964), pp. 211–12.

28. See Patricia Mellenkamp, "Jokes and Their Relationships to the Marx Brothers," in Stephen Heath and Patricia Mellenkamp, *Cinema and Language* (Frederick, Md.: University Publications of America, 1983).

29. See Norbert Elias, *The Civilizing Process,* vol. 1 (New York: Pantheon, 1978).

30. See Pierre Bourdieu, *Outline of a Theory of Practice,* trans. Richard Nice (Cambridge: Cambridge University Press, 1977).

31. See Ella Shohat, "Ethnicities in Relation: Film, Parody, and the Musical," forthcoming in Lester Friedman, ed., *Unspeakable Images: Ethnicity and American Cinema* (Champaign: University of Illinois Press).

32. Arthur Waskow, in *Seasons of Our Joy* (New York: Bantam, 1982), describes Purim as "the hilarious noisemaker among all the holy days, the day of merriment and buffoonery, parody and satire," whose laughter is not gentle: "It is a kind of angry, blood-red humor that celebrates the tyrants overthrow." In medieval Europe, he further explains, "an already lively Purim was quick to enhance its own hilarity by borrowing the carnival masquerades and mystery plays. . . . The Purimshpiel or Ahashverosh-shpiel—a burlesque of the Purim story itself—became a staple of the celebration, sometimes sexually obscene enough that the rabbis tried to stop them. The custom grew of making Purim-Torah—parodying the prayers themselves on Purim night, parodying the rabbis' Talmudic debates and discussions over how to apply the Torah to life-dilemmas."

33. From an unpublished paper on Pasolini by Joel Kanoff.

34. See Joan Magretta and William R. Magretta, "Lina Wertmuller and the Tradition of Italian Carnivalesque Comedy," *Genre* 12 (Spring 1979).

35. Jurij Lotman, *Semiotics of Cinema,* trans. Mark E. Suino, Michigan Slavic Contributions, no. 5 (Ann Arbor: Department of Slavic Languages and Literature, University of Michigan, 1976), p. 22.

36. M. M. Bakhtin, "Epic and Novel," in *The Dialogical Imagination,* p. 23.

37. Georges Bataille, "Sacrifice," in *October* 36 (Spring 1986): 68–69.

38. Helene Cixous, "The Laugh of the Medusa," *Signs* 1, no. 4 (1976): 888; and Ruby Rich, "In the Name of Feminist Criticism," in *Movies and Methods,* vol. 2, ed. Bill Nichols (Berkeley and Los Angeles: University of California Press, 1985).

39. See Linda Williams, "A Jury of Their Peers," in *Postmodernism and Its Discontents,* ed. Ann Kaplan (London: Verso, 1988).

40. M. M. Bakhtin, "From Notes Made in 1970–1971," in *Speech Genres and Other Late Essays,* trans. Vern W. McGee, ed. Caryl Emerson and Michael Holquist (Austin: University of Texas Press, 1986), p. 135.

41. Mary Russo, "Female Grotesques," in *Feminist Studies/Critical Studies,* ed. Teresa de Lauretis (Bloomington: Indiana University Press, 1986), p. 226.

Chapter 4. Of Cannibals and Carnivals

1. Bakhtin's only reference to Latin American literature, to my knowledge, is in *Rabelais and His World,* to Pablo Neruda, in the context of "grotesque realism."

2. See Emir Rodriguez Monegal, "Carnaval/Antropofagia/Parodia," and Haroldo de Campos, "A Escritura Mefistofelica," in *Tempo Brasileiro,* no. 62 (July-September 1980).

3. See René Menil, *Traces: Identité, Negritude, Esthetique aux Antilles* (Paris: Robert Lafont, 1981).

4. Modernist pronouncements on the Indian, cannibalism, and so forth, are gathered under rubrics in Maria Eugenia Boaventura, *A Vanguarda Antropofágica* (São Paulo: Attica, 1985), pp. 91–100.

5. See Monegal, "Carnaval/Antropofagia/Parodia."

6. Oswald de Andrade, *Obras Completas,* vol. 6 (Rio de Janeiro: Editora Civilização Brasileira, 1971), p. 169.

7. The quotation from "Anthropophagie" appears in Augusto de Campos, *Revista de Antropofagia* (São Paulo: Divisão de Arquivo do Estado de São Paulo, 1984), p. 1. For "Almanachs du Père Ubu," see Alfred Jarry, *Tout Ubu* (Paris: Librairie Generale Française, 1962).

8. From "A Descida Antropofágica" (The Anthropophagic Descent), a manifesto signed by "Oswaldo Costa," in all probability a pseudonym for Oswald de Andrade, and included in *Revista da Antropofagia* (São Paulo: Municipalidade de São Paulo, 1975).

9. Alejo Carpentier, "De lo Real Maravilloso Americano," *Cine Cubano,* no. 102 (1982), pp. 12–14.

10. Quoted by Augusto Tamayo Vargas in "Interpretacões da America Latina," in *America Latina em Sua Literatura,* ed. César Fernández Moreno (São Paulo: Perspectiva, 1972), p. 472.

11. Quoted by Randal Johnson in *Literatura e Cinema: Macunaima: Do Modernismo na Literatura ao Cinema Novo* (São Paulo: T. A. Queiroz, 1982), p. 59.

12. Quoted by Haroldo de Campos in "Ruptura dos Generos na Literatura Latino-Americana," in *America Latina em Sua Literatura,* p. 293.

13. Quoted in Boaventura, *A Vanguarda Antropofágica,* p. 114.

14. In *The Formal Method in Literary Scholarship,* trans. Albert J. Wehrle (Cambridge, Mass.: Harvard University Press, 1985), M. M. Bakhtin and P. M. Medvedev note that Europe was liberated from the provincialism of its verism through contact with non-European cultures, a factor that contributed to the development of European modernism. Since these non-European cultural currents were even more prevalent in Latin America, the eagerness with which some Latin American cultures "took" to modernism is quite comprehensible.

15. See *Folha de São Paulo* (*Folha Ilustrada*), March 25, 1988.

16. Roberto da Matta, *Carnavais, Malandros e Herois* (Rio de Janeiro: Zahar, 1980).

17. José Guilherme Merquior, *Saudades do Carnaval* (Rio de Janeiro: Forense, 1972), p. 117.

18. Oswald de Andrade, "Manifesto da Poesia Pau-Brasil," *Do Pau-Brasil a Antropofagia e as Utopias* (Rio de Janeiro: Editora Civilização Brasileira, 1972), p. 5.

19. Jorge Mautner, *Panfletos da Nova Era* (São Paulo: Global, 1980), p. 147.

20. See Peter Fry, *Para Ingles Ver: Identidade e Politica na Cultura Brasileira* (Rio de Janeiro: Zahar, 1982).

21. See Antonio Riserio, *Carnaval Ijexa* (São Paulo: Hucitec, 1984).

22. See Charles A. Perrone, "Open Mike: Brazilian Popular Music and Redemocratization," in *Studies in Latin American Popular Culture,* ed. Randal Johnson, vol. 7 (1988).

23. Mario de Andrade, *Macunaima: O Heroi Sem Nemhum Carater* (São Paulo: Martins, 1970), English translation by E. A. Goodland (New York: Random House, 1984). The English translation, unfortunately, is egregiously inadequate. While the Brazilian novel is linguistically polyphonic, taking advantage of words of African and indigenous origin as well as latinate words, the translation tends to reduce the text to its lowest common denominator of denotation. Where Mario de Andrade uses *cunha,* the indigenous Tupi word for "woman," the translator renders it simply as "woman," when the Native American word for "squaw" would have been more suggestive. A key exclamation in the novel—"Ai! Que preguiça!" (literally, "What laziness!" but in fact evocative of a delicious stretch in a hammock)—is rendered as "What a fucking life!" (a phrase more evocative of Manhattan punks than of Brazil's Amazonian modernism).

24. See Theodor Koch-Grunberg, *Vom Roroima Zum Orinoco: Ergebnisse einer Reise in Nord Brasilien und Venezuela in den Jahren 1911–1913,* vol. 2, *Mythen und Legenden der Taulipang und Arekuna Indianer* (Stuttgart: Strocker & Schroder, 1924).

25. Brazilian critic Suzana Camargo explores *Macunaima* in terms of the Menippe in her *Macunaima: Ruptura e Tradicão* (São Paulo: Massão Ohno/ João Farkas, 1977).

26. M. M. Bakhtin, *Rabelais and His World,* trans. Helene Iswolsky (Cambridge, Mass.: MIT Press, 1968), p. 19.

27. Quoted by M. Cavalcanti Proença in *Roteiro de Macunaima* (Rio de Janeiro: Civilização Brasileira, 1969), p. 17.

28. See Haroldo de Campos, *Morfologia de Macunaima* (São Paulo: Perspectiva, 1973).

29. Mario de Andrade, *A Escrava Que Não é Isaura,* in Mario de Andrade, *Obra Imatura* (São Paulo: Livraria Martins Editora), p. 268.

30. M. M. Bakhtin, "Forms of Time and Chronotope in the Novel," in *The Dialogical Imagination,* trans. Caryl Emerson and Michael Holquist (Austin: University of Texas Press, 1981), p. 198.

31. For expositions on dependency analysis, see A. G. Frank, *Capitalism and Underdevelopment in Latin America* (New York: Monthly Review Press, 1966); and James Cockroft, A. G. Frank, and Dale Johnson, *Dependency and Underdevelopment: Latin America's Political Economy* (New York: Anchor Books,

1971). For a critical view of the literature on dependency, see Fernando Henrique Cardoso, "The Consumption of Dependency Theory in the United States," in *Latin American Research Review*, 1977, pp. 7–24.

32. Welles's *oeuvre* and personality, in our view, virtually pleads for a Bakhtinian analysis. His Rabelaisian spirit and "excessive" body, constantly displayed in films, plays, talk shows, and commercials, reminds us in its gigantism of countless passages from *Rabelais and His World*. It is a body cut to the measure of Falstaff, the most carnivalesque of Shakespeare's protagonists, a body reminiscent of Bacchus, or of the fat lords of misrule, called *Rei Momos,* invariably corpulent, that launch the carnival celebrations in Brazil, and that Welles himself registered in *It's All True*. The biographical Welles was a profoundly antipuritanical personality, the laughing partisan of excess and the banquet. (Even the products he advertised, such as wines, were consistent with his Dionysian persona.) In relation to official art, Welles was always the breaker of rules, a rebel figure who placed himself in opposition to dominant theatrical and cinematic practice. In his films we find strategies, themes, and characters eminently suitable to a Bakhtinian dialogical analysis. Throughout his work we find the following:

a. a central place accorded to parody—think, for example, of the spoof on the Hearst movie-tone newsreel in *Citizen Kane;* the reflexive play with the forms of the conventional art-documentary in *F for Fake;* or the parodic avant-garde footage in the unfinished *The Other Side of the Wind;*

b. a polyphonic approach to voices, point of view, and genre; *Citizen Kane,* as Mary Desjardins demonstrates, is eminently dialogical, offering us not only the polyphonic orchestration of multiple-voice memories but also the dialogization of (literary and filmic) genres: tragedy, melodrama, documentary, detective film, Gothic horror story, newspaper film;

c. a predilection for Menippean space-time dislocations in an aesthetic that is little preoccupied with verisimilitude;

d. a fondness for popular culture and "low" genres (vaudeville, magic shows);

e. in his films, the recurrent trope of crowning and uncrowning, from *Kane* to *Macbeth* to *Chimes at Midnight;*

f. a carnivalesque capacity to assume other roles, adopt other voices;

g. the filmic foregrounding of carnivals (*It's All True*), pageants (*The Merchant of Venice*), and masques (*Journey into Fear?*);

h. the *parti pris* for the interspersing and mutual illumination of genres;

i. the constant self-irony, implicit in the earlier films and brought to its paroxysm in *F for Fake*;

j. Bakhtin's refusal of the "final word," his constant relativization of truth and of the multiplicity of perspectives.

33. Vinicius de Morais's observations on Welles's visit to Brazil were recorded in the Brazilian newspaper *A Manhã*, April 30, 1942.

34. Welles's written observations about the carnival sequence of *It's All true* can be found in the Welles collection at the Lilly Library, Indiana University, Bloomington.

35. Some of the shots and sequences from *It's All True* can be seen in a BBC documentary concerning RKO which includes a half-hour on *It's All true;* in the promotional short *Four Men on a Raft,* by Welles's collaborator Richard Wil-

son; and in two Brazilian films by Rogerio Sganzerla (*Brasil* [1981] and *Nem Tudo é Verdade* [It's Not All True, 1984]). I have also gained knowledge of the film by looking at stills, talking to Welles's close collaborators Richard Wilson and George Fanto, reading critical and journalistic accounts of the film, and examining the various memoranda, scripts, and presentations from the production gathered in the Lilly Library. I would like to thank Catherine Benamou, João Luiz Vieira, and Heloisa Buarque de Holanda for providing materials relevant to *It's All True*.

36. The conventional version of the *It's All True* experience, as presented by such critics as Charles Higham and John Russell Taylor, has generally been hostile to Welles, describing him as profligate, susceptible to tropical temptations, guilty of unseemly behavior, and irrationally reluctant to mold his materials into a conventional story with box-office appeal. The bill of particulars against Welles recalls, ironically, the perennial accusations made against carnival itself—debauched, dissipated, dissolute. For more on *It's All True,* see Robert Stam, "Orson Welles, Brazil, and the Power of Blackness," forthcoming in a special issue of *Persistence of Vision* dedicated to Welles.

37. João Luiz Vieira, *Hegemony and Resistance: Parody and Carnival in Brazilian Cinema* (Ph.D. diss., Cinema Studies, New York University, 1984).

38. Oswald de Andrade's various manifestoes are collected in his *Do Pau-Brasil a Antropofagia as Utopias*. The translations here are mine.

39. Oswald de Andrade's vision is confirmed by Pierre Clastres's anthropological research into the same Brazilian indigenous groups of which de Andrade spoke. Clastres describes these groups as tropical "affluent societies" (not in the contemporary sense, but in the sense of having surplus food) and as societies without social hierarchy or political coercion. See Pierre Clastres, *Society against the State* (New York: Zone Books, 1987).

40. See Clastres, *Society against the State*, for a critique of the ethnocentrism of a classical anthropology accustomed to conceiving of political power in terms of hierarchized and authoritarian relations of command and obedience and therefore incapable of theorizing Tupinamba culture and society.

41. Quoted in Augusto de Campos, *Poesia, Antipoesia, Antropofagia* (São Paulo: Cortez e Moraes, 1978), p. 123.

42. Randal Johnson and Robert Stam, *Brazilian Cinema* (East Brunswick, N.J.: Fairleigh Dickinson University Press, 1982), pp. 82–83.

43. Bakhtin, *Rabelais and His World,* p. 308.

44. Bakhtin, "Forms of Time and Chronotope in the Novel," p. 219.

45. Ibid., p. 198.

46. Randal Johnson, "Macunaíma: From Modernism to Cinema Novo" (Ph.D. diss., University of Texas, 1977).

47. For a thoroughly researched and closely observed textual analysis of *Macunaíma,* see Randal Johnson, "Cinema Novo and Cannibalism: *Macunaíma,*" in Johnson and Stam, *Brazilian Cinema,* pp. 178–90.

48. See Ismail Xavier, "Allegories of Underdevelopment: From the 'Aesthetics of Hunger' to the 'Aesthetics of Garbage'" (Ph.D. diss., New York University, 1982).

Chapter 5. The Grotesque Body and Cinematic Eroticism

1. M. M. Bakhtin, *Rabelais and His World,* trans. Helene Iswolsky (Cambridge, Mass.: MIT Press, 1968), p. 317.

2. Stephen Greenblatt, "Filthy Rites," *Daedalus* 3 (1982): 1–16.

3. Bakhtin, *Rabelais and His World,* p. 32.

4. Ibid., p. 40.

5. Ibid., p. 26.

6. Quoted in M. F. Hans and G. Lapouge, eds., *Les Femmes, La Pornographie, L'erotisme* (Paris: Seuil, 1978), p. 50.

7. Bakhtin, *Rabelais and His World,* pp. 353–54.

8. Ibid., p. 21.

9. Ibid., p. 26.

10. See Mary Russo, "Female Grotesques: Carnival and Theory," in *Feminist Studies/Critical Studies,* ed. Teresa de Lauretis (Bloomington: Indiana University Press, 1986).

11. Montaigne *Essays* (trans. George B. Ivez) 3.5.

12. M. M. Bakhtin, "Forms of Time and of the Chronotope in the Novel," in *The Dialogical Imagination,* trans. Caryl Emerson and Michael Holquist (Austin: University of Texas Press, 1981), p. 215.

13. Ibid.

14. Bakhtin, *Rabelais and His World,* p. 240.

15. Wayne Booth, "Freedom of Interpretation: Bakhtin and the Challenge of Feminist Criticism," in *Bakhtin: Essays and Dialogues on His Work,* ed. Gary Saul Morson (Chicago: University of Chicago Press, 1986), pp. 165–66.

16. Jacques Lacan, "Seminar of 21 January 1975," quoted in Juliet Mitchell and Jacqueline Rose, *Female Sexuality* (New York: Norton, 1983), p. 164.

17. See Russo, "Female Grotesques," p. 225.

18. See J. C. Flugel, *The Psychology of Clothes* (London: Hogarth, 1930).

19. See Kaja Silverman, *The Acoustic Mirror: The Female Voice in Psychoanalysis and Cinema* (Bloomington: Indiana University Press, 1988).

20. See Andrew Ross, "Demonstrating Sexual Difference," in *Men in Feminism,* ed. Alice Jardine and Paul Smith (New York: Methuen, 1987).

21. Lonnie Barbach, ed., *Erotic Interludes* (New York: Harper & Row, 1987), pp. 46–47.

22. Susan Griffin, "Viyella," in *Pleasures: Women Write Erotica,* ed. Lonnie Barbach (New York: Harper & Row, 1984), p. 65.

23. Susan Block, "Leaving Sasha; or, The Bed Makes the Man," in *Erotic Interludes,* ed. Lonnie Barbach (New York: Harper & Row, 1987), p. 137.

24. See Pascal Bruckner and Alain Finkelraut, *Le Nouveau Desordre Amoureux* (Paris: Seuil, 1977).

25. Luce Iragaray, *This Sex Which Is Not One* (Ithaca: Cornell University Press, 1985), p. 200.

26. Ellen Willis, *"Deep Throat:* Hard to Swallow," in *Sexuality in the Movies,* ed. Thomas R. Atkins (New York: Da Capo, 1984).

27. E. Ann Kaplan, "Pornography and/as Representation," *Enclitic* 9, nos. 1–2 (Fall 1977).

28. Bakhtin, "Forms of Time," p. 128.

29. See Arthur Kroker and Michael Dorland, "Panic Cinema: Sex in the Age of the Hyperreal," *Cineaction!* no. 10 (Fall 1987).

30. See Susan Sontag, "The Pornographic Imagination," *Styles of Radical Will* (New York: Delta, 1981); and Susan Suleiman, "Pornography and the Avant-Garde," in *The Poetics of Gender,* ed. Nancy K. Miller (New York: Columbia University Press, 1986).

31. Georges Bataille, *The Story of the Eye,* trans. Joachim Neugroschel (New York: Urizen, 1977), p. 6.

32. Georges Bataille, "L'Esprit Moderne et le Jeu des Transpositions," *Ouevres Completes,* vol. 1 (Paris: Gallimard, 1970), p. 273.

33. From an interview with Carlos Fuentes, in Joan Mellen, *The World of Luis Bunuel* (New York: Oxford University Press, 1978), pp. 69–70.

34. Ibid.

35. In the wake of Bunuel, many filmmakers have mined this vein of sexualized sacrilege. I am thinking, for example, of Pedro Almovodar's *Dark Habits* and Ana Carolina's *Sonhos da Valsa.*

36. See Stephen Heath, *The Sexual Fix* (London: Macmillan & Co., 1982).

37. The words are Amos Vogel's in *Film as a Subversive Art* (New York: Random House, 1974).

38. Roland Barthes, *A Lover's Discourse: Fragments* (New York: Hill & Wang, 1978), pp. 142 and 173.

39. Ibid., p. 73.

40. Barbara Ehrenreich, Elizabeth Hess, and Gloria Jacobs, *Remaking Love* (Garden City, N.Y.: Anchor, 1986), p. 202.

41. George Steiner, *After Babel: Aspects of Language and Translation* (New York: Oxford University Press, 1975), p. 43.

42. One of the pleasing inversions of *Sauve Qui Peut/(la Vie)* and another film about prostitution, Lizzie Borden's *Working Girls,* is that each ultimately depersonalizes the johns and repersonalizes the prostitutes.

43. David James's talk, entitled "Hardcore: Resistance(?) in the Postmodern," was presented as part of a panel chaired by Michael Renov at the Conference of the Society for Cinema Studies in Montreal in June 1987.

Chapter 6. From Dialogism to *Zelig*

1. M. M. Bakhtin, "The Problem of the Text," in *Speech Genres and Other Late Essays,* trans. Vern W. McGee (Austin: University of Texas Press, 1986), p. 119.

2. M. M. Bakhtin, *Problems of Dostoevsky's Poetics,* trans. Caryl Emerson (Minneapolis: University of Minnesota Press, 1984), p. 252.

3. M. M. Bakhtin, "The Problem of Speech Genres," in *Speech Genres and Other Late Essays,* p. 91.

4. Dana B. Polan, "The Text between Monologue and Dialogue," *Poetics Today* 4, no. 1 (1983): 145–52.

5. M. M. Bakhtin, "Discourse in the Novel," in *The Dialogical Imagination,* trans. Caryl Emerson and Michael Holquist (Austin: University of Texas Press, 1981), p. 281.

6. Ibid., p. 293.

7. Bakhtin, "The Problem of the Text," pp. 121–22.

8. M. M. Bakhtin, "Response to a Question from the *Novy Mir* editorial staff," in *Speech Genres and Other Late Essays,* p. 5.

9. Ibid., p. 2.

10. Ibid., p. 3.

11. See David Toop, *The Rap Attack: African Jive to New York Hip Hop* (New York: Pluto Press, 1984).

12. See Dick Hebdige, *Cut 'n' Mix: Culture, Identity, and Caribbean Music* (New York: Methuen, 1987).

13. Betsy Wheeler's paper was presented at a C.U.N.Y. colloquium on Bakhtin in November 1986.

14. Some of the material included here appeared as part of an article entitled "*Zelig* and Contemporary Theory," *Enclitic* 9, nos. 1–2 (Fall 1987), which I coauthored with Ella Shohat. I would like to thank Ella for her generosity in allowing me to include some of the "shared territory" of our article here.

15. V. N. Voloshinov, *Marxism and the Philosophy of Language*, trans. Ladislav Matejka and I. R. Titunik (Cambridge, Mass.: Harvard University Press, 1986), p. 95.

16. See Northrop Frye, *Anatomy of Criticism* (Princeton: Princeton University Press, 1957).

17. In his essay "The Uncanny," Freud comments on one of the themes of the uncanny, defining "the double" as a situation in which one possesses knowledge, feeling, and experience in common with the other, identifies oneself with the other, so that the self becomes confounded, or the foreign self is substituted for one's own through the doubling, dividing, and interchanging of the self. Art Simon, in an as yet unpublished paper entitled "Tracing Zelig," has usefully explored the relevance of Freud's ideas on the "uncanny" to the "interchanges of self" in the Allen film. Freud's essay can be found in *On Creativity and the Unconscious* (New York: Harper & Row, 1958).

18. See Hayden White, *Metahistory: The Historical Imagination in Nineteenth-Century Europe* (Baltimore: Johns Hopkins University Press, 1973). White was not the first, obviously, to stress the inseparability of "history" and "fiction." Many cultures do not apply the concept of fiction to traditional narrations, so that what the West calls "myths" are from their point of view comparable to historical events. White's line of thought, as he would doubtless be the first to point out, goes back to classical antiquity (for the Greeks, Homeric epic was at once "history" and "fiction") and, in the modern period, to Nietzsche, Becker, and Lèvi-Strauss. "History," argues the historian-protagonist of Sartre's *La Nausée*, "is a complete fabrication," a "work of pure imagination."

19. For technical information on how this filmic chameleonism was achieved, see "Gordon Willis, ASC, and *Zelig*," *American Cinematographer*, April 1984.

20. See Richard Grenier, "*Zelig*," *Commentary*, November 1983.

21. Friedrich Nietzsche, "Nietzsche contra Wagner," in *Nietzsche Werke*, ed. Alfred Baeumler, vol. 5/2 (Leipzig: Alfred Kröner, 1930), p. 56 (translation by Robert and James Stam).

22. See Jean-Louis Schefer, *L'Homme Ordinaire du Cinema* (Paris: Gallimard, 1980).

23. See Edgar Morin, *Le Cinema ou L'Homme Imaginaire* (Paris: Gonthier, 1958).

24. The evolution of the *theatrum mundi* trope over the course of literary history is inventoried in Ernst Curtius, *European Literature and the Latin Middle Ages* (Princeton: Princeton University Press, 1973).

25. See Hannah Arendt, *The Origins of Totalitarianism* (New York: Harcourt Brace, 1951); Georg Simmel, *On Individuality and Social Forms* (Chicago: University of Chicago Press, 1971); and Helmuth Plessner, *Anthropologie der Sinne* (Frankfurt: Suhrkamp, 1980).

26. See Friedrich Nietzsche, *Joyful Wisdom,* trans. Thomas Common (New York: Ungar, 1960).

27. Paul de Man, "Dialogue and Dialogism," *Poetics Today* 4, no. 1 (1983): 100.

28. See Leon Poliakov, *The History of Anti-Semitism: From Mohammed to the Marranos,* trans. Richard Howard (New York: Vanguard, 1973).

29. See Tzvetan Todorov, *The Conquest of America: The Question of the Other,* trans. Richard Howard (New York: Harper & Row, 1984).

30. On the medieval diabolization of Jews, see Joshua Trachtenberg, *The Devil and the Jews: The Medieval Conception of the Jew and Its Relation to Modern Anti-Semitism* (New York: Harper, 1943).

31. See Otto Weininger, *Sex and Character* (New York: G. P. Putnam, 1906). Weininger's *selbst-hass* fused anti-Semitism with misogyny, since he equated Judaism with the female principle and saw human bisexuality as the source of evil in social life.

32. The idea of a Jew-into-Nazi transformation was anticipated, on a more frankly comic register, by an early Allen stand-up monologue alluding to a rabbi who was "very reform, in fact, a Nazi."

33. See Homi K. Bhabha, "Signs Taken for Wonders: Questions of Ambivalence and Authority under a Tree outside Delhi, May 1817," *Critical Inquiry* 12, no. 1 (Autumn, 1985).

34. See Stephen Greenblatt, *Renaissance Self-Fashioning* (Chicago: University of Chicago Press, 1980).

35. Bakhtin, "Discourse in the Novel," p. 345.

36. Ibid., p. 346.

37. Ibid.

38. See John Murray Cuddihy, *The Ordeal of Civility: Freud, Marx, Lèvi-Strauss, and the Jewish Struggle with Modernity* (Boston: Beacon, 1974).

39. Irving Howe, *World of Our Fathers* (New York: Bantam, 1976), p. 387.

40. Dr. B., "Die Rassenmerkmale der Juden," *Der Sturmer* 38 (1928): 2, quoted in Sander L. Gilman, *Jewish Self-Hatred: Anti-Semitism and the Hidden Language of the Jews* (Baltimore: Johns Hopkins University Press, 1986).

41. Howe, *World of Our Fathers,* p. 553.

42. Ibid.

43. *Zelig* at first glance would appear to partake of certain characteristics of neoconservative postmodernism: a style rooted in pastiche, the eclectic historicism of recycled texts, the view of the past as available only through stereotypical representations, a kind of blank irony (Jameson). I would argue, however, that while Zelig the character, at least in his chameleon phase (and it might be argued that he never leaves his chameleon phase), does represent postmodernism, *Zelig* the film cannot be so characterized. *Zelig* does not so much trivialize history, as is sometimes charged, as shed light on the constructed, manipulable nature of history as mediated by the culture industry. While it would be an exaggeration to see *Zelig* as an example of what Hal Foster calls "oppositional postmodernism," it is still possible to coax an oppositional, anticipatory reading out of what is in some ways a recalcitrant text.

44. Our reading of *Zelig* goes "against the grain" also in the sense that Allen's work, generally, is not terribly open to the voice of the ethnic other. The dialogue, in Allen's films, is often reducible to one between assimilated Jews and Anglo-America. Films such as *Annie Hall* and *Manhattan* reveal a New York

virtually devoid of blacks, while *Radio Days* evokes "latinidad" as a sentimental, nostalgic presence.

45. It is this "taking oneself as object" that distinguishes Bakhtinian dialogism from romantic megalomania and the "egotistical sublime."

46. See Jacques Derrida, "Racism's Last Word," *Critical Inquiry*, Autumn 1985.

Envoi: Bakhtin and Mass-Media Critique

1. See Hans Magnus Enzensberger, "Constituents of a Theory of the Media," *The Consciousness Industry* (New York: Seabury Press, 1974).

2. See Tania Modleski, *Studies in Entertainment: Critical Approaches to Mass Culture* (Bloomington: Indiana University Press, 1986); and Colin MacCabe, *High Theory/Low Culture: Analyzing Popular Television and Film* (New York: St. Martin's, 1986).

3. Horace M. Newcombe deploys a Bakhtinian framework to speak of the "heteroglot environment" and "dialogic nature" of the televisual medium, arguing that television is in many ways more "novelistic" than the novel. "From the collaborative writing process common in film and television, to the negotiation between writer and producer, producer and network, network and internal censor—dialogue is the defining element in the creation of television content." See Horace M. Newcombe and Paul M. Hirsch, "Television as a Cultural Forum: Implications for Research," *Quarterly Review of Film Studies,* Summer 1983.

4. For further analysis of television news, see Robert Stam, "Television News and Its Spectator," in *Regarding Television* (Frederick, Md.: University Publications of America, 1983).

5. Newcombe and Hirsch, "Television as a Cultural Forum," p. 27.

6. John Fiske, *Television Culture* (London: Methuen, 1987), pp. 243–50. I should add that I found most of the analyses in *Television Culture* immensely suggestive from a Bakhtinian perspective. One could perform a similar analysis of the carnivalesque aspects of the Mort Downey show. This self-proclaimed populist stages a show where studio audiences assume positions of power, and grants home viewers access to this apparently anarchical realm. The carnival leitmotif is signaled by the program logo of a huge, gaping mouth—perennial symbol of carnival's defiant orality—and in the frequent mouthings of the kind of obscenities which Bakhtin called "marketplace speech." Part of the pleasure of the program derives from the irreverent dethroning of the avatars of liberal (and occasionally conservative) authority, as Mort and his supporting chorus of barking seals hoot and insult them into submission. We get the sense of a carnivalesque overturning, but it is not always clear precisely what is being overturned. King Mort, as magister ludi of these revels, is never himself dethroned, and always retains the regal power of censure (encapsulated in the royal dictum "Zip it"). A compendium of political contradictions, equally enthusiastic in his denunciations of racism and affirmative action programs, Downey works what Jamin Raskin calls the "essential fault lines of power in America." But what is interesting from a Bakhtinian perspective is the show's boisterous heteroglossia, its noisy confrontation of diverse social discourses, and its appropriation of the imagery and practices of carnival, ultimately, to solidify official culture even while providing the enjoyment found in the exercise of a verbal gestural freedom.

7. Some of these reflections were formulated in a document authored by William Boddy, Marty Lucas, Jonathon Buchsbaum, and myself, entitled "Charisma, Jujitsu, and the Democrats," and sent to those in charge of the television spots for Mondale and Ferraro—all, obviously, to precious little effect. How little the Democrats have learned was obvious in the calamitous 1988 Dukakis campaign, in which the Democrats showed themselves unable to either carnivalize Reagan-Bush or propose any counterutopia beyond competence. See Ed McCabe, "The Campaign You Never Saw," *New Yorker* 21, no. 49 (Dec. 12, 1988), for a detailed account of what McCabe calls one of the greatest "communications disasters of the 20th century."

8. M. M. Bakhtin, "The Problem of Speech Genres," in *Speech Genres and Other Late Essays,* trans. Vern W. McGee (Austin: University of Texas Press, 1986), p. 91.

9. See Charlotte Bunch, "Making Common Cause: Diversity and Coalitions," in *Ikon,* no. 7 (Spring/Summer 1987).

10. See, for example, Karl Marx, *Surveys from Exile,* trans. David Fernbach (London: Allen Lane, 1973), p. 320. Leon Poliakov, in his *De Voltaire a Wagner* (São Paulo: Perspectivo, 1985), cites examples of anti-Semitic and antiblack prejudice in Marx's personal correspondence. For instance, "The form of his head and his hair [Marx wrote of Lasalle] show that he descends from blacks who joined the tribe of Moses on the occasion of the exodus from Egypt" (p. 359, translation mine).

11. Ernst Bloch, *The Principle of Hope,* vol. 1 (Cambridge, Mass.: MIT Press, 1986), p. 394.

12. George Yudice, "Reading/Hearing Marginality" (unpublished paper given to me by author).

13. Elizabeth Fox-Genovese, "The Claims of a Common Culture: Gender, Race, Class, and the Canon," *Salmagundi,* 72 (Fall 1986): 121.

14. See James Clifford, *The Predicament of Culture* (Cambridge, Mass.: Harvard University Press, 1988).

15. Nelly Richard, "Postmodernism and Periphery," in *Third Text* 2 (Winter 1987/88): 11.

16. Quoted in Fiske, *Television Culture,* p. 81.

Index

Works by Bakhtin will be found under
"Bakhtin, Mikhail—works"

A Banana Mecanica (film), 144
Acting: as allegory in Zelig, 209–11;
  and oppression, 211
Adorno, Theodor, 219, 234
Adventures in Babysitting (film), 47
A Escrava que Não é Isaura (De An-
  drade): language in, 136
Africa: influence on Brazilian culture,
  127, 133, 136, 195–96, 230
After Babel (Steiner), 182–83
Against Interpretation (Sontag), 203
Age d'Or, L' (film), 104–6, 175, 176–77
AIDS (disease), 170–73; in cinema,
  172–73
Alencar, José de, 133
Aleph, El (Borges): carnivalesque in,
  123
Alienness: Bakhtin on, 214; in Zelig,
  214–16
Allen, Woody, 25, 43, 110, 152, 200,
  203–5, 210, 218; derivativeness of
  his films, 197–98; "Getting Even,"
  211; intertextuality in his films, 197,
  200; as stand-up comic, 197; in Stardust Memories, 196–97
"All Night Long" (music video), 225

"Almanach du Père Ubu, L'" (Jarry),
  125
Alô Alô Brasil (film), 139
Alô Alô Carnaval (film), 138, 139
Althusser, Louis, 53, 61
Amado, Jorge: Pais do Carnaval, 128
American Friend, The (film), 79
Amerikanische Freund, Der (film), 79
Anatomy of Criticism, The (Frye), 199–
  200
Animal Crackers (film), 113
"Anthropophagie" (Jarry), 125
Anti-Semitism: as theme in Zelig, 211–
  15
"Apesar de Voce" (samba), 132–33
A Propos de Nice (film): carnivalesque
  in, 110, 117–18
Apuleius, 134; The Golden Ass, 169;
  The Metamorphoses, 97
Arabian Nights, The (film), 115
Aristophanes: The Birds, 172
Art: formalism and, 36; Shklovsky on,
  36
Artaud, Antonin, 127; The Theatre and
  Its Double, 113–14
Artistic originality: Bakhtin and, 199–
  200
Assis, Machado de, 128; and carnival,
  123; Dom Casmurro, 123

As You Like It (Shakespeare), 97
Atalante, L' (film), 185
Audience: participation in cinema, 63–
64, 111; for pornography, 168, 185
Authorship: Bakhtin's concept of, 3,
135

Bacalhau (film), 144, 155
*Bakhtin: Essays and Dialogues on His
Work* (Morson), 13
Bakhtin, Mikhail: on alienness, 214;
and artistic originality, 199–200; on
carnival, 10, 17, 20, 22–24, 85–86,
89–90, 122–23, 125, 128–29, 136,
140–41, 155, 173, 175, 224–27, 234,
238; on the clown, 112–13; compared
to Lacan, 4–6, 162–63; compared to
Nietzsche, 87–90; concept of authorship, 3, 135; concept of polyphony,
136, 145, 180, 198–99, 216, 229–34;
concept of the body, 23, 24, 157–60,
171; and consciousness of self, 4–6;
and cultural self-awareness, 122–23;
and culture, 195, 229–30, 231, 233;
definition of language, 7–8; on dialogism, 60, 187–88, 213–14, 218,
229, 231–32, 237; dissertation, 158;
feminist interpretations of, 6, 22,
159–60, 162, 164; on folklore, 135;
and formalism, 6–7, 20, 28, 31–32;
on formalism, 34–36, 49–50, 55; on
Freudianism, 3–4, 6; hellenistic influence on, 87; influence in Brazil,
128; influence on *Macunaíma*, 133;
on inner speech, 64, 68; interpretations of, 15–16; on Jarry, 99; Kristeva on, 1, 2–3, 16, 69; and language,
40, 79, 80, 178; on language, 29, 32–
33, 49, 51–53, 57–59, 78, 82–84,
183, 187–88, 201, 213–14, 216; on
laughter, 89, 119–21; on linguistics,
31–33; on Marr, 83; and Marxism,
7–8, 15–16, 32, 39, 220, 233–34,
238–39; and music, 136; and oppression, 21–22; on parody, 92, 156; personal life, 2, 72; on polyglossia, 72,
78, 155; and postmodernism, 134–
36; on Rabelais, 85–87, 98–99, 109,
134, 157–58, 161–62, 204; and realism, 236; on the Renaissance, 122;
and role of interlocutor, 46–47; on
Saussure, 28–33, 48; and the self,
216–18; on semiotics, 59; and sexism, 161–62; and sexuality, 158–63,
165, 169, 177–78, 181–82; on Shakespeare, 190, 208; and Soviet authorities, 158, 188; on speech genres, 66,
191–92; and unitary language, 57–
59; White on, 2–3; and Zelinsky, 87
—works: *The Dialogical Imagination*,
1, 10–12; "Discourse on the Novel,"
44, 49, 51, 188, 189; "Epic and
Novel," 72, 78; *The Formal Method
in Literary Scholarship*, 1, 3, 6–7,
22, 23, 32–33, 34, 39, 45, 49–50,
234; "Forms of Time and Chronotope
in the Novel," 11, 112–13, 161, 169;
Freudianism: A Marxist Critique, 1,
3, 9; *Marxism and the Philosophy
of Language*, 1, 3, 7, 9, 13, 23, 28–31,
62, 85; "The Problem of Speech
Genres," 8, 20–21, 33–34, 58,
65, 187; "The Problem of the Text,"
13–14, 40, 58, 187; *Problems of Dostoevsky's Poetics*, 1, 5, 9–10, 14, 21,
24, 85, 97, 116, 128, 136, 172, 187,
197; *Rabelais and His World*, 1, 10,
24, 85, 90, 96, 99, 114, 116–17, 128,
157–60, 169; *Speech Genres and
Other Late Essays*, 1, 12
Bald Soprano, The (Ionesco), 106
Bandido da Luz Vermelha (film), 151–
52; Sganzerla on, 151
Bangue, Bangue (film)
Barber, C. L.: *Shakespeare's Festive
Comedy: A Study of Dramatic Form
and Its Relation to Social Custom*,
96; on suppression of carnival, 92
Barthes, Roland, 36, 53, 61; on lan-
guage, 180; *A Lover's Discourse*, 180
Bataille, Robert, 93, 127; and eroti-
cism, 175–77; *Grammaire Cinégra-
phique*, 27; on laughter, 120; *The
Story of the Eye*, 175, 176
Battle between Carnival and Lent
(film): carnivalesque in, 116
Baudrillard, Alexandre E.: on
postmodernism, 235
Baudry, Jean-Louis, 53, 55
Bauer, Dale: *Feminist Dialogics*, 22

Beckett, Samuel: *Endgame,* 106
Bed, The (film), 169
Behind the Green Door (film), 166
Bellow, Saul: in *Zelig,* 198, 203
Benjamin, Jessica, 219; *The Bonds of Love,* 6
Bergman, Ingmar, 74, 179, 198
Berkeley, Busby, 115, 150
Bettelheim, Bruno, 116, 203
Biculturalism. *See* Cultural self-awareness
Big (film): carnivalesque in, 113
Birds, The (Aristophanes), 172
Birth of a Nation (film): social context of, 41, 43
Birth of Tragedy, The (Nietzsche), 87, 88
Black, David: on language in cinema, 69
Black Orpheus (film), 110, 138, 140
Black Orpheus (Morais), 140
Blacks: compared to Jews, 215–16
Black Sunday (film), 47
Blazing Saddles (film), 74, 210
Bloch, Ernst, 227, 228, 237, 238–39; *The Principle of Hope,* 234
Block, Susan: on eroticism, 165
Blue Movie (film), 169
Blum, Morton: in *Zelig,* 203, 207, 208
Body: Bakhtin's concept of, 23, 24, 157–60, 171; carnival and, 86, 89, 93, 137, 163, 166–67; Lacan and, 162–63; Rabelais and, 157–58
—grotesque: concept of, 158–62; and pornography, 166–67
Boëthius: *De Consolatione Philosophiae,* 97
Bonds of Love, The (Benjamin), 6
Booth, Wayne, 15; "Freedom of Interpretation: Bakhtin and the Challenge of Feminist Criticism," 161–62
Borden, Lizzie, 110, 120
Borges, Jorge Luis, 152; and carnival, 123; *El Aleph,* 123; "Everything and Nothing," 209
Born in Flames (film), 110, 120
Bra for Daddy, A (film), 173
Brazil, 23, 24, 74, 77, 81–82, 110; African influence on culture of, 127, 133, 136, 195–96, 230; Bakhtin's influ-

ence in, 128; carnival in, 91, 126–33, 136–40, 147–49, 152–54; cultural cannibalism in, 124–26; Dadaism in, 126, 145; De Gaulle on, 129; modernism in, 124–25, 127, 133–34, 155
Brazilian Independence Day: carnival compared to military parade, 130
Brazilian television: postsynchronization in, 76
"Brazil-Wood Manifesto" (De Andrade), 129
Brecht, Bertolt, 92, 94, 96, 99; and epic theatre, 48
Breton, André, 145, 152
Broadway Danny Rose (film), 210
Brooks, Mel, 24, 74, 110, 112, 115, 210; Shohat on, 114–15; "2,000 Year Old Man," 211
Bruckner, Pascal: on pornography, 167
Buarque de Holanda, Chico, 81; "Fado Tropical," 193; and samba, 132–33, 193
Buarque de Holanda, Sergio: on carnival, 129
Bunuel, Luis, 10, 67, 93, 103–4, 218; background of, 102; and carnival in cinema, 102–7; and death, 103–4; and eroticism, 175–77; and laughter, 103; and religious parody in films, 103, 177; and speech genres, 67
Burn (film), 78
Bush Mama (film), 43
"By a Waterfall" (song), 150
Bye Bye Brazil (film): language in, 81–82

Cabrera Infante, Guillermo: *Tres Tristes Tigres,* 123
Café Flesh (film): pornography in, 170–71
Camargo, Suzana, 128; on *Macunaíma,* 134
Camões, Luis de: *Os Lusíados,* 194
Campos, Augusto de: on cannibalism as metaphor, 126
Campos, Haroldo de, 128; and cultural self-awareness, 123; on *Macunaima,* 135
Candido, Antonio: on carnival, 127, 129

Canetti, Elias: on carnival, 93
Cannibale (periodical), 125
Cannibalism: and anticolonialism, 124;
as cultural metaphor, 124–26, 145–
46, 155; De Andrade on, 126, 145–
46; in *Gargantua and Pantagruel*,
137; in *Macunaíma*, 137; in *Macu-
naíma* (film), 146; Melville on, 125;
in *Triste Tropico*, 152; Tupinamba
Indians and, 124, 127
—cultural: in Brazil, 124–26
Cannibalistic Review (periodical), 126
Cannibal Manifesto (De Andrade), 124
Canterbury Tales (film), 110, 115–16
Carabiniers, Les (film): carnivalesque
in, 107–9; critical reaction to, 109
Carnavais, Malandros e Herois (De
Mata), 128–29
Carnaval Atlantida (film), 141–42
Carnaval de 1908, O (film), 138
Carnaval de Romans, Le (Ladurie),
95–96
Carnaval Ijexa (Riserio), 131
Carnival: aggression in, 137; American
cinema as literal outgrowth of, 113;
Assis and, 123; Bakhtin on, 10, 17,
20, 22–24, 85–86, 89–90, 122–23,
125, 128–29, 136, 140–41, 155, 173,
175, 224–27, 234, 238; and the body,
86, 89, 93, 137, 163, 166–67; Borges
and, 123; in Brazil, 91, 126–33, 136–
40, 147–49, 152–54; Brazilian
cinema and, 138–44, 146–47, 153–
55; Buarque de Holanda on, 129,
132–33; in Bunuel's films, 102–7;
Candido on, 127, 129; Carpentier on,
126–27; and the Catholic Church,
86, 105, 111–12; Cervantes and, 96,
98, 102; chanchadas and, 138, 141;
class division in, 131; and comic violence, 108–9; compared to Brazilian
Independence Day military parade,
130; co-optation of, 94–95; and
Dadaism, 98, 125; Da Matta on,
129–31; De Andrade on, 125, 127; de-
generation of, 90, 94; Diderot and,
96, 98; Dionysian nature of, 90, 129,
153; Dostoevsky and, 97, 98; dynamic qualities of, 90–91; Eco on,
91–92; effect on literature, 96; eroticism in, 170–71, 176; in Europe,
126–28, 137, 169; Falstaff and, 97;
and feminism, 95; and folk culture,
85–86, 89, 91–92, 95–96, 124–27,
128–33, 225; Fry on, 131; Godard
and, 107–10; Halloween compared
to, 90; in Italian cultural tradition,
115–17; and language, 94, 99, 112–
13, 114, 135–36; in Latin America
and the Caribbean, 90, 122–23, 126–
28; laughter and, 89, 103, 119–20;
mass media and, 90, 92, 93; Mautner on, 129; in Mexico, 127; and music, 89, 92–93, 118; and musical
comedy, 92–93, 114–15; nature of,
86, 89, 93–95, 129–31, 170, 180; in
New York, 90–91; Nietzsche on, 88–
89; origins of, 86, 89; parody in, 173;
as participatory theatre, 94, 130–31;
Paz on, 127; Perrone on, 133; and
plague, 171; pornography as, 169–
70; in Purim tradition, 115; Rabelais
and, 10, 86–87, 98–99, 100–101, 102,
131; and racism, 92, 139; and revolution, 95, 118–19; in Russia, 90; and
samba in Brazil, 126, 140, 154; and
sausages, 87, 100–101; and self-
mockery, 86–87; Shakespeare and,
96–98, 101; social-political content
of, 95, 117–19, 130–31; as subversive
force, 85–86, 89–90, 93–94, 95, 98,
114, 122, 128–30; suppression of, 92,
98; toleration of, 92, 119; translinguistics and, 85; and transvestism, 93, 163–64, 173; Welles and,
139–41; White on, 92, 95, 98. *See
also* Dionysian, the
Carnival!, 91
Carnival at Flanders (Ladurie), 119
Carpentier, Alejo, 96; on carnival,
126–27
Carson, Johnny, 222–23, 225
Casablanca (film), 81
Catholic Church: carnival and the, 86,
105, 111–12
Cervantes, Miguel de, 15, 45, 98; and
carnival, 96, 98, 102; *Don Quixote*,
190, 196, 203; influence on *Macunaíma*, 134
Chairs, The (Ionesco), 106

Chanchadas (Brazilian musical comedies), 138–39, 141, 144, 146–47, 150, 153, 155, 173–74; and carnival, 138, 141; nature of, 139; as parody, 141–43, 150, 153, 155. *See also* Pornochanchadas
Changing Man, The (film), 205
Chant d'Amour (film), 169
Chaplin, Charlie, 106, 112
"Chicklets with Banana" (Gil), 196
Chico Rei (film), 154
Chien Andalou, Un (film), 104, 176–77
Chimes at Midnight (film), 97, 110
Chinoise, La (film), 107
Chronotope: concept of, 11–12, 41–42; Morson on, 41
Cinco Vezes Favela (film), 154
Cinema: AIDS in, 172–73; anticolonialism in, 79–80; audience participation in, 63–64, 111; Black on language in, 69; Bunuel and carnival in, 102–7; categories of the carnivalesque in, 110–11; compared to music, 45–46; dialogism in, 196; effect of subtitles in, 61, 68, 72, 75; English language in, 78–79; eroticism in, 166–70, 175–77, 180–81, 183; formalism and, 27, 44; Godard and language in, 69–70; Gorin and language in, 70–72; inner speech in, 64–65; Japanese conventions in, 63; language in, 57, 59–65, 68–70, 78–83; nature of, 16–17; postsynchronization in, 74–77; racial content of language in, 79–83; role of dialogue in, 59–60, 65–66, 183; semiotic interpretation of, 27–28; semiotic role of music in, 62; social context in, 41–44, 47; sound in, 45–46, 60; theory and criticism in France, 27; translation in, 72–75; visual images in, 62–63
—American: as literal outgrowth of the carnival, 113
—Brazilian: and carnival, 138–44, 146–47, 153–55; and commercial films, 144–45; effect of *Macunaima* on, 146–47; and Hollywood, 139, 141–42, 144, 151; political content of, 153; Vieira on, 141–43; Xavier on, 150, 155

—feminist: Iragaray on, 120; laughter in, 120; and Medusan films, 120
Cinema Novo movement, 144–45, 147, 150–52, 154, 173
Cinesemiotics: concept of, 38; concept of heteroglossia, 11, 17, 20, 24, 43, 50, 53, 59, 70–71, 116, 180, 220–22, 229, 237; concept of intonation, 45, 84, 168, 182, 184; concept of polyglossia, 53, 58, 72, 77–78, 155, 210; concept of social accent, 45, 168; concept of social evaluation, 45; concept of speech genres, 8, 12, 14, 65; concept of tact, 18, 20, 22, 45–48, 52, 79, 80, 182–85, 222–24; concept of text, 18–19, 41–42, 48–50; and psychoanalysis, 53–54; and Saussure, 53–54, 57; translinguistics and, 37, 44, 53, 56, 57, 62, 72, 166, 180; vocabulary of, 44–45
Citizen Kane (film), 204, 206
Cixous, Helene, 162, 182, 186; "Laugh of the Medusa," 120
Clark, Katerina, 16, 87, 158
Clifford, James, 19; on postmodernism, 236
Clockwork Orange, A (film), 144
Conner, Bruce, 51, 204
Conquest of America, The (Todorov), 212
Conrad, Joseph, 11; *Heart of Darkness*, 152
Consciousness of self: Bakhtin and, 4–6
"Constituents of a Theory of the Media" (Enzensberger), 219, 220
Contempt (film), 79
Cosmonautas, Os (film), 155
Costinha e o King-Mong (film), 144
Course in General Linguistics (Saussure), 26, 28
"Creátion du Monde, La" (play), 127
Cuddihy, John Murray: *The Ordeal of Civility: Freud, Marx, Lèvi-Strauss, and the Jewish Struggle with Modernity*, 114, 213–14
Cultural self-awareness: Bakhtin and, 122–23; Campos and, 123; in Latin America and the Caribbean, 122–23, 126–28, 156, 230; Monegal and, 123, 125; in Russia, 122–23

Culture: Bakhtin and, 195, 229–30, 231, 233
Cultures, marginal. See Postmodernism
Curtis, James M.: "Mikhail Bakhtin, Nietzsche, and Russian Pre-Revolutionary Thought," 87

Dadaism: in Brazil, 126, 145; carnival and, 98, 125
Dak Van de Walvis, Het (film): language in, 83–84
Da Matta, Roberto: on carnival, 129–31
"Dance Party" (music video), 225
Date with Judy, A (film), 81
"Dating Game, The" (television program), 225
Day for Night (film), 73
De Andrade, Joaquim Pedro, 146, 173–74; on Macunaíma (film), 146
De Andrade, Mario: concept of polyphony, 136; A Escrava que Não é Isaura, 136; Macunaíma, 128, 133–36, 146, 149; on Macunaíma, 135; musical background of, 136
De Andrade, Oswald, "Brazil-Wood Manifesto," 129; on cannibalism, 126; on cannibalism as metaphor, 145–46; Cannibal Manifesto, 124; on carnival, 125, 127; as film character, 153; on laughter, 125; Serafim Ponte Grande, 128
Death: Bunuel and, 103–4; in Macunaíma, 137
Decameron (film), 110, 115–16
De Consolatione Philosophiae (Boëthius), 97
De Laurentis, Dino, 144
De Man, Paul: on dialogism, 13, 211
De Mata, Roberto: Carnavais, Malandros e Herois, 128–29
De Mille, Cecil B., 78
Derrida, Jacques, 26, 48, 218
"Des Cannibales" (Montaigne), 125
Dialectics: dialogism and, 188, 237
Dialectique Peut-Elle Casser les Briques?, La (film), 75
Dialogism: Bakhtin on, 60, 187–88, 213–14, 218, 229, 231–32, 237; in

cinema, 196; concept of, 12–15, 17, 20, 24–25, 34, 54, 125, 187–91, 229; De Man on, 13, 211; and dialectics, 188, 237; and formalism, 34, 37; in the novel, 189–90; Polan on, 187; rap music and, 192; in Stardust Memories, 196–97; in Zelig, 196, 198
Dialogue: Godard's use of, 65–66; role in cinema, 59–60, 65–66, 183
Diderot, Denis, 15; and carnival, 96, 98; Le Neveu de Rameau, 190
Diegues, Carlos, 81, 154
Dionysian, the: function of, 88–89; and nature of carnival, 90, 129, 153; Nietzsche and, 87–90; origins of, 89. See also Carnival
Doctor Strangelove (film), 62
Dom Casmurro (Assis): carnivalesque in, 123
Donahue, Phil, 222–23, 225
Don Quixote (Cervantes), 190, 196, 203
Don's Party (film): carnivalesque in, 111
Dora (film), 61
Dostoevsky, Feodor, 5, 9–10, 15, 52, 181, 189–90, 196–97, 200; and carnival, 97, 98; compared to Tolstoy, 188; and polyphony, 229
Douglas, Mary, 2; on carnival, 93
Down Argentine Way (film), 42
Dubbing in films. See Postsynchronization
Duck Soup (film), 110
Duluth (Vidal), 15
Duras, Marguerite: Moderato Cantabile, 73
Dyer, Richard: "Entertainment and Utopia," 92–93; and mass media, 220, 224

E. Teia a Mulher do Extraterrestre em Sua Aventura no Rio de Janeiro (film), 144
E.T. (film), 144
Eagleton, Terry, 15, 29
Easy Rider (film): carnivalesque in, 113
Eco, Umberto, 27, 37; on carnival, 91–92; as elitist, 91
Economics: semiotic interpretation of, 27

8 1/2 (film), 115, 196, 197
Eijanaika! (film): carnivalesque in, 110, 118–19
Eikhenbaum, Boris, 62, 64
Eisenstein, Sergei M., 31, 64
Eliade, Mircea: on carnival, 93
Elias, Norbert: on good manners, 114
Endgame (Beckett), 106
English language: "Black," 77, 82; in cinema, 78–79; and power, 78–79; Steiner on, 79
"Entertainment and Utopia" (Dyer), 92–93
Enzensberger, Hans Magnus: "Constituents of a Theory of the Media," 219, 220; and mass media, 219, 220, 224, 238
Erotic Interludes, 164
Eroticism: Bataille and, 175–77; Block on, 165; Bunuel and, 175–77; in carnival, 170–71, 176; in cinema, 166–70, 175–77, 180–81, 183; Griffin on, 165; in home-produced videotapes, 185–86; and pornography, 166–70; women and, 164–65. *See also* Sexuality
Europe: carnival in, 126–27, 137, 169
"Everything and Nothing" (Borges), 209
Exorcist, The (film), 144
Exterminating Angel, The (film), 67, 104, 176; carnivalesque in, 106

"Fado Tropical" (Buarque), 193
Fame (film), 230–31
"Fantasy Island" (television program), 225
Fellini, Federico, 110, 115, 196, 197
Feminism: carnival and, 95; and interpretations of Bakhtin, 6, 22, 159–60, 162, 164; Iragaray and, 159
Feminist cinema. *See* Cinema—feminist
Feminist Dialogics (Bauer), 22
Femme est une Femme, Une (film), 59
Femme Mariee, Une (film), 64
Festival. *See* Carnival; Dionysian, the
F for Fake (film), 204
Filho, Antunes: on laughter, 128
Film language: Metz and concept of,

37–40, 44, 48–49, 50, 52–53, 55–56, 57, 186, 200
Finkelraut, Alain: on pornography, 167
Fireworks (film), 169
Fiske, John, 21; on television, 226–27, 233
Five Easy Pieces (film), 73
Flaubert, Gustave: *Madame Bovary,* 196
Flugel, J. C.: *The Psychology of Clothes,* 163
Folk culture: carnival and, 85–86, 89, 91–92, 95–96, 124–27, 128–33, 225; Rabelais and, 86–87; rap music as, 191–92
Folklore: Bakhtin on, 135
Footlight Parade (film), 149
Formalism: and art, 36; Bakhtin and, 6–7, 20, 28, 31–32; Bakhtin on, 34–36, 49–50, 55; dialogism and, 34, 37; Jakobson on, 36–37; and linguistic interpretation of cinema, 27, 44; nature of, 35–36; Pechey on, 49–50; the Prague School and, 37; in Russia, 36–37, 39; Tynyanov on, 36–37
Fox-Genovese, Elizabeth: on postmodernism, 235
France: film theory and criticism in, 27
Freaks (film), 72
Fred and Ginger (film), 115
"Freedom of Interpretation: Bakhtin and the Challenge of Feminist Criticism" (Booth), 161–62
Freudianism: Bakhtin on, 3–4, 6
Fry, Peter: on carnival, 131
Frye, Northrop: *The Anatomy of Criticism,* 199–200
Funeral, The (film), 66–67

Garcia Márquez, Gabriel: *A Hundred Years of Solitude,* 123
Gargantua and Pantagruel (Rabelais), 87, 133, 137, 147; cannibalism in, 137
Gaulle, Charles de: on Brazil, 129
Genet, Jean, 169; *The Maids,* 98
"Getting Even" (Allen), 211
Gil, Gilberto: "Chicklets with Banana," 196

Godard, Jean-Luc, 10, 42, 48, 59, 61, 75, 174–75, 183–85, 191; and carnival, 107–10; and cinesemiotic concept of heteroglossia, 51–52; film adaptation of *Ubu Roi,* 108–9; and language in cinema, 69–70; on mass media, 219; and pornography, 178–80; and postsynchronization, 74–75; use of dialogue, 65–66; use of inner speech, 64
Golden Ass, The (Apuleius), 169
Golden Positions, The (film), 169
Gold Rush, The (film), 106
Gorin, Jean-Pierre, 51; and language in cinema, 70–72
Go West (film), 112
Grammaire Cinégraphique (Bataille), 27
Grammar of Film (Spottiswoode), 27
Grease (film), 144
Greenblatt, Stephen, 158; *Renaissance Self-Fashioning,* 213
Grenada: invasion of, 228
Grenier, Richard: on *Zelig,* 203–4
Griffin, Susan: on eroticism, 165
Griffith, D. W., 41, 112

Hail Mary (film), 107
Hall, Stuart, 21; on language and power, 77
Halloween: compared to carnival, 90
Halloween (film): carnivalesque in, 111
Hamlet (Shakespeare), 101
Hammer, Signe: "Strangers in the Universe," 165
"Hardcore: Resistance(?) in the Postmodern" (James), 185
Harder They Come, The (film), 82
Heart of Darkness (Conrad), 152
Heat (film), 169
Heath, Stephen, 42, 177
Hebdige, Dick: and mass media, 220
Hegel, Georg W. F.: on parody, 156
Hellenism: influence on Bakhtin, 87
Henry IV (Shakespeare), 97
Herman, Pee Wee, 43, 220
Heteroglossia: cinesemiotic concept of, 11, 17, 20, 24, 43, 50, 53, 59, 70–71, 116, 180, 220–22, 229, 237; Godard and cinesemiotic concept of, 51–52; in television, 220–22, 232–33

High Noon (film), 142–43
High Theory/Low Culture (MacCabe), 220
Hirsch, Paul: on mass media, 225
History of the World, Part I (film): carnivalesque in, 110, 114–15
Hitchcock, Alfred, 47, 63
Holding (film), 169
Hollywood: Brazilian cinema and, 139, 141–42, 144, 151
Holquist, Michael, 16, 87, 158
"Homeland as Text, The" (Steiner), 213
Hora de los Hornos, La (film), 63
Horkheimer, Max, 219
Horse's Mouth, The (film), 74
Howe, Irving, 215–16; *World of Our Fathers,* 203; in *Zelig,* 198, 203
Huis Clos (Sartre), 106
Hundred Years of Solitude, A (Garcia Márquez): carnivalesque in, 123

Idade da Terra (film), 154
I Love You Rosa (film), 180–81
Images, visual: in cinema, 62–63
Imaginary Signifier, The (Metz), 55
Imamura, Shohei, 24, 110, 118–19
Inner speech: Bakhtin on, 64, 68; in cinema, 64–65; Godard's use of, 64
Interlocutor: Bakhtin and role of, 46–47; newscaster as, 46–47; role of, 45, 46–47, 183; in *Zelig,* 200
Intertextuality: in Woody Allen's films, 197, 200; in *Zelig,* 198, 203–4, 206–8
Intonation: cinesemiotic concept of, 45, 84, 168, 182, 184
Ionesco, Eugene: *The Bald Soprano,* 106; *The Chairs,* 106; *Rhinoceros,* 106
Iragaray, Luce, 22, 178, 182; and feminism, 159; on feminist cinema, 120; on pornography, 167
Irish: compared to Jews, 214–15
Ishtar (film), 47
Italian cultural tradition: carnival in, 115–17
"It's All True" (unfinished film), 139–41

Jakobson, Roman, 30, 44; on formalism, 36–37; and linguistics, 26

James, David: "Hardcore: Resis-
tance(?) in the Postmodern," 185
Jameson, Fredric, 15, 95, 188, 201; and
mass media, 220, 221, 224; on semio-
tics, 26, 70
Japan: cinematic conventions in, 63
Jarry, Alfred, 24, 127, 143; "An-
thropophagie," 125; Bakhtin on, 99;
"L'Almanach du Père Ubu," 125;
Ubu Roi, 99–102, 106, 107–9, 125
Jaws (film), 144
Jazz Singer, The (film), 215
Jeca Contra o Capeta, O (film), 144
Jews: compared to blacks, 215–16;
compared to Irish, 214–15
Johnson, Randal: on Macunaima
(film), 149–50
Joyce, James, 96; Ulysses, 64
Joyful Wisdom, The (Nietzsche), 88
Julius Caesar (Shakespeare), 101

Kaplan, Ann: on pornography, 167–68
Keaton, Buster, 110, 112
King, Martin Luther, 192, 232
King Kong (film), 144
King of Comedy, The (film), 223, 230
Kings of the Road (film), 79
Kis'ot Lohatim (film), 74
Koch-Grunberg, Theodor: Vom
Roroima zum Orinoco: Ergebnisse
einer Reise in Nord Bresilien und
Venezuela in den Jahren 1911–1913,
133
Konsky Pysk (film), 74
Kristeva, Julia, 17, 26, 36, 48, 125, 201;
on Bakhtin, 1, 2–3, 16, 69; "Une Po-
etique Ruinée," 3
Kroker, Arthur, 170, 171
Kubrick, Stanley, 62, 112, 144

Lacan, Jacques, 51, 53–55, 61, 209;
Bakhtin compared to, 4–6, 162–63;
and the body, 162–63; and linguistic
interpretation of psychoanalysis, 27
"La-Di-Da-Di" (song), 192
Ladrões de Cinema (film), 154
Ladurie, Emmanuel le Roy, 2; Carni-
val at Flanders, 119; Le Carnaval de
Romans, 95–96
Langage et Cinema (Metz), 38–39, 48–
49, 52, 59

Language: Bakhtin and, 40, 79, 80,
178; Bakhtin on, 29, 32–33, 49, 51–
53, 57–59, 78, 82–84, 183, 187–88,
201, 213–14, 216; Bakhtin's definition of, 7–8; Barthes on, 180; in Bye
Bye Brazil, 81–82; carnival and, 94,
99, 112–13, 114, 135–36; in cinema,
57, 59–65, 68–70, 78–83; in Der
Leone Have Sept Cabecas, 83; in Het
Dak Van de Walvis, 83–84; in Macunaíma, 134, 136–37; Marr on, 83;
and oppression, 8–9, 77; political dimension of, 77–78; as political issue
in South Africa, 77; and power, 77,
79–84; Rabelais and, 99, 104; racial
content in cinema, 79–83; and sexuality, 180–83; and structuralism,
27–28; Trouble in Paradise and nature of, 76; in Zelig, 216. See also
Linguistics; Semiotics; Translinguistics
—unitary: Bakhtin and, 57–59
Latin America and the Caribbean: carnival in, 90, 122–23, 126–28; cultural self-awareness in, 122–23, 126–
28, 156, 230
Latin Lovers (film), 81
Latino (film), 47
"Laugh of the Medusa" (Cixous), 120
Laughter: Bakhtin on, 89, 119–21;
Bataille on, 120; Bunuel and, 103;
and carnival, 89, 103, 119–20; De
Andrade on, 125; in feminist cine-
ma, 120; Filho on, 128; Nietzsche
and, 89; Rabelais and, 87, 89, 125,
204
Lawrence of Arabia (film), 81
Lear (film), 107
Lefebvre, Henri: on carnival, 93
Leibnitz, Gottfried Wilhelm, 29, 58
Leone Have Sept Cabecas, Der (film):
language in, 83
Letter to Jane (film), 107
Lèvi-Strauss, Claude, 152, 153; and
linguistics, 26–27
Life of Brian, The (film): carnivalesque
in, 111–12
"Lingua" (Veloso), 192–95
Linguistics: Bakhtin on, 31–33; defini-
tion of, 28–29; development of, 26–

Linguistics (*continued*)
27; Jakobson and, 26; Lèvi-Strauss
and, 26–27; Metz and, 28; Saus-
sure's system of, 23, 28–33, 37, 40,
44, 52, 59, 70, 84, 187, 194; Trou-
betskoy and, 26. *See also* Language;
Semiotics; Translinguistics
Lira do Delirio (film), 153
Literature: carnival's effect on, 96
Lolita (Nabokov), 167
"Lounge Time: Post-war Crises and
the Chronotope of Film Noir" (Sob-
chack), 12
Love: sexuality and, 161
Love and Anarchy (film), 117
Love and Death (film), 110
"Love Boat" (television program), 225
Lover's Discourse, A (Barthes), 180
Lubitsch, Ernst, 76
Lusiados, Os (Camões), 194

Macbeth (Shakespeare), 101
MacCabe, Colin: *High Theory/Low
Culture: Analyzing Popular Television and Film*, 220
Macunaima (De Andrade), 128, 133–
36, 146, 149; Bakhtinian themes in,
133; Brazilian folklore in, 133–36;
Camargo on, 134; Campos on, 135;
cannibalism in, 137; carnivalesque
in, 133, 136; Cervantes' influence on,
134; characterization in, 135; De Andrade on, 135; death in, 137; language in, 134, 136–37; Rabelaisian
influence on, 134
Macunaima (film), 146–50, 230; cannibalism in, 146; carnivalesque in,
145–49; critical reaction to, 149; De
Andrade on, 146; effect on Brazilian
cinema, 146–47; Johnson on, 149–
50; political content of, 149–50
Madame Bovary (Flaubert), 196
Made in U.S.A. (film), 107
Maffesoli, Michael: on carnival, 93
Maids, The (Genet), 98
Makavejev, Dusan, 110, 200
Male Fantasies (Theweleit), 165
Malek, Anwar Abdul: on postmodern-
ism, 235
Manga, Carlos, 142–43, 155

"Manifeste Cannibale Dada" (Picabia),
125
Man Who Envied Women, The (film),
51
Mardi gras. *See* Carnival
Marnie (film): compared to *Zelig*, 206–
7
Marr, Nikolai Y.: Bakhtin on, 83; on
language, 83
Marx, Karl, 145, 233–34; on parody,
156
Marx Brothers, 24, 110, 112; subversion in their films, 114
Marxism: Bakhtin and, 7–8, 15–16,
32, 39, 220, 233–34, 238–39
Masculin, Féminin (film), 66, 75; as
parody, 179–80
"Masque of the Red Death" (Poe), 172
Mass media: and carnival, 90, 92, 93;
Dyer and, 220, 224; Enzensberger
and, 219, 220, 224, 238; Godard on,
219; Hebdige and, 220; Hirsch on,
225; Jameson and, 220, 221, 224;
leftist criticism of, 219–20, 227–28,
238; Newcombe on, 225; political
content of, 219–20, 227–29; Rapping
on, 225. *See also* Television
Matar ou Correr (film), 142–43, 155
Mautner, Jorge: on carnival, 129
Mazursky, Paul, 43, 230
Medium Cool (film), 185
"Medusan" films. *See* Cinema, feminist
Medvedev, P. M., 3, 23, 34, 49
Mellenkamp, Patricia, 51, 114
Melville, Herman, 11; and cannibalism
as metaphor, 125; *Moby Dick*, 208,
216
Menippean satire, 9, 96–100, 102, 104–
5, 107–10, 116, 125, 128, 134, 137,
147, 148–49, 172, 198, 208, 210; na-
ture of, 97–98, 198–99; *Zelig* as,
198–200
Menippus of Gadara, 97
Mépris, Le (film), 66, 74–75
Merquior, José Guilherme: *Saudades
do Carnaval*, 129
"Message, The" (song), 192
Metahistory (White), 200
Metamorphoses, The (Apuleius), 97
Metz, Christian, 10, 32; and concept of

film language, 37–40, 44, 48–49, 50, 52–53, 55–56, 57, 186, 200; *The Imaginary Signifier*, 55; *Langage et Cinema*, 38–39, 48–49, 52, 59; and linguistics, 28; and Saussurean linguistic system, 40, 44; "The Perceived and the Named," 64
Midsummer Night's Dream, A (Shakespeare), 97, 210
Midsummer Night's Sex Comedy, A (film), 198
Miéville, Anne-Marie, 174–75, 178, 183–84
"Mikhail Bakhtin, Nietzsche, and Russian Pre-Revolutionary Thought" (Curtis), 87
Mikhail Bakhtine: Le Principe Dialogique (Todorov), 2, 12–13, 18
Milhouse: A White Comedy (film), 232
Miranda, Carmen, 43, 81, 138
Missing (film), 47
Moby Dick (Melville), 208, 216
Moderato Cantabile (Duras), 73
Moderato Cantabile (film), 73
Modernism: in Brazil, 124–25, 127, 133–34, 155
Modleski, Tania, 21; *Studies in Entertainment: Critical Approaches to Mass Culture*, 220
Mondale, Walter: scripting of presidential campaign (1984), 228–29
Monegal, Emir Rodriguez: and cultural self-awareness, 123, 125
Monkey Business (film), 113–14
Montaigne, Michel de, 145, 190; "Des Cannibales," 125; and sexuality, 160–61
Monty Python and the Holy Grail (film): carnivalesque in, 111
Monty Python Live at the Hollywood Bowl (film): carnivalesque in, 111–12
Morais, Vinicius de: *Black Orpheus*, 140
Moravia, Alberto: *The Odyssey*, 74
Morson, Gary Saul, 16; *Bakhtin: Essays and Dialogues on His Work*, 13; on chronotope, 41
Moscow on the Hudson (film), 230–31
Music: Bakhtin and, 136; carnival and, 89, 92–93, 118; cinema compared to, 45–46; semiotic role in cinema, 62

Musical comedy: carnival and, 92–93, 114–15
My Dinner with André (film), 60–61
My Last Sigh (Bunuel), 103–4

Nabokov, Vladimir: *Lolita*, 167
Natal de Portella (film), 154
Nausée, Le (Sartre), 178
Nem Sansão nem Dalila (film), 142, 155
Neveu de Rameau, Le (Diderot), 190
Newcombe, Horace: on mass media, 225
Newscaster: as interlocutor, 46–47
New York City: polyphony in, 230–31
Nietzsche, Friedrich, 129, 145; Bakhtin compared to, 87–90; *The Birth of Tragedy*, 87, 88; on carnival, 88–89; and Christianity, 89; and the Dionysian, 87–90; as elitist, 90; *The Joyful Wisdom*, 88; and laughter, 89; *Nietzsche against Wagner*, 209
Nietzsche against Wagner (Nietzsche), 209
"Nightline" (television program), 47
Nin, Anais, 164, 182
Noire de . . . , La (film), 79–80
Nos Tempos da Vasolina (film), 144
Nothing But the Best (film), 82
Novel: dialogism in the, 189–90
Numero Deux (film), 48, 185

Odyssey, The (Moravia), 74
Oedipus Rex (Sophocles), 99
Olvidados, Los (film), 106–7
O'Neill, Eileen: on pornography, 168
One Potato, Two Potato (film), 42–43
Oppression: acting and, 211; Bakhtin and, 21–22; language and, 8–9, 77; Vigo and, 117–18
Ordeal of Civility (Cuddihy), 114, 213–14
Oscarito (actor), 143, 155
Otelo, Colé, 142, 153
Otelo, Grande, 142, 143, 147, 148, 150
Othello (Shakespeare), 123

Pais do Carnaval (Amado), 128
Palmer, R. Barton: on Saussure, 30
Parody: Bakhtin on, 92, 156; in carnival, 173; chanchadas as, 141–43, 150,

Parody (continued)
153, 155; Hegel on, 156; Marx on,
156; Masculin, Féminin as, 179–80;
Sauve Qui Peut/(la Vie) as, 174–75,
183–84; Shakespeare's use of, 97;
Vereda Tropical as, 173–74; Zelig
as, 201, 205–6
Pasolini, Pier Pãolo, 27–28, 37, 110,
115–16
Paz, Octavio: on carnival, 127
Pechey, Graham, 15, 17; on formalism,
49–50
"People's Court, The" (television pro-
gram), 225
Pepe le Moko (film), 81
"Perceived and the Named, The"
(Metz), 64
Perrone, Charles: on carnival, 133
Persona (film), 74
Pessoa, Fernando, 194, 195
Petronius, 134; Satyricon, 97
Picabia, Francis: "Manifeste Can-
nibale Dada," 125
Pink Flamingos (film), 110
Plague: carnival and, 171; Rabelais
and, 171
Play It Again, Sam (film), 198
Pleasures: Women Write Erotica, 164
Poe, Edgar Allan: "Masque of the Red
Death," 172
Poetica Kino, 27
"Poetique Ruinée, Une" (Kristeva), 3
Polan, Dana: on dialogism, 187
Polyester (film), 110
Polyglossia: Bakhtin on, 72, 78, 155;
cinesemiotic concept of, 53, 58, 72,
77–78, 155, 210
Polyphony: Bakhtin's concept of, 136,
145, 180, 198–99, 216, 229–34; De
Andrade's concept of, 136; Dostoev-
sky and, 229; in New York City,
230–31
Popular culture. See Folk culture
Pornochanchadas (Brazilian film
genre), 173–74. See also
Chanchadas
Pornographic Imagination, The (Son-
tag), 176
Pornography: audience for, 168, 185;
Bruckner on, 167; in Café Flesh,
170–71; as carnival, 169–70; carnivalesque in, 166; eroticism and, 166–
70; Finkelraut on, 167; Godard and,
178–80; grotesque body and, 166–
67; Iragaray on, 167; Kaplan on,
167–68; nature of, 166–70, 174–75;
O'Neill on, 168; and sexism, 167–68,
182; types of, 168–69; Waugh on,
168; Willis on, 167
"Pornography and the Avant-Garde"
(Suleiman), 176
Postmodernism: Bakhtin and, 134–36;
Baudrillard on, 235; Clifford on,
236; Fox-Genovese on, 235; Malek
on, 235; Richard on, 236; Yudice on,
235
Postsynchronization: in Brazilian television, 76; in cinema, 74–77; Godard
and, 74–75; as plot point in Voz do
Brasil, 77; as plot point in Women
on the Verge of a Nervous Break-
down, 76–77. See also Subtitles
Poto and Cabengo (film), 70–72; Sob-
chack on, 71
Power: English language and, 78–79;
language and, 77, 79–84
Prenom Carmen (film), 107
Principle of Hope, The (Bloch), 234
Producers, The (film): carnivalesque
in, 115
Propp, Vladimir, 135, 206
Pryor, Richard, 110, 113
Psycho (film), 63
Psychoanalysis: cinesemiotics and,
53–54; linguistic interpretation of,
27
Psychology of Clothes, The (Flugel),
163
Puig, Manuel, 123–24
Purim: carnival tradition in, 115
Python, Monty, 24, 111

Quando as Mulheres Pecam (film), 74
Quando o Carnaval Chegar (film), 138
Question of Silence, A (film): carni-
valesque in, 120–21
Quilombo (film), 154

Rabelais, François, 15, 24; Bakhtin on,
85–87, 98–99, 109, 134, 157–58,

161–62, 204; and banquet imagery, 87; and the body, 157–58; and carnival, 10, 86–87, 98–99, 100–101, 102, 131; death of, 104; and folk culture, 86–87; *Gargantua and Pantagruel*, 87, 133, 137, 147; influence on *Macunaima*, 134; and language, 99, 104; and laughter, 87, 89, 125, 204; and plague, 171; and sexism, 161–62
Racism: carnival and, 92, 139
Rainier, Yvonne, 51, 52
Rambo (film), 42
Rap music, 194, 196; and dialogism, 192; as folk culture, 191–92; Toop on, 191
Rapping, Elayne: on mass media, 225
Reagan, Ronald: scripting of presidential campaign (1984), 228–29
Realism: Bakhtin and, 236
Reception theory, 20–21
Reds (film), 206
Remaking Love, 95
Remedial Reading Comprehension (film), 61
Renaissance: Bakhtin on the, 122
Renaissance Self-Fashioning (Greenblatt), 213
Revista de Antropofagia (periodical), 124
Revolution: carnival and, 95, 118–19
Rhinoceros (Ionesco), 106
Richard, Nelly: on postmodernism, 236
Riddles of the Sphynx (film), 61
Riserio, Antonio: *Carnaval Ijexa*, 131
"Rock-'n'-Wrestling" (television program), 226–27
Rocky Horror Picture Show, The (film), 64, 111
Romeo and Juliet (Shakespeare), 97
Ronde, La (film), 45
Ruiz, Raul, 10, 52, 83, 191
Russia: carnival celebrated in, 90; cultural self-awareness in, 122–23; formalism in, 36–37, 39; semiotics in, 28, 30–31, 34
Russo, Mary, 121, 160, 162; on transvestism, 163

Samba, 193–95; in Brazilian carnival, 126, 140, 154; Buarque de Holanda

and, 132–33, 193; political content of, 132–33
Samba da Criacão do Mundo (film), 154
Sartre, Jean-Paul, 208, 210, 213; *Huis Clos*, 106; *Le Nausée*, 178
"Saturday Night Live" (television program), 225
Satyricon (film), 110, 115
Satyricon (Petronius), 97
Saudades do Carnaval (Merquior), 129
Sausages: carnival and, 87, 100–101
Saussure, Ferdinand de: Bakhtin on, 28–33, 48; cinesemiotics and, 53–54, 57; *Course in General Linguistics*, 26, 28; linguistic system of, 23, 28–33, 37, 40, 44, 52, 59, 70, 84, 187, 194; Metz and linguistic system of, 40, 44; Palmer on, 30
Sauve Qui Peut/(la Vie) (film): as parody, 174–75, 183–84
Scorcese, Martin, 223
Sea of Roses (film), 120
Secretaries Who Do . . . Everything!, The (film), 173
Seduction of Mimi, The (film), 116–17
Self: Bakhtin and the, 216–18
Sembene, Ousmane, 79–80
Semiotics: Bakhtin on, 59; Jameson on, 26, 70; in Russia, 28, 30–31, 34. *See also* Language; Linguistics; Translinguistics
Serafim Ponte Grande (De Andrade), 128
Servant, The (film), 46
Seven Beauties (film), 116
Sexism: Bakhtin and, 161–62; pornography and, 167–68, 182; Rabelais and, 161–62
Sexuality: Bakhtin and, 158–63, 165, 169, 177–78, 181–82; language and, 180–83; and love, 161; Montaigne and, 160–61. *See also* Eroticism
Sganzerla, Rogerio: on *Bandido da Luz Vermelha*, 151
Shakespeare, William, 24, 91, 100, 198; Bakhtin on, 190, 208; and carnival, 96–98, 101; *Hamlet*, 101; *Henry IV*, 97; *Julius Caesar*, 101; *Macbeth*, 101; *A Midsummer Night's Dream*, 97,

Shakespeare (*continued*)
210; *Othello,* 123; *Romeo and Juliet,*
97; *The Tempest,* 84; *Twelfth Night,*
97; use of parody by, 97; *As You Like
It,* 97
Shakespeare's Festive Comedy (Bar-
ber), 96
"She Works Hard for the Money" (mu-
sic video), 225
Shklovsky, Viktor, 27, 49; on art, 36
Shohat, Ella: on Brooks, 114–15
Show People (film), 112
Silence, The (film), 179
Silverman, Kaja: on transvestism,
163–64
Simon of the Desert (film), 103
"Six Million Cruzeiro Man, The," 155
Snow, Michael, 61, 73
Sobchack, Vivian: "Lounge Time: Post-
war Crises and the Chronotope of
Film Noir," 12; on *Poto and
Cabengo,* 71
Social accent: cinesemiotic concept of,
45, 168
Social evaluation: cinesemiotic concept
of, 45
Socialism: popular American view of,
238
So Is This (film), 61
Sontag, Susan: *Against Interpretation,*
203; *The Pornographic Imagination,*
176; in *Zelig,* 198, 202–3
Sophocles: *Oedipus Rex,* 99
Speech genres: Bakhtin on, 66, 191–
92; Bunuel and, 67; cinesemiotic
concept of, 8, 12, 14, 65; and trans-
linguistics, 65–67
Spellbound (film): compared to *Zelig,*
206–7
Spielberg, Stephen, 144
Spinoza, Benedict de: *Tractatus
Theologico-Politicus,* 212
Spottiswoode, Raymond: *Grammar of
Film,* 27
Stallybrass, Peter, 15; on carnival, 92,
95
Stardust Memories (film): Allen in,
196–97; compared to *Zelig,* 207; crit-
ical reaction to, 197; dialogism in,
196–97

"Star Search" (television program),
225
Steiner, George: *After Babel,* 182–83;
on English language, 79; "The
Homeland as Text," 213
Sterne, Laurence: *Tristram Shandy,*
196
Story of the Eye, The (Bataille), 175,
176
"Strangers in the Universe" (Ham-
mer), 165
Strangers on a Train (film), 43, 113
Studies in Entertainment (Modleski),
220
Subtitles: cinematic effect of, 61, 68,
72; as social-political control, 75. *See
also* Postsynchronization
Suleiman, Susan: "Pornography and
the Avant-Garde," 176
Sweet Sweetback's Baadasssss Song
(film), 82
Swept Away (film), 117

Tabu (film): carnivalesque in, 153
Tact: and cinematic tension, 48;
cinesemiotic concept of, 18, 20, 22,
45–48, 52, 54, 79, 80, 182–85, 222–
24; in television, 222–24
Tampopo (film), 181
Tati, Jacques, 62, 226
Television: Bakhtinian perspective on,
220–25, 229; carnivalesque in, 224–
27; Fiske on, 226–27, 233; heteroglossia in, 220–22, 232–33; news
programs, 223–24; sponsors, 221,
223; tact in, 222–24; talk shows,
222–23. *See also* Mass media
Tempest, The (Shakespeare), 84
Tennyson, Alfred: *Ulysses,* 209
Tension, cinematic: tact and, 48
Text: cinesemiotic concept of, 18–19,
41–42, 48–50
That Obscure Object of Desire (film),
104, 177
Theatre
—epic: Brecht and, 48
—participatory: carnival as, 94, 130–
31
Theatre and Its Double, The (Artaud),
113–14

"Theses on the Commune," 95
Theweleit, Klaus: *Male Fantasies,* 165
Three Ages, The (film), 110, 112
Todorov, Tzvetan, 15, 206; *The Conquest of America,* 212; *Mikhail Bakhtine: Le Principe Dialogique,* 2, 12–13, 18
Tolstoy, Leo: compared to Dostoevsky, 188
Tom Jones (film), 181
Toop, David: on rap music, 191
Touch of Evil (film), 79
Tout Va Bien (film), 51, 178
Tractatus Theologico-Politicus (Spinoza), 212
Translation: in cinema, 72–75
Translinguistics: and carnival, 85; and cinesemiotics, 37, 44, 53, 56, 57, 62, 72, 166, 180; concept of, 30–31, 40–41, 58, 166, 186; speech genres and, 65–67. *See also* Language; Linguistics; Semiotics
Transvestism: carnival and, 93, 163–64, 173; Russo on, 163; Silverman on, 163–64
Trash (film), 169
Tres Tristes Tigres (Cabrera Infante): carnivalesque in, 123
Tricia's Wedding (film), 173
Triste Tropico (film), 152–53; cannibalism in, 152; carnivalesque in, 152–53
Tristram Shandy (Sterne), 196
Tropical Serenade (film), 42
Troubetskoy, Eugene S.: and linguistics, 26
Trouble in Paradise (film): and nature of language, 76
Truffaut, François, 73
Tupinamba Indians: and cannibalism, 124, 127
Turner, Victor, 2, 129; on carnival, 93
Twelfth Night (Shakespeare), 97
Twelve Chairs (film), 74
Twentieth Century (television series), 204
Two or Three Things I Know about Her (film), 64, 69–70
"2,000 Year Old Man" (Brooks), 211

Tynyanov, J., 27, 44, 49; on formalism, 36–37
Tzara, Tristan, 99, 127

Ubu Roi (film), 108–9
Ubu Roi (Jarry), 106, 107–9; carnivalesque in, 99–102, 125
Ulysses (Joyce), 64
Ulysses (Tennyson), 209

"Vai Passar" (samba), 132–33
Van Peebles, Melvin, 82
Veloso, Caetano, 153; "Lingua," 192–95
Vereda Tropical (film): as parody, 173–74
Very Curious Girl, A (film), 120
Victory at Sea (television series), 204
Vidal, Gore: *Duluth,* 15
Videotapes, home-produced: eroticism in, 185–86
Vidor, King, 112
Vieira, João Luiz: on Brazilian cinema, 141–43
Vigo, Jean, 24, 110; and class oppression, 117–18
Violence, comic: carnival and, 108–9
Virgin and the Macho, The (film), 173
Viridiana (film), 103, 177
Virus Kennt Keine Moral, Ein (film), 172–73
Visualism: concept of, 19; Yudice on, 19. *See also* Images, visual
Vivre sa Vie (film), 66
Voloshinov, V. N., 23, 28, 62
Vom Roroima zum Orinoco (Koch-Grunberg), 133
Voz do Brasil (film): postsynchronization as plot point in, 77
Vygotsky, Leon S., 31, 64

Warhol, Andy, 169, 225
Waugh, Tom: on pornography, 168
Wavelength (film), 73
"We Are the World" (music video), 232
Welles, Orson, 42, 97, 110, 204; and carnival, 139–41; Wise on, 140
Wertmuller, Lina, 24, 116–17
Wheeler, Elizabeth: "Why Is It Fresh? Rap Music and Bakhtin," 192, 194

White, Allon, 15; on Bakhtin, 2–3; on carnival, 92, 95, 98

White, Hayden: *Metahistory: The Historical Imagination in Nineteenth-Century Europe,* 200

Who's Afraid of Virginia Woolf? (film): carnivalesque in, 111

"Why Is It Fresh? Rap Music and Bakhtin" (Wheeler), 192, 194

Williams, Robin, 113, 230

Willis, Ellen: on pornography, 167

Winfrey, Oprah, 222–23

Wise, Robert: on Welles, 140

Women: and eroticism, 164–65

Women on the Verge of a Nervous Breakdown (film): postsynchronization as plot point in, 76–77

World of Our Fathers (Howe), 203

WR (film), 200

Wrong Man, The (film), 47, 63

Xala (film), 80

Xavier, Ismail: on Brazilian cinema, 150, 155

Xica da Silva (film), 128, 154

Yiddish theatre: influence on *Zelig,* 210–11

Yudice, George: on postmodernism, 235; on visualism, 19

Zelig (film), 23, 24–25, 152, 230–31; acting as allegory in, 209–11; alienness in, 214–16; anti-Semitism as theme in, 211–15; Bellow in, 198, 203; Blum in, 203, 207, 208; carnivalesque in, 201; compared to *Marnie,* 206–7; compared to *Spellbound,* 206–7; compared to *Stardust Memories,* 207; critical reaction to, 198; dialogism in, 196, 198; Grenier on, 203–4; Howe in, 198, 203; interlocutor in, 200; intertextuality in, 198, 203–4, 206–8; language in, 216; as Menippean satire, 198–200; as parody, 201, 205–6; as pseudo-documentary, 200–205; resolution of, 216–17; Sontag in, 198, 202–3; special effects in, 201–2; structure of, 200–202, 204–6, 208, 216; use of archival film footage in, 201–2; Yiddish theatre's influence on, 210–11

Zelinsky, Tadeusz: Bakhtin and, 87

Zero de Conduite (film), 110